CHRIST-CENTERED

Exposition

"Look, I enjoy as much as the next guy a commentary that spends four pages exploring the ins and outs of the aorist, passive, optative in 1 Peter 1:2. And yet, does anyone else sometimes feel like there are commentaries that have lost sight of the fact that these details, as important as they are, are but a means to an end? God did not preserve the Scriptures until today in order to school you in the intricacies of literary voice! If the Word of God is a two-edged sword, designed to do something important in the reader, here is the handle to help you wield it effectively in preaching and teaching, written by two scholars (Danny Akin and James Merritt) who have worked through the scholastic issues, have given you the most relevant data from their research, and have done all of that without losing their focus on the proclamation of the Word and the equipping of the saints. The need is no greater anywhere else than for the believer who will tackle 1 Corinthians, because this book plays a critical role in forming the Christian understanding of how to address conflict, to conduct oneself in romantic relationships, to observe the Lord's Supper, to practice church discipline, to sort out claims about spiritual gifts, and to celebrate the resurrection of Jesus Christ, among other things. For the preacher, the teacher, and the serious student alike, this volume will be a sound investment."

C. Bart Barber, president, Southern Baptist Convention; pastor, First Baptist Church, Farmersville, TX

"Akin and Merritt are obviously skilled at teaching and preaching the Bible. But what I love about this treatment of 1 Corinthians is that they not only offer a reliable commentary on the text, but they also provide an exegetical outline of the text that is useful for communicating the message of the book. Preachers would do well to have this book in their arsenal when preparing sermons or Bible studies."

Benjamin L. Merkle, Dr. M. O. Owens Jr. Chair of New Testament Studies and professor of New Testament & Greek, Southeastern Baptist Theological Seminary, Wake Forest, NC

"The apostle Paul's letters to the church at Corinth contain some of the most urgently needed instruction for Christ's church today. In this commentary on 1 Corinthians, James Merritt and Danny Akin combine keen pastoral wisdom, theological insight, and gospel urgency. Merritt and Akin combine decades of expository commitment in this volume.

Preachers, Bible teachers, and students of God's Word will find this commentary both helpful and timely."

R. Albert Mohler Jr., president, The Southern Baptist Theological Seminary, Louisville, KY

"Every pastor should soon preach through 1 Corinthians! This powerful book directly addresses many of the most pressing issues that Christians face today. Yet preaching through this letter faithfully requires careful study and firm resolve. The preacher must address issues like Christian celebrity culture, immorality in the church, church discipline, litigation between Christians, sacramentalism, gender confusion, and spiritual gifts. Any preacher will benefit from the wise counsel of seasoned preachers as they navigate the potential minefields of this book. Danny Akin and James Merritt are experienced expositors who offer valuable guidance in handling this important book accurately and boldly."

Charles Quarles, research professor of New Testament studies and biblical theology, Charles Page Chair of Biblical Theology, Southeastern Baptist Theological Seminary, Wake Forest, NC

"I'm often asked about the people who have influenced my life and served as models for my ministry. Danny Akin and James Merritt both are at the top of that list. These brothers are passionate about Bible exposition, and they are passionate about the local church. In 1 Corinthians in the Christ-Centered Exposition Series, they combine those passions with their wealth of local church ministry experience to show how the gospel of Christ is the only answer for the conflict, chaos, confusion, and complications that characterized the Corinthian church in the first century and still mark many churches in the twenty-first century. Pastors, Bible teachers, and all who love God's Word will be helped by it."

Jim Shaddix, W. A. Criswell Chair of Expository Preaching, Southeastern Baptist Theological Seminary, Wake Forest, NC

AUTHORS Daniel L. Akin and James Merritt
SERIES EDITORS David Platt, Daniel L. Akin, and Tony Merida

CHRIST-CENTERED

Exposition

EXALTING JESUS IN

1 CORINTHIANS

HOLMAN®
REFERENCE
BRENTWOOD, TENNESSEE

Copyright information continued on page 329.

SERIES DEDICATION

Dedicated to Adrian Rogers and John Piper. They have taught us to love the gospel of Jesus Christ, to preach the Bible as the inerrant Word of God, to pastor the church for which our Savior died, and to have a passion to see all nations gladly worship the Lamb.

—David Platt, Tony Merida, and Danny Akin
March 2013

AUTHORS' DEDICATIONS

To the preaching department at Southeastern Baptist Theological Seminary who faithfully teach and model expository preaching. What an honor it is to work alongside each of you for the glory of King Jesus.

—Danny Akin

To Rev. LaVay McCullough. He was the pastor that gave me my start in ministry and taught me by his example to have a love for the Greek New Testament.

— James Merritt

TABLE OF CONTENTS

Acknowledgments   xi
Series Introduction   xiii

Commentary by Daniel L. Akin

Introduction   3
Jesus, Yes! The Church, Yes!   1 Corinthians 1:1-9   6
How Do You Divide and Nearly
    Destroy a Church?   1 Corinthians 1:10-17   16
The Power of the Cross   1 Corinthians 1:18-25   24
No Superstars but a Savior   1 Corinthians 1:26-31   33
Jesus Christ and Him Crucified   1 Corinthians 2:1-9   42
What Kind of Person Are You?   1 Corinthians 2:10–3:4   51
The Church of God   1 Corinthians 3:5-17   60
In Christ We Have It All   1 Corinthians 3:18-23   69
Four Truths a Minister of God
    Must Never Forget   1 Corinthians 4:1-5   75
Just Who Do You Think You Are?   1 Corinthians 4:6-13   84
Listen to Your Father   1 Corinthians 4:14-21   93
The Basics of Church Discipline   1 Corinthians 5   102
Why Christians Should Not Sue
    Christians in Civil Court   1 Corinthians 6:1-11   114
My Body Belongs to God   1 Corinthians 6:12-20   128
God's Wisdom for a Biblical Marriage 1 Corinthians 7:1-16   137
Find Your Contentment in Christ   1 Corinthians 7:17-24   148
The Savior's Superlative Single   1 Corinthians 7:25-40   156
Am I My Brother's Keeper?   1 Corinthians 8   166
The Gospel Above All   1 Corinthians 9:1-18   176
The Heart of a Soul Winner   1 Corinthians 9:19-27   185

A History Lesson from God   1 Corinthians 10:1-13   193
Don't Dine with Demons   1 Corinthians 10:14-22   202
My One Ambition: Glorifying God   1 Corinthians 10:23–11:1   210
Seven Principles for Worship That
      Pleases God   1 Corinthians 11:2-16   218
The Lord's Supper Manuscript   1 Corinthians 11:17-34   229

Commentary by James Merritt

You Are a Gifted Child   1 Corinthians 12:1-11   238
Unwrapping Spiritual Gifts   1 Corinthians 12:8-31   246
Love from Above   1 Corinthians 13   257
Control Your Tongues   1 Corinthians 14   264
The Gospel   1 Corinthians 15:1-11   274
What If?   1 Corinthians 15:12-19   279
Resurrection Guaranteed   1 Corinthians 15:20-34   284
No Body Like This Body   1 Corinthians 15:35-58   290
Now about the Collection   1 Corinthians 16:1-4   298
Parting Words   1 Corinthians 16:5-24   305

Works Cited   310
Scripture Index   317

ACKNOWLEDGMENTS

Akin: Words are not adequate to express my gratitude to Devin Moncada, Kimberly Rochelle, and Kim Humphrey for their invaluable assistance in my part of this commentary on First Corinthians. They are God's good gift to me.

Merritt: I would like to acknowledge Cross Pointe Church that allows me to be their pastor and gives me the time to extend the ministry of the church beyond the four walls with opportunities like this.

I would also like to acknowledge the joy of being allowed to collaborate with my best friend Dr. Danny Akin in joining this wonderful commentary series.

I would like to acknowledge—always the love of my life, my partner in ministry, my best friend and soulmate, and the best thing that ever happened to me next to Jesus—my precious wife Teresa. Ministry is hard, but she has made the journey so much easier.

Finally, I'm so grateful that the author of the entire Bible and the creator of the universe and the Savior of the world not only saved me as a nine-year-old boy, but called me into the ministry. I gladly and joyfully acknowledge Jesus Christ as my Lord every day of my life, and I will do so with my last breath.

SERIES INTRODUCTION

Augustine said, "Where Scripture speaks, God speaks." The editors of the Christ-Centered Exposition Commentary series believe that where God speaks, the pastor must speak. God speaks through his written Word. We must speak from that Word. We believe the Bible is God breathed, authoritative, inerrant, sufficient, understandable, necessary, and timeless. We also affirm that the Bible is a Christ-centered book; that is, it contains a unified story of redemptive history of which Jesus is the hero. Because of this Christ-centered trajectory that runs from Genesis 1 through Revelation 22, we believe the Bible has a corresponding global-missions thrust. From beginning to end, we see God's mission as one of making worshipers of Christ from every tribe and tongue worked out through this redemptive drama in Scripture. To that end we must preach the Word.

In addition to these distinct convictions, the Christ-Centered Exposition Commentary series has some distinguishing characteristics. First, this series seeks to display exegetical accuracy. What the Bible says is what we want to say. While not every volume in the series will be a verse-by-verse commentary, we nevertheless desire to handle the text carefully and explain it rightly. Those who teach and preach bear the heavy responsibility of saying what God has said in his Word and declaring what God has done in Christ. We desire to handle God's Word faithfully, knowing that we must give an account for how we have fulfilled this holy calling (Jas 3:1).

Second, the Christ-Centered Exposition Commentary series has pastors in view. While we hope others will read this series, such as parents, teachers, small-group leaders, and student ministers, we desire to provide a commentary busy pastors will use for weekly preparation of biblically faithful and gospel-saturated sermons. This series is not academic in nature. Our aim is to present a readable and pastoral style of commentaries. We believe this aim will serve the church of the Lord Jesus Christ.

Third, we want the Christ-Centered Exposition Commentary series to be known for the inclusion of helpful illustrations and theologically driven applications. Many commentaries offer no help in illustrations, and few offer any kind of help in application. Often those that do offer illustrative material and application unfortunately give little serious attention to the text. While giving ourselves primarily to explanation, we also hope to serve readers by providing inspiring and illuminating illustrations coupled with timely and timeless application.

Finally, as the name suggests, the editors seek to exalt Jesus from every book of the Bible. In saying this, we are not commending wild allegory or fanciful typology. We certainly believe we must be constrained to the meaning intended by the divine Author himself, the Holy Spirit of God. However, we also believe the Bible has a messianic focus, and our hope is that the individual authors will exalt Christ from particular texts. Luke 24:25-27,44-47 and John 5:39,46 inform both our hermeneutics and our homiletics. Not every author will do this the same way or have the same degree of Christ-centered emphasis. That is fine with us. We believe faithful exposition that is Christ centered is not monolithic. We do believe, however, that we must read the whole Bible as Christian Scripture. Therefore, our aim is both to honor the historical particularity of each biblical passage and to highlight its intrinsic connection to the Redeemer.

The editors are indebted to the contributors of each volume. The reader will detect a unique style from each writer, and we celebrate these unique gifts and traits. While distinctive in their approaches, the authors share a common characteristic in that they are pastoral theologians. They love the church, and they regularly preach and teach God's Word to God's people. Further, many of these contributors are younger voices. We think these new, fresh voices can serve the church well, especially among a rising generation that has the task of proclaiming the Word of Christ and the Christ of the Word to the lost world.

We hope and pray this series will serve the body of Christ well in these ways until our Savior returns in glory. If it does, we will have succeeded in our assignment.

David Platt
Daniel L. Akin
Tony Merida
Series Editors
February 2013

1 Corinthians

Introduction

Church life can be messy business. It's messy because the church is filled with people, which means it is filled with sinners. There are no perfect people or perfect churches. Everyone has flaws, defects, and weaknesses. Perhaps no church exhibited this more than the church in Corinth in the first century. Although its members had been sanctified, called to be saints, enriched in grace and gifts, and called into fellowship with the Son of God, Jesus Christ (1:1-9), the congregation was a carnal, sinful mess. It was a mess theologically, practically, and morally. People were divided, since the cult of personality had taken over (1:10-17). Sexual immorality was being tolerated (5:1-13; 6:12-20). Believers were suing believers in civil court (6:1-11). There was confusion about God's design for marriage and singleness (7:1-40), Christian liberty (8:1–11:1), attire for worship (11:2-16), the Lord's Supper (11:17-34), spiritual gifts—especially the gift of tongues (chs. 12–14)—and the doctrine of bodily resurrection and its implications for the resurrection of Jesus (ch. 15). This, then, is not the kind of church that testifies to the lost world about the power and beauty of the gospel. No, as Warren Wiersbe well says, the church at Corinth was "a defiled church, a divided church, a disgraced church!" (*Be Wise*, 25).

The ancient city of Corinth was strategically located as a sentry of the four-and-a-half-mile Isthmus of Corinth in Achaia (modern Greece). It was approximately fifty miles due west of Athens and was on major land and sea travel routes. It sat at the base of the 1,886-foot-high Acrocorinth and controlled two harbors—Cenchreae leading to Asia and Lechaeum leading to Italy. From its beginning, Corinth was prosperous due to this strategic location. But it also became famous for luxury and immorality. The city contained at least twenty-six sacred places, including one dedicated to Aphrodite, the goddess of love. At one point, her temple had a thousand prostitute slaves of varied ethnicities. Indeed, the Greek word *korinthiazo* means "to commit immorality." Plato even used the phrase "Corinthian girl" to refer to a prostitute (Köstenberger et al., *Cradle*, 547–49).

In Paul's day, the population of the city was about two hundred thousand, though some estimate it to have been much larger. It was five to eight times larger than Athens. Corinth was the New York, Los Angeles, New Orleans, or San Francisco of the ancient world (Köstenberger et al., *Cradle*, 547–49). In 27 BC it became the capital of the Roman province of Achaia, what is now southern Greece. The city contained Jews and Greeks, both slaves and free. It was proud of its Hellenistic culture, international Isthmian games (second only to the Olympics in prestige), philosophical schools, and esoteric mystery religions. It was pluralistic, open-minded, religious, wealthy, and progressive. From Paul's perspective, it was a gospel-strategic city.

Paul's relationship with Corinth, though, was complex. We know from this letter that he wrote it from Ephesus during his third missionary journey (16:8). The date of writing is around AD 53–55, probably the spring of AD 54, according to Tom Schreiner (*1 Corinthians*, 8). Almost all New Testament scholars agree that the New Testament indicates Paul wrote four letters to the church at Corinth and visited them three times. The following chart, adapted from Wayne House's *Chronological and Background Charts of the New Testament*, summarizes the interactions between the apostle and the Corinthians (*Chronological*, 135).

Paul's Four Corinthian Letters and His Three Visits

Paul's Work	Scripture Reference
Founds the church on second missionary journey	Acts 18:1-17
Leaves Corinth and goes to Ephesus	Acts 18:18-21
Writes a letter now lost to us, a previous letter (first letter)	1 Cor 5:9-13
Receives a bad report from "Chloe's people" and a letter from Corinth	1 Cor 1:11; 7:1
Writes 1 Corinthians (second letter)	1 Corinthians
Sends Timothy and Erastus to Corinth	Acts 19:22; 1 Cor 4:17; 16:10
Hears of a crisis in Corinth caused by Jewish troublemakers who question Paul's authority	2 Cor 10:10; 11:21b-23; 12:6-7
Makes a quick trip to Corinth (a "painful visit")	2 Cor 2:1; 12:14; 13:1

Writes severe letter to Corinth (third letter, now lost to us)	2 Cor 2:3-9; 7:8-12
Looks for Titus in Troas and Macedonia	2 Cor 2:12-13
Finds Titus, who brings a positive report about Corinth	2 Cor 7:6-16
Writes 2 Corinthians (fourth letter)	2 Corinthians
Makes third visit to Corinth	Acts 19:21; 20:2-3; 2 Cor 13:1

Paul was informed of the mess at Corinth by a report from "Chloe's people" (1 Cor 1:11) and a letter from the church asking for his counsel (1 Cor 7:1), leading to the writing of 1 Corinthians. Their request is understandable since Paul had evangelized Corinth on his second missionary journey (Acts 15:36–18:22) as recorded in Acts 18:1-17. Paul had spent eighteen months in Corinth (Acts 18:11). The only city Paul spent more time in was Ephesus (Acts 19:8-10). So, we can state Paul's purpose in penning this letter this way: Paul, who planted the church at Corinth, wrote **in response to** a report from Chloe's people—and possibly Stephanas, Fortunatus, and Achaicus—and to a letter from the church who needed to know how to deal with the specifics of divisions, disorders, and difficulties in their midst (e.g., those involving marriage, the role of women, worship, spiritual gifts, and resurrection) **in order to correct** the worldly attitudes and arrogance of the church **and to encourage** them to pursue a godly lifestyle and doctrinal purity.

In a day when the church is mocked and ridiculed, those of us who follow Jesus Christ need to ask, "Why is this happening? Why has our witness to the gospel been compromised?" I can think of no better book in the Bible to help us answer that than 1 Corinthians. Paul wrote a letter that, if heeded, will show us the beauty and attractiveness of the church and Christ, of the saints and the Savior, in a day when people were impressed with Jesus—usually a Jesus of their creation and not the Jesus of the Bible—but not his church. Despite all the mess in the church at Corinth, Paul says, "Jesus, yes! The church, yes!" God has not given up on his people, and neither should we! Let's begin our journey and see how Paul, as John Piper writes, explains "the centrality of who we are in relation to God" ("Sustained by the Faithfulness of God").

Jesus, Yes! The Church, Yes!

1 CORINTHIANS 1:1-9

Main Idea: The people of God are those whom God has graciously called to be saints, who continually profess faith in Christ, and who humbly use their gifts for God's glory as they wait for Christ to return and fulfill his promises.

I. **God Builds His Church in a Specific Way (1:1-3).**
   A. God calls out leaders to serve us (1:1).
   B. God calls out sinners to be saints (1:2-3).
II. **God Gives Gifts to His Church, with Nothing Missing (1:4-7).**
   A. We are rich in grace (1:4).
   B. We are rich in gifts (1:5-7).
III. **God Provides Hope for His Church with Powerful Promises (1:7-9).**
   A. We can expect Jesus to return (1:7-8).
   B. We can expect God to be faithful (1:8-9).

When one considers the church at Corinth, a church body all too like many congregations today, the words of Charles Spurgeon are particularly appropriate:

> The Corinthians were what we should call nowadays, judging them by the usual standard, a first-class church. They had many who understood much of the learning of the Greeks; they were men of classic taste, and men of good understanding, men of profound knowledge; and yet, in spiritual health, that church was one of the worst in all Greece, and perhaps in the world. Amongst the whole of them, you would not find another church sunk so low as this one, although it was the most gifted. ("Confirming the Witness," 133)

Despite this accurate assessment, Paul remained hopeful for the church's future. His hope was not grounded in the Corinthians. It was rooted in the God who gave it birth. Therefore, Paul opens his letter by describing the many ways God works in his church.

God Builds His Church in a Specific Way
1 CORINTHIANS 1:1-3

No matter what is happening in the life of a faithful New Testament church, we must never forget that the church is God's church. Where the Word of God is preached, the ordinances of baptism and the Lord's Supper administered, regenerate church membership is honored, church discipline is practiced, and the Great Commandments and Great Commission are pursued, there exists the Lord's church regardless of what may be going wrong otherwise. God is still building faithful churches, imperfections and all, among the nations. And he builds them in two primary ways.

God Calls Out Leaders to Serve Us (1:1)

Paul is the author of this letter. He would write a total of thirteen New Testament letters. Formerly known as Saul (see Acts 13:9), Paul was a devout Jew, Pharisee, and persecutor of the church (Acts 7:58–8:3; 9:1-2; Phil 3:4-6). The Lord Jesus, however, called him to be an apostle, specifically but not exclusively, to the Gentiles (Acts 9:15-17; Gal 1:16). He accomplished three missionary journeys, which are recorded in the book of Acts. It is also likely he went on a fourth mission, parts of which can be reconstructed from the Pastoral Epistles (1 & 2 Timothy and Titus). He would be imprisoned twice in Rome (Acts 28; 2 Timothy) and was executed after his second imprisonment, around AD 65–68. New Testament scholar John Polhill says, "A date in late 67 or early 68 seems more likely" (*Paul and His Letters,* 438).

In 1 Corinthians 1, Paul immediately calls attention to three things concerning himself: he is "an apostle of Christ Jesus," he was "called" to this divine assignment, and his calling was "God's will." An apostle is sent on behalf of another, and Paul was endowed with divine, apostolic authority as an emissary of the Lord Jesus Christ. His ministry as an apostle had a divine origin. He was supernaturally called by the sovereign will of God. In fact, he was seized! He was arrested by God! Therefore, the Corinthians must understand, as Gordon Fee writes, that Paul has a "position of authority in relationship to the church in Corinth" (*Corinthians,* 2014, 26).

Paul also notes that "Sosthenes our brother" is with him. It is likely that this is the same Sosthenes of Acts 18:17, "the leader of the synagogue" who was seized by the Jews and beaten during Paul's mission in Corinth. I believe the Christian church came to his aid, cared for him, and led him to faith in Jesus, leading to his becoming a missionary serving alongside Paul in Ephesus. It is possible he even served as Paul's amanuensis, or secretary, for 1 Corinthians. Our wonderful God works in wonderful ways to call out leaders to serve his church.

God Calls Out Sinners to Be Saints (1:2-3)

Paul writes "to the church of God at Corinth" (v. 2). Corinth, a strategically located city (see Introduction), was the geographical location of this particular church. But the congregation also had a *spiritual* location. It was "the church of God." This church, like every other, is his church, his possession. And the Lord's church, regardless of each's location, has certain defining characteristics.

First, each is comprised of "those sanctified in Christ Jesus." The word *sanctification* or *sanctified* appears several times (vv. 1,2,3,4,6,7,8,9). Normally when we see the word, we think of God's work in us to make us holy and to conform us more and more into the image of his Son, the Lord Jesus Christ. And it is certainly used like this in the New Testament (see 1 Thess 4:3). Here, however, Paul is not talking about "experiential sanctification" but "positional sanctification," which is not something believers are pursuing but something we already have from the moment of conversion. Tom Schreiner puts it well:

> The participle word *sanctified* (*hēgiasmenois*) is in the perfect tense in Greek (and here the focus is on the resultant state) and designates what is often called "positional" or "definitive" sanctification. . . . The Corinthians are God's holy people in Christ! (*1 Corinthians*, 52–53).

Second, all true believers within a congregation are "called as saints." Just as God had sovereignly called Paul to be an apostle, he had sovereignly, effectually called believers at Corinth to be saints (holy ones). Saints are much more than participants on an American football team in New Orleans. Moreover, a saint is much more than a uniquely holy person formally recognized by the Catholic or Orthodox Church. The Bible refers to any and every person who calls in faith "on the name of Jesus Christ our Lord" as a saint.

Third, saints have one Lord, but they are not limited to one locale; rather, each is part of the larger church scattered among the nations. No one geographical country or location has a special claim on Christ! The church is "all those in every place who call on the name of Jesus Christ our Lord." This is probably an allusion to Malachi 1:11 where the Lord says, "My name will be great among the nations." God's people, his saints, cannot be contained by borders or even walls.

Fourth, believers comprising the church are sovereignly *called* by God to salvation, but they must also be those "who *call* on the name of Jesus Christ." This alludes to the beautiful biblical balance between divine sovereignty and human responsibility.

Fifth, the Lord builds his church and blesses his saints with two essential kindnesses: grace and peace (v. 3). "Grace" is God's unmerited favor. We could summarize its meaning with an acronym: **G**od's **R**iches **A**t **C**hrist's **E**xpense. "Peace" draws on the Hebrew idea of *shalom*, which speaks of God's total well-being and wholeness of blessing in our lives. I love the way Gordon Fee addresses these twin Christian blessings:

> In a sense this sums up the whole of Paul's theological outlook. The sum total of all of God's activity toward his human creatures is found in the word "grace"; God has given himself to them mercifully and bountifully in Christ. Nothing is deserved; nothing can be achieved: "'Tis mercy all, immense and free." And the sum total of those benefits as they are experienced by the recipients of God's grace is found in the word "peace," meaning "well-being, wholeness, welfare." The one flows out of the other, and both together flow from "God our Father" and were made effective in human history through our "Lord Jesus Christ." (*Corinthians*, 2014, 31)

Don't miss this important theological truth. Grace and peace flow equally from "God our Father and the Lord Jesus Christ"—who are equal in deity and yet distinct in person. Curtis Vaughn is right: "These words by Paul are actually a prayer in which he urges the Corinthians to look again to the Father and the Son as the sources of full salvation" (*1 Corinthians*, 22). Charles Hodge would add, "All Christians regard God as their Father and Christ as their Lord. His person they love, his voice they obey, and in his protection they trust" (*Exposition*, 6).

God Gives Gifts to His Church, with Nothing Missing
1 CORINTHIANS 1:4-7

Our God is a good and gracious God. He delights in showering his children with gifts. Psalm 84:11 says it beautifully: "For the LORD God is a sun and shield. The LORD grants favor and honor; he does not withhold the good from those who live with integrity." The Corinthian Christians, though, were not walking in integrity! They were divisive, idolatrous, prideful, sexually immoral, and greedy. But they were still God's people and an actual church. He still loved them and was committed to working with them and in them for their good and his glory. Here Paul emphasizes two ways that God acts for his children.

We Are Rich in Grace (1:4)

Verse 3 is a prayer wish. Verse 4 begins a prayer of thanksgiving for God's grace. Normally Paul will start his letters by commending a certain church. The notable exception is Galatians, where Paul critiques a church for its failures. In 1 Corinthians too, though, Paul is silent in terms of praise for the Corinthians' love, faith, or works. Rather, he focuses where they need to focus: on God and his grace through Jesus Christ. "I always thank my God for you because of the grace of God given to you in Christ Jesus," he says. God's gracious activity toward the Corinthians and all believers is supremely revealed in the Lord Jesus Christ. It is a grace given, not earned or merited. It is something the Corinthians certainly did not deserve. Its origin was the Father, and its means was the Son. "Marvelous grace, infinite grace! Grace that will pardon and cleanse within. Grace, grace, God's grace! Grace that is greater than all our sin!" (Johnston, "Grace Greater Than Our Sin"). Mark Taylor is right: "Grace profoundly shaped Paul's outlook in every way, and his gratitude for grace anticipates a major emphasis of [this] letter" (*1 Corinthians*, 42). Oh, how we need God's grace. Oh, how we need to extend grace to one another.

We Are Rich in Gifts (1:5-7)

One evidence of God's grace in our lives is his blessing of spiritual gifts (grace gifts), which are listed in four different places in the New Testament (Rom 12:3-8; 1 Cor 12:4-11,28-30; Eph 4:11; 1 Pet 4:10-11). Paul will provide an extensive discussion of spiritual gifts in chapters 12–14, especially the gift of tongues in chapter 14. Here Paul lays the groundwork for what he will say later by simply noting that spiritual gifts, like every other blessing in the Christian life, have their source in God's grace revealed in Jesus. Paul says he is thankful believers are enriched (GNT, "have become rich") in him. And to what extent did they become rich in Christ? Well, spiritually, "in every way"! Their gracious Father holds nothing back. But Paul draws attention to the gifts of "all speech and all knowledge." Schreiner notes, "We see a connection with 1 Corinthians 12:8, where two spiritual gifts are named: a 'message of wisdom' (*logos sophia*) and a 'message of knowledge' (*logos gnōseōs*)" (*1 Corinthians*, 55). As we will see later, all spiritual gifts generally fall under one of three categories: knowledge, speaking, or service.

Paul is convinced the Corinthian church has been enriched in "all speech and all knowledge," areas highly valued by the Corinthians. However, for all who are in Christ, there is no place for boasting or pride. God did this for those in Christ (v. 5). These gifts, then, are simply the evidence of the power of the gospel in our lives. The activity of spiritual gifts, according to verse 6, demonstrates that "the testimony [GNT, "the message"; NLT, "what I told you"] about Christ was confirmed among [them]." Fee says, "God himself 'guaranteed' the truth of the message by enriching them with every kind of spiritual gift" (*Corinthians*, 2014, 39).

The believing community does "not lack any spiritual gift" (v. 7). Indeed, in Christ we get all that we will ever need to be pleasing to God and effective for God. This occurs the moment one is saved, not later in the Christian experience. So, Calvin says it is "as if [Paul] had said, 'The Lord has not merely honored you with the light of the gospel, but has eminently endowed you with all the graces that may be of service to the saints for helping them forward in the way of salvation'" (*1 Corinthians*, 57). Oh, how rich is the believer in Jesus. Nothing is missing. Nothing lacking. He provides all we need.

God Provides Hope for His Church with Powerful Promises
1 CORINTHIANS 1:7-9

Hope is a powerful concept in any language. However, real hope is only as effective as its object. The Bible does not teach a "Well, I hope so" way of thinking. It teaches an "I hope because I know so" way of thinking. We hope because we know Christ! We hope because we know the promises of God, which are too many to count. Isaiah 40:31 tells us, "[T]hose who hope in the LORD will renew their strength" (NIV). In 1 Corinthians

1:7-9 Paul identifies two particular promises of God that we can trust: the return of the Lord Jesus Christ and the faithfulness of God.

We Can Expect Jesus to Return (1:7-8)

Interestingly, Paul connects spiritual gifts and the second coming of Jesus. Could it be that a waning passion for the Lord's return had contributed to this church's abuse of spiritual gifts? I think his argument goes something like this: To exercise your abundance of spiritual gifts effectively and rightly you must "eagerly wait for the revelation of our Lord Jesus Christ" (v. 7). Otherwise, you will get things out of spiritual balance, and all sorts of mischief will ensue. As C. K. Barrett perfectly says,

> Christians are what they are because through the Holy Spirit they have received gifts of grace, and they are what they are because, having been redeemed and called by the historic work of Christ they now look for his coming to consummate his achievement. They live in remembrance of what he has done, and in expectation of what he will do (cf. xi. 26). It was a characteristic Corinthian error (cf. iv. 8; note the *already*) to concentrate on the present with its religious excitement, and to overlook the cost at which the present was purchased. (*First Epistle*, 39)

In other words, being heavenly minded will make you of earthly good! Never lose sight of the truth that what you have now is good, but the best is yet to come! Work and wait! Work and watch! Philippians 3:20 is a wonderful reminder: "Our citizenship is in heaven, and we eagerly wait for a Savior from there, the Lord Jesus Christ" (cf. 1 Thess 1:10; 4:13-18; 5:23-24; Rev 19:11-21).

We Can Expect God to Be Faithful (1:8-9)

First Thessalonians 5:23-24 parallels the final two verses in this opening paragraph. There Paul writes,

> *Now may the God of peace himself sanctify you completely. And may your whole spirit, soul, and body be kept sound and blameless at the coming of our Lord Jesus Christ. He who calls you is faithful; he will do it.*

Paul says there is both blessing and hope in longing for the coming of "our Lord Jesus Christ" (v. 7). First, believer, "He will also strengthen

[ESV, "sustain"] you to the end" (v. 8). You will persevere because God will preserve you. The one who called you to salvation (v. 2) will keep you in salvation to the end. This is another confirmation of what is called the doctrine of eternal security or perseverance of the saints (cf. John 10:27-29; Rom 8:28-39; Eph 1:13-14; 2 Tim 1:12; Jude 24-25). Christ will faithfully get his people home. Second, we will arrive "blameless [ESV, "guiltless"] in the day of the Lord Jesus Christ." Schreiner writes,

> It is quite remarkable that Paul speaks of *the day of our Lord Jesus Christ*. The Old Testament repeatedly speaks of "the day of the LORD," that is, the day of Yahweh. Paul, however, conceives of that same day as the day of Christ (see also Rom. 2:16; Phil. 1:6, 10; 2:16). Relating that day to Christ demonstrates that Jesus Christ has divine status and exercises divine functions. (*1 Corinthians*, 56; emphasis in original)

He is our God!

The wonderful hope and security the Christian enjoys are grounded in a basic theological truth: "God is faithful" (v. 9). You can trust him. You can count on him. And "you were called by him into fellowship [Gk. *koinonia*; NLT, "partnership"] with his Son, Jesus Christ our Lord." The church at Corinth may be fragmenting and headed toward a split, but God nevertheless has a hold of the believers there by his Son. He will not let his people go, no matter what. He may have to exercise some tough love, but they are his and will remain his forever. You can count on it. He has promised, and God always keeps his word to his Son and to us who are called and sanctified and made rich in him.

Conclusion

These opening verses of 1 Corinthians are so important to me personally. They help explain the spiritual biography of Danny Akin. I was called to be a saint at the age of ten at the Ben Hill Baptist Church in Atlanta, Georgia. And I can testify to God's faithfulness to sustain us in our call to salvation because I did not walk closely with the Lord during my teenage years. Honestly, I was a Corinthianesque mess. But when I was nineteen, our perfect heavenly Father got my attention and brought me back to himself (see Heb 12:5-13). Then, in July 1977, when I was on a mission trip to Sells, Arizona, to work among the Tohono O'odham Nation (a name meaning "desert people"), the Lord, by his will, called me into the gospel ministry. Like Paul, I felt seized! I could not say no, nor have I ever wanted to. And in his grace the Lord took a not very smart twenty-year-old and graced him with his gift for the gospel assignment he had sovereignly given him. Ministry has not always been easy, but it has always been good! I could not imagine doing anything else. I don't want to do anything else. Despite the mess that is Danny Akin and despite the mess that is the church this side of heaven, I say "Jesus, yes! The church, yes!" We all have been "called by [God] into fellowship with his Son" (v. 9) and with one another (v. 2). Why would anyone want to be anywhere else?

Reflect and Discuss

1. Does Paul's greeting to the Corinthian church differ from what you would expect given what he knows about them? How would you have responded to the same report? How does grace shape Paul's outlook?
2. What are some ways that you can serve and encourage the leaders who are in your church? How can regularly praying for your leaders serve them?
3. What does this passage teach you about God's work in salvation? What does it teach you about the Christian's identity?
4. In what ways does this passage emphasize God's role from the beginning to the completion of your salvation? How can this give you hope and rest?
5. Can Christians begin to believe a church is theirs instead of God's? If so, how? What are the fruits of this belief? How does the church's identity as God's possession refocus what a church prioritizes?
6. What is the difference between positional sanctification and experiential sanctification? Why is it important that we understand the difference between the two?
7. How does God's role as the builder of his church shape your role? How does it give both power and freedom to your role?
8. How does being heavenly minded make you of earthly good? How does waiting eagerly for Christ's return help Christians to use their spiritual gifts properly? In what ways does neglecting to do this cause Christians to abuse their gifts?

9. Have you ever begun to believe that, even now that you are a believer, God is *against* you instead of *for* you? What does this passage teach that might help you work through such thoughts?

10. What does it mean that God will sustain believers to the end? In what ways does he do this?

How Do You Divide and Nearly Destroy a Church?

1 CORINTHIANS 1:10-17

Main Idea: The family of God should unite with one another in Christ, refusing to create divisions or to elevate anyone as more important.

I. You Stop Thinking Like Jesus (1:10).
II. You Start Fussing and Fighting with One Another (1:11).
III. You Buy into the Cult of Personality (1:12-13).
IV. You Forget What Matters Most (1:14-17).

On the night that he was betrayed, our Lord Jesus prayed for his church. John records our Savior's prayer for the church's unity:

> *Holy Father, protect them by your name that you have given me, so that they may be one as we are one. . . . May they all be one, as you, Father, are in me and I am in you. May they also be in us, so that the world may believe you sent me. I have given them the glory you have given me, so that they may be one as we are one. I am in them and you are in me, so that they may be made completely one, that the world may know you have sent me and have loved them as you have loved me. . . . I made your name known to them and will continue to make it known, so that the love you have loved me with may be in them and I may be in them.* (John 17:11,21-23,26)

These verses lead us to an unalterable conviction: our Lord is heartbroken by division in his church. Now, to be sure, sometimes division must take place when the issue is moral or theological. In chapter 5 Paul tells the Corinthians to exercise church discipline (in line with what Jesus taught in Matt 18:15-20) and to remove from the fellowship a man who was committing sexual immorality with his stepmother. In 1 Corinthians 11:19-20 we are informed that divisions or factions in a church can be used by God to distinguish between those who truly belong to God and those who don't. And Paul, in Romans 16:17-18 and Titus 3:9-11, warns us to avoid those who cause division because of false doctrine. But when division takes place in a church because of the cult of personality or a factious spirit, our Lord weeps in heaven. It dishonors his glory, makes a mockery of the gospel, and does massive damage to the church's reputation in the world.

Sadly, division of the last sort was the situation in Corinth. Within the church there was a Paul faction, an Apollos faction, a Peter or Cephas faction, and possibly a Jesus faction (1:12). Paul was horrified by this development and would spend 1:10–4:21 pleading with the church to pursue unity, not division. Dividing into political parties may be the way of the world, but it should not be the practice of the people of God. There could not be a more relevant word for the twenty-first-century church. Our eyes and ears need to be wide open to the counsel of God's appointed apostle here. God is speaking through him. So, let us explore what divides and even destroys a church. Paul makes four observations in 1:10-17.

You Stop Thinking Like Jesus
1 CORINTHIANS 1:10

Paul is an apostle with God-given authority. However, he begins his exhortation with gentleness: "Now, I urge [ESV, "appeal to"] you, brothers and sisters." Paul does not get in their faces. He comes alongside them and puts his arm around them. He does not pull rank as an apostle. He approaches them as their spiritual father (4:14-15). He is a spiritual dad talking to his children about their shared faith.

He appeals to "brothers and sisters," and does so "in the name of our Lord Jesus Christ." The use of the full, majestic title of our Savior "reminds the [Corinthians] that Paul's words are not merely his private opinion" (Schreiner, *1 Corinthians*, 61). They come in the authority of the one who is God (Lord), Savior (Jesus), and Messiah (Christ). Leon Morris rightly says, "The full title heightens the solemnity of his appeal and the one name [that] stands over against all party names" (*1 Corinthians*, 39). The Corinthians are in the mess they find themselves in because they have lost sight of their Master!

Paul's appeal is threefold and laid out in the remainder of verse 10: "all of you agree in what you say," let "there be no divisions among you," and "be united with the same understanding and the same conviction." These words reflect Paul's instructions to the church at Philippi where he sought to reconcile Euodia and Syntyche. There he asked these sisters in Christ "to agree in the Lord" (Phil 4:2). He grounded that request in his call to the entire church to "adopt the same [mind] as that of Christ Jesus" (Phil 2:5), an attitude characterized by "thinking

the same way, having the same love, united in spirit, intent on one purpose" (Phil 2:2). The Corinthians had forgotten the mind of Christ.
They had stopped thinking like Jesus. As a result, they were disagreeing,
not pulling together. They were divided, not united in speech, mind,
or convictions. They deserved an "F" when it came to obeying the two
great commandments (see Matt 22:37-40). They were not loving either
God or one another well. My hero in the faith and mentor in ministry is
Adrian Rogers. In a private conversation he told me the church is at its
best when it is on the battlefield fighting the real enemies of Satan, sin,
death, hell, and the grave. She is at her worst when she is in the barracks
fighting her own members. Jesus said love God, love one another, and
go to the nations with the gospel. The Corinthians were doing none of
this. They had stopped thinking and acting like Jesus.

You Start Fussing and Fighting with One Another
1 CORINTHIANS 1:11

In verse 11 Paul specifies what he knows and how he learned it. He
heard of the divisions from "members of Chloe's people." This is the
only mention of Chloe in Scripture. We know nothing about her or her
people, but Mark Taylor gives us a few possibilities. He writes,

> "Those of Chloe" . . . could indicate family and extended
> household members, such as slaves, or those who acted on
> behalf of Chloe as business agents. Some think that since
> Paul was in Ephesus at the time of the writing of the letter,
> Chloe may have been a wealthy Asian with business interests
> that required her representatives to travel to Corinth. We do
> not know for certain that she was a believer, but it is probable
> since she had a presence in Corinth and was known to the
> church, even if through her business agents. The report itself
> regarding the Corinthian quarrels does not come from Chloe
> but rather from her household. (*1 Corinthians*, 53)

I believe Chloe was a believer and member of the church at
Corinth, as were those who reached out to Paul. This answers the "how"
Paul heard the question. The "what" he learned question was partially
answered in verse 10: there are divisions. Verse 11 expounds on that:
"there is rivalry [ESV, "quarreling"; MSG, "fighting"] among you." The
concept is found only in Paul's writings in the New Testament. It usually

appears in vice lists like Romans 1:29; 13:13; Galatians 5:20; 1 Timothy 6:4; and Titus 3:9 (Taylor, *1 Corinthians*, 53). What was in the minds of this church in verse 10 manifested itself out of their mouths in verse 11. And what was coming out of their mouths led to verbal sparring! *Public* and *ugly* describe what was going on. Brothers and sisters in Christ were treating one another like enemies. And a watching world was being turned off the gospel of Jesus Christ in the process.

Today our divisive words may be hushed in face-to-face encounters. In times past, and still today, church business conferences have been a favorite arena for verbal combat. But more often today, we shoot disgruntled emails or post negativity on social media. We may even say things online we would never say in person. For some, a keyboard becomes a weapon of choice as he or she rips and tears at others, doing serious harm to the body of Christ. Leon Morris is right: "*Quarrels* are one of the 'acts of the sinful nature.' . . . They do not belong among God's people" (*1 Corinthians*, 40; emphasis in original). Do not downplay fussing and fighting. If you participate, you may divide the church. You may even destroy your local congregation.

You Buy into the Cult of Personality
1 CORINTHIANS 1:12-13

What do I mean by the phrase "cult of personality"? The *Merriam-Webster Dictionary* says it refers to when "a public figure (such as a political leader) is deliberately presented to the people of a country as a great person who should be admired and loved" ("Cult of Personality"). Most discussions relate the concept to politics, often with negative connotations. Tragically, this idolization of a person can work its way into the church with devastating consequences. Churches might put a person on a pedestal that belongs only to Jesus.

Corinth had a battle royal going over who was the greatest at preaching. Four candidates were in the running (v. 12):

- Paul: their **founder**, who was just an average preacher
- Apollos: the eloquent **preacher** from Alexandria, expositor extraordinaire
- Cephas (i.e., Peter): the Jewish apostle and **pillar** of the church from the inner circle of Jesus
- Jesus: the **Savior**!

Competition among the Corinthians—not the four men themselves—raged as different camps touted their choices. Each party within the church claimed an allegiance: "I belong to Paul," "I belong to Apollos," "I belong to Cephas," or "I belong to Christ." Determining the precise details leading to the situation is difficult. Verlyn Verbrugge suggests, "We should note that if the church at Corinth was composed of several worship centers in different homes, these 'parties' may represent different worshiping communities" (*1 and 2 Corinthians*, 265). And if there was a Christ party among the four, those in this group "were trying to rise above any human leaders and claim allegiance to Christ alone" (ibid., 266).

Paul was scandalized by the presence of party politics in the body of Christ. He expresses his alarm with three rhetorical questions in verse 13 that have clear-cut answers. "Is Christ divided?" No! "Was Paul crucified for you?" No! "Were you baptized in Paul's name?" No! Christ is one and his body is one. Christ and only Christ was crucified on the cross for our sins. Jesus, and Jesus alone, is the name into which we are immersed and identified in the waters of baptism. To say anything else is spiritual insanity! Christ has preeminence in all things (Col 1:18). Lose sight of that and only spiritual disaster will result. Don't take pride in being associated with people you and others esteem as important. Take pride in Jesus and only him! As Paul says in Galatians 6:14, "I will never boast about anything except the cross of our Lord Jesus Christ."

You Forget What Matters Most
1 CORINTHIANS 1:14-17

The church of the Lord Jesus Christ does many good and important things. In Matthew 28:18-20 Jesus tells us to "make disciples of all nations" by going, baptizing, and teaching. In Acts 2:41-47 the church was birthed on the day of Pentecost. Thereafter we see the infant church baptizing, teaching, fellowshipping, sharing the Lord's Supper, praying, caring for one another, and doing evangelism. In Ephesians 4:1-16 Paul informs us that the church is to pursue doctrinal unity and ministry diversity as all members are equipped for their work of ministry. However, all these good and essential activities rest on a single foundation: the gospel! Every good thing the church does must flow out of the good news of the gospel that Jesus Christ, the sinless Son of God, died on the cross for our sins according to the Scriptures, was buried, and rose again the third day according to the same (see 1 Cor 15:3-6). Christ and the cross must always remain of first importance in the life of a church! Otherwise, we can expect division and the absence of God's power.

It seems Corinth divided in part over who administered baptism. The books of Matthew, Acts, and Ephesians make abundantly clear the importance of baptism for the Christian community. No one in the first century would have understood a Christian's refusal to be baptized. It would have been nonsensical. To be a Christian is to publicly identify as a follower of Jesus Christ, which is beautifully symbolized through baptism by immersion (Rom 6:1-11). Biblical baptism involves three elements: a right *member*—that is, a believer in the gospel of Jesus Christ; the right *meaning*—a believer's identification with Christ in his death, burial, and resurrection; and also the right *mode*—immersion. Baptism is important, but it does not matter the most. The gospel matters most!

So Paul says in 1 Corinthians 1:14-16,

> *I thank God that I baptized none of you except Crispus and Gaius, so that no one can say you were baptized in my name. I did, in fact, baptize the household of Stephanas; beyond that, I don't recall if I baptized anyone else.*

Curtis Vaughn notes,

> Crispus is likely the synagogue ruler whose conversion is narrated in Acts 18:8. Gaius is probably Paul's host in Corinth mentioned in Romans 16:23. Stephanas is mentioned in 1 Corinthians 16:15, 17. (*1 Corinthians*, 28)

Paul was likely honored to have baptized these people. But what the Corinthians had done with baptism, specifically the status they'd given to the baptizer, was a travesty and mockery. Schreiner nails why:

> The person who performed the baptism is utterly insignificant. By paying attention to the person who baptized them, they were missing out on the true import of baptism . . . baptism must be subordinated to and understood within the context of the gospel. (*1 Corinthians*, 64)

Paul makes this clear in verse 17: "For Christ did not send me to baptize, but to preach the gospel." This is what Jesus called him to do, and this is why Jesus sent him to Corinth and the nations. Further, he was sent to preach the gospel "not with eloquent wisdom," not with *sophia* (wisdom) of *logos* (word). What all believers should be interested in is the substance of the gospel, not the style of one's delivery. Paul, for example, was not interested in Greek rhetorical "oratory and showmanship" (Schreiner, *1 Corinthians*, 65). Paul knew it was better to speak truth poorly than to say nothing with flair. Paul certainly cared nothing about the *delivery* of the gospel. Paul would agree that what you say and how you say it are important, yet the point is the medium must not get in the way of the message. The power is in the message! The power is in the preaching of the cross! If an impressive delivery overshadows the preaching of the good news, then the cross will be emptied of its power. The power of salvation is never in the messenger. The power of salvation is always in the message, the gospel, the cross of Christ.

Conclusion

I love the simple words of missionary Amy Carmichael in her reflection on the cross: "God hold us to that which drew us first, when the Cross was the attraction, and we wanted nothing else" (*Gold Cord*, 6). Believer, stay with Jesus and the cross. As we do, the church will be filled with life and unity for the glory of God.

Reflect and Discuss

1. In what ways does division in the church distort the gospel and ruin the church's reputation? How does unity promote the gospel to a lost world?
2. What does it mean to be of the "same understanding" and "same conviction"?
3. Do Christians downplay or accept quarreling in the church? If so, how?
4. In what ways do Christians attempt to justify their divisive and quarrelsome attitudes?
5. Some Corinthians divided over who baptized them. What issues are Christians currently quarreling and dividing over? Assess your heart and actions to see if you are participating in these.
6. Why do quarreling and divisiveness indicate that someone has lost sight of Christ?
7. Does the idea of unity in the church mean there must be complete agreement on every issue? Why or why not? What are the essentials that Christians must be united around? What can we disagree over

while still preserving unity? And what can we biblically, yet peace-fully, divide over?

8. What is ultimately behind divisiveness and quarreling within the body of Christ?

9. What does this passage teach about the church's identity? How can remembering this identity lead to unity? Why does forgetting it lead to division?

10. In what does Jesus exemplify the perfect pursuit of unity?

The Power of the Cross

1 CORINTHIANS 1:18-25

Main Idea: God displays his power and subverts worldly wisdom by bringing salvation through the message of a crucified Savior.

I. **The Word of the Cross Separates the Lost and Saved (1:18).**
   A. It is foolishness to the lost.
   B. It is the power of God to the saved.
II. **The Wisdom of the Cross Highlights the Foolishness of Worldly Wisdom (1:19-21).**
   A. It reveals the impotency of prideful people (1:19-20).
   B. It reveals the inadequacy of prideful ideas (1:21).
III. **The Witness to the Cross Is a Hindrance to Some but the Power of God to Others (1:22-25).**
   A. Some reject and ridicule the cross (1:22-23).
   B. Some receive and rejoice in the cross (1:24-25).

The wonderful pastor and Bible teacher James Boice well said, "The cross stands as the focal point of the Christian faith. Without the cross the Bible is an enigma, and the Gospel of salvation is an empty hope" (*Philippians*, 144). John Piper, in *Don't Waste Your Life*, adds to Boice's thoughts and prepares us for our study of 1 Corinthians 1:18-25. He writes,

> Life is wasted if we do not grasp the glory of the cross, cherish it for the treasure that it is, and cleave to it as the highest price of every pleasure and the deepest comfort in every pain. What was once foolishness to us—a crucified God—must become our wisdom and our power and our only boast in this world. (*Don't Waste Your Life*, 46)

Christianity is a Jesus Christ religion. It is a cross religion. Without the cross of Christ, there is no Christianity. And without a biblical understanding of the cross, there is no authentic Christianity. Salvation for fallen, lost, spiritually dead people comes only through a crucified and risen Savior. Faith in him is the one way to God. Billy Graham is reported as saying, "God proves his love on the cross. When Christ hung, bled, and died, it was God saying to the world, 'I love you.'" Paul, in 1:18-25, teaches that God also proved his power on the cross. Its message alone can give us spiritual and eternal life.

Paul will make three important theological observations about the cross of Christ in these verses. They are essential to a right understanding of what Jesus did when he died on a Roman cross in AD 33. They deserve careful meditation and reflection.

The Word of the Cross Separates the Lost and Saved
1 CORINTHIANS 1:18

Verses 18-25 naturally follow 1:10-17, as the word "for" indicates. Human wisdom exalts the cult of personality. Human wisdom seeks to empty the cross of Christ of its power. And both human wisdom and human power are at odds with God's plan of salvation. John Polhill writes,

> Paul considered the Corinthian espousal of their favorite teachers as the pursuit of human wisdom. He dealt with the problem in 1:18–3:23. First, he argued the incompatibility of divine and human wisdom. By human standards God's wisdom is foolishness (1:18–2:5). The cross is the ultimate demonstration of this (1:18-25). By all standards of human wisdom, the cross is foolishness—folly to the Greek way of wisdom as well as to the Jewish way of divine manifestation by sign. But God's way of salvation is through the cross. The cross is thus the negation of all human attempts to know God. One can only know God by first being known by God and called by God in the wisdom and power of Christ and his atoning death (v. 24). (*Paul and His Letters*, 237)

The cross divides all of humanity into two camps: the perishing and the saved. Paul will explain this idea throughout this paragraph, but he sets the table here in verse 18.

It Is Foolishness to the Lost

"The word of the cross is foolishness to those who are perishing." The phrase "the word of the cross" is synonymous with "preaching the gospel" (v. 17). There is no gospel without the cross, and there is no gospel without the resurrection (15:1-20). The ancients despised and loathed death by crucifixion. The Roman orator Cicero wrote, "The very word 'cross' should be far removed not only from the person of a Roman citizen but from his thoughts, his eyes and his ears" (*Pro Rabirio Perduellionis Reo* 5.16). The idea that this heinous act could bring humanity to God is unimaginable to the wisdom of this world. Yet, that is exactly what God chose to use. This message is received as "foolishness" (Gk. *moria*) by the spiritually lost, those described as in the process of "perishing," which Schreiner says, "is a common word in Paul for eschatological [end-time and final] destruction (e.g., Rom. 2:12; 1 Cor. 15:18; 2 Cor. 2:15; 4:3; 2 Thess. 2:10)" (*1 Corinthians*, 67). The perishing simply cannot believe the cross is the way of salvation: that seems absurd.

It Is the Power of God to the Saved

In verse 18 Paul contrasts those who are perishing with those "who are being saved." For the saved, the message of the cross is not foolishness. It is the power of God for our salvation (cf. Rom 1:16; also Rom 5:9; 1 Cor 5:5; 2 Cor 2:15; 1 Thess 2:16). In fact, the cross of Christ is the power of God that saves us in three tenses! It *delivered* us in the past from the *penalty* of sin (justification). It *delivers* us in the present from the *power* of sin (sanctification). It *will deliver* us in the future from the *presence* of sin (glorification). Nothing other than Jesus's death on the cross could save us. Indeed,

> Nothing can for sin atone, nothing but the blood of Jesus;
> Naught of good that I have done, nothing but the blood of
>   Jesus. (Robert Lowry, "Nothing but the Blood")

The cross of Christ is the great divide. Notice the contrast between what the cross means to the saved in comparison to the lost:

The Cross

The Saved	The Perishing (Lost)
Power	Weakness
Wisdom	Foolishness
Eternal Deliverance	Eternal Destruction

Power and Wisdom	Stumbling Block and Foolishness
Wisdom of God That Saves	Wisdom of the World That Condemns
Heaven	Hell
Righteousness	Unrighteousness
Sanctification	Uncleanness
Redemption	Slavery
Boast in the Lord	Boast in Self

The cross of Christ divides all humanity. For believers, this cross means God's power for us. But the cross was costly. C. S. Lewis points out, "It costs God nothing, so far as we know, to create nice things: but to convert rebellious wills cost [the] crucifixion [of His Son]" (*Mere Christianity*, 212).

The Wisdom of the Cross Highlights the Foolishness of Worldly Wisdom
1 CORINTHIANS 1:19-21

The Bible does not disapprove of knowledge or wisdom. Its question is, "Is it the right knowledge and wisdom you're accepting?" In Matthew 22:37, quoting Deuteronomy 6:5, Jesus commands us to love the Lord our God with all that we are. James 3:17 teaches that there is a "wisdom from above [that] is first pure, then peace-loving, gentle, compliant, full of mercy and good fruits, unwavering, without pretense." However, James also warns about worldly wisdom characterized by "bitter envy and selfish ambition. . . . Such wisdom does not come down from above but is earthly, unspiritual, demonic" (Jas 3:14-15). It does not reflect love for God.

We are in perpetual danger of being seduced by the inferior wisdom of this world. Our intellectual pride and arrogance find the world's wisdom attractive. It seduces us into boasting about ourselves and not in Christ, trusting in the pride of our intellects and not in the wisdom found in the cross. In 1 Corinthians 1:19-21 Paul shows the absolute folly and foolishness of trusting in any wisdom other than the wisdom of God revealed in Christ and his Word.

It Reveals the Impotency of Prideful People (1:19-20)

God tells us in Isaiah 55:8-9, "[M]y thoughts are not your thoughts, and your ways are not my ways. . . . For as heaven is higher than earth, so my ways are higher than your ways, and my thoughts than your thoughts." In 1 Corinthians 1:19 Paul affirms this truth by quoting Isaiah 29:14, where so-called prophets completely missed God's plan: "For it is written, I [God] will destroy the wisdom of the wise, and I will set aside the intelligence of the intelligent." (Jesus alludes to this same passage in Matt 15:8-9.) Curtis Vaughn correctly comments:

> [Paul] indicates that worldly cleverness fails in dealing with the things of God. Isaiah sees the failure of worldly statesmanship in Judah in the face of the judgment of the Assyrian invasion. Paul takes this principle and applies it to the failure of worldly wisdom in the face of the cross. (*1 Corinthians*, 29)

In 1 Corinthians 1:20 Paul teaches God's rejection of human wisdom with three stinging and sarcastic questions having clear-cut answers. First, "where is the one who is wise?" He is not here! Second, "where is the teacher of the law," the Jewish scholar? Even should one show up, he is not qualified to speak! Third, "where is the debater of this age," the person gifted in philosophy and rhetoric? He is nowhere to be found, but would have nothing valid to say! Even gifted people cannot contribute to what God has accomplished in the cross of Christ. God has shown the bankruptcy and foolishness of all mere human brilliance. God has "made the world's wisdom foolish." Fee sums it up perfectly:

> The cross is foolishness to the perishing (v. 18), but by means of it God has himself thereby rendered as foolish the world's wisdom; wisdom that belongs merely to the sphere of human self-sufficiency. God has not simply made such wisdom *appear* foolish; by means of the cross God has actually turned the tables on such wisdom altogether, so that it has been made into its very opposite—foolishness." (*Corinthians*, 2014, 75; emphasis in original)

Humans think they can reason their way to God, but God says, "No!" All who desire salvation must come to him through the cross! No matter how smart you think you are, God says, you are a fool to do life without Christ and his cross.

It Reveals the Inadequacy of Prideful Ideas (1:21)

Arrogant humans and their prideful ideas cannot be separated. They are a package deal. God has made both fallen people and their ideas foolish by his wisdom in the preaching of the cross. This was God's plan. Paul teaches, "In God's wisdom [that is, his sovereign plan], the world [meaning the whole human race] did not know God through wisdom." We couldn't. Fallen human reasoning and brilliance can never possess a saving knowledge of God or a relationship with him. As Paul says in Romans 1:22, "Claiming to be wise, they [only] became fools." We need salvation, not information. We need a Savior, not an educator. With irony and a bit of sarcasm, Paul declares, "God was pleased to save those who believe through the foolishness of what is preached." Gordon Fee comments,

> A God discovered by human wisdom will be both a projection
> of human fallenness and a source of human pride, and this
> constitutes the worship of the creature, not the Creator. The
> gods of the "wise" are seldom gracious to the undeserving,
> and they tend to make considerable demands on the ability
> of people to understand them; hence they become gods only
> for the elite and "deserving." It should be noted that Paul
> is here acknowledging that there is another *Sophia*, God's
> wisdom, which he is about to explicate (see v. 24); but that
> wisdom turns out to be the exact opposite of human wisdom.
> (*Corinthians*, 2014, 76)

And opposite it is! People do not save themselves. God does! Humans are not saved by what they know (by a philosophy) but by the one they believe in (a person brutally executed on a cross for the forgiveness of sins). The message of a crucified Savior strips prideful humans of all their genius and intellectual achievements. It drives us to our knees at the foot of a horrible instrument of execution and says, "Here and only here may we be forgiven. Here and only here may we find God!" In fact,

> I must needs go home by the way of the cross,
> There's no other way but this;
> I shall ne'er get sight of the gates of light,
> If the way of the cross I miss.
> The way of the cross leads home,
> The way of the cross leads home;

It is sweet to know as I onward go,
the way of the cross leads home. (Jessie Brown Pounds, "The
    Way of the Cross Leads Home")

Foolishness to the world. Salvation for those who believe. Oh, how amazing is the old rugged cross!

The Witness of the Cross Is a Hindrance to Some but the Power of God to Others
1 CORINTHIANS 1:22-25

The final verses of 1:18-25 reinforce and summarize Paul's argument. Wisdom continues to be the dominant theme. Paul has divided the world into two categories in verse 18: those who are perishing and those who are being saved. He will address both groups with greater detail in verses 22-25, revealing some additional subdivisions that provide historical and theological insight.

Some Reject and Ridicule the Cross (1:22-23)

Those who are perishing and headed for eternal damnation are subdivided into two categories: Jews and Greeks (by extension, think Gentiles). Paul divides them based on their particular rejection of the message of the cross. The Jews rejected the message because they asked for signs—the miraculous. Nothing could be more antithetical to their request than their Messiah dying like a bloody criminal on a cross. The idea of a crucified Messiah hanging on a tree, in fact, is repugnant and inconceivable to many Jews. Deuteronomy 21:23 even teaches, "anyone hung on a tree is under God's curse" (but see Gal 3:10-14). A crucified Jew on a Roman cross is as far away from the miraculous as you can get. Sadly, the Jews did not correctly interpret texts like Psalm 22 and Isaiah 53 that point to that very thing. They did not heed the words of Jesus either (Matt 12:38-42; 16:1-4; John 2:18-22; 6:30-66).

    In contrast to the Jews, "the Greeks seek wisdom." Knowledge was their pride, their idol. Heirs to Socrates, Plato, and Aristotle, the Greeks lifted sophists (traveling teachers of wisdom), popular rhetoricians, and debaters as the celebrities of the day. How could an ignorant Jew, crucified as a criminal, compare to their intellectual titans? *What a joke*, many no doubt thought. To such persons, the preaching of Christ crucified was not acceptable. Therefore, the cross was a "stumbling block" (Gk. *skandalon*), an offense to the Jews, and "foolish-ness [*morian*] to the Gentiles [*ethnē*]." It was utterly unimaginable to them. It was a message to be rejected and ridiculed for its lack of power and its foolishness.

Some Receive and Rejoice in the Cross (1:24-25)

The perishing (that is, the spiritually lost) stumble over the cross of Christ and find it foolish. It does not fit their ideas about how one encounters the divine. "Yet to those who are called [by divine initiative, cf. 1:2,9], both Jews and Greeks, Christ is the power of God and the wisdom of God." This is a divine work. God effectually calls sinners to himself by his power and wisdom. This is also an indiscriminate work. God calls both Jews and Greeks (Gentiles). And God's saving power is alive and active in the saved. God's wisdom, not man's, is thus alive and active in all whom he calls. Leon Morris says it well:

> The power in the cross opens the way for the humblest to
> know God and overcome evil, and that is a wisdom superior by
> far to anything the philosophers could produce. On the level
> of the search for wisdom the "foolishness" of God proved to be
> the true wisdom. (*1 Corinthians*, 46)

Paul concludes his argument by noting the paradox of the gospel of a crucified Savior. He uses two phrases we would not expect: "God's foolishness" and "God's weakness." We know that God is neither fool-ish nor weak. But the cross *looks* both foolish and weak to the world. Nevertheless, in reality, it is power and wisdom for salvation. It is how God saved us and how he will judge sinful humanity. By the cross God outsmarted the wise and overpowered the strong. God's seemingly fool-ish and weak thing is wiser and more powerful than anything mere mor-tals can come up with. Truly, the cross is what all who are being saved rejoice and boast in (1:31). We need nothing else. We want nothing more. It is all we need today and forever.

Conclusion

Keith and Kristyn Getty capture the truth of this passage in their song "The Power of the Cross." The cross has power because it is where Christ took our sin and died for us. The cross is where we are forgiven. Matthew Henry would add,

> Come and see the victories of the cross. . . . Christ's wounds
> are thy healing, his agonies thy repose, his conflicts thy
> conquests, his groans thy songs, his pains thine ease, his
> shame thy glory, his death thy life, his sufferings thy salvation.
> (*Communicant's Companion*, 130)

This is the beauty, the glory, the power of the cross! Hallelujah! What a
Savior we have in Jesus!

Review and Discuss

1. What is the message of the cross? What happens to the Bible without the cross?
2. How does one move from thinking the message of the cross is foolish to believing it is the power of God?
3. Why would God be pleased to offer salvation through a means the world considers foolish? How does the "foolishness" of the cross make the gospel message more accessible to everyone?
4. What types of boasting can we be tempted to make about ourselves instead of Christ?
5. In what other ways does God turn the tables on what the world considers foolish and wise?
6. The message of the cross was foolishness and offensive to the first-century Jews and Greeks. In what ways is it foolish or offensive to those around you?
7. How does God disrupt our ideas about how we "ought" to encounter the divine?
8. How does the message of the gospel prove that God is wiser than the world's standard?
9. In what ways may we be tempted to change the message of the gospel so that it does not appear foolish?
10. In what ways would it be true, as Fee stated, that "a God discovered by human wisdom will be both a projection of human fallenness and a source of human pride"?

No Superstars but a Savior

1 CORINTHIANS 1:26-31

Main Idea: God saves people of humble origins so that they only boast about him.

I. God Calls the Unlikely (1:26).
    A. He seldom calls the intelligent.
    B. He seldom calls the influential.
    C. He seldom calls the important.

II. God Chooses the Unimpressive (1:27-29).
    A. He chooses the foolish (1:27).
    B. He chooses the weak (1:27).
    C. He chooses the insignificant (1:28).
    D. He chooses the despised (1:28).
    E. He chooses the nobodies (1:28-29).

III. God Changes the Unworthy (1:30-31).
    A. Wisdom delivers us from sin's perspective (1:30).
    B. Righteousness delivers us from sin's penalty (1:30).
    C. Sanctification delivers us from sin's power (1:30).
    D. Redemption delivers us from sin's presence (1:30).
    E. Boasting in the Lord delivers us from sin's pride (1:31).

Many idolize celebrities and superstars. We elevate athletes, intellectuals, movie stars, musicians, and even politicians. We follow their every move and hang on their every word. We wish we could be like them, have their influence, and enjoy their wealth and popularity. We should expect those of the world to act and to think this way. There is nothing surprising about it. But when it comes to the church of the Lord Jesus Christ, such actions are inappropriate and wrongheaded. They fail to value and prioritize what all believers are to pursue: personal humility and service to others (Phil 2:3-5).

By extension, there is no place in the church for superstars. We have a Savior. His name is Jesus (Matt 1:21), and he is all we need. Further, God seldom (but occasionally!) calls the superstars of this world to himself. As Paul makes clear, he often calls the unlikely, the unimpressive, the unworthy, the nobodies of this world so that no one will boast in anything or anyone but their Lord Jesus (1 Cor 1:31). Martyred missionary Jim Elliot's words about missionaries also give an appropriate reminder for all followers of our Savior, King Jesus: "Missionaries [Christians] are very human folks, just doing what they are asked. Simply a bunch of nobodies trying to exalt Somebody" (Elliot, *Shadow*, 46). The only worthy Somebody. God turns the value systems of this world upside down. He did it by saving Jews and Gentiles through a crucified Savior (1:18-25), and he does it again in the types of people he calls to himself. This calls for a marvelous reversal and a radical transformation of thinking. I like Guy Waters's summation of the text:

> From the standpoint of God's wisdom, this world's values of
> worldly wisdom, power, and noble birth are null (1:26). God's
> wisdom exalts what is weak and despised in order to nullify
> human boasting (1:27-29) and to direct all boasting to God
> himself (1:31). These principles are nowhere more clearly
> on display than in the sufficiency of Christ for the believer's
> salvation (1:30). ("1–2 Corinthians," 229)

God Calls the Unlikely
1 CORINTHIANS 1:26

God's message of the cross is unimpressive to many Jews and Greeks (1:18-25). To them, it is not spectacular enough nor intellectually persuasive. People who demand such a standard from God and that he meet them on their terms are "too wise" and "too powerful" to come to him by way of a crucified man on a cross. Therefore, we should not be surprised or shocked at the kinds of people God typically draws to himself and who bow their knees to King Jesus at the cross. It is a motley crew to be sure! This is why Paul says to the proud Corinthians, you need to "consider your calling." He asks them to remember who they were and where they were when Jesus saved them! They were not an impressive lot! Warren Wiersbe is right: "God called them, not *because of* what they were, but *in spite of* what they were!" (*Be Wise*, 22; emphasis in original).

He Seldom Calls the Intelligent

Paul asks us to reflect on our lost state and condition before God effectually called us to himself in salvation. "Not many [he does *not* say "not any"] were wise from a human perspective" (lit. "wise according to the flesh"). The ESV says not many "were wise according to worldly standards." John Calvin aids our understanding when he writes,

> Paul, however, does not say here, that there are none of the noble and mighty that have been called by God, but that there are few. He states the design of this—that the Lord might bring down the glory of the flesh, by preferring the contemptible before the great. (*1 Corinthians*, 91)

A high IQ, an Ivy League education, or numerous degrees hanging on your wall will not give you an edge with God. It is not the wisdom of people that saves; it is the message of the cross. Being smart will not save you. Paul says in effect to the Corinthians, "Take a look!" There are not many PhDs holders among you. The intellectual elites are few in the kingdom.

He Seldom Calls the Influential

God does not often call the "powerful," the movers and shakers of the world, to salvation. Why? Like their intellectual companions, they do not see any need for God in their lives. "Look at all my money. Look at all I have. Look at who I am," they say. Jesus has a response to those who would claim security in position, prestige, and possessions: "Again I tell you, it is easier for a camel to go through the eye of a needle than for a rich person to enter the kingdom of God" (Matt 19:24).

He Seldom Calls the Important

God does not often call "many of noble birth" (MSG, "many from high society families"). These are the elite of society by virtue of their birth and connections. In Paul's day this group would include the Sanhedrin in the nation of Israel. It included the patricians or aristocrats of Roman society. These families "formed the privileged class of Roman citizens" ("Patricians"). Such groups carried enormous weight and influence. They were proud and self-sufficient. They felt they needed nothing and no one, including God with his ridiculous message of salvation based on a Jew dying on a cross.

God Chooses the Unimpressive
1 CORINTHIANS 1:27-29

Paul continues his argument by emphasizing God's work in calling us to himself in salvation. Three times Paul uses the phrase "God has chosen" (vv. 27-28). Our salvation has its origin and source in the divine will and purpose of God. It was God's plan to call the nobodies of this world through the cross of Christ. Schreiner is right:

> Just as the cross reverses human expectations in terms of how the world will be saved, so too God chose to save the most unlikely candidates—the *foolish* and *weak*. Those who are not esteemed for their wisdom and those who lack political power are among those whom God has savingly called to himself. (*1 Corinthians*, 72–73; emphasis in original)

Paul names five specific groups as the objects of God's gracious call to salvation.

He Chooses the Foolish (1:27)

God does not call to salvation many who are wise, powerful, and of noble birth (v. 26). Instead, he often calls the "foolish in this world to shame the wise." The word for "foolish" is *mōra*. It means the unintelligent, the stupid. *The Message* says, "I don't see many of the 'brightest and the best' among you." Not much room for boasting or pride is left after processing a statement like that. Shame on the "wise guys" who think they can reason their way to God with their powerful and impressive minds.

He Chooses the Weak (1:27)

God has also "chosen what is weak in the world to shame the strong." Choosing the weak of this world to bring glory to himself, began when God called small, insignificant Israel (Deut 7:7). Often in Scripture it appears God's typical pattern is to choose the most unlikely and unimpressive. In a world that idolizes but also cowers at power, God has decided to do his greatest work through weakness. What could be weaker than a poor, homeless Jew, bloody and beaten, hanging on a cross though innocent? Yet what could be more powerful than the salvation his death brought to the world?

He Chooses the Insignificant (1:28)

"God has chosen what is insignificant." God delights in saving the lowly over those of significance. He chooses common people over those of "noble birth." People that the world pays no attention to, God notices and uses them greatly for his glory! A shepherd boy named David whom he made a king. An uneducated farmer and tender of sycamore trees named Amos whom he made a prophet. An old woman named Anna whom he called to be a prophetess and who testified to the redemption of Jerusalem when she saw the baby Jesus (Luke 2:26-38). All of them are insignificant to the world but not to God.

He Chooses the Despised (1:28)

God has chosen what is "despised in the world." This word "despised" may simply amplify the word "insignificant" or "lowly." However, it would apply to all that the world holds in disdain, those deemed unimportant and pathetic by high society. Today some speak of "trailer trash" or people "from the hood." People this world categorically insults and treats poorly are prime candidates for God's grace and salvation.

He Chooses the Nobodies (1:28-29)

God has chosen "what is viewed as nothing" (ESV, "things that are not"), that is, the nobodies of this world. The world looks down on some people as worthless and useless zeros! God, however, prefers and often chooses the nobodies over the somebodies! He picks them first for his team. Why do things this way? First, "to bring to nothing what is viewed as something." Second, "so that no one may boast in his presence." Richard Hays notes there are echoes both of Hannah's prayer in 1 Samuel 2:1-10 and Mary's Song in Luke 1:46-53 here (*First Corinthians*, 77). Psalm 83:16,18 also adds a helpful commentary on these verses:

> Cover their faces with shame
> so that they will seek your name, LORD.
> . . .
> May they know that you alone—
> whose name is the LORD—
> are the Most High over the whole earth.

The third-century church father Origen of Alexandria wrote *Against Celsus* to counter the writings of that pagan philosopher. In it, he quoted Celsus's observations concerning the quality of Christian converts:

> The following are the rules laid down by them. Let no one come to us who has been instructed, or who is wise or prudent (for such qualifications are deemed evil by us); but if there be any ignorant, or unintelligent, or uninstructed, or foolish person, let them come with confidence. By which words, acknowledging that such individuals are worthy of their God, they manifestly show that they desire and are able to gain over only the silly, and the mean, and the stupid, with women and children. (Origen, *Against Celsus*, III.44)

Celsus's words are not entirely true, but they are not completely false either. God is in the habit of calling the unimpressive by the world's standards.

God Changes the Unworthy
1 CORINTHIANS 1:30-31

God hates pride. It is at the heart of all sin. A good question to ask and answer is, "What is pride?" Pastor John Piper provides a helpful description:

- It is boasting in self and not the Lord.
- It is taking credit ourselves for what God alone can do.
- It is relying on self and not God.
- It is feeling sufficiency in our own strength and not in God's.
- It is the disinclination to admit that we are mere earthen vessels so that another gets the glory.
- It is the unwillingness to admit weaknesses that may accent the power of Christ. ("Let Him Who Boasts Boast in the Lord!")

Paul has presented an argument that completely dismantles any claim to bringing about one's own salvation. Now he puts the nail in the coffin of any such arrogant thinking, noting once again that every good thing we have comes to us from God through his Son the Lord Jesus Christ.

Wisdom Delivers Us from Sin's Perspective (1:30)

Paul begins verse 30 by reminding us that "it is from [God] that [believers] are in Christ Jesus." Salvation is of God, not man. All praise and all boasting must be directed to God, never people. Salvation is in Christ and only Christ. Here is true wisdom, a wisdom older than creation itself (Prov 8:22-31) and made evident in the most unexpected way, in the cross. Sin told us we could save ourselves. The cross tells us only Christ can save us.

Righteousness Delivers Us from Sin's Penalty (1:30)

Three wonderful blessings of salvation are connected to God's wisdom in verse 30. They are "righteousness, sanctification, and redemption." The first one means that we are delivered from sin's penalty by the righteousness of Christ imputed to our accounts. It speaks to the great exchange! We give Christ our sin, and he gives us his righteousness (see 2 Cor 5:21).

Sanctification Delivers Us from Sin's Power (1:30)

"Sanctification" or "holiness" (NIV) delivers us from sin's power positionally and progressively. Schreiner says here Paul speaks of "the holiness that belongs to all believers by virtue of their union with Christ" (*1 Corinthians*, 75). In salvation, God sets us apart from sin and unto himself as his personal possessions. We are set apart *from* sin and *for* the Savior as holy priests called to serve him (1 Pet 2:9-10).

Redemption Delivers Us from Sin's Presence (1:30)

The word "redemption" recalls God's deliverance of the Hebrews out of Egyptian bondage. It also carries the idea of a price paid to purchase a slave. God has rescued sinners from their sin, and the price paid for each one is the precious blood of the Son of God (1 Pet 1:18-19).

Boasting in the Lord Delivers Us from Sin's Pride (1:31)

Verse 31 brings this section to a close. Once again Paul anchors his argument in the Old Testament, drawing from Jeremiah 9:23-24:

> *This is what the LORD says: The wise person should not boast in his wisdom; the strong should not boast in his strength; the wealthy should*

not boast in his wealth. But the one who boasts should boast in this:
that he understands and knows me—that I am the Lord, *showing*
faithful love, justice, and righteousness on the earth, for I delight in
these things. This is the Lord's *declaration.*

There is a place and time for boasting. The place is the cross and the
time—better, the person!—is in the Lord. The prideful will refuse to
come to God by the way of the cross and be saved. The humble, on the
other hand, will bow their knees to Christ and raise their voices to God:
"You did it all! You did it all!"

Conclusion

The gospel of Jesus Christ is an amazing story of God's great reversal in
his grand redemptive plan. The nobodies of earth can now become the
somebodies of heaven, because the great Somebody of heaven came for
the nobodies of earth! His weakness became our strength. His "foolishness" became our wisdom. His loss became our gain. His crucifixion
became our salvation! So let us boast loud and long, and let our boast
be in the Lord. Galatians 6:14 sums it up perfectly: "But as for me, I will
never boast about anything except the cross of our Lord Jesus Christ.
The world has been crucified to me through the cross, and I to the
world." Only to the cross should we ever and always cling.

Reflect and Discuss

1. In what ways could you be categorized as part of the following
   groups: the intelligent, influential, important? How might compar-
   ing yourself to the majority of the world help you to answer this
   question more honestly? How could this help you guard your heart
   against pride and other sins?
2. Is it possible for the church to implicitly communicate that it values
   or requires a certain social or economic status? If so, how?
3. How should the church handle the topic of Christian celebrities?
   What are some dangers or blessings that come when certain people
   are given more influence or status among believers?
4. Why is boasting so common in our culture? Why does God not want
   anyone to boast in his presence?
5. Since God calls the foolish, weak, and insignificant in the world,
   should Christians ever aspire to fame or political power? How might

achieving such things begin to lead believers toward pride? In what ways have Christians used personal influence for good?

6. Where do you see Jesus's relationships in the Gospels exemplifying God's choice of the unlikely, unimpressive, and unworthy? Who in your circle would fall into such categories?

7. How does God's choice of the unlikely, unimpressive, and unworthy contribute to what you value? How can you better value those deemed unworthy by most? How does your church make sure such people feel welcomed?

8. Does someone's character always match his or her intelligence? Why or why not? Are you ever tempted to think that low intelligence means less holiness or that high intelligence means more holiness? If so, explain why.

9. Why do both an inflated ego and a deflated ego evidence pride?

10. How should this passage influence your evangelism?

Jesus Christ and Him Crucified

1 CORINTHIANS 2:1-9

Main Idea: The church preaches the simple gospel message of Jesus Christ because God's power and God's wisdom are in the cross.

I. **The Cross Reveals the Power of God (2:1-5).**
   A. The method must be simple (2:1).
   B. The message must be clear (2:2).
   C. The messenger must be dependent on God (2:3-4).
   D. The motive must be sincere (2:5).
II. **The Cross Imparts the Wisdom of God (2:6-9).**
   A. There is a wisdom that will not last (2:6).
   B. There is a wisdom for our glory (2:7-9).

Those who love the Lord Jesus love his cross. They love it because wrath and mercy made peace there. Righteousness and grace united there. Because of the salvation made possible by the cross, Christians boast in it and nothing else (Gal 6:14). The cross is our delight, our joy, our hope, our all. Therefore, it grieves us when the spiritually lost, the "perishing" of 1:18, do not love the cross as we do. The Bible explains, however, why this is so: They can't make sense of it. They can't make sense of how a first-century Jew dying on a cross could be the means of anyone's salvation. Those who are intellectually driven will even call it "foolishness" (1:23). The simple message of the cross has no attraction for them. This reality opens the door to a dangerous temptation. We start to wonder if perhaps what we need to do is adorn the cross and make the message more attractive with eloquence and stirring rhetoric. Maybe if we spruce up the presentation, people will respond. To such thinking Paul gives a resounding "No!" The power is in the content of the message, not the delivery of the messenger. It is in the work of the Spirit, not in the wisdom of man.

Paul arrived in Corinth after a tough time in Athens (see Acts 17–18). Few there had believed the gospel of Jesus Christ. He could have been questioning his methods. Perhaps he even asked himself, "Should I adjust the message?" His conclusion is clear: "I will not change a thing!"

The gospel of Jesus Christ and him crucified is both the *power* of God and the *wisdom* of God. Paul addresses both in 1 Corinthians 2:1-9.

The Cross Reveals the Power of God
1 CORINTHIANS 2:1-5

Paul had determined in his soul that "he was an ambassador, not a 'Christian salesman'" (Wiersbe, *Be Wise*, 27). God had saved and called him to preach, not perform. The power to give spiritual life to spiritually dead people, he knew, came from the preaching of the cross. To faithfully carry out this assignment, Paul relied on four essential elements.

The Method Must Be Simple (2:1)

Paul says, "When I came to you, brothers and sisters, announcing the mystery [ESV, "testimony"] of God to you, I did not come with brilliance [NIV, "eloquence"] of speech or wisdom." Paul was not interested in impressing people with his oratorical abilities. He was not interested in people saying, "What a great preacher!" Paul knew there is always a danger of the messenger getting in the way of the message. He was always on guard to prevent this from happening. He knew people needed to see Christ and him crucified to be saved. John Henry Jowett (1863–1923), pastor of Westminster Chapel in London, is reported to have said,

> What we are after is not that folks shall say at the end of it all, "What an excellent sermon!" That is a measured failure. You are there to have them say when it is over, "What a great [Savior]!" It is something for men not to have been in your presence but in his. ("Preaching," *Christianity Today*, July 2002, 62)

When you preach or share the gospel, keep the method simple. Be sure to point others to Jesus, not you.

The Message Must Be Clear (2:2)

When we share the gospel, regardless of the context, our message must be clear. It is "Jesus Christ and him crucified." Paul said he had "decided to know nothing" among the Corinthians other than this. He knew this gospel is the only way of salvation. Paul certainly believed there are many important issues that the church needs to address. The rest of 1 Corinthians affirms this. But the gospel of a crucified and resurrected

Savior is the most important (1:18; 15:3-6). If Christianity ever loses the centrality of the cross, it will lose Christianity. Its message is simple and must always be presented clearly, repeatedly. It needs no addition, and we must never subtract from it. That Jesus died in our place (substitution) and paid in full the penalty of our sin (penal) is a nonnegotiable biblical truth. This message needs no adjustment. Share it in unvarnished clarity and trust God's Spirit to do his work. My friend Paul Tripp is spot on: "The cross confronts us with how we really are (sinners) and what we need (rescuing and forgiving grace)" (*Journey to the Cross*, 9). Present the gospel simply. Present the gospel clearly.

The Messenger Must Be Dependent on God (2:3-4)

Paul is autobiographical and transparent in verses 3-4. In verse 3 he bares his soul and says his time in Corinth was marked by three deficiencies in the world's eyes: his "weakness," "fear," and "much trembling." These phrases describe Paul's state of mind when he arrived at Corinth. He was not self-confident or cocky. He was scared and weak. His heart was pounding, and he was weak in the knees. The apostle knew that if anything good happened, it would be God's doing, not his. Today a man might claim an intimidating assignment is "beyond me," "over my head," or "above my pay grade." But dependence suggests we are exactly where God wants us. This is where God can use us greatly. Paul later says in 2 Corinthians 12:10, "For when I am weak, then I am strong." God delights in working through weak, God-dependent vessels.

A God-dependent mindset impacted Paul's approach to ministry and preaching, as verse 4 makes clear: "My speech [NIV, "message"] and my preaching were not with persuasive words of wisdom." Paul refused to fall into the trap of the Greek rhetoricians and sophists who would flatter, entice, and manipulate their audiences to gain applause and to line their own pockets. He knew if he talked the Corinthians into making commitments or decisions, then someone else could talk them out of them. Therefore, Paul would rely on "a demonstration of the Spirit's power." Paul would preach, and the Spirit would work. Paul would preach, but the Spirit would convert.

Tom Schreiner points out that Paul's ministry echoes Jesus's ministry: "The life of the apostle replicates . . . and matches the life of our Lord. The pathway to power is through weakness" (*1 Corinthians*, 77). Although Paul did not preach to entertain or receive applause, he did recognize the need to be clear and persuasive in the right way. He knew that *what* we say is more important than *how* we say it. But he also knew that how we say things is important too. We do not honor Christ and him crucified with poor preparation and presentation. Our great Savior always deserves our best, weak and feeble as it may be. Curtis Vaughn is a help when he writes:

> Nothing in Paul's words should be seen as an invitation to the contemporary preacher to make his words dull and insipid. God's message is to be presented in a creative arresting manner. The gospel must also be plain, clear, and undiluted. Paul feared greatly the dilution of the gospel by an excessive emphasis on form. So long as the content of the gospel is kept intact, the method of presenting it may be adjusted to the audience. (*1 Corinthians*, 34)

A God-dependent worker is still a hard worker.

It is better to say something poorly than to say nothing well. But it is better still to say something well and depend on the Spirit to do his work. It is said of Charles Spurgeon that as he would enter the pulpit he would repeat the words, "I believe in the ministry of the Holy Spirit." If this is true of the "Prince of Preachers," how much more should it be true of us?

The Motive Must Be Sincere (2:5)

When it comes to preaching or sharing the gospel, we must ask ourselves about our motives. Am I seeking my glory or God's? His praise or mine? I know of contemporary evangelists who guarantee that a certain percentage of those attending their meetings will "make decisions." That is, become believers. Such men—I dare not call them preachers—are masters of manipulation. Their ability to move people from one geographical location in an auditorium to another may be impressive for a moment to human eyes, but it borders on blasphemy to God's. As those who faithfully proclaim the gospel, we should never seek to add anyone to our spiritual trophy cases. No, our goal is to simply proclaim "Christ and him crucified" and to trust in the power of God to give saving faith to those who hear (v. 2). Proclaiming "Christ and him crucified" opens the door to "the Spirit's power" (v. 4), "God's power" (v. 5). Saving faith cannot be found in "human wisdom" no matter how brilliant and attractive it may be. Saving faith must have a saving object.

That object is "Christ and him crucified." As G. B. Wilson says, "A faith that depends on clever reasoning may be demolished by a more acute argument, but the faith which is produced by the power of God can never be overthrown" (quoted in Morris, *1 Corinthians*, 52).

The Cross Imparts the Wisdom of God
1 CORINTHIANS 2:6-9

The cross is both God's power (2:1-5) and God's wisdom (2:6-9). Unfortunately, those familiar with the cross are always in danger of losing both. By neglect or adjustment, the message of the cross can be explained away and lost. A. W. Tozer expressed this concern when he wrote:

> If I see aright, the cross of popular evangelicalism is not the cross of the New Testament. It is, rather, a new bright ornament upon the bosom of a self-assured and carnal Christianity whose hands are indeed the hands of Abel, but whose voice is the voice of Cain. The old cross slew men; the new cross entertains them. The old cross condemned; the new cross amuses. The old cross destroyed confidence in the flesh; the new cross encourages it. The old cross brought tears and blood; the new cross brings laughter. The flesh, smiling and confident, preaches and sings about the cross; before that cross it bows and toward that cross it points with carefully staged histrionics—but upon that cross it will not die, and the reproach of that cross it stubbornly refuses to bear. (*God's Pursuit of Man*, 62)

Paul wrote this letter to the church, not to the world. He wrote to the saved, not to the lost. He feared that blood-bought believers could lose the power of the cross and miss the wisdom of the cross. He was aware of the evil seductions of the flesh, the world, and Satan. He has addressed the power of the cross. Now, he turns to address its wisdom, building on what he previously wrote in 1:18-31. Once more Paul instructs us by making a sharp contrast.

There Is a Wisdom That Will Not Last (2:6)

Paul begins by saying there is a wisdom in Christ and him crucified, but it is not connected in any way to "human wisdom" (v. 5) or the "wisdom of this age" (v. 6). However, it requires spiritual maturity to rightly appreciate God's wisdom. In one sense Paul considers all Christians as "the mature" in contrast to the lost. However, he also recognizes that Christians don't always act mature. Amazingly, God's wisdom is quite simple. It is the preaching of the cross. To go beyond the cross or away from the cross reveals one is essentially a spiritual baby (3:1). Further, the wisdom of this world will not last. It is a wisdom that is at home in this present evil age (cf. Gal 1:4; 1 Tim 6:17) and characteristic of the evil rulers of this age (those that are human, not demonic). Such a wisdom is "coming to nothing" (1 Cor 2:6). It's headed nowhere. The way this world thinks and evaluates life is a dead end that will not deliver what it promises. Fee is right: "Those whom the Corinthians would especially give deference do not really know true wisdom; indeed they are themselves 'coming to nothing'" (*Corinthians*, 2014, 111).

There Is a Wisdom for Our Glory (2:7-9)

Romans 1:22 says of fallen, sinful humanity, "Claiming to be wise, they became fools." Perhaps nothing proves this truth more than what "the rulers of this age" did when they "crucified the Lord of glory" (1 Cor 2:8). Paul likely had in mind both Jewish and Roman leaders, particularly the Sanhedrin, Herod, and Pilate. The wisdom of this age is bankrupt indeed. But true and authentic wisdom, a wisdom of God, still exists. John Piper is right: "The Bible may condemn the wisdom of men but it will not surrender wisdom to the enemy" ("The Wisdom We Speak"). Only the wisdom of this age is "coming to nothing" (v. 6). Paul writes, "[W]e speak God's hidden wisdom in a mystery, a wisdom God predestined before the ages for our glory" (v. 7). Let's unwrap what Paul is saying here.

First, the idea of a "hidden wisdom in a mystery" draws from the language of Daniel 2 (see 2:18,19,27,28,29,30,47; also 4:9). A "mystery" in the New Testament speaks of something previously hidden but now revealed. It speaks of something humans could only know by divine revelation.

Second, God's hidden wisdom has a paradoxical nature to it. God had promised a deliverer, a Savior, throughout the Old Testament. There were prophecies, shadows, and types. However, because of human sinfulness, those promises were misunderstood and misinterpreted. Two things are a part of God's hidden mystery that brought clarity: the cross/resurrection and the teaching ministry of the Holy Spirit (1 Cor 2:10-13,15-16). Don Carson writes,

The point is that however much the Old Testament points
to Jesus, much of this prophecy is in veiled terms—in types
and shadows and structures of thought. The sacrificial system
prepares the way for the supreme sacrifice; the office of
high priest anticipates the supreme intermediary between
God and sinful human beings, the man Christ Jesus; the
passover displays God's wrath and provides a picture of
the ultimate passover lamb whose blood averts that wrath;
the announcement of a new covenant (Jer. 31) and a new
priesthood (Ps. 110) pronounce the obsolescence in principle
of the old covenant and priesthood. Hypothetically, if there
had been some perfect people around to observe what was
going on, people with an unblemished heart for God, they
might well have observed the patterns and understood the
plan. But the world has been peopled with sinners since the
fall, and the Old Testament Scriptures God gave were often in
some measure misunderstood. That there was human fault in
this misunderstanding is presupposed by Jesus himself when
he berates his followers: "How foolish you are, and how slow of
heart to believe all that the prophets have spoken! Did not the
Christ have to suffer these things and then enter his glory?"
(Luke 24:25-26). (*The Cross*, 49)

Third, Paul notes that this marvelous wisdom was "predestined before
the ages" (1 Cor 2:7). This was not a new idea in the mind of God, as if that
ever happens! (See Acts 4:28; Rom 8:29-30; Eph 1:5,11.) God planned
what would happen and when it would happen (cf. 1 Pet 1:10-12,20).

Fourth, the hidden and mysterious wisdom of God revealed in
"Christ and him crucified" is "for our glory" (1 Cor 2:2,7). This is unexpected but so wonderful. We know the cross brings glory to God, but
now we learn it is for our glory, too! This glory begins the moment one
is saved, and it will grow and increase until the day of his or her glorification and perfect conformation to the image of the Son (Rom 8:28-30).
Contrasting our destiny with that of the rulers of this age, J. B. Lightfoot
writes, "Our glory increases, while their glory wanes" (*Notes*, 175).

First Corinthians 2:8 drives home the point that "the rulers of this
age" completely missed this marvelous mystery and hidden wisdom.
Indeed, "None of the rulers of this age knew this wisdom, because if they

had known it, they would not have crucified the Lord of glory" (NLT, "glorious Lord"; cf. Jas 2:1). What sinful humanity did to the "Lord of glory" by nailing him to the cross reveals just how evil our hearts are and how blind our eyes are. The phrase "King of glory" is used of God in the Old Testament (Ps 24:10). Paul applies similar wording to Jesus. Leon Morris notes,

> More than one scholar has thought that this is the loftiest title Paul ever applied to Christ. It stands fitly alongside the application to him of words originally referring to Yahweh (1:31). Both show that Paul habitually assigned to Christ the highest place of all. (*1 Corinthians*, 55)

Paul's words bring us back to our ongoing effort to understand the dance in Scripture between divine sovereignty and human responsibility. The cross was God's plan that he marked out before time began. The cross is also the responsibility of the wicked "rulers of this age" who "crucified the Lord of glory" (1 Cor 2:8). Perhaps the apostle Peter says it in the simplest way in Acts 4:27-28:

> *For, in fact, in this city both Herod and Pontius Pilate, with the Gentiles and the people of Israel, assembled together against your holy servant Jesus, whom you anointed, to do whatever your hand and your will had predestined to take place.*

The evil "rulers of this age" did it, and God determined it would happen (1 Cor 2:6). A divine mystery indeed!

Paul's words in verse 9 are often read at funerals to speak about the wonderful glories that will be ours in heaven. However, in context, Paul is not talking about what will be ours in the future but what belongs to believers right now. Paul brings together several Old Testament texts (Isa 64:4; also Isa 52:15; 65:17; Jer 3:16). They demonstrate that humans could never learn the wonderful wisdom of Christ crucified on their own. No eye, ear, or heart could conceive (ESV, "imagine") such a thing. God had to reveal it. He has revealed it "for those who love him." Rationalism cannot reason to God. Empiricism cannot locate God. But as John MacArthur puts so well, "What man cannot find God has given. Man cannot come to God on his own, but God has come to him" (*1 Corinthians*, 62).

Conclusion

I conclude this chapter with a word from the wonderful medieval writer
Thomas à Kempis (1380–1471). He describes the gospel message so simply and so beautifully:

> In the Cross is salvation; in the Cross is life; in the Cross is
> protection against our enemies; in the Cross is infusion of
> heavenly sweetness; in the Cross is strength of mind; in the
> Cross is joy of spirit; in the Cross is excellence of virtue; in the
> Cross is perfection of holiness. There is no salvation of soul,
> nor hope of eternal life, save in the Cross. (*Inner Life*, 16)

Reflect and Discuss

1. In what ways can "brilliance of speech" (v. 1) distort the gospel message? Is persuasive rhetoric always harmful? Why or why not?
2. What is the difference between effective communication and human-centered rhetoric? How do you ensure that you effectively preach the gospel without deviating from the power of the message? What practices and motivations are necessary to do this well?
3. How can the loss of right motive for preaching the gospel lead one to start having impure motives?
4. What does having a simple method of presenting the gospel look like in your particular context?
5. How does Paul's focus on simple and clear preaching relieve the burdens we place on ourselves or the fears we have in evangelism?
6. Why does God delight to use people who are dependent on him? How is God able to display himself better through our weakness?
7. What is the difference between the wisdom of people (vv. 1,4) and the wisdom of the Spirit (vv. 6-7)?
8. How can the phrase "for our glory" (v. 7) help us to trust God as we attempt to understand his sovereign will?
9. In what ways does the title "Lord of glory" (v. 8) reveal both God's power and God's wisdom?
10. How would you summarize the gospel message in a clear and simple way?

What Kind of Person Are You?

1 CORINTHIANS 2:10–3:4

Main Idea: How a person thinks and lives will reveal whether he or she has the Spirit and is growing in maturity in Christ.

I. **The Natural Person Does What Comes Naturally (2:14).**
    A. The natural person does not accept spiritual things.
    B. The natural person does not appreciate spiritual things.
II. **The Spiritual Person Does What Comes Supernaturally (2:10-13, 15-16).**
    A. The spiritual person is informed by the Spirit (2:10-11).
    B. The spiritual person is instructed by the Spirit (2:12-13).
    C. The spiritual person is given insight by the Spirit (2:15).
    D. The spiritual person is made incomprehensible by the Spirit (2:15-16).
III. **The Carnal Person Does What Comes Unnaturally (3:1-4).**
    A. They are weak spiritually (3:1-2).
    B. They are willful in sin (3:3-4).

Several times in 1 Corinthians Paul divides the human race into categories for our spiritual instruction and edification. When he does so, he is not making a value judgment. He is not denying the image of God that exists in all people nor their innate value and worth (Gen 1:26-27). He is pointing us to spiritual truths and realities. In 1 Corinthians 1:18 he says the whole world can be divided into "those who are perishing" and those "who are being saved." In 1:22-23 he divides those who are lost spiritually into "Jews" and "Greeks" (Gentiles) to help us understand why they reject the "word of the cross" (1:18). To one it is a "stumbling block" (Jews), and to the other it is "foolishness" (Greeks/Gentiles).

In 2:10–3:4 Paul will again divide the human race into spiritual categories. But the division will be different from previous assessments. Just as he subdivided the perishing into Jews and Gentiles, he subdivides the saved into spiritual/mature and carnal/worldly. Unfortunately, this latter category of carnal/worldly/fleshly has opened the door for some terrible theology and a misunderstanding of the Christian life. I will do my best to work through this and bring biblical clarity. These verses, especially 3:1-4, will require a most careful study and investigation.

The Natural Person Does What Comes Naturally
1 CORINTHIANS 2:14

In 2:14 Paul refers to the lost person, the "perishing" of 1:18. These are lost people who act like lost people. They lack the Spirit of God and are enslaved to their fallen nature, their unregenerate souls. Paul says two things are true of the lost man or woman, "the person without the Spirit."

The Natural Person Does Not Accept Spiritual Things

"[T]he person without the Spirit [ESV, "the natural person"; KJV, "the natural man"] does not receive [ESV, "accept"] what comes from God's Spirit." The natural person is spiritually dead (Eph 2:1). There is no spiritual life within these people. They lack the necessary spiritual equipment to correctly process spiritual truth. Tom Schreiner writes,

> It is not that unbelievers cannot mentally grasp or
> comprehend the message of the gospel . . . they are unable
> to understand the truth and significance of the gospel
> because such things can be *discerned only through the Spirit.*
> (*1 Corinthians*, 84–85; emphasis in original)

They can hear the message, but they cannot translate it as spiritually valuable and wonderful. Only the Holy Spirit can do that, but they don't have him working on them.

The Natural Person Does Not Appreciate Spiritual Things

Commenting on the natural person, "the person without the Spirit," John Piper says one's "basic problem is not an *intellectual* inability to construe the meaning of Paul's message; the problem is the *moral* inability to assign the right value to it" ("How the Spirit Helps Us Understand"; emphasis in original). This explanation helps us to understand what Paul means in the latter part of verse 14. The gospel of "Jesus Christ and him crucified" (2:2) is once again deemed as "foolishness" (Gk. *moria*) to the person without the Spirit. On a certain level, such can understand it, evaluate it, and consider it. But they will determine it is "foolishness" (MSG, "silliness"). The reason they don't appreciate the gospel is clear: the natural person "is not able to understand it since it is evaluated [ESV, "discerned"] spiritually." The natural person without the Spirit cannot "make appropriate 'judgments' about what God is doing in the world" (Fee, *Corinthians*, 2014, 125). The natural person can read the Bible, hear the gospel, and weigh its meaning. However, without the work of the Spirit, he or she will never boast in it (1:31; Gal 6:14). They will never see it as beautiful, precious, and valuable. They are blind to its beauty, deaf to its melody, and insensitive to its fragrant aroma.

The Spiritual Person Does What Comes Supernaturally
1 CORINTHIANS 2:10-13,15-16

We now move to examine the second category of people Paul discusses in these verses: the "spiritual person[s]" (v. 15). These are saved persons who act like saved people. They are captive to the Spirit of God who has taken up residence in them as his temple (1 Cor 3:16; 6:19-20). These are men and women who love the Bible, God, Jesus, the gospel, the cross, holiness, the lost, the nations, and all things that glorify God (1 Cor 10:31). Paul makes four important observations about these spiritual persons.

The Spiritual Person Is Informed by the Spirit (2:10-11)

In John 14:16 Jesus promised us that the Spirit would come as our Counselor. Paul affirms this wonderful truth. He tells us that "God has revealed these things to us by the Spirit" (1 Cor 2:10). "These things" refers back to 2:1-9 and the wisdom of God revealed in the gospel of "Christ and him crucified." Our understanding and believing the gospel are gifts of the Spirit. We did not need human information. We needed divine revelation. We needed the Holy Spirit of God to take the truth of the crucifixion and resurrection of Jesus and drive its significance and value home to our hearts in the work of regeneration (Titus 3:5). The Spirit is perfectly equipped to do this "since the Spirit searches everything, even the depths of God"—that is, his wisdom and all it entails (1 Cor 2:10). Don Carson pinpoints what Paul means in this verse:

> Even though God has now so definitively brought his all-wise
> plan to fruition in the gospel of the crucified Messiah, people
> still do not believe. They still do not see that his plan is wise. If

we the "mature" have come to grasp it, it is because "God has revealed it to us by his Spirit" (2:10).

In other words, there has not only been an objective, public act of divine self-disclosure in the crucifixion of God's own Son, but there must also be a private work of God, by his Spirit, in the mind and heart of the individual. That is what distinguishes the believer from the unbeliever, the "mature" from the people of this age and the rulers of this age. If we "see" the truth of the gospel, therefore, it has nothing to do with our brilliance or insight; it has to do with the Spirit of God. If we should express unqualified gratitude to God for the gift of his Son, we should express no less gratitude to God for the gift of the Spirit who enables us to grasp the gospel of his Son. (*The Cross*, 52)

Paul provides an illustration in verse 11 to make his point. He asks, "For who knows a person's thoughts except his spirit within him?" The answer is no one unless we tell them. Well, that is also true of God. "In the same way, no one knows the thoughts of God except the Spirit of God," who of course is God! And as an act of amazing grace, God has informed us, "revealed these things to us by the Spirit."

The Spiritual Person Is Instructed by the Spirit (2:12-13)

The spiritual person stands in striking contrast to the natural person of verse 14. We have a different Spirit within us as our guide and instructor. Paul boldly declares, "Now we have not received the spirit of the world, but the Spirit who comes from God" (v. 12; see Rom 8:9,15; 12:2; Gal 3:2,14; 4:6). And why, at least in part, did God give us his Spirit? "So that we may understand what has been freely given to us by God." In other words, God does not play hide-and-seek with his sons and daughters. He has put himself in us so that we may know him truly and genuinely. Paul explains how this is accomplished in verse 13. Having the Spirit of God within us, we are equipped to "speak these things," the things (teachings) of God. We do so "not in words taught by human wisdom, but in those taught by the Spirit, explaining spiritual things to spiritual people." The CSB has a marginal reading: "spiritual things with spiritual words." I prefer this marginal reading. Believers explain and interpret spiritual matters with words that are given by the Spirit of God. As Andy Davis explains,

The spirit of the world, Satan, is teaching worldlings,
the people of the world, the language of the world. The
language of wealth, the language of power, the language of
pleasure, the language of self. . . . But the Spirit from God
teaches us the language of spiritual riches that God is freely
giving us. ("Wisdom")

The Spirit instructs us with his spiritual words. Today we have this wonderful gift of "spiritual words" in the Bible. We have an obligation to pass on the wonderful, spiritual words of Holy Scripture to others. A good teacher will gladly honor the teachings of his or her Master.

The Spiritual Person Is Given Insight by the Spirit (2:15)

Because spiritual persons are indwelt and instructed by the Spirit of God, they are given insight that the lost person does not have. Further, the lost person cannot understand or evaluate (ESV, "judge") the saved person. This is the meaning of verse 15. Warren Wiersbe puts it well: "The unsaved person does not understand the Christian; they live in two different worlds. But, the Christian understands the unsaved person" (*Be Wise*, 38). Conversion opens our eyes to see life in a new way, a more accurate way. The glasses provided by the Spirit change our perspective, our values, how we see the world. Leon Morris adds,

When the Spirit enters the life everything is changed and
one new thing that appears is the ability to make a right
judgment. This does not mean that the man has acquired
greatness; it means that the Spirit of God is guiding him. He
has the point of reference within himself and is thus able to
make judgments *about all things*. The force of *all* should not be
overlooked. The spiritual principle is the basis of judgment on
what we call the secular as well as the sacred. (*1 Corinthians*,
59–60; emphasis in original)

The Spiritual Person Is Made Incomprehensible by the Spirit (2:15-16)

Paul tells us the spiritual person "cannot be evaluated by anyone." *The Message* says they "can't be judged by unspiritual critics." Leon Morris again helps us to understand what Paul is saying. He writes,

> It is clear from the whole tenor of Paul's writings that he did
> not hold that men in whom was the Spirit of God could not be
> called upon to account for their actions (cf. 14:29). Much of this
> epistle is a criticism, if a loving and spiritual criticism, of *spiritual*
> men. His point is that the *spiritual* man cannot be judged by the
> natural man for precisely the same reason that he himself can
> judge all things. He has the Spirit of God within him and the
> natural man has not. This makes him an enigma to the natural
> man. What does the natural man know of spiritual things?
> Because he cannot know spiritual things (v. 14), he cannot
> judge spiritual people. (*1 Corinthians*, 60; emphasis in original)

Paul seals his argument in verse 16 with a question and another
affirmation of the deity of the Lord Jesus Christ. Paul asks, referring to
Isaiah 40:13, "For who has known the Lord's mind, that he may instruct
him?" The answer is no one. As Carson puts it, "[N]o one can successfully probe the depths of God's thoughts, let alone match wits with God"
(*The Cross*, 60). However, what the natural or worldly person cannot do,
we can because "we have the mind of Christ" (1 Cor 2:16). By means of
the indwelling Holy Spirit, the mind of the Lord Jesus is ours. His perspective is ours. This wonderful truth does not mean there is no need
for growth and maturing in our understanding of the things of God.
Some of us have a long way to go, as 3:1-4 makes abundantly clear.

The Carnal Person Does What Comes Unnaturally
1 CORINTHIANS 3:1-4

Paul now introduces us to a third category of persons, those he refers to
as "carnal" (KJV), "fleshly" (ESV), "worldly" (CSB). These are persons
who are saved but too often act like the lost. Paul says they are captive
to the flesh. Many have misunderstood these verses. So, let me provide a
simple list of what they mean and what they don't mean. Let's start with
what they *don't* mean:

- They don't mean you can accept Jesus as Savior but reject him
  as Lord.
- They don't mean you will never bear tangible fruit as a Christian.
- They don't mean you can become an unbelieving believer.
- They don't mean you can live your Christian life no differently
  than a non-Christian.

- They don't mean you can sit on the throne of your heart with Christ at your feet.
- They don't mean that though we are saved without works, we may have a faith without works.

Now, here's what they mean:

- Christians can be slow to mature in their faith without proper nourishment.
- Christians can sometimes act like spiritual babies when they should act like spiritual adults.
- Christians need to be reminded of the basics of the gospel even as they grow in their depth of understanding the gospel. The gospel is both milk and meat!
- Nominal Christianity is inauthentic Christianity.
- Spiritual backsliding is possible, but it should not be permanent (see 1 Cor 6:9-11; Gal 5:16-21).

With these preliminary observations in mind, let's see two points Paul makes with respect to the carnal person.

They Are Weak Spiritually (3:1-2)

Paul begins with a gentle touch by calling his readers "brothers and sisters." He believes they are spiritual family. Yet he tells them that because of their status as "babies in Christ" (v. 1), he had to acquaint them once again with the basics of the gospel (1 Cor 1–2) just like he did when he first evangelized them (Acts 18:1-17). He was "not able to speak to [them] as spiritual people but as people of the flesh," as spiritual infants. He adds in 1 Corinthians 3:2, "I gave you milk to drink, not solid food, since you were not yet ready for it. In fact, you are still not ready." We can sense the intensity and passion behind Paul's words. There was nothing wrong with Paul giving them milk (cf. Heb 5:12; 1 Pet 2:2) when they were first converted. They were spiritually weak, newborns. All they could digest was milk. Morris is exactly correct:

> He did not push the infant believers beyond their capacity, but gave them the teaching that was suited to their state. There was nothing blameworthy in their being "not yet ready for it." But it is otherwise when he says *you are still not ready*. . . . It was all very well for the Corinthians to have been in the

position of "infants" whey they actually were "infants." But they should have outgrown that state long since. (*1 Corinthians*, 61; emphasis in original)

Acting like a baby is cute when one is little but not when one is grown. The Corinthians were still weak when they should have been strong.

They Are Willful in Sin (3:3-4)

Babies are not accountable for their actions, but adults are. Paul hits the Corinthians with this reality and calls them out in verse 3: "you are still worldly" (ESV, "of the flesh"; KJV, "carnal"; NLT, "controlled by your sinful nature"). Paul cites their actions as evidence: "there is envy and strife among you." He concludes, "[A]re you not worldly and behaving like mere humans?" To provide a precise example, Paul draws on what he previously wrote in 1:10-12: "For whenever someone says, 'I belong to Paul,' and another, 'I belong to Apollos,' are you not acting like mere humans?" Bottom line, they were acting like pagans, persons without the Spirit. Division and factionalism are the way of the world, not the way of Christ. Demanding one's way and rights is the way of the flesh. Carnality gets us lost in the weeds, caring more about little things than big things. Always arguing but never content. Always fighting but never satisfied. Carnal Christians never build up the church; they always drag it down. And carnal Christians never exalt Christ; they ignore Christ.

> I lived for myself, I thought for myself,
> For myself, and none besides—
> Just as if Jesus had never lived,
> As if he had never died. (Drummond, *The Greatest*, 63)

Conclusion

What kind of person are you? It is important for all of us to answer that question. Salvation gets the Christian out of the world. Sanctification gets the world out of the Christian. What kind of person are you? If you are a person of natural depravity, come to Christ and be saved today. If you are a person of carnal immaturity, repent of your sins and flee to Christ as the rightful Lord of your life. And if you are a person of spiritual maturity, keep on growing and going for the glory of God that you may help win the natural person to Jesus and that you may influence the carnal person for Jesus.

Reflect and Discuss

1. If the lost person does what comes naturally, how important is prayer for him or her? In what ways should the spiritual state of lost people drive Christians to have compassion for them? Why is compassion often missing from believers' interactions with unbelievers online and in person?
2. What does it mean to be a "spiritual" person according to this passage?
3. How do you see the Trinity at work in this passage? What works does each member of the Trinity perform?
4. Are Christians ever without the need of the Spirit to teach them the things of God? Why should our past need for the Spirit to change us lead us to depend daily on the Spirit to teach us?
5. Paul addresses the immature believers as "brothers and sisters." How does this reflect the mercy of God?
6. According to 3:1-3, what makes a believer a spiritual baby? What happens when the church begins to associate maturity in Christ with knowledge as opposed to having godly character?
7. What has God given to the church so that believers can grow into maturity?
8. Is it surprising to you that Paul highlights envy and strife as indicative of spiritual infancy? Why are these matters so dangerous to us as individuals and to the church of which we are a part? What reasons might Christians give to excuse strife and envy in their midst?
9. Review the list on pages 56–57 regarding what 3:1-4 does and does not mean. How do these compare to what you have believed up to this point? How does this list reshape your thinking?
10. Why is nominal Christianity inauthentic Christianity? What is the solution for nominal Christianity?

The Church of God

1 CORINTHIANS 3:5-17

Main Idea: God uses his servants to build the church and will judge the quality of each person's work, but he is responsible for the church's growth.

I. **The Church Is God's Field (3:5-9).**
   A. We are servants who work together (3:5-6,8-9).
   B. God is the Lord who gives the growth (3:6-7).
II. **The Church Is God's Building (3:9-15).**
   A. The foundation is Christ (3:9-11).
   B. Our construction must be careful (3:12-13).
   C. God's evaluation will be correct (3:13-15).
III. **The Church Is God's Temple (3:16-17).**
   A. We are his sanctuary (3:16).
   B. We have his Spirit (3:16).
   C. We are special (3:17).
   D. We are sacred (3:17).

There are two words in the English language that will make almost all students cringe, their blood pressure go up, and sweat break out on their brows: final exam. And like students, every Christian is going to face a final exam before God. Second Corinthians 5:10 says, "For we must all appear before the judgment seat of Christ, so that each may be repaid for what he has done in the body, whether good or evil." You cannot cram for this exam because in an unusual twist you are taking it right now. You have been taking it since the day you were saved and born again. This exam is not about your salvation but your service. Every believer in Jesus Christ will give an account for his or her service as a Christian, and those who do the work of teaching are being graded more strictly. James 3:1 thus points out, "Not many should become teachers, my brothers, because you know that we will receive a stricter judgment." Report cards, of a sort, will come on judgment day.

Paul will use three pictures to describe the church of God in verses 5-17: a field (vv. 5-9), a building (vv. 9-15), and a temple (vv. 16-17). His goal is to put dedicated ministers and the ministry in proper perspective for the divisive, quarreling Corinthians. In the work of the Lord there are no superstars, only servants who point others to Jesus Christ and him crucified (2:2). He is the only way to salvation. He is the church's foundation (3:11). Let us glorify God by making much of his Son, the Savior, not the Lord's servants.

The Church Is God's Field
1 CORINTHIANS 3:5-9

The congregation at Corinth was in trouble. They had allowed politics to infiltrate the church. As a result, they were acting more like rival political parties than brothers and sisters in Christ. Members were exalting Paul, Apollos, or Cephas (3:22). They were putting them on inappropriate pedestals. Paul, therefore, wants to set the record straight. Christian teachers are servants whom God sovereignly assigns. They do what they do because God called them to their tasks. Further, they are ultimately responsible to him, as everyone is, and he will hold them accountable for their work. Paul puts it perfectly in 4:1 when he writes, "A person should think of us in this way: as servants of Christ."

We Are Servants Who Work Together (3:5-6,8-9)

Paul begins verse 5 with two rhetorical questions: "What then is Apollos? What is Paul?" He answers: "They are servants [*diakonoi*] through whom you believed." They are instruments used by God, and "each has the role [NLT, "work"] the Lord has given." They are doing what God has called them to do. In verse 6 Paul focuses on how God used his servants in the church at Corinth. Paul "planted, Apollos watered." Verses 8-9 reinforce this image and draw attention to the fact we are on the same team striving for the same goal in ministry. "Now he who plants and he who waters are one," working to the same end or purpose. "We are God's coworkers" working in "God's field" (v. 9). Here "God's field" references the local church at Corinth. And God takes notice of his servants, his "fellow workers" (ESV). "Each will receive his own reward according to his labor" (v. 8). Schreiner says, "God will evaluate quality of work and apportion rewards accordingly" (*1 Corinthians*, 89). God makes the assignments and "gives the growth" (v. 7). However, how we serve matters. What we do and why we do it matter. Our service to Christ is essential and meaningful, even to the "intentions of the hearts" (4:5).

God's servants are teammates, working with one another. We are not in competition with one another. I like the way Vaughn and Lea put it: "Paul notes the essential unity between planter and waterer (v. 8). They are one in the aim, result, and motivating power of their work. They are allies and not rivals" (*1 Corinthians*, 41).

God Is the Lord Who Gives the Growth (3:6-7)

In terms of working in God's field, the Lord's servants do their part by planting and watering faithfully. However, they cannot make people grow spiritually any more than a farmer can make a carrot grow physically. God and God alone "gave the growth" in Corinth (v. 6). The words of Jesus in John 4:34-38 and Matthew 9:38 can be heard ringing in the background. God is the "Lord of the harvest"!

In 1 Corinthians 3:7 Paul gives the proper perspective on God's economy. The words are humbling but necessary when the cult of personality has wormed its way into the church. "So, then, neither the one who plants [Paul] nor the one who waters [Apollos] is anything, but only God who gives the growth." Carson says,

> To heap unqualified and exclusive praise on the sower is to focus too narrowly; to praise those who handle the irrigation and forget those who sow the seed is to be myopic. In any case it is God alone who makes things grow. Should not he be praised? (*The Cross*, 76)

Exalting a person to divine status is idolatry and robs God of the glory that rightly belongs only to him. Thank him for the service of his servants, but praise him for the growth in his field that only he can give. As Matthew 9:38 says, he is "the Lord of the harvest." Compared to God, Paul would say, "Apollos and I amount to nothing!"

The Church Is God's Building
1 CORINTHIANS 3:9-15

Paul shifts from an agricultural image to an architectural image in verses 9-15. The church of the Lord Jesus is his field in which he sends his servants and coworkers to plant, water, cultivate, and reap a harvest. It is also his "building" (v. 9) where he sends his "skilled master builder" (v. 10) and other laborers and workers to build with materials of excellence that will withstand the purifying fires of revelation on "the day" of judgment (v. 13), which Paul calls in 2 Corinthians 5:10 "the judgment seat of Christ."

The Foundation Is Christ (3:9-11)

Salvation is by grace, and so is anyone's service in ministry. Paul says, "According to God's grace that was given to me, I have laid a foundation as a skilled master builder [Gk. *architekton*]," a foundation on which "another builds." This indicates Christians work together as a team. They work to build a local church that will flourish for the glory of God and the good of all nations. And because it is the church of the Lord Jesus, "each one is to be careful how he builds." We are to serve Christ and build up his church with excellence and integrity. We work with good motives, methods, and goals. *How* we work in and for the church matters. *Why* we work in and for the church matters. The reason is made clear in verse 11 as Paul draws attention to the foundation of the building: "For no one can lay any foundation other than what has been laid down. That foundation is Jesus Christ" (v. 11). The founding principle for every church is Jesus Christ and him crucified (2:2). It is the gospel. No other starting place is acceptable before God. If we have any foundation but Jesus and his Word, we will not have a true church! Warren Wiersbe writes,

> The foundation is laid by the proclaiming of the gospel of Jesus Christ. The foundation is the most important part of the building because it determines the size, shape, and strength of the superstructure. A ministry may seem successful for a time, but if it is not founded on Christ, it will eventually collapse and disappear. (*Be Wise*, 46)

What a critically important word for our day when many so-called churches are building on personalities, programs, politics, and social agendas. What is your church known for? What is it standing on? Christ and him crucified are the only things that will last!

Our Construction Must Be Careful (3:12-13)

The foundation has been laid. It is the gospel as explained in Scripture. Now workers build on this rock-solid, unbreakable, and eternal foundation. But there is a question: How will we build? Paul uses an illustration to show that how we build is important, particularly in terms of the materials we use. Some materials are long-lasting and valuable. They will survive the test of fire (v. 13). Paul equates quality, right-focused work done for God with "gold, silver, and costly stones." However, it is possible to do ministry and service in the church that lacks lasting value. Some efforts are of little value. Paul calls these "wood, hay, or straw." Spiritually speaking, the key in many cases between good and cheap building material is motive. Think, *Why do I do what I do? Whose glory do I work for?* Although we may not always be able to tell the difference between quality kingdom work and its opposite due to our limited and finite perspective, God can. Paul tells us, "Each one's work will become obvious" (v. 13). There is coming a day, a day of judgment for the believer, when the quality of our service for Christ will be revealed. Verses 13-15 tell us exactly how this will happen.

God's Evaluation Will Be Correct (3:13-15)
(cf. Rom 14:10; 2 Cor 5:10)

Revelation 19:12 teaches us that the exalted Lord Jesus has eyes "like a fiery flame." This language speaks of his omniscience and penetrating judgment into the innermost depths of the human soul. Those eyes judge the works of believers done in service to our Lord, and we will hear his ruling on what Paul calls "the day" (1 Cor 3:13). This is the day of the Lord when Christ returns. On that day the works of each believer will be disclosed because they "will be revealed by fire." This fire "will test the quality of each one's work. If anyone's work that he has built survives, he will receive a reward. If anyone's work is burned up, he will experience loss, but he himself will be saved—but only as through fire" (vv. 13-15). We need to understand several theological truths about this text and others like it.

- This is a judgment of service, not salvation.
- This is the judgment seat of Christ for believers (2 Cor 5:10), not the great white throne judgment of unbelievers (Rev 20:11-15).
- This judgment will be impartial and perfect.
- This judgment involves the quality of our work, not its quantity.
- This judgment will evaluate both actions and motives (1 Cor 4:5).

Christ will judge what we taught, believed, and lived before others. Ministers of the Word and leaders in the church will be held to a higher standard of responsibility and judgment.

Just as there are degrees of punishment in hell (Matt 11:20-24), there will be degrees of reward in heaven. However, no believer will be jealous, envious, or unfulfilled. The Puritan Thomas Watson said it well:

> And let me tell you, the more labour you have put forth for the kingdom of heaven, the more degrees of glory you shall have. As there are degrees of torment in hell (Matthew 23:14 [KJV]), so of glory in heaven. As one star differs from another in glory, so shall one saint (1 Corinthians 15:41). Though every vessel of mercy shall be full, yet one may hold more than another. (*A Body of Practical Divinity*, 632)

The Church Is God's Temple
1 CORINTHIANS 3:16-17

Paul now introduces a third metaphor or image to describe the Lord's church, though it is possible to see it as an extension of the "building" metaphor of verses 9-15. The image is that of "God's temple." The phrase is used three times in verses 16-17. Later Paul will talk about the believer's body as a "temple of the Holy Spirit" (6:19), but here he is talking about the church, the "body of Christ" (see 1 Cor 12:27; Eph 4:12; 5:23). Paul will make four observations that naturally flow from this picture of the Lord's church.

We Are His Sanctuary (3:16)

Paul raises a rhetorical question, which is something of a rebuke: "Don't you yourselves know you are God's temple?" The Greek word for "not" is fronted for emphasis. This text was first written in Greek. The word translated "temple" was originally the Greek word *naos*, which refers to the temple's inner sanctuary. That would have powerfully impacted the first readers of this letter. Christians are God's special, holy creation. They are also God's temple, his holy place. What an amazing statement of their identity in Christ and their status before God. But there is more.

We Have His Spirit (3:16)

As God's temple, "the Spirit of God lives in you." Vaughn says, "In believers the very presence of God exists" (*1 Corinthians*, 44). Schreiner adds, "Just as Yahweh resided in the temple under the old covenant and in Israel (Exod. 25:8; 29:45; Lev. 26:11-12; Ps. 114:2), so now *God's Spirit* dwells in the new temple, the church of Jesus Christ" (*1 Corinthians*, 93; emphasis in original). Paul will emphasize the church as God's temple again in 2 Corinthians 6:16 and Ephesians 2:19-22. Jewish and Gentile believers of the first century would be stunned by this declaration. The sovereign God of the universe now dwells in a small, insignificant people called the church. It is the current temple of God.

We Are Special (3:17)

God loves and cares deeply for his church, which was purchased by the precious blood of his dear Son (Acts 20:28). Therefore, those who minister as his servants and workers should take great care in how they treat it. Paul sounds the strongest possible warning: "If anyone destroys God's temple, God will destroy him" (v. 17). These words should take our breath away and call for the most careful reflection. If "anyone" is inclusive and comprehensive, no one is excluded. Carson notes,

> The ways of destroying [a] church are many and colorful. Raw factionalism will do it. Rank heresy will do it. Taking your eyes off the cross and letting other, more peripheral matters dominate the agenda will do it—admittedly more slowly than frank heresy, but just as effectively on the long haul. (*The Cross*, 83)

A focus on entertainment, false conversions, preaching a watered-down gospel, spending resources on fancy programs or impressive buildings, weak preaching, acceptance of gossip and materialism, lack of prayer, loss of missions and evangelistic passion, and much more will drain a local church of its life.

But destroy God's temple, and "God will destroy [us]." We have been told those who build the Lord's church well will be properly rewarded. Now we are told that those who destroy his church, his temple, will themselves be destroyed. The warning of Galatians 1:8-9 immediately comes to my mind:

But even if we or an angel from heaven should preach to you a gospel
contrary to what we have preached to you, a curse be on him! As we
have said before, I now say again: If anyone is preaching to you a
gospel contrary to what you received, a curse be on him!

Paul does not specify the destruction. Perhaps Vaughn puts it best: "It
refers to something grave. It represents some terrible ruin and eternal
loss" (*1 Corinthians*, 44).

We Are Sacred (3:17)

Paul concludes this section with a final reason why those who serve the
church should watch that they serve it properly: "For God's temple is
holy, and that is what you are." The idea of "holy" is separation. Through
faith in the crucified Christ, the church is now separated from the world
unto him for purity of life and devotion. We are now his. We are those
chosen by God. Amazingly, God chooses to live in and among his people, the church! What a blessing. What a privilege. What a responsibility.
We must serve her well. We are under examination.

Conclusion

Salvation is by grace alone through faith alone in Christ alone. It is a gift
we cannot earn. It is not a reward for the things we do. Jesus lived as we
should have lived but didn't. He died the death we should have died but
now don't have to. He offers us the gift of eternal life we do not deserve
but can freely receive by faith alone. All of this makes many Christians
hesitant to talk about rewards. We even get spiritually squeamish.
However, that should not be the case when rewards are correctly understood. Jesus taught us that God will reward his servants and coworkers for the good works of service they have performed as Christians
(Matt 6:4,6,18). He admonishes us to "store up . . . treasures in heaven"
(Matt 6:20). So, as we anticipate standing before the "judgment seat of
Christ" (2 Cor 5:10), what kind of works will our Savior reward? Andy
Davis's supreme book on heaven, *The Glory Now Revealed*, lists ten kinds
of good works we should pursue every day of our Christian lives. We
choose good works out of gratitude for our salvation and a desire to
glorify our Savior in all we do (1 Cor 10:31; Eph 2:10). These gospel-
inspired pursuits provide a fitting conclusion to this chapter:

1. Anything done for the glory of God (even simple daily tasks; 1 Cor 10:31)
2. Humble servanthood (Matt 20:26-28)
3. Sacrificial giving (2 Sam 24:24; Luke 21:3; 2 Cor 9:6-7)
4. Suffering for the kingdom (Matt 5:11-12)
5. Advancing the gospel (1 Thess 2:19)
6. Giving to the poor (Luke 14:12-14)
7. Secret acts of piety—fasting and prayer (Matt 6:6,18)
8. Anything done to help those advancing the gospel (Matt 10:42)
9. Anything done to help other Christians in any way (Heb 6:10)
10. An honorable life of hard work (1 Thess 4:11-12)

Reflect and Discuss

1. What role has the Lord currently given you to serve the church? Are you serving in that role well?
2. Do you think it would have been easy for Paul or Apollos to be jealous of the other's role in the church? Why or why not? Have you ever been jealous of another's role? Why should you be joyful about where God has placed you?
3. How does the phrase "but only God gives the growth" (v. 7) free you from the burden of producing results?
4. What steps do you need to take to avoid elevating your view of yourself or another's role in the church?
5. Should Christians be motivated in ministry by the reward(s) God promises? Why or why not?
6. How can motives contribute to whether a person builds the church with permanent/valuable materials or temporary/cheap materials?
7. What difference does it make that God judges Christians for the *quality* of their work, not the *quantity*? Also, why is it important he judges actions *and* motives?
8. How will knowing that each person will be judged for his or her work help you fight against jealousy and rivalry?
9. How does verse 17 function as both a warning and a blessing?
10. What stands out about the above list of works that God will reward? Are any of these out of reach for the ordinary Christian?

In Christ We Have It All

1 CORINTHIANS 3:18-23

Main Idea: Worldly wisdom fuels competition in the church and causes Christians to forget they have everything in Christ.

I. Do Not Deceive Yourself; Know What True Wisdom Is (3:18).
II. Remember, God Sees Every Action and Knows Every Thought (3:19-20).
III. Enjoy Every Blessing of God Because All Things Belong to You (3:21-23).

In 1987, singing sensation Whitney Houston released her hit "Didn't We Almost Have It All." It quickly shot to number one on the Billboard Hot 100 and was nominated for a Grammy Song of the Year. Tragically, its lyrics serve as a commentary on many people who have so much but still lack. Sadly, many strive in this life to have it "all" in what this world offers only to find heartache, disappointment, and regret in the end. The world promises, but it fails to deliver. Thankfully, there is one who delivers all that he promises and even more. It is Christ and him crucified (2:2).

Paul returns to themes he addressed in 1:10–2:9. There is a wisdom from the world and a wisdom from God. One leads to foolishness and spiritual death. The other leads to true wisdom and spiritual life. One will make promises it cannot keep. The other will give you more than you could ever hope or imagine!

Verse 21 unlocks these final verses in 1 Corinthians 3: "For everything is yours." This verse is a wonderful and comprehensive promise because "[we] belong to Christ, and Christ belongs to God" (v. 23). Therefore, in light of these wonderful truths, how should we live? Paul provides us three directives.

Do Not Deceive Yourself; Know What True Wisdom Is
1 CORINTHIANS 3:18

Paul informs us in 3:5-17 that the church is God's field, building, and temple. God cares about his church and will condemn and destroy anyone who destroys that temple (v. 17). In light of this reality Paul gives a command in verse 18 that functions as a hinge verse that looks backward and forward: "Let no one deceive himself." Be on guard against self-deception. *The Message* reads, "Don't fool yourself." Paul is concerned about the Corinthians because they were acting like infants (3:1). They were thinking more of themselves and their leaders than they should. They were adopting the mind of the world, not "the mind of Christ" (2:16).

Paul pushes the point with what follows: "If anyone among you thinks he is wise in this age, let him become [third-person imperative] a fool so that he can become wise." Carson notes well that we must see that . . .

> the Almighty utterly reverses so many of the values cherished
> by the world. What the world judges wise, God dismisses as
> folly; what the world rejects as foolishness is nothing less than
> God's wisdom. (*The Cross*, 84)

Our evidence is the cross of Christ! The world delights in power and might. God works in weakness and suffering. The wisdom of this world mocks the cross. The wisdom of God glories in the cross. In terms of ministry, God works through servants, not superstars. He works through the nobodies, rarely the somebodies (1:26-29). God operates in a great reversal of values and norms. This is true wisdom. Don't be deceived and led away from the wisdom of the cross. The crucified life must accompany us all the days of our lives (Mark 8:34). The crucified life gives us new eyes through which we can see clearly.

Remember, God Sees Every Action and Knows Every Thought
1 CORINTHIANS 3:19-20

Tom Schreiner writes,

> If believers, then, are "wise" during the present era, they are
> joining forces with those who deem the cross to be foolishness.
> They may think they are on the right side of history, but they
> are actually on the wrong side of history. (*1 Corinthians*, 95)

What Schreiner refers to as this "present era," Paul calls "this age" (cf. 2:6-8) in verse 18 and "this world" in verse 19. Buying into the wisdom of this "present evil age" (Gal 1:4) is evidence of being self-deceived. It is to have a wisdom that "is foolishness with God" (1 Cor 3:19). Paul cites two Old Testament texts to give his thesis warrant: Job 5:13 and Psalm 94:11. God, Job says, turns the craftiness of the wise of this world back on them. Vaughn says, "The tricky measures of the wise become a net with which God captures them" (*1 Corinthians*, 45). They think they are wise. They even boast of their wisdom, only to discover it is their demise and destruction. The psalmist citation carries Paul's argument one step further, peering into the souls of the so-called wise. It says, "The Lord knows that the reasonings of the wise are futile" (1 Cor 3:20). In their actions and their thinking, the wise of this age demonstrate their foolishness. They are especially foolish in their boasting about men, not God, and in their idolization of leaders and power. That such thinking could make its way into the churches is scandalous, shameful, and maddening. Anthony Thiselton notes the appeal of Psalm 94:11 to the Corinthian dilemma:

> Psalm 94 stresses that in spite of manipulative and corrupt
> leadership by those in authority (Ps. 94:5-7,16) the "schemes"
> of these human persons fail because their best "thinkers" are
> fallible (Ps. 94:11). (*First Epistle*, 323)

The plans of the wise of the world are foolish, empty, and ineffective. In the great and grand reversal, "God, by use of what men call foolishness, has set man free from sin, provided him righteousness, and set him on the path to holiness" (Vaughn, *1 Corinthians*, 45).

God sees every action and knows every thought of every person. If we desire to be wise in the eyes of God, we must believe, live, think, and act in ways that this world sees as foolish. Run the other way from worldly fads and ideologies. They will only let you down. In the end you will have played the fool.

Enjoy Every Blessing of God Because All Things Belong to You
1 CORINTHIANS 3:21-23

Paul will now pick up a theme he positively laid down in 1:31: "Let the one who boasts, boast in the Lord." Now in chapter 3 he says it negatively and with specificity: "So let no one boast [third-person imperative] in human leaders" (v. 21). The context is the factionalism and party politics that were tearing the church apart. This secular, worldly way of acting was problematic for at least two reasons. As Carson notes,

> It is wrong because the focus is wrong; the concentration is on some human being and not on the Lord God . . . the second reason why it is wrong to boast about some human leader or other is that it cuts you off from the wider heritage that is rightfully yours. (*The Cross*, 85–86)

Paul addresses this latter error in verses 21-23, beginning with a statement that is nothing less than breathtaking: "For everything is yours." What an amazing statement of the blessings and wealth the believer has in Christ! God has made all unsinful things for our blessing, good, joy, and pleasure. For instance, God does not bless us with one teacher of the gospel but every teacher. He blesses us in life and death. He blesses us now and in the future. Everything is ours!

Now, let's get specific and see the eight examples of this concept Paul gives us in verses 22-23. The list is selective, not exhaustive. It is tailored to address the issues plaguing the Corinthian church. As we process Paul's words to the Corinthians, we should remember that they have importance for us too.

Paul is theirs, for one thing. Their father in the faith is theirs. The great apostle to the Gentiles, the missionary extraordinaire, the author of thirteen New Testament letters belongs to them and to all of us.

Apollos is theirs, too. The Alexandrian prince of preachers is theirs. With all his eloquence, rhetorical skill, brilliance, and apologetical gifting, he belongs to them and to all of us.

Cephas is theirs. Peter, the rock, one of the inner circle of Jesus, is theirs. His life and perspective coloring the Gospel of Mark, his two letters building up the church, his humanity and frailty, his powerful preaching and miraculous works belong to them and to all of us.

The world is theirs as well. Vaughn correctly says that here "the term 'world' is not used in its ethical sense [see v. 19], but it refers to the entirety of creation seen as the proper inheritance for the Christian" (*1 Corinthians*, 45). This whole world belongs to them and to all of us.

Life is theirs. Every waking moment and every sleeping hour is theirs. They do not belong to this life. It belongs to them. And because they belong to Jesus, "to live is Christ" (Phil 1:21). Life in Christ belongs to them and to all of us.

Death is theirs, too. Paul says for the Christian, "to die is gain!" (Phil 1:21). The sting of death is thus gone. The garden tomb is empty. Death has become their servant to usher them into the presence of King Jesus. To be away from the body is to be present with the Lord (2 Cor 5:8). Death, thanks to Jesus, now belongs to them and to all of us.

The **present** is also theirs. All things are theirs right now. Every moment is in the hands of a loving Father who is using each one to conform them more and more to "the image of his Son" (Rom 8:29). The present, that is, today, belongs to them and to all of us.

Finally, the **future** is theirs. The future in Christ is not uncertain, scary, ominous, or nerve-racking. The one who holds my present also holds my future. We've read about the end, and we win! There is a rider who will arrive on a white horse. He is King of kings and Lord of lords, and all things are under his control (Rev 19:11-21). The future belongs to them and to all of us (see Rom 8:35-39 for a comparable list).

Paul concludes by telling us that all these glorious realities are ours because we "belong to Christ, and Christ belongs to God" (1 Cor 3:23). Jesus is God's Messiah, God's Son (Matt 3:17), God's Word (John 1:1), God's essence (Phil 2:6), God's image (Col 1:15), God's radiance (Heb 1:3). And because we are Christ's and Christ is God's, we who are in Christ are God's too. Everything we have has the double stamp of the Son and the Father. Therefore, as Warren Wiersbe says so well, "How rich we are in Christ! If all things belong to all believers, then why should there be competition and rivalry?" (*Be Wise*, 50). Why indeed?

Conclusion

Fallen, sinful humanity tends to be afflicted with one of two great sicknesses. One is pride and the feeling of self-sufficiency, and the other is insecurity and the feeling of inferiority. Both groups seek to heal their problems by boasting, either in themselves or in others. Both problems are evidence of self-deception, which Paul warns us about in 3:18. At this point, the only cure for these deadly illnesses is the grace of God found in Christ and him crucified. Grace cures pride and insecurity. Grace will lead you to humility: I need help. Grace will lead you to the cross: there is help. Both will lead you to boast, not in yourself or any mere human but only in Christ. All things are yours in him. Be wise in the eyes of God and look to and boast only in Jesus.

Reflect and Discuss

1. Consider what the world says is wise concerning money, intelligence, power, and popularity. How do God's standards of wisdom counter the world's standards?

2. How does pride function as the root for what Paul addresses? How does human wisdom feed pride?

3. In what ways does Paul's warning not to be deceived help us avoid unconsciously adopting the world's standard of wisdom?

4. How could the world's so-called wisdom cause you to take advantage of others for personal gain?

5. Why does Paul use the language *this* age and *this* world? How does the knowledge of *another* age and *another* world help refine your standards of wisdom?

6. Describe an experience where the wisdom of God appeared foolish at first but turned out to be wise. In what ways will Christians need to wait for Christ's return to see God's wisdom ultimately prevail?

7. What is the difference between valuing human leaders and boasting in them? What drives one to boast in human leaders?

8. How did the Corinthians' boasting in particular leaders cause them to lose sight of the greater gifts that God had given them? In what other ways does pride cause us to be shortsighted?

9. What does it mean to "belong to Christ" (v. 23)? How does remembering our identity affect how we view human leaders?

10. How does competition within the church reveal a lack of love? How does rivalry suggest a lack of love for both God and others?

Four Truths a Minister of God Must Never Forget

1 CORINTHIANS 4:1-5

Main Idea: Ministers are servants God will hold accountable for their good and bad service when Christ returns.

I.   A Minister Is a Servant of God (4:1).
II. A Minister Is a Manager of the Mysteries of God (4:1-2).
III. A Minister Will Ultimately Be Judged Only by God (4:3-5).
IV. A Minister Will Receive His Reward from God (4:5).

In Jerry Bridges's classic work *Respectable Sins*, he addresses one of the most poisonous sins for Christians: the sin of judgmentalism. Concerning this spiritual serpent, Bridges writes,

> The sin of judgmentalism is one of the most subtle of our "respectable" sins because it is often practiced under the guise of being zealous for what is right. It is obvious that within our conservative evangelical circle there are myriads of opinions on everything from theology to conduct to lifestyle and politics. Not only are there multiple opinions but we usually assume our opinion is correct. That's where our trouble with judgmentalism begins. We equate our opinions with truth. (*Respectable Sins*, 141)

A critical spirit and a condemning attitude in the church are like cancer to the human body. If they are allowed to spread, fatality may result. Paul knew this to be true, especially as it relates to ministry. The church at Corinth was still under the seduction of the world's value systems. As Don Carson puts it, one-upmanship was tearing the church apart (*The Cross*, 93). "My preacher or Christian leader is better than yours" was being bantered about. The Corinthians used Paul, Peter, Apollos, and even Jesus as pawns in a popularity contest that resulted in division, quarreling, jealousy, and strife (1 Cor 1–3). The church had lost the proper perspective on just what a minister is, and Paul seeks to correct their wrong way of thinking. As Paul helps us rightly see what ministers of the gospel of Jesus Christ are, he also provides valuable instruction on the ever-present danger of judgmentalism. Four truths are presented for our edification.

A Minister Is a Servant of God
1 CORINTHIANS 4:1

The Corinthians had elevated Paul, Apollos, and Cephas (Peter) to celebrity status. Paul finds this scandalous and sets out to quickly correct their error. Paul writes, "A person should think of us in this way" (v. 1). *The Message* paraphrases it: "Don't imagine us leaders to be something we aren't." Paul Gardner writes, "Paul is not making a suggestion that may help the Corinthians see things in a better light. Rather, this is the way it is in God's church" (*1 Corinthians*, 191). And what are ministers of God? First, they are servants (Gk. *hypēretai*). Gordon Fee states,

> This word originated to describe the slaves who rowed in
> the lower tier of a trireme (a ship with 3 levels of oarsmen).
> Eventually, it came to be used of any who were in a subservient
> position, with emphasis on the relationship of one who served
> a superior. (*Corinthians*, 2014, 173)

Ministers are servants, not captains. They are humble servants of their sovereign Master and King, the Lord Jesus Christ. Their assignment is clear and singular. Their status is plain and certain. They serve Christ and his churches. They live and serve by one simple dictum: "All that matters in life and ministry is that I please Christ!" What liberty! What responsibility! What a calling! We are "servants of Christ."

A Minister Is a Manager of the Mysteries of God
1 CORINTHIANS 4:1-2

Paul adds a second descriptor to the ministers of God in verse 1: "managers [ESV, "stewards"] of the mysteries of God." Mark Taylor says the word *manager* . . .

> denotes one who has authority and responsibility for
> something such as an administrator or manager of a
> household. The term denotes a person in a position of trust
> and who is accountable to others. (*1 Corinthians*, 112)

Ministers are accountable to Christ alone. Further, our trust is in the gospel and all it entails, which Paul calls "the mysteries of God." Ministers have a special calling to proclaim the gospel (2:2) and protect the gospel. When the gospel is misrepresented or compromised, added to or subtracted from, the minister of God must sound an immediate warning. That is why Paul adds in verse 2 of chapter 4, "In this regard, it is required that managers be found faithful." To be faithful in ministry requires walking in the footsteps of Jesus as a servant of God and a servant to others (Mark 10:42-45). It requires a passion for faithfulness and obedience to our heavenly Father that envelopes everything we do. The end result can be powerful. Spurgeon put it beautifully: "It is not great talents God blesses so much as likeness to Jesus. A holy minister is an awful weapon in the hand of God" (*Lectures to My Students*, 8).

A Minister Will Ultimately Be Judged Only by God
1 CORINTHIANS 4:3-5

One of the most egregious aspects of judgmentalism is that we put ourselves in the place of God, who is the rightful Judge of us all. James 4:12 makes this clear: "There is one lawgiver and judge who is able to save and to destroy. But who are you to judge your neighbor?" Paul develops this principle in light of how the Corinthians carnally evaluated the worth of different leaders in the church. Paul could not care less about any human assessment. Ultimately God will render an accurate and final judgment of each person's service.

Paul places things in proper perspective when it comes to how others see him and his ministry for Christ and the church. First, "It is of little importance to me that I should be judged by you." Paul knows what they say about him. He knows their opinion of him. He considers it, but it does not consume him. Second, it does not matter to him if he is judged by "any human court." Their opinion doesn't matter all that much either. Anticipating what Paul will say in verses 4-5, Mark Taylor writes, "A human 'day' in court is quite insignificant in comparison with the judgment day of God" (*1 Corinthians*, 114). Third, Paul boldly states, "I don't even judge myself." He explains what he means in the following verse: "For I am not conscious of anything against myself, but I am not justified by this. It is the Lord who judges" (v. 4). Tom Schreiner writes,

> Paul is not "conscious of anything against myself" (CSB), but
> his own subjective assessment of his ministry is not decisive,
> for it is the Lord who gives the definitive word, who assesses
> (*anakrinō* again) how faithful Paul has been in his ministry.
> Since the Lord assesses, it follows that he is also the one who
> "justifies" (*dedikaiōmai*) and acquits. Paul reflects, then, on the
> final day, the day when the Lord will judge ministers in terms
> of their faithfulness to their stewardship. The Corinthians,
> then, should not presume to render final judgment on the
> effectiveness of ministers or anyone else before the time of the
> final judgment—the day the Lord returns. The Corinthians
> are engaging in an assessment of ministers, but they must
> desist since their knowledge of others is limited and partial.
> (*1 Corinthians*, 99)

Paul seals his argument in verse 5 with a command and a theological
observation. He commands, "Don't judge anything prematurely, before
the Lord comes." Paul bases this command on a theological principle:
It is the Lord "who will both bring to light what is hidden in darkness
and reveal the intentions of the heart." Christians are not to make judgments now because they are the wrong judges and because they judge
at the wrong time. The Lord is the only rightful Judge, and his second
coming signals the right time. This principle also implies that record of
our work for Jesus does not end at death! It continues into the future,
for good or evil, by how our lives affected others. This realization is an
especially somber reality for the servants and managers of Christ.

The theological principle gets to the core of Paul's concern. Divine
judgment, and only divine judgment, will accomplish two things: it "will
both bring to light what is hidden in darkness" and "reveal the intentions of the heart." I like the way *The Message* paraphrases verse 5:

> *So don't get ahead of the Master and jump to conclusions with your
> judgments before all the evidence is in. When he comes, he will bring
> out in the open and place in evidence all kinds of things we never even
> dreamed of—inner motives and purposes and prayers.*

Paul's points are powerful. Mere humans can never see all the evidence.
Only God can. Mere humans cannot see into the dark recesses of the
soul. Only God can. Mere humans cannot know why people do what
they do, "the intentions of the heart." Only God can.

When we trespass into these territories that rightly belong only to God, we cross the line from righteous judgment to sinful judgmentalism. Ken Sande says that the "most insidious type of critical judgment is to assume the worst about others' motives" ("Judging Others: The Danger of Playing God [Part 2]"). He notes,

> Some people are habitually cynical (distrustful or suspicious of others' nature or motives); others assume the worst only in certain people. In either case, the effect is the same: they are quick to attribute others' actions to an unworthy motive, such as pride, greed, selfishness, control, rebellion, stubbornness, or favoritism. (Ibid.)

Sande then gives proper advice for discerning when our judgments are pure:

> So, is there ever a time when we can properly form a firm opinion about someone's motives? Yes, we may do so whenever the other person expressly admits to such motives, or when there is a pattern of incontrovertible facts that can lead to no other reasonable conclusion. But when such clear proof is not present, it is wrong to presume we can look into others' hearts and judge the motives for their actions. Scripture teaches that God alone can see into the heart and discern a person's motive (see 1 Sam. 16:7; Ps. 44:21; Prov. 16:2). When we believe that we also are able to do this, we are guilty of sinful presumption. (Ibid.)

Scripture calls us to make important and even necessary judgments. However, it also calls us to be charitable, gracious, and wise. Sande notes there are at least four limits on making charitable judgments:

> First, God's command to be charitable does not require us to believe that an action is good when there is significant evidence to the contrary. Although we should always give people the benefit of the doubt, we should not ignore clear indications that things are not as they should be. In fact, excessive charity can lead to denial and blind us to issues that need to be faced.
>
> Second, charity does not require that we accept without question everything people tell us. Nor does it require that we

naively entrust ourselves to people who do not have legitimate authority or have not proven themselves to be worthy of our trust. Since we live in a fallen world, charity must always walk hand in hand with discernment and wisdom (Phil. 1:9-10; James 3:14-17).

Third, the call for charitable judgments should not be used to stifle appropriate discussion, questioning, and debate. If people have sincere concerns about a matter, they should not be brushed aside with, "Just trust us."

Finally, charity does not prevent the exercise of redemptive church discipline. When the leaders of a church believe a member is caught in a sin, they have a responsibility to seek after him, like shepherds looking for a straying sheep (Matt. 18:12-14; Gal. 6:1). (Sande, "Judging Others: The Danger of Playing God [Part 2]")

A Minister Will Receive His Reward from God
1 CORINTHIANS 4:5

Paul concludes this short paragraph with a word of encouragement about future rewards for God's servants (cf. 3:10-15). He writes, "And then praise [ESV, "commendation"] will come to each one from God." Schreiner notes, "God's reward will be just, since he understands the motives of the hearts and knows everything about every person" (*1 Corinthians*, 99). Carson adds a nice pastoral touch as he writes,

> Perhaps the most remarkable feature of this paragraph of 1 Corinthians is how it ends. With the final day of judgement in view, Paul might have been expected to say, "At that time each will receive his rebuke from God." But instead, he says, "At that time each will receive his praise from God" (4:5c). How wonderful! The King of the universe, the Sovereign who has endured our endless rebellion and sought us out at the cost of his Son's death, climaxes our redemption by praising us! He is a wise Father who knows how to encourage even the feeblest efforts of his children. (*The Cross*, 101)

God is omniscient, and God is just. He will do right by his servants. We can rest in that. We can rejoice in it, too.

Conclusion

The New Testament's teaching about judging can be confusing at first. On the one hand, there are places in the Bible where we are told to make judgments, to evaluate people, their teaching and action. Paul's instruction in 1 Corinthians 5 about the man living in an immoral relationship "with his father's wife" (5:1) makes this clear. On the other hand, Jesus condemns being judgmental in Matthew 7:1-5, only to follow immediately in verse 6 with the command, "Don't give what is holy to dogs or toss your pearls before pigs." Thus, the Bible teaches an important distinction between being wrongly judgmental and rightly judging sin. We must find a way to judge graciously and righteously. I want to conclude this chapter with some practical and biblical applications. How can those of us who have been redeemed from all our sins by the precious blood of Christ rightly make judgments without wrongly being judgmental? Below are some thoughts for consideration.

1. **Check your motives.** Why am I doing this? Have I checked my heart, knowing that ultimately only God knows the motives and intentions of the heart (Prov 16:2; 1 Cor 4:3-5)?
2. **Examine your walk with the Lord first.** Am I walking in the Spirit and characterized by a gentle spirit, careful to monitor my sin even as I seek to restore another (Gal 6:1-2)?
3. **Seek out the wisdom of God's Word and godly counsel before acting** (Prov 10:13-14; 11:14; 15:22). Don't play the Lone Ranger in this area
4. **Practice the Golden Rule.** Think about how you would want to be treated if you were receiving correction (Matt 7:12).
5. **Be careful not to make a snap decision or quick judgment.** Take the time to get the facts and listen before acting, recognizing you will never know everything (Prov 18:13).
6. **Pray for the one who appears to be caught in sin before correcting them** (Jas 5:15-16).
7. **Remember the example of Jesus and how he helped and ministered to sinners.** Jesus was condemned and ridiculed for how he cared for and loved sinners, tax collectors, pagans, and the woman caught in adultery (John 7:53–8:11).
8. **Speak the truth, but do it in love** (Eph 4:15).
9. **Remember that some things are right or wrong, but some things are just different** (Rom 14:1-6,13-23).

10. **Never forget that ultimately everyone must give an account to the Lord, not to you or anyone else** (Rom 14:7-12; 1 Cor 4:4-5; 2 Cor 5:10).

Ken Sande provides a wonderful word to bring this message to a close—good words for our careful consideration.

Help Me to Judge Rightly
Lord, help me to judge others
as I want them to judge me:
Charitably, not critically,
Privately, not publicly,
Gently, not harshly,
In humility, not pride.
Help me to believe the best about others,
until facts prove otherwise—
To assume nothing,
to seek all sides of the story,
And to judge no one until I've removed
the log from my own eye.
May I never bring only the Law,
to find fault and condemn.
Help me always to bring the Gospel,
to give hope and deliverance,
As you, my Judge and Friend,
have so graciously done for me. ("Judging Others: The Danger
    of Playing God [Part 3]")

Reflect and Discuss

1. How does judgmentalism disguise itself under a zeal for what is right? How can you discern whether your opinions are correct or misguided?
2. Does the label "servant of Christ" apply to career ministers only or all Christians? Is there anything particular about a pastor service?
3. How does the minister's identity as a servant and manager shape how you view gifted teachers?
4. How would you rank the importance of holiness for a minister on a scale of 1 to 10? How would you also rank the importance of gifted-ness? Based on your rankings, how should holiness and giftedness

relate to each other? What are some ways you could live and think in ways contrary to the proper order?

5. How should the minister's *identity* shape the minister's *practice?* How does a minister's identity shape what he values as essential?

6. What does the phrase "It is the Lord who judges me" (v. 4) stir inside you? How does this give you freedom when you feel others judge you incorrectly? How should this help you when you have judgmental thoughts?

7. What parts of God's identity and character should increase your trust in him to judge yourself and others correctly?

8. How would you define "success" for a career minister and a local church?

9. Is there a difference between being a successful minister and a faithful minister? Why or why not?

10. How does Paul's view of Christ's return in the future shape how he lives in the present?

Just Who Do You Think You Are?

1 CORINTHIANS 4:6-13

Main Idea: Because Christians have received every good thing from God, they should avoid superiority, expect opposition, and live humbly.

I. **Be Careful about Being Prideful about Whom You Follow (4:6-7).**
   A. Don't pit one servant of God against another (4:6).
   B. Don't forget everything you have is a gift of grace (4:7).
II. **Be Careful about Being Arrogant about Who You Are (4:8-13).**
   A. Before the world and angels, we are condemned (4:8-9).
   B. Before the world and angels, we are a spectacle (4:9).
   C. Before the world and angels, we are fools (4:10).
   D. Before the world and angels, we are weak (4:10).
   E. Before the world and angels, we are dishonored (4:10).
   F. Before the world and angels, we are hungry (4:11).
   G. Before the world and angels, we are thirsty (4:11).
   H. Before the world and angels, we are poorly clothed (4:11).
   I. Before the world and angels, we are roughly treated (4:11).
   J. Before the world and angels, we are homeless (4:11).
   K. Before the world and angels, we are mere laborers (4:12).
   L. Before the world and angels, we are reviled (4:12).
   M. Before the world and angels, we are persecuted (4:12).
   N. Before the world and angels, we are slandered (4:13).
   O. Before the world and angels, we are scum (4:13).
   P. Before the world and angels, we are garbage (4:13).

These are some of the hardest verses in 1 Corinthians to understand and apply. They are difficult to understand because Paul uses irony and sarcasm. They are difficult to apply because they are so foreign to almost all of us in our twenty-first-century, comfortable, Western context. Yet we desperately need these words because they strike at the heart of the great enemy of God's people: pride. John Piper is right:

> There is a very close relationship between unbelief and pride. . . . Unbelief is a turning away from Jesus (or God) in order to seek satisfaction in other things. Pride is a turning

away from God specifically to take satisfaction in self. ("Battling the Unbelief of a Haughty Spirit")

The Corinthians had both a pride and an unbelief problem. They were taking pride in particular spiritual leaders and were arrogant in terms of who they thought they were and what they had achieved. Paul knew how deadly these twin sins can be in the body of Christ, the local church. So he confronts them head-on with biting sarcasm and irony. He does it "for [their] benefit" (v. 6), praying it will have the kind of sting of a topical medicine that aids healing.

Be Careful about Being Prideful about Whom You Follow
1 CORINTHIANS 4:6-7

Paul continues to plead for unity in the church. His plea began in 1:10 and will conclude in 4:21. The Corinthians were in turmoil because they misunderstood the *nature* of the Christian *message* (the gospel of Christ and him crucified as the wisdom of God), the *role* of the Christian *minister* (a servant), and the *attitude* of the Christian *minister* (humility). Paul, one final time, will try to put the ministries of himself, Apollos, and the apostles in proper perspective. If he is successful, the church will unite for gospel advancement. If he fails, their witness will be compromised, and their future effectiveness will be fatally harmed.

Don't Pit One Servant of God Against Another (4:6-7)

Paul again addresses the Corinthian church with tact and gentleness, calling them "brothers and sisters" (v. 6). He tells them that he has "applied these things to myself and Apollos for your benefit." They are examples for them. "These things" refers to the various images in 3:5– 4:5 of servants, coworkers, master builders, and managers as appropriate analogies for their leaders. These men are servants sent by God to fulfill their assigned tasks. To unduly exalt them or unwisely judge them is wrong. It is to view ministers of the church contrary to how God sees them. It is to tell God they have a more accurate understanding of who their ministers are than Paul did.

Paul says his goal is that the church "may learn from us the meaning of the saying: 'Nothing beyond what is written.'" "The purpose," he writes, "is that none of you will be arrogant, favoring one person over another." The phrase "nothing beyond what is written" is difficult. It is not found in the Old Testament. Paul may be referring, in general, to what the Old Testament teaches about arrogance and pride (Schreiner, *1 Corinthians*, 101). He may also be referring to a common or popular slogan in the early church (Carson, *The Cross*, 102). We can't be certain. However, his main point is clear. He does not want the church to be arrogant, prideful, or puffed up, choosing favorites like worldly political parties do. We need to hear the same warning. Don't be seduced by the ways of the world when it comes to your leaders. Think biblically! Don't line up behind Calvin or Luther, Whitfield or Wesley, Lloyd-Jones or Stott, MacArthur or Piper. Don't fall into the trap of pride by thinking you are smarter and wiser than others. Be wise? Sure. Be arrogant? God forbid!

Don't Forget Everything You Have Is a Gift of Grace (4:7)

Verse 6 teaches us not to boast about whom we follow. Verse 7 teaches us not to boast about what we have. After all, it is all because of grace. Paul employs three rhetorical questions in verse 7 to remind the church that any good thing they have is the result of God's grace in their lives.

Of the first question, "For who makes you so superior?," Fee says,

> The English equivalent . . . would be, "Who in the world do
> you think you are, anyway? What kind of self-delusion is it
> that allows you to put yourself in a position to judge another
> person's servant?" (*Corinthians*, 2014, 186)

What incredible presumption they were demonstrating is his point.

Second, Paul asks, "What do you have that you didn't receive?" The Corinthians forgot that everything they had was grace, a gift. Absolutely everything! Again Fee is right: "All is grace; nothing is deserved, nothing earned" (*Corinthians*, 2014, 186). Calvin pointedly adds, "There is no man that has anything of excellency from himself; therefore, the man that extols himself is a fool and an idiot" (*1 Corinthians*, 160).

Third, Paul says, "If, in fact, you did receive it, why do you boast as if you hadn't received it?" Grace leads to gratitude. Pride leads to boasting. Grace says, "Thank you, Lord." Pride says, "Look at me, Lord." Warren Wiersbe gets to the heart of this issue when he writes,

> The best commentary of 1 Corinthians 4:7 is the witness of
> John the Baptist: "A man can receive nothing, except it be
> given him from heaven. . . . He [Christ] must increase, but I
> must decrease" (John 3:27,30). (*Be Wise*, 56)

Grace gives us what we have and what we need. It gives us what we do not deserve and cannot earn. It saves us. It sustains us. It gives glory to the one who rightly deserves it: God, not us.

Be Careful about Being Arrogant about Who You Are
1 CORINTHIANS 4:8-13

Paul will now employ some sanctified, spiritual sarcasm. It is biting. He will use contrasts and strong statements to shame the Corinthians. You can almost sense the desperation in Paul's words as he writes them. He has tried everything he knows to do. Maybe a little (or a lot!) of sarcasm and playful ridicule will do the trick.

Sixteen different points are made. I will note each one only briefly. Cumulatively, they constitute a mountain of evidence and a compelling argument.

Before the World and Angels, We Are Condemned (4:8-9)

Paul tells the church that our lives are always on display "to the world, both to angels and to people" (v. 9). The whole universe is always watching the church. Arrogantly and pridefully, the Corinthian believers saw themselves as "already full" (v. 8). They thought they had arrived and had all they needed. "How foolish!" Paul says in effect. They were thinking like pagans. Schreiner is persuasive here, arguing that the problem was not primarily their eschatology (an over-realized eschatology) but their ethics. They were thinking like the Stoic-Cynic philosophers of the day. He notes Epictetus's example:

> "Who, when he lays eyes upon me, does not feel that he is seeing his king and master?" (*Diatr.* 3.22.49). The Corinthians believe they are spiritually filled, abounding in riches, and ruling the world. (Schreiner, *1 Corinthians*, 102)

Paul is brutal in his sarcasm: "You are already full [ESV, "have all you want"]! You are already rich! You have begun to reign as kings without us." But—and here is the brutal truth—Paul responds, "I wish you did reign, so that we could also reign with you!" (v. 8). He wished their perspective was correct. He wished the kingdom were present in all its fulness and glory. But it wasn't. If they needed proof, they need only look at the apostles. Paul says, "For I think God has displayed [ESV, "exhibited"] us, the apostles, in last place, like men condemned to die" (v. 9).

The apostles were not first. They were last. They were not thriving. They were dying. And the deaths they were dying were not taking place privately or in secret, as what follows makes clear.

Before the World and Angels, We Are a Spectacle (4:9)

"We have become a spectacle to the world." In this Paul likens the apostles to "condemned criminals in the amphitheater" (Vaughn and Lea, *1 Corinthians*, 50). The word "spectacle" is *theatron*, from which we get our word "theater." Paul Gardner says, "They are living pictures of the one they follow" (*1 Corinthians*, 209). Believers are put on shameful, public display for the world to mock and lampoon, just like Jesus was. Angels look in amazement at this spectacle. Demons no doubt laugh and shout with glee and joy.

Before the World and Angels, We Are Fools (4:10)

Verse 10 adds needed perspective. Paul says, "We [the apostles] are fools for Christ!" Paul knows the Corinthians think themselves "wise in Christ." But they have it all wrong. It's better to be a fool before the world than take a stance like that, Paul says. Let the world sneer at the crucified Galilean and those who follow him. It's better to receive the approval of Christ than the world. It is his "well done" we should long to hear.

Before the World and Angels, We Are Weak (4:10)

In their pride, arrogance, and adoption of worldly standards, the Corinthians saw themselves as strong, powerful, and influential. In contrast, the suffering apostles appeared weak and insignificant. Had the Corinthians already forgotten that God "has chosen what is weak in the world to shame the strong" (1:27)? Wiersbe is right:

> Paul discovered that his spiritual strength was the result of personal weakness (2 Cor. 12:7-10). Strength that knows itself to be strength is weakness; but weakness that knows itself to be weakness [in Christ] becomes strength. (*Be Wise*, 57–58)

Before the World and Angels, We Are Dishonored (4:10)

The Corinthians saw themselves as "distinguished." But Paul said in effect it is better to see yourself as "dishonored"! Morris notes the word for dishonor (Gk. *atimos*) is "sometimes used of those deprived of citizenship" (*1 Corinthians*, 78). In this world we believers are nomads, foreigners without a home country, because this world is not our home.

Before the World and Angels, We Are Hungry (4:11)

Paul will now introduce a list of deprivations and sufferings he and the other apostles experienced as servants of Christ. It anticipates a similar list in 2 Corinthians 11:23-29. It also further reinforces his argument that the kingdom has not arrived and that boasting and pride are the ways of the fool. "Up to this present hour we are . . . hungry," he admits. "Up to this present hour" tells us this was not unusual. Today is like yesterday and the day before that. Sometimes food has been in short supply, and sometimes there has been no food. Unlike the Corinthians, Paul has never had all he wanted (v. 8). But Paul would say he has always been content in Christ (Phil 4:11-12).

Before the World and Angels, We Are Thirsty (4:11)

The apostles were hungry and thirsty, often without water. Having an abundance of the necessities of life was not their experience.

Before the World and Angels, We Are Poorly Clothed (4:11)

"Poorly clothed" is the apostles' Sunday best! They are not personally acquainted with the current styles of the cultured people of society. No new spring or fall wardrobe for them! If each has a single, decent article of clothing and a pair of sandals, he considers himself blessed! (I know people like this!)

Before the World and Angels, We Are Roughly Treated (4:11)

Far from being treated like kings and the rich, the apostles are "roughly treated." Morris notes, "Paul's word (*kolaphizō*) is that used of the ill-treatment accorded Jesus (Mt. 26:67)" (*1 Corinthians*, 78). "Insulted and abused" captures well the apostle's intent.

Before the World and Angels, We Are Homeless (4:11)

Those accustomed to a comfortable and culturally convenient Christianity struggle to identify with the apostle's words here in this section. In that respect we are once again much like the Corinthians. However, as Gardner notes, "'Homeless' is the lot of a missionary who is constantly traveling. We are reminded of Jesus who had nowhere to call home (Matt. 8:20)" (*1 Corinthians*, 210). Vagabonds for Christ have no place to call home in this world.

Before the World and Angels, We Are Mere Laborers (4:12)

Servants of Christ rarely live like kings and wealthy nobles. Of the apostles, Paul writes, "[W]e labor, working with our own hands." Paul gladly supported himself in gospel ministry, as the Corinthians well knew (see Acts 18:3). He would not be a hindrance nor put a stumbling block in the way of the gospel by being pampered. The Greco-Roman world might despise manual labor, "thinking of it as fit only for slaves" (Morris, *1 Corinthians*, 78). Paul and the apostles thought otherwise.

Before the World and Angels, We Are Reviled (4:12)

Fee notes what follows "are clear reflections of the teaching of Jesus and as such anticipate the 'imitation of Christ' motif in the next paragraph" (*Corinthians*, 2014, 195). Indeed, "When we are reviled, we bless" is a reflection of the Lord Jesus by word (Luke 6:28) and example (Luke 23:34). Paul repeats this ethic in Romans 12:17 and 1 Thessalonians 5:15. This is not the response of a slave to this world. It is the response of a slave to Christ.

Before the World and Angels, We Are Persecuted (4:12)

"When we are persecuted, we endure it." Paul's eyes were drawn to Golgotha in this statement. When persecuted, the apostles do not quit, drop out of the race, or throw in the towel. They persevere, hang in there, and refuse to stop. Simon Kistemaker points out, "The verbs that Paul writes in this passage are in the present tense to indicate that the apostles were constantly mocked and persecuted" (*Exposition*, 141).

Before the World and Angels, We Are Slandered (4:13)

Paul says, "When we are slandered, we respond graciously." Vaughn notes, "The Greeks would see this as cowardliness, but Paul sees this as a demonstration of the virtues of Christianity" (*1 Corinthians*, 51). The world may speak ill of Christians and seek our harm, but we cannot play the world's game. A kind word, a soft answer, should always be what slanderers receive in return (note Prov 15:1).

Before the World and Angels, We Are Scum (4:13)

Paul's last two words in this list are striking: "scum" and "garbage" (ESV, "refuse"). Paul says, "Even now, we are like the scum of the earth." This reflects Lamentations 3:45 ("You have made us disgusting filth among the peoples"). That means that in the world's eyes, God's faithful people are no better than the stuff removed when you clean a filthy body, the floor, or a toilet.

Before the World and Angels, We Are Garbage (4:13)

Scum and garbage are virtually synonymous in this instance. Repetition intensifies the word picture. MacArthur states,

> The words were commonly used figuratively of the lowest, most degraded criminals, who often were sacrificed in pagan ceremonies. That is the way the world looked at the apostles. They were religious scum and dregs. (*1 Corinthians*, 112)

Conclusion

Amy Carmichael (1867–1951) was a wonderful and faithful missionary to India. She built an orphanage and rescued little girls from lives of Hindu temple prostitution. She never took a furlough from this work, though she suffered from neuralgia, a disease of the nerves, that greatly weakened her body. Carmichael was severely injured from a fall in 1931 and was basically bedridden for the last twenty years of her life. Still, she pressed on, endured in missions ministry for her Master, and went to be with her Savior at the age of 83. How did she think of life for the servant of Christ? I think we should let her speak for herself. Echoes of 1 Corinthians 4:8-13 can be heard ringing in the background!

> Do not be surprised if there is an attack on your work, on you who are called to do it, on your innermost nature—the hidden person of the heart. The great thing is not to be surprised, nor to count it strange—for that plays into the hand of the enemy. Is it possible that anyone should set himself to exalt

our beloved Lord and not instantly become a target for many arrows? (*Candles in the Dark*, 42)

Reflect and Discuss

1. What does Paul's correction of the Corinthians teach you about life in the church among believers?

2. Why are arrogance and pride so detrimental to the church? How does grace destroy the root of our pride?

3. How does pride distort our view of ourselves? How does it distort our view of others?

4. In what ways can our pride lead us to despise grace and forgiveness for others but assume grace and forgiveness for ourselves?

5. If grace leads to gratitude, what does a lack of gratitude in one's life signal? How can you use gratitude to fight pride?

6. Do you think it is easy or difficult for Christians to remember that following Jesus often condemns you in the world? Explain.

7. What similarities can you find between the apostles' suffering and Christ's? What contrasts can you find between the negative experiences of the apostles and the eternal promises of God? Where in Scripture do you find these promises?

8. Should Christians be wary of having all they want? Why or why not?

9. How should Christians reconcile the experience of the apostles with commands in the Gospels that tell us not to be anxious about basic provisions (Matt 6:25-34)?

10. What is dangerous about a comfortable and culturally convenient Christianity? How do you guard yourself against moving toward this type of Christianity?

Listen to Your Father

1 CORINTHIANS 4:14-21

Main Idea: The church needs spiritual fathers to live exemplary lives and provide gentle, firm correction to help others mature in Christ.

I. **Spiritual Fathers Have a Unique Relationship with Their Children (4:14-15).**
    A. They care for us (4:14).
    B. They gave us birth (4:15).
II. **Spiritual Fathers Provide an Example to Follow (4:16-17).**
    A. We imitate them (4:16).
    B. We follow their teaching (4:17).
III. **Spiritual Fathers Confront Us When We Sin (4:18-19).**
    A. They confront our sinful attitudes (4:18).
    B. They confront our sinful actions (4:19).
IV. **Spiritual Fathers Correct Us as Needed (4:20-21).**
    A. They provide spiritual perspective (4:20).
    B. They provide spiritual discipline (4:21).

The Bible speaks a lot about the wisdom of listening to our fathers. Just a sampling from Proverbs makes this clear:

- Proverbs 1:8: "Listen, my son, to your father's instruction, and don't reject your mother's teaching."
- Proverbs 2:1-5: "My son, if you accept my words and store up my commands within you, listening closely to wisdom and directing your heart to understanding; furthermore, if you call out to insight and lift your voice to understanding, if you seek it like silver and search for it like hidden treasure, then you will understand the fear of the LORD and discover the knowledge of God."
- Proverbs 3:1-2: "My son, don't forget my teaching, but let your heart keep my commands; for they will bring you many days, a full life, and well-being."
- Proverbs 4:1-2: "Listen, sons, to a father's discipline, and pay attention so that you may gain understanding, for I am giving you good instruction."

- Proverbs 6:20-22: "My son, keep your father's command, and don't reject your mother's teaching. Always bind them to your heart; tie them around your neck. When you walk here and there, they will guide you; when you lie down, they will watch over you; when you wake up, they will talk to you."
- Proverbs 23:22: "Listen to your father who gave you life."

I wonder if Paul had this biblical theme and these proverbs in his mind when he penned the words of our text. Eva Lassen points out, "For Paul, the use of the father-image seems to have been a fundamental one for expressing his relationship to congregations, which he had founded" ("The Use of the Father Image," 127). In using it, "He is invoking an authoritative relationship over the congregation as its founding father" (ibid., 136). The call for church unity that began in 1 Corinthians 1:10 now reaches its conclusion (4:21). Here Paul exposes his heart and bares his soul. He says, you are my children because "I became your father in Christ Jesus through the gospel" (4:15). This text comes from the heart of a father. He only wants God's best for them.

Four truths in these verses should inform every spiritual relationship between spiritual fathers and their spiritual children.

Spiritual Fathers Have a Unique Relationship with Their Children
1 CORINTHIANS 4:14-15

Paul's words in 4:8-13 were ironic and sarcastic. They were sharp and cutting. Now his words are tender and personal. A good minister recognizes the value of both. The key is what to say and when to say it. As Paul closes this section (1:10–4:21) and prepares to tackle several complex issues (chs. 5–6), he places all that he says in the context of the father-child relationship between himself and the church at Corinth.

They Care for Us (4:14)

Paul wants the church to know his tough words (vv. 8-13) flow from a tender heart, a heart of love and concern. He did not write to "shame" them "but to warn (ESV, "admonish") [them] as [his] dear children." The verse literally begins, "not shaming you I write." This word order allows him to emphasize the point that his goal is not to put them to shame. Rather, he wants to warn those he sees as precious and "dear [ESV, "beloved"] children." Paul is a father talking to his sons and daughters. His concerns are parental and relational. He will correct their immature behavior, but he will do so with tender care and encouragement. *The Message* paraphrase is too good to pass over: "I'm not writing all this as a neighborhood scold to shame you. I'm writing as a father to you, my children. I love you and want you to grow up well, not spoiled."

They Gave Us Birth (4:16)

Paul's firm but tender care for the Corinthians is not difficult to understand. It is quite natural (or supernatural). He alone was used by Christ, by means of the gospel, to bring about their spiritual birth, their conversion. "For I became your father in Christ Jesus through the gospel," he says in verse 15. Paul planted the church in Corinth (Acts 18:1-17). He is, on the human plane, their spiritual father. In God's providence, then, he has a special relationship with and authority over the Corinthians.

Now, his role as a father does not negate how God used others (like Apollos, Peter, Aquila, Priscilla, Silas, and Timothy) to bless and nurture the Corinthians. Paul gladly acknowledges, "For you . . . have countless instructors [ESV, "guides; NIV, "guardians"] in Christ, but you don't have many fathers." Fee notes Paul uses "unusually hyperbolic language: 'Even though you *may end up having countless thousands* of guardians in Christ, *at least* you do not have many fathers'" (*Corinthians*, 2014, 201; emphasis in original). The word "instructors" or "guardians" is the Greek word *paidagōgos*. Again, Fee's comments are instructive at this point:

> The "guardian," to be distinguished from a "teacher," was ordinarily a trusted slave to whom a father turned over his children (usually sons), whom the guardian was to conduct to and from school and whose conduct in general he was to oversee. This is not intended to be a putdown of their other teachers, of whom Paul has thus far spoken favorably. Rather, the metaphor intends simply to distinguish his own relationship to them from that of all others, including of course Apollos and Peter. But it also includes those within their community who are currently exercising influence, not to mention all others who ever would. Paul's unique relationship to them was that of a "father," and that gave him a special authority over and responsibility toward them. With this language, therefore, he is both reasserting his authority

and appealing to their loyalty, which had obviously eroded in this church. (*Corinthians*, 2014, 201–2)

Fathers should be viewed in a special way in the natural family. They should be viewed in a special way in our spiritual family, too. Others are important in our growth and instruction, but no one can take a father's place. Paul brought the Corinthians the life-changing gospel of Jesus Christ. He spent time nurturing them and loving them. No one else did for them what he did. They should never forget that.

Spiritual Fathers Provide an Example to Follow
1 CORINTHIANS 4:16-17

In 3 John 11 the apostle John writes, "Dear friend [Gaius], do not imitate what is evil, but what is good. The one who does good is of God; the one who does evil has not seen God." The Bible often refers to the wisdom of following and imitating good, godly examples. The importance of role models is found throughout Scripture. To the direction given in 3 John 11 we can add the following:

- Ephesians 5:1: "Be imitators of God, as dearly loved children."
- Philippians 2:5: "Adopt the same attitude as that of Christ Jesus."
- 1 Peter 2:21: "For you were called to this, because Christ also suffered for you, leaving you an example, that you should follow in his steps."
- 1 Peter 5:2-3: "Shepherd God's flock among you . . . not lording it over those entrusted to you, but being examples to God's flock."

Paul will draw on this biblical pattern twice in 1 Corinthians (4:16; 11:1). Here, he will tie it to his father-child relationship with the Corinthians. "Like father, like son," we could say!

We Imitate Them (4:16)

Paul says, "I urge you to imitate me." The word translated "urge" is *parakalō*. It means to beg (GNT) or encourage (NET). Here it suggests coming up beside someone, putting your arm around him or her in a friendly embrace, and encouraging. Paul's specific encouragement to his spiritual children is "imitate me." The Greek word translated "imitate" is *mimetai*, from which we get our word *mimic*. Schreiner notes, "In

context, the imitation centers on Paul's suffering as an apostle (4:9-13)"
(*1 Corinthians*, 105). I agree with this, though I would not limit it only to
the sufferings of Paul. He has provided a pattern, a life worthy of emula-
tion because his role model is Christ! Calvin argues,

> But to what extend he wishes them to be imitators of him,
> he shows elsewhere, when he adds, as he was of Christ
> (1 Cor. xi. 1). This limitation must always be observed, so as
> not to follow any man, except so far as he leads us to Christ.
> (*1 Corinthians*, 173)

I like Carson's simple summation: "What Paul wants them to imitate is
his passion to live life in the light of the cross" (*The Cross*, 110).

We Follow Their Teaching (4:17)

In addition to the letter of 1 Corinthians, Paul also sent Timothy to this
church. We do not know whether Timothy or the letter arrived first.
Concerning Timothy, Schreiner writes,

> [He] frequently travelled with Paul as he journeyed and
> proclaimed the gospel (Acts 16:1; 17:14-15; 18:5; 19:22; 20:4).
> Timothy was also present when the gospel was proclaimed
> to the Corinthians (Acts 18:5; 2 Cor. 1:19). He was a valued
> and trusted co-worker of Paul's (see esp. Phil. 2:19-24; cf. also
> Rom. 16:21; 1 Thess. 3:2) and was particularly beloved by Paul
> (1 Tim. 1:2, 18; 6:20; 2 Tim. 1:2-5). We see from 1 Corinthians
> 16:10-11 that Paul anticipates Timothy visiting the Corinthians.
> (*1 Corinthians*, 105)

Acts 16:1 informs us that Timothy's mother was a Jewish believer, but his
father was an unbelieving Greek. Paul notes that he and Timothy also
have a father-son relationship: "He is my dearly loved and faithful child
in the Lord." Because Paul trusts him, he sends Timothy, to "remind
[them] about [his] ways in Christ Jesus, just as [Paul taught] everywhere
in every church." Timothy would remind them of Paul's life of faithfulness and integrity, which had been on display before them for eighteen months when he planted the church. Further, they should know
that not only is Paul's life one of faithful consistency, so is his teaching.
Paul does not teach one thing at this church and something different at
another church. Wiersbe is right:

> God does not have one standard for one church and a
> different standard for another church. He may work out His
> will in different ways (Phil. 2:12-13), but the basic doctrines
> and principles are the same. (*Be Wise*, 61)

Paul was the same man with the same message in Galatia, at Thessalonica, at Corinth, and everywhere else. There was a remarkable consistency to his message and methods. How desperately we need men and women like that today.

Spiritual Fathers Confront Us When We Sin
1 CORINTHIANS 4:18-19

A father and mother who love their children will not look the other way when they disobey and misbehave. Because they love them, they will discipline them (Eph 6:4; Col 3:20-21; see also Prov 13:24; 22:6; 29:15). This parental pattern for the home is once again followed in the church as Paul now begins to demonstrate tough with the Corinthians. He began with a gentle hand, but now the rod of discipline is threatened if they do not respond to his gracious appeal.

They Confront Our Sinful Attitudes (4:18)

There was a small but vocal group stirring things up at Corinth. (Some things that plague congregations never change!) They were arrogantly claiming that although Paul said he was coming to see them, he would never show up. Paul called them out for their arrogance in 4:6 and does so again here. A heart of pride and a spirit of arrogance often go hand in hand. A superiority complex is deadly to the family of God and cannot be allowed to go unchecked and without confrontation, as Paul makes clear in the next verse.

They Confront Our Sinful Actions (4:19)

Paul counters the unfounded gossip at Corinth by informing the church, "But I will come to you soon, if the Lord wills." Paul absolutely intends to visit Corinth, but he willingly submits his plans to the sovereign will of the Lord (cf. Jas 4:15-16). He will not presume on the Lord's plans for his life. Nevertheless, trusting that the Lord will allow him to return to Corinth, he lets them know his plan to rebuke the arrogant: "I will find out not the talk, but the power of those who are arrogant." *The Message* says, "We'll see if they're full of anything but hot air." I like the comments of Schreiner here:

> During his visit, [Paul] plans not to hold discussions but to uncover the *power* of those in sin because power, as 1 Corinthians 1:18–2:5 demonstrates, is manifested in an astonishing way, namely, through the preaching of Christ crucified. (*1 Corinthians*, 105; emphasis in original)

Gossip wilts when it is exposed to the searing light of the gospel. Sinful attitudes and sinful actions cannot flourish when the gospel's purifying heat is applied.

Spiritual Fathers Correct Us as Needed
1 CORINTHIANS 4:20-21

Paul brings his call for unity in 1:10–4:21 to an end. He knows how harmful division and disunity can be in the church when we act more like rival political parties than we do family. His final words in chapter 4 contain a powerful affirmation and a stern warning. Once more we see the spiritual value of listening to our spiritual fathers.

They Provide Spiritual Perspective (4:20)

"The kingdom of God," his reign and realm, "is not a matter of talk," of mere words. Persuasive and flowery rhetoric may gain the world's attention and applause, but not God's. No, the kingdom of God is about "power" found in the gospel of Christ and him crucified (2:1-5). Paul Gardner writes on this verse:

> When Paul comes to Corinth, he will be seeking to discover evidence that God in Christ is at work through these leaders. He fears that their grace-gifts, abused to buy them status and honor within the community, will offer no such evidence. The irony is that real evidence will be offered as people's lives are so changed that they become Christ-like and even "apostle-like," as has been described earlier. It is in weakness, in being the scum of the earth and yet living for God and his rule that kingdom power will be manifest. This is what Paul desires to see, and so he ends with a statement that is regarded by most as harsh or heavy-handed. (*1 Corinthians*, 217)

They Provide Spiritual Discipline (4:21)

Paul concludes with two rhetorical questions that would certainly get the church's attention. First, "What do you want?" The idea is, what would you like me to do? How I respond will depend on you and how you respond to my letter. Second, "Should I come to you with a rod, or in love and a spirit of gentleness?" *The Message* paraphrases: "So how should I prepare to come to you? As a severe disciplinarian who makes you walk the line? Or as a good friend and counselor who wants to share heart-to-heart with you? You decide." The children would prefer hugs and kisses, not discipline! Paul would prefer the same. The key will be their response. Paul loves them as his children. He will do whatever he must. He loves them too much to let them go on acting like fools and embarrassing themselves. After all, he is a good father!

Conclusion

Proverbs 3:11-12 reads, "Do not despise the Lord's instruction, my son, and do not loathe his discipline, for the Lord disciplines the one he loves, just as a father disciplines the son in whom he delights" (cf. Heb. 12:5-6). This is how our heavenly Father treats his children whom he has adopted through the work of his Son, the Lord Jesus Christ. This is also how our earthly spiritual fathers are to treat us. Wise children will listen when their heavenly Father speaks. Wise children will also listen when their earthly spiritual fathers speak. Those who faithfully lead us to trust in Jesus alone have the right to be loved and listened to as they follow in the footsteps of Jesus (1 Cor 11:1). Obeying them may not always be pleasant, but it will be for our good. Let's make our heavenly Father and earthly fathers happy. The world, after all, is always watching.

Reflect and Discuss

1. Do you have a spiritual father in your life who has been an excellent example of your heavenly Father? What about this person do you find the most valuable?
2. What is the difference between a spiritual instructor and a spiritual father?
3. Is authority inherently wrong? Why or why not? What signals abusive authority?

4. How does a good fatherly figure best express love and authority? What pitfalls does a spiritual figure have if love or authority is missing?

5. If Paul had wanted to shame the Corinthians, what would he have said? What false promises does our sinful nature make when it tempts us to shame others? In what ways does the gospel free us from feeling shame and from shaming others?

6. Why does it matter that Paul calls the Corinthians to imitate a life for Jesus that he is already living?

7. Why must all spiritual leaders have faithful teaching *and* faithful consistency in their lives?

8. How should the church address divisive people?

9. Has anyone ever confronted your sin in a gentle but firm way? What made that person's efforts to confront your sin so effective?

10. How can God's good spiritual gifts be abused in the church?

The Basics of Church Discipline

1 CORINTHIANS 5

Main Idea: Christians must lovingly confront sin through church discipline to preserve the church's holiness and to rescue the sinner's soul.

I. Neglecting Church Discipline Invites the Ridicule of the World (5:1).
II. Pride Instead of Sorrow Leads Us to Ignore Church Discipline (5:2).
III. Church Discipline Must Be Exercised Under the Lordship of Jesus Christ for the Good of the Whole Body (5:3-5).
IV. The Absence of Church Discipline Will Lead to the Church Being Infected with Sin (5:6).
V. Church Discipline Is Grounded in the Redemptive Work of Christ (5:7-8).
VI. Church Discipline Must Be Exercised in the Community of Faith, Not the World (5:9-11).
VII. God Judges Those on the Outside While We Judge Those on the Inside (5:12-13).

Dietrich Bonhoeffer wrote, "Nothing can be more cruel than the tenderness that consigns another to his sin. Nothing can be more compassionate than that severe rebuke that calls a brother back from the path of sin" (*Life Together*, 107). Church discipline is a loving and necessary biblical process of confrontation and correction carried out by individual Christians, leaders of the church, and sometimes the whole community. It occurs when a member of the body is in public, continuous, unrepentant, and serious sin. The goal is always to reclaim and restore the brother or sister to fellowship with Christians and his or her local congregation.

The New Testament says a great deal about church discipline. Jesus addresses it in Matthew 18:15-20, and Paul does so repeatedly in texts like Romans 16:17-18; 1 Corinthians 5:1-13; 2 Corinthians 2:5-11; 13:1-3; Galatians 6:1-2; 2 Thessalonians 3:6-12; and Titus 3:9-15. The abundance of attention given to this topic makes it even more remarkable that no aspect of church life in our day is more neglected than this one. And it is a dangerous neglect. Baptist theologian John Dagg warns, "When discipline leaves a [local] church, Christ goes with it" (*Manual*, 274). Carl Laney adds,

> The church that neglects to confront and correct its members lovingly is not being kind, forgiving, or gracious. Such a church is really hindering the Lord's work and the advance of the gospel. The church without discipline is a church without purity (Eph. 5:25-27) and power (cf. Josh. 7:11-12a). By neglecting church discipline a church endangers not only its spiritual effectiveness but also its very existence. God snuffed out the candle of the church at Thyatira because of moral compromise (Rev. 2:20-24). Churches today are in danger of following this first-century precedent. ("Biblical," 354)

First Corinthians 5 reminds us that avoiding and neglecting church discipline is not new. It also provides us with theological and practical guidance for recovering a jewel that is missing from the treasury of too many churches. Alistair Begg is right: "Church discipline brings glory to God as his people obey his word" ("Discipline"). How, then, do we travel the road in glorifying God through obedience to his Word in the ministry of church discipline, what I like to call "the ministry of loving confrontation"? Seven considerations arise from this text.

Neglecting Church Discipline Invites the Ridicule of the World
1 CORINTHIANS 5:1

Paul receives a report that has already gone viral in Corinth. Perhaps he received the bad news from Chloe's people (1:11) or from Stephanas, Fortunatus, and Achaicus (16:17). It is a case of *porneia*, of "sexual immorality" (twice in 5:1; also 5:9,10,11; 6:9,13,18 twice; 7:2). Specifically, it is a case of incest: "A man is sleeping with his father's wife," almost certainly his stepmother, not his biological mother. The present tense seems to indicate "an ongoing, habitual relationship, not a one-time affair." And "Paul makes no mention about taking action against the woman, indicating that she is not a believer (5:12)" (Taylor, *1 Corinthians*, 133).

Incest is condemned repeatedly in the Old Testament (Lev 18:8; Deut 22:30; 27:20). Even the pagan Romans found such behavior

scandalous. The Roman orator Cicero, in fact, said incest was virtually
unheard of in Roman society (Vaughn, *1 Corinthians*, 56). But amazingly,
what Hebrews and Romans found inconceivable, the Corinthians con-
doned. This church out-tolerated the tolerance of an obscene Roman
culture. In the process they invited the criticism and ridicule of the lost
world. The pagan Romans did not applaud the super-tolerant church.
They mocked it. They did not cheer. They jeered.

An impure church will soon be a powerless church. The tolerance
of habitual, unrepentant, and public sin robs the gospel of its beauty
and the church of its witness. Perhaps, for a season, the church's
open-mindedness will be celebrated. In time, however, it will be lam-
pooned and scorned. Eventually, a morally compromising church will
be ignored altogether. A church that looks and acts like the world is of
the world. There is no difference. Why suggest otherwise? Why would
anyone believe it?

Robert Saucy is right:

> Church discipline in all its forms was given by the Head of the
> church for the health and welfare of the body. To avoid its
> practice when necessary for the sake of reputation or what is
> really a false unity can only lead to a sick and weak church life.
> (*The Church*, 126)

Sacrifice the church's purity, and you will soon forfeit the church's
power and the church's witness.

Pride Instead of Sorrow Leads Us to Ignore Church Discipline
1 CORINTHIANS 5:2

My friend and colleague at Southeastern Seminary, Chuck Lawless, wrote
an article entitled "11 Reasons Churches Don't Practice Discipline":
1. They don't know the Bible's teaching on discipline.
2. They have never seen it done before.
3. They don't want to appear judgmental.
4. The church has a wide-open front door.
5. They have had a bad experience with discipline in the past.
6. The church is afraid to open "Pandora's box."
7. They have no guidelines for discipline.
8. They fear losing members (or dollars).
9. They fear being "legalistic."

10. They hope transfer growth will fix the problem.

11. Leaders are sometimes dealing with their own sin.

There is merit and truth in each of these observations. Paul adds another reason that certainly undergirds many of those noted by Lawless: pride! The Corinthians were "arrogant" (NIV, "proud," NKJV, "puffed up"). The verb is in the perfect tense. It indicates they are settled and abiding in their pride. Paul has already and repeatedly confronted the Corinthians about their spiritual pride (1:31; 3:21; 4:6,18-19). In 4:21 he warned them that their response to his letter would determine whether he would come to them "with a rod, or in love and a spirit of gentleness." Whether the Corinthians suffered from a false dualism that said "the spiritual" no longer should concern themselves with the issues of the physical (Platonism) or a heretical understanding of Christian liberty that resulted from a misunderstanding of grace, we cannot be sure. What is certain is they took great pride in their tolerance of sin when the proper response to it should have been "grief." In the spirit of Ezra, who owned and mourned over the nation's sins (Ezra 9), the church should mourn over the sins of its members.

A sin-sick church will boast, "We are affirming and accepting." A gospel-filled church will mourn, "We are sinful and undone." It will readily acknowledge it is a community of repenting sinners. What God calls sin, this church calls sin. What God fights against, this church fights against. The issue is not one of perfection; it is an issue of purity.

Daniel Wray is correct. We practice church discipline . . .

> to maintain the purity of the church and her worship
> (1 Cor. 5:6-8) and to avoid profaning the sacrament of the
> Lord's Supper (1 Cor. 11:27). We shall never be able to keep
> the visible church in perfect purity since we are but fallible
> men. Our inability to achieve perfection in this matter,
> however, is no excuse for giving up the attempt. We must
> maintain the purity of Christ's visible church to the full extent
> of our knowledge and power. This is all the more evident
> once we recognize that false doctrine and bad conduct are
> infectious. If these are tolerated in the church all members
> will receive hurt. (*Biblical Church Discipline*, 4)

Given the seriousness of the situation, Paul's directive is straightforward at the end of verse 2: "Let him who has done this be removed from among you" (ESV). The details of this excommunication are expounded in verses 3-5.

Church Discipline Must Be Exercised Under the Lordship of Jesus Christ for the Good of the Whole Body
1 CORINTHIANS 5:3-5

R. C. Sproul notes, "The church is called not only to a ministry of reconciliation, but a ministry of nurture to those within her gates. Part of that nurture includes church discipline" (*In Search of Dignity*, 182). Correction is essential to spiritual health, growth, and maturity in the body of Christ. John MacArthur adds with a pleading pastoral voice,

> The purpose of church discipline is the spiritual restoration of fallen members and the consequent strengthening of the church and glorifying of the Lord. When a sinning believer is rebuked and he turns from his sin and is forgiven, he is won back to fellowship with the body and with its head, Jesus Christ. The goal of church discipline, then, is not to throw people out of the church or to feed the self-righteous pride of those who administer the discipline. It is not to embarrass people or to exercise authority and power in some unbiblical manner. The purpose is to restore a sinning believer to holiness and bring him back into a pure relationship within the assembly. ("Church Discipline")

Paul's attitude on this matter of sexual immorality contrasts with the proud and conceited Corinthians'. Invoking his apostolic authority, he stated he is there with them even if he is "absent" in body (v. 3). Further, he has "already pronounced judgment on the one who has been doing such a thing," thereby nullifying the Corinthian's lax moral position on the sexually immoral man who calls himself a "brother" in the Lord (v. 11). Vaughn notes the perfect-tense verb "gives an air of finality to the sentence" (*1 Corinthians*, 57).

Verses 4 and 5 contain a clear, logical outline for how the church adjudicates this matter. The prior steps Jesus gave in Matthew 18:15-20 are assumed to have already been followed. A grievous situation like this could necessitate moving quickly to the final step of excommunication.

First, they are to assemble "in the name" and under the authority ("with the power") of the "Lord Jesus" and with apostolic witness ("I am with you in spirit," 1 Cor 5:4). This gathering is congregational. Church discipline is no place for a Lone Ranger.

Second, "With the power [or authority/name] of our Lord Jesus," they are to "remove" this man from their fellowship (v. 2) and deliver him (v. 5) to the realm of Satan (i.e., the world).

Third, the goal of excommunication is to destroy the sinful desires and impulses of his fleshly nature "so that his spirit may be saved in the day of the Lord" (v. 5). Some view this as a pronouncement of a curse that potentially leads to physical death. This view draws from the story of Ananias and Sapphira in Acts 5:1-11 and the death of some Corinthians for abusing the Lord's Supper in 1 Corinthians 11:30. Such a position has merit and weight. Still, correction and restoration seem to be the better understanding of this text (cf. 1 Tim 1:19-20 and the situation of Hymenaeus and Alexander). John Piper follows the correction and restoration interpretation, drawing an analogy from Job:

> What seems to be in view is something like what happened in the book of Job. The only other place in the Bible outside Paul's letters where "handing someone over to Satan" with these very words occurs is Job 2:6, which says, literally, "And the Lord said to the Devil, 'Behold I hand him [Job] over to you. Only spare his life.'"
>
> The next verse says, "Satan went out from the presence of the Lord and smote Job with sore boils from the sole of his foot to the crown of his head." And the result of God's gracious purpose? Job 42:6-7: "Now my eye sees you [O Lord] and I despise myself and repent in dust and ashes."
>
> So Satan became the means under God's sovereign control of purifying Job's heart and bringing him closer than ever to God. This is not the only place where God uses Satan to do that. In 2 Corinthians 12 Paul describes his thorn in the flesh as a messenger of Satan which God appoints for Paul's humility and Christ's glory. Verse 7: "To keep me from exalting myself, there was given me a thorn in the flesh, a messenger of Satan to buffet me—to keep me from exalting myself!" . . .
>
> Jesus is Satan's ruler. And he uses Satan, our archenemy, to save and sanctify his people. He brought Job to penitence

and prosperity. He brought Paul to the point where he could exult in tribulation and make the power of Christ manifest.

And Paul hopes that the result of handing over this man to Satan will be the salvation of his spirit at the day of Christ. In other words, Paul's aim—our aim—in handing someone over to Satan is that some striking misery will come in such a way that the person will say with Job, "My eyes have seen the Lord, and I despise myself and repent in dust and ashes." ("How Satan Saves the Soul"; brackets in original)

The Absence of Church Discipline Will Lead to the Church Being Infected with Sin
1 CORINTHIANS 5:6

This verse contains a statement of fact accompanied by a warning. Paul states, "Your boasting is not good," which connects back to verse 2. Indeed, their arrogance, boasting, and tolerance of ongoing sin are something they should be ashamed of, not proud of. Their spiritual value system has been turned upside down. Their carnal boasting may soon lead to spiritual blindness infecting the whole body.

Paul warned the Corinthians with a popular and well-known saying among the Hebrews. It is analogous to our modern proverb, "One bad apple can spoil the whole barrel." Rooting his words in the event of Passover and the common understanding of leaven representing evil, Paul warns the church that "a little leaven leavens the whole batch of dough." There is a contaminating element to sin. Like cancer, it can spread widely and quickly, infecting the whole body. Indeed, "one corrupt member could corrupt an entire church" (Vaughn and Lea, *1 Corinthians*, 59).

Church discipline recognizes a simple spiritual truth: Sin is bad for the church. Left unchecked, it will spread like a wild, invasive weed through a fellowship. It will grow wide and deep. It will choke out the church's purity and its wonder at the gospel. Passion for the unreached and underserved will wither. Love for the Word will die. Respect for the ministers of the Word will disappear. Satan would rather have a little leaven inside the church than a whole batch of risen dough outside it. Attitudes and actions are contagious. In James Boyce's "Three Changes in Theological Institutions," delivered at Furman University on July 30, 1856, he warned, "It is with a single man that error usually commences;

and when such a man has influence or position, it is impossible to estimate that evil that will attend it" (Broadus, *A Gentleman*, 139).

Church Discipline Is Grounded in the Redemptive Work of Christ
1 CORINTHIANS 5:7-8

Paul grounds his argument for critical issues in the gospel of Jesus Christ. In these verses he draws from the imagery of the Passover (Exod 12). Sin must be removed like old leaven was cleaned out before the Passover was observed. Thus, the sinning brother who remains unrepentant must go. After all, by their repentance of sin and faith in Christ, believers "may be a new unleavened batch." They are new creations in Christ. The old has passed (v. 7; 2 Cor 5:17). Paul challenges them to be who they already are in Christ because Christ, the true Passover Lamb, "has been sacrificed" (v. 7). His blood covers our sin and separates us from sin. We are new in him, never again to live in the old ways of slavery to sin. MacArthur is helpful here:

> As pictured in the Passover in Egypt, the sacrifice of Jesus Christ, God's perfect Passover Lamb, and the placing of His blood over us, completely separates us from the dominion of sin and the penalty of judgment. We, too, are to remove everything from the old life that would taint and permeate the new. As Israel was set free from Egypt as a result of the Passover and was to make a clean break with that oppressor, so the believer is to be totally separated from his old life, with its sinful attitudes, standards, and habits. Christ died to separate us from bondage to sin and give us a new bondage to righteousness (Rom. 6:19), which is the only true freedom. (*1 Corinthians*, 129)

Verse 8 pictures life in Christ as a party, a joyful feast that celebrates the mentality, "out with the old and in with the new"! Out go things like "malice and evil [NIV, "wickedness"],", and in come qualities like "sincerity and truth." We will gladly pursue what honors and glorifies Christ when we have grasped the magnitude of his sacrifice on our behalf. He stayed the hand of the angel of death by his blood. Obedience to this Savior is not a burden. It is a blessing! We should delight in who we are and who we are becoming in him.

David Brainerd, who died at twenty-nine and spent his short adult life as a missionary to the American Indians, wrote in his diary:

> I never got away from Jesus, and him crucified, and I found that when my people were gripped by this great evangelical doctrine of Christ and him crucified, I had no need to give them instructions about morality. I found that one followed as the sure and inevitable fruit of the other. . . . I found my Indians begin to put on the garments of holiness and their common life begins to be sanctified even in small matters when they are possessed by the doctrine of Christ and him crucified. (Jowett, *Apostolic Optimism*, 84)[1]

Church Discipline Must Be Exercised in the Community of Faith, Not the World
1 CORINTHIANS 5:9-11

There is an important relationship between the ministries of church discipline and evangelism that Paul helps us see in these verses. In a real sense church discipline and evangelism are flip sides of the coin of salvation. Church discipline is a natural component of discipleship that functions as the corollary of evangelism. Laney says, "Evangelism ministers to those *outside* the church who are in bondage to sin. Congregational discipline ministers to those *within* the church who are in bondage to sin" ("Biblical" 353; emphasis in original). Paul makes this argument in verses 9-11.

In a previous letter now lost to us and therefore not intended by God to be a part of inspired Scripture, Paul wrote to the Corinthians telling them "not to associate with sexually immoral people" who profess to follow Christ and believe the gospel (v. 9). They apparently misunderstood his instructions, either accidentally or intentionally, as verse 10 makes clear.

Paul quickly and directly corrects them, providing a representative list of the kinds of public, continuous, and unrepentant sins we must lovingly confront in the life of a professing believer in Jesus (vv. 10-11).

---

[1] To the best I can determine, this quote appears to be Jowett's paraphrase of the content found in David Brainerd's journal (Edwards, *Memoirs*, 321–27).

There are six categories in total. David Garland points out that each is especially addressed in 1 Corinthians (*1 Corinthians*, 189).

(1) Sexual immorality (5:1; also 6:9,13-18; 7:1-6)
(2) Greed (6:1-11)
(3) Swindling (robbers; 6:1-11)
(4) Idolatry (chs. 8;10)
(5) Verbal abuse (slanderers; 1:18–4:21)
(6) Drunkenness (11:21)

Though believers are not to be *of* the world (John 17:17-19; Rom 12:1-2), we are to be *in* the world. Removing ourselves from sin and sinners would require us to exit the world. This is not God's plan in the present age. Jesus was clear in John 17:18, saying, "As [God] sent me into the world, I also have sent [my followers] into the world." We are to be in this world and active in loving our neighbors, sharing the gospel, and bearing witness to Christ. We must spend time with the lost to win the lost. By contrast, the professing brother or sister in Christ who is living in sin is to be shunned. We are not to "associate" with them, nor should we "even eat with such a person" (1 Cor 5:11). This would certainly include taking the Lord's Supper. It may have included breaking all social ties except those engagements and social interactions that had the specific purpose of restoration and reconciliation. MacArthur once more helps us:

> The command not to have fellowship or even social contact
> with the unrepentant brother does not exclude all contact.
> When there is an opportunity to admonish him and try to
> call him back, the opportunity should be taken. In fact, such
> opportunities should be sought. But the contact should be for
> the purpose of admonishment and restoration and no other.
> ("Church Discipline")

God Judges Those on the Outside While We Judge Those on the Inside
1 CORINTHIANS 5:12-13

Verses 12-13 conclude the argument of chapter 5. Paul draws clear lines of demarcation and responsibility. God judges those outside the church (the lost), and we as his people judge those inside the church. After applying Jesus's teaching in Matthew 18:15-17, we have three responsibilities to an unrepentant sinning brother: we must remove him (v. 2), deliver him "to Satan for the destruction of the flesh" (v. 5), and "expel the wicked person from among [us]" (NIV, cf. Deut 17:7). Expelling or removing the wicked from among God's people is a consistent theme in Deuteronomy (Deut 17:7,12; 19:19; 21:21; 22:21-22,24; 24:7). Its repetitive nature makes clear its importance.

Such a serious action must be bathed in the sentiments commended in Galatians 6:1-2. When taking this final step of church discipline, we do so with sorrow and broken hearts. There is no joy in a person's sin, but there is joy in our obedience to Christ. We do not truly love our brother or sister if we do nothing. We must love them enough to hurt them, even though it hurts us.

- Overlooking sin is not loving; it is sinful.
- Overlooking sin is not gracious; it is cowardice.
- Overlooking sin is not merciful; it is dangerous.
- Overlooking sin is not kind; it is hateful.

I often tell my friends the only way you can truly hurt my feelings is by seeing me do something that dishonors the Lord and hurts his kingdom and not confronting me. It means you did not love me enough to point out my sin. Church discipline loves people enough to point out their sin and then guide them to the place of repentance and then on to restoration (see 2 Cor 2 for a hopeful resolution of 1 Cor 5).

Conclusion

One minister said, "If you see your neighbor sin, and you pass by and neglect to reprove him, it is just as cruel as if you should see his house on fire, and pass by and not warn him of it" (Finney, *Lectures*, 45). Marlin Jeschke summarizes well the heart of the matter:

> In discipline, as in the presentation of the good news to a non-Christian, a person is presented the opportunity of being liberated from the power of sin in all its forms by coming under the rule of Christ and walking in His way. (*Discipling*, 181–82)

Let us be zealous in presenting that good news, and let us be faithful in the practice of the ministry of loving confrontation. In both we will be helping to save souls.

Reflect and Discuss

1. Why does Bonhoeffer say that nothing could be more cruel than giving someone leniency that allows him or her to sin? Why is nothing more compassionate than a reprimand that calls someone back to the Christian community?

2. How does practicing regular, loving confrontation on small matters help protect the church from having to deal with sin issues that require excommunication?

3. What heart posture must someone have to engage in loving confrontation?

4. Why is it incorrect to think that covering up sin will help the church?

5. Which of the eleven reasons from the article on why churches don't practice discipline most tempts you?

6. What causes someone to slowly move from being humbly sick over the presence of sin to being pridefully okay with its presence? What must you do to protect your heart from this shift?

7. Describe a time when someone lovingly corrected you. How did it help you repent of your sin?

8. In what ways is Christians' pursuit of holiness dependent on their identity in Christ? How does working against sin as those who already have a new identity allow the church to pursue holiness correctly?

9. How would the church benefit if each Christian cultivated an attitude that welcomes correction?

10. Does Paul's language in 1 Corinthians 5:9 imply you should not be discerning in whom you associate with? When is it harmful to associate with immoral people?

Why Christians Should Not Sue Christians in Civil Court

1 CORINTHIANS 6:1-11

Main Idea: Christians should avoid greed and selfish disputes that defame the church because Jesus has radically saved and changed them.

I. **Suing a Fellow Believer Is Inconsistent with Our Future Responsibilities (6:1-3).**
   A. We will be judges over the world (6:1-2).
   B. We will be judges over the angels (6:3).

II. **Suing a Fellow Believer Is Inconsistent with How the Church Should Work (6:4-8).**
   A. The church should be able to handle matters like these (6:4).
   B. The church's witness to unbelievers must not be compromised (6:5-7).

III. **Suing a Fellow Believer Is Inconsistent with New Life in Christ (6:9-11).**
   A. It forgets who we were before Christ (6:9-10).
   B. It forgets who we are in Christ (6:11).

Sometimes Christians, by their actions and attitudes, cast a dark cloud over the beauty of the gospel. They turn unbelievers away from the Lord Jesus because their lives contradict the message that salvation in Christ makes one different. Examples of such bad behavior run throughout 1 Corinthians. The body of Christ, which should be characterized by grace and truth (John 1:14), is being torn apart over division, disputes, and party politics. It is being ripped to shreds by sexual immorality and a demand for personal rights. In chapter 6 further shame comes on the church in the public arena as believers take one another to the secular courts to settle their "dispute[s]," their "grievance[s]" (ESV), and their "complaint[s] (civil dispute[s])" (AMP). Paul is scandalized at their behavior because it is shameful (v. 5), and it admits "defeat" (v. 7) for the gospel and the reputation of the redeemed community who ought to be different. The great Baptist preacher from London, Charles Spurgeon (1834–1892), knew what was at stake for the church before a watching world. He said,

The eagle-eyed world acts as a policeman for the church. . . . [It] becomes a watch-dog over the sheep, barking furiously as soon as one goes astray. . . . Be careful, be careful of your private lives . . . and I believe your public lives will be sure to be right. [But] remember that it is upon your public life that the verdict of the world will very much depend. ("The Parent's and Pastor's Joy," 717–18)

Paul provides three arguments for why Christians should not sue Christians in civil court. Now, let's be clear as we begin to walk through the text. Criminal matters are not the issue in this chapter. Criminal acts like sexual or physical abuse, theft, or any crime at all for that matter should be immediately reported to legal authorities. The church has its place to deal with others (see Rom 13:1-5), and the government has its place to deal with certain issues. When it comes to an actual crime, the wrongheaded idea that "what happens in the church stays in the church" is dangerous and sometimes criminal itself. The church must know its place and responsibilities in these matters.

Suing a Fellow Believer Is Inconsistent with Our Future Responsibilities
1 CORINTHIANS 6:1-3

Jesus said, "By this everyone will know that you are my disciples, if you love one another" (John 13:35). The Corinthians had forgotten this statement, or they did not think it had any bearing on whether or not to take a brother or sister in Christ to civil court. They failed to see the inconsistency of unbelievers being called upon to judge believers.

We Will Be Judges Over the World (6:1-2)

Paul begins with a direct and confrontational question: "If any of you has a dispute against another, how dare you take it to court before the unrighteous, and not before the saints?" Schreiner agrees with what I said earlier: "The Corinthians' lawsuits were not criminal cases, such as murder, rape or theft, but the kind of minor matters that lead to litigation" (*1 Corinthians*, 117). *The Message* provides a powerful paraphrase of verse 1: "How dare you take each other to court! When you think you have been wronged, does it make any sense to go before a court that knows nothing of God's ways instead of a family of Christians?" The thought of doing such a thing over small claims is unthinkable!

Paul adds to his initial salvo in verse 2 with a point of theology and the first of six don't-you-know statements in chapter 6 (cf. 5:6). "Or don't you know that the saints will judge the world? And if the world is judged by you, are you unworthy [ESV, "incompetent"] to judge the trivial cases?" Texts like Matthew 19:28; Luke 22:29-30; and Revelation 20:4 speak of believers being involved in future judgment. But there is more that we must consider. The doctrine of our union with Christ in salvation enters the discussion. Paul Gardner writes,

> For Paul and the early church, it is a given that God's
> judgment will be carried out by the Christ who is himself
> the "Lord." . . . Paul believes that God's people are involved
> with the work of their Lord and caught up in his status,
> being found "in Christ" and *participating* covenantally with
> him. They are involved in his work and are incorporated in
> him as they are represented by him . . . so he can envisage
> God's people caught up in all that is true of the Lord Jesus.
> If Christ is judge of the world, it stands to reason that those
> "in Christ" will judge the world. (*1 Corinthians*, 252; emphasis
> in original)

We Will Be Judges Over the Angels (6:3)

Paul extends his argument in verse 3 to the spiritual realm and angels. "Don't you know that we will judge angels—how much more matters of this life?" In the eschaton believers will judge these other intelligent creatures. Whether Paul means their good, their bad, or both is not specified. However, Paul's main point is clear as he employs a greater-to-lesser argument. Angels, as Morris notes, "are by nature the highest class of created beings" (*1 Corinthians*, 91). If you will someday judge these extraordinary creatures, you certainly should be able to handle the mundane matters of this life. Kyle Dillon sounds a helpful reminder: "We do not use worldly methods to achieve worldly aims. Rather, in all things, we should be set apart as people governed by God's Word and empowered by God's Spirit" ("What Does It Mean?"). Are you as wise as you claim to be? Your current behavior may say, "No!"

Suing a Fellow Believer Is Inconsistent with How the Church Should Work
1 CORINTHIANS 6:4-8

In commenting on 1 Corinthians 6, John Piper writes, "I can't think of any reason why a Christian would take another Christian to court. Peacemakers ought to go to peace with each other. What you want to do is model for the world you're not a lover of money" ("Is It Ever Okay?"). We cannot ignore that love for money is part of the equation of the need for this chapter. It is probably the driving component. I think verse 7 seals this argument. Paul moves his argument in this direction, especially in his use of rhetorical questions.

The Church Should Be Able to Handle Matters Like These (6:4)

Paul begins this section with a question: "So if you have such matters [ESV, "cases"], do you appoint as your judges those who have no standing in the church?" The irony, the sarcasm, is biting. The Corinthians invited pagan judges who had no status in the church to arbitrate matters within the church. This is mind-boggling! The church should be able to handle small claims matters. We are family. We need to act like it![2]

The Church's Witness to Unbelievers Must Not Be Compromised (6:5-8)

The Corinthians should have been ashamed of themselves, and Paul tells them so. This is not spiritual abuse; it is spiritual admonition! Paul again raises a rhetorical question to make his point: "Can it be that there is not one wise person among you who is able to arbitrate between fellow believers?" (v. 5). Again, the sarcasm is biting given how the Corinthian church boasted about its wisdom and how smart they were. However, their actions prove otherwise, as verse 6 makes painfully clear: "Instead, brother goes to court against brother, and that before unbelievers!" Shame on all such troublemakers, Paul says, for the harm they continually bring to Christ and the gospel as they repeatedly ask unbelievers to handle their disputes and disagreements.

If addressing their minor problem situation were an athletic contest, the church lost before the event ever began. Paul says, "[T]o have

---

[2] For an alternative understanding of verse 4, see Taylor, *1 Corinthians*, 146–47.

legal disputes [ESV, "lawsuits"] against one another is already a defeat for you" (v. 7). Regardless of the outcome of the lawsuit, they all lost for going to a pagan judge in the first place.

Perhaps drawing from the words of Jesus in Matthew 5:39-42, Paul asks, "Why not rather be wronged? Why not rather be cheated [ESV, "defrauded"]?" Pastor Warren Wiersbe puts it well: "Better to lose money and possession than to lose a brother or lose your testimony" (*Be Wise*, 69). I readily acknowledge what Paul says here is a tough pill to swallow, but it is what the Bible tells us to do. Unfortunately, the Corinthians, and too many Christians today, love money more than they love Christ, the gospel, and the reputation of the church. That's why Paul says, "[Y]ou yourselves do wrong and cheat—and you do this to brothers and sisters" (v. 8). Curtis Vaughn says, "The Corinthian Christians had double problems. They sinned against ethical standards, for they actually defrauded. They also wounded brotherly love" (*1 Corinthians*, 63). Such behavior was inconsistent with their new identity in Christ, which Paul will now make clear.

Suing a Fellow Believer Is Inconsistent with New Life in Christ
1 CORINTHIANS 6:9-11

Paul writes in 2 Corinthians 5:17, "Therefore, if anyone is in Christ, he is a new creation; the old has passed away, and see, the new has come!" This wonderful verse is a marvelous summary of 1 Corinthians 6:9-11. Here Paul draws a stark and striking contrast between who we were before Jesus saved us and who we are after Jesus saved us. These verses serve the dual purpose of rejoicing and warning.

Don't Forget Who You Were Before Christ (6:9-10)

Verses 9-10 constitute what we call a vice list. It is similar to Romans 1:29-31; 1 Corinthians 5:11; Galatians 5:19-21; Ephesians 5:3-6; and Colossians 3:5-9. They address the believer's nature and lifestyle before accepting Christ and also the eternal destiny of those who never trust Christ and thus are never regenerated or justified.

These Corinthians were living like the unrighteous, and they needed to be reminded that "the unrighteous will not inherit God's kingdom" (1 Cor 6:9). They will not escape eschatological judgment. They will not enjoy the new heaven, the new earth, or the new Jerusalem (Rev 21–22).

They will not spend eternity with God. Tragically, their eternal destiny is "the lake of fire" (Rev 20:14-15).

"Do not be deceived" is a present imperative and sounds a strong warning (1 Cor 6:9). What follows is a selective list of nine sinful groups representing those who will not inherit the kingdom of God. Such sinful behavior is not occasional and rare, and it is possible that a Christian might commit any sin. The list, however, identifies those whose lives are characterized by these sins. Such habits represent who they are, and they have no regard for what God thinks or desires. What follows is the list and a brief description of those indulging each vice:

"Sexually immoral people." The Greek word *porneia* used here is a general term for those engaged in sexual sin contrary to the teachings of the Bible. This covers sexual activity that occurs outside the marriage covenant between a man and a woman.

"Idolaters" refers to those practicing perhaps the most basic and fundamental of all sins (see Exod 20:3-6). They give status and position to people and things that rightly belongs only to God. Schreiner points out idolatry is repeatedly addressed in the New Testament (Rom 1:18-25; 1 Cor 5:10-11; 10:7,14; Gal 5:20; Eph 5:5; Col 3:5; Rev 21:8).

"Adulterers" are those who are unfaithful to their covenantal marriage vows (1 Cor 6:9).

"Males who have sex with males" refers to both passive homosexual participants (Gk. *malakoi*) and active homosexual participants (Gk. *arsenokoitai*). In spite of cultural accommodation and liberal reinterpretations, the Bible is consistent in its condemnation of homosexuality as sinful and contrary to the design and plan of God (see Lev 18:22; 20:13; Rom 1:26-27; 1 Tim 1:10; Jude 7-8). Jesus spoke to this issue as well in Matthew 19:4-6. (For an excellent treatment of the issue, see Gardner, *1 Corinthians*, 264–69.)

"Thieves" are those who steal secretly, attempting to avoid attention.

"Greedy people" refers to those who never have enough and always seek to gain more by any means.

"Drunkards" are those who abuse alcohol to the point of drunkenness (cf. Eph 5:18). A sure way to avoid drunkenness is abstinence from alcohol.

"Verbally abusive people" (ESV, "revilers") are those who use harsh and abusive language to mock or scoff or even slander others.

"Swindlers" are those "who forcibly steal from others" (Schreiner, *1 Corinthians*, 121–22, 238).

The phrase "not inherit the kingdom of God" brackets verse 9. This reinforces the seriousness of the warning to those clinging to their sin. God does not make light of or wink at sin. Neither can we. Those who practice these things should be excluded from the church (ch. 5). If they persist and do not repent, they will be excluded from the kingdom of God (ch. 6).

Don't Forget Who We Are in Christ (6:11)

Paul knows many of us have not just sinful, but ugly and wicked pasts. Some of us were prime examples of those in the groups of verses 9-10. But praise God, not anymore. That is in our BC—our before Christ! That is who we used to be, but are not now! Three powerful theological truths describe who believers have become. Before I explain that, consider this wording: "In the name of the Lord Jesus Christ [note his full majestic title] and by the Spirit of our God." Do not pass over too quickly the Trinitarian nature of our salvation. God sent the Son, the Son accomplished redemption, and the Spirit applies the Son's work!

Now for the first of the three new identity truths I mentioned. "Washed." This speaks of the believer's new birth (John 3) and our regeneration (Titus 3:5). The early church would have seen its connection with baptism as well. Schreiner is right:

> Baptism is part of a series of events that occur at conversion;
> those who are converted also repent, believe and confess Jesus
> as Lord. Hence, the washing takes place upon conversion,
> when one repents and believes in Jesus Christ, and thus
> baptism symbolizes cleaning from sin. (*1 Corinthians*, 123)

"Sanctified" is the next identity truth. Usually we think of sanctification as progressive growth in Christlikeness, but here "positional sanctification" is in view. When we were saved, washed, and regenerated, we also received a new status of being holy or set apart to God. We became "saints," holy ones, who belong to God (cf. 1 Cor 1:2; Eph 5:26).

"Justified" is the next identity truth mentioned. We now stand before God acquitted, innocent because of the imputed righteousness of Christ in our accounts. We are not made justified. We are declared to be justified based on what Jesus has done for us. Morris explains that justified . . .

> is a legal term used of acquittal, "reckon as righteous,"
> "declare righteous," "acquit." Paul uses it for the act of
> God whereby, on the basis of Christ's atoning death, he

declares believers to be just, and accepts them as his own.
(*1 Corinthians*, 94)

The Father, through the Son, by the Spirit, has done all this for us. How utterly inconceivable that we would live and act like we did before our great God saved us.

Conclusion

I want to conclude our study on a practical note that expands the application of our text to how we should handle conflict in a number of areas. Ken Sande is the founder of Peacemaker Ministries and Relational Wisdom 360. His article "20 Ways to Prevent and Resolve Conflict in the Church" is a goldmine of biblical truth and wisdom. It provides a helpful way to bring our study of 1 Corinthians 6 to a close. The following is a closely followed and extensively quoted summation of the article that includes a few adjustments for the sake of clarity and space. It beautifully demonstrates the gospel in action for those who have been washed, sanctified, and justified "in the name of Lord Jesus Christ and by the Spirit of our God" (6:11).

1. Remember the Golden Result.

We all know the Golden Rule: "Do to others as you would have them do to you." But do you know the Golden Result? It's a direct corollary to the Golden Rule: "Other people will usually treat you the way you treat them." So anytime you're in a conflict, ask yourself, "How do I want to be treated?" Then engage others by treating them exactly the same way (Matt 7:12).

2. Bring the Gospel into Every Conflict.

When Christians are in conflict, our tendency is to resort to "the law." We love to use God's Word to show where we're right and others are wrong. This approach usually just drives us further apart. Instead of bringing the law to others, bring them the gospel. Remind others of the forgiveness we all have in Christ. If we trust in him, our sins have been paid in full. As you remind yourself and others of these promises, you can bring hope, reduce defensiveness, make it safe to confess sin, and inspire Christ-like behavior.

3. Expose the Idols that Drive Conflict.

James 4:1 [ESV] provides a key insight on conflict: "What causes quarrels and what causes fights among you? Is it not this, that your passions are at war within you?"

In many church conflicts, the passions involved are not inherently sinful. They are often linked to good things we want too much. This gives rise to a downward spiral, which I often refer to as the "progression of an idol": a good desire turns into a *consuming demand* that leads us to *judge others* and eventually *punish them* if they don't give us what we want.

4. Guard Against Amygdala Hijacking in Yourself and Others.

This process typically involves sudden, intense emotions that trigger an impulsive reaction that will be deeply regretted. The good news is that the Bible describes four simple steps you can follow to avoid this destructive dynamic: This process is summarized in the simple acrostic: **READ** (**R**ecognize and name your emotions; **E**valuate their source; **A**nticipate the consequences of following them; and **D**irect the power of your emotions on a constructive course).

5. Weave Relational Wisdom into Your Church.

When we get into a conflict, most of us have a tendency to go "two-dimensional." We focus obsessively on our own righteousness and the other persons' wrongs.

Relational wisdom, which is a gospel-driven form of emotional intelligence, helps people always view their relationships "three-dimensionally" by seeking to be *God-aware*, *self-aware* and *other-aware* in every relational interaction, just as Jesus taught (Matt 22:37-40).

6. Communicate So Clearly You Cannot Be Misunderstood.

Many conflicts in the church are triggered or inflamed by poor communication, often by leaders themselves. For a leader, it's not good enough to communicate so you can be understood. You must communicate so clearly that you *cannot be misunderstood*. Make clarity and charity your goals.

7. Work Patiently with People as They Process Their Emotions and Experiences.

People are always interpreting our words and actions through their own life experiences and emotions. As a result, a seemingly innocent statement can trigger an intense emotional reaction in others. Our natural tendency in such situations is to defend ourselves and point out how unwarranted their responses are. It takes time and patience, but it's possible to turn these types of interactions into opportunities for life-changing ministry if you'll take the time to gently and patiently help people process their emotions and life experiences.

8. Don't Be Misled by the Three Faces of Fear.

When people react to you with control, anger, or withdrawal, it's natural to become defensive and judgmental. But has that response ever helped, whether in your family or in your church? Probably not. Instead, realize that control, anger, and withdrawal are often triggered by fear. Once you understand this, you can resist the temptation to become defensive and instead seek to discern and address whatever fear is triggering another's behavior.

9. Practice the Three Ps of Satisfaction.

If helping others work through a conflict, you are far more likely to see a positive outcome if you work diligently to provide these:

- **Process satisfaction** requires a fair, orderly, and even-handed process where everyone feels that they've had a reasonable opportunity to present their side of the matter.
- **Personal satisfaction** requires treating everyone with respect, courtesy, and equality, just as we would want to be treated ourselves.
- **Product satisfaction** requires a final solution that is as reasonable, just, and equitable as is humanly possible. I cannot emphasize this point too much: Give people process satisfaction (the opportunity to fully and candidly share their views), as well as personal satisfaction (treating them with sincere courtesy and respect), and you'll be surprised how content they'll be even if they disagree with your substantive decision.

10. Constantly Build Passport.

A passport is an authorization to go someplace you have no
inherent right to be. In relational terms, it is the permission
that people give to you to enter into their lives, to learn
their secrets, to know their struggles, and to offer advice and
correction. The best way to earn and maintain that is to relate
to others in such a way that they would automatically answer
"yes" to three key questions:

- Can I trust you?
- Do you really care about me?
- Can you actually help me?

11. Teach Your People to Practice Charitable Judgments.

Many of the conflicts that arise in a church begin or grow
worse because people assume the worst about others' actions
or motives. The best way for you to prevent this tendency is
to proactively teach your congregation to practice "charitable
judgments" in every area of life. Making a charitable judgment
means that out of love for God, you strive to believe the best
about others until you have facts to prove otherwise.

12. When You Need to Negotiate, PAUSE.

- **P**repare (pray, get the facts, seek godly counsel, develop options).
- **A**ffirm relationships (show genuine concern and respect for
  others).
- **U**nderstand interests (identify others' concerns, desires, needs,
  limitations, or fears).
- **S**earch for creative solutions (prayerful brainstorming).
- **E**valuate options objectively and reasonably (evaluate, don't
  argue).

13. Defuse Explosive Meetings with a Six-Part Format.

Turn volatile meetings into times of humble self-examination
and constructive problem solving by summarizing the issue to
be discussed and then indicating that everyone who speaks will
be expected to follow a six-part format:

- Briefly stated, how do you feel because of this problem?
- What have you done that might have contributed to this problem?
- What do you think would please God as we work through this situation?
- What steps have you already taken to make things better?
- What are you now willing to do to help resolve this problem?
- What do you suggest others do to help resolve this problem?

14. Teach People to Focus on the Good Before Itemizing the Bad.

When any of us get into a conflict, our tendency is to see our opponents in an increasingly negative light, highlighting their faults and recounting their wrongs. This is a perfect strategy for destroying relationships and dividing churches.

Since God commands us to seek unity and reconciliation in the body of Christ, he graciously provides wisdom principles that enable us to overcome our tendency to focus on others' flaws (see Phil 4:8-9). God can use this passage to change the course of bitter divorces, lawsuits, and church divisions.

15. Be Approachable.

Conflicts in churches often begin with misunderstandings and minor differences in opinion. Unfortunately, many Christians are afraid to approach their church leaders with their concerns, which sometimes allows those concerns to fester and grow until they finally explode into an intense conflict. One of the most effective ways to encourage church members to share their concerns before they become major problems is for church leaders to strive earnestly to make themselves "approachable." This requires the development of a variety of relational skills, including humility, empathy, reading subtle emotional cues, and attentive listening.

16. Unleash the Power of Confession.

If you confess your contribution to a problem, it's amazing how often others will follow your lead and begin to acknowledge how they have contributed to the situation as well.

17. Follow the Example of Lincoln and Reagan.

One of the many characteristics that these two American presidents shared was their exceptional ability to understand and manage not only their own emotions and interests but also the emotions and interests of the people they led and the opponents they wished to turn into friends.

18. Deploy God's Full Array of Peacemaking Processes.

The Bible provides a variety of ways for Christians to resolve conflict, including overlooking minor offenses (Prov 19:11), talking privately with each other (Matt 18:15), seeking advice from wise counselors (Prov 20:18), pursuing mediation (Matt 18:16), and submitting to binding arbitration (1 Cor 6:1-6).

Although some conflicts are so complex that professionally trained conciliators may be needed, the vast majority of conflicts involving Christians can be fully resolved by spiritually mature leaders in the local church, just as God instructs in 1 Corinthians 6:4-5.

19. Practice Redemptive, Gospel-Centered Church Discipline.

Jesus knew that believers will occasionally refuse to receive guidance and correction from church leaders. This is why the Matthew 18:15-20 (see also 1 Cor 5–6) process includes instructions on how to carry out formal discipline with believers who refuse to listen to godly counsel.

Jesus calls us to approach such ministry as a gospel-centered "rescue mission" rather than a time to impose guilt and condemnation (see Matt 18:12-14).

20. An Ounce of Prevention Is Worth Many of Hours of Conflict Resolution.

There is one thing that is even better than successfully resolving a conflict; *preventing* a conflict in the first place. Train others to improve their own relational wisdom and peacemaking skills.

Remember what James 3:18 [NIV] promises:
"Peacemakers who sow in peace reap a harvest of
righteousness." (Adapted from "20 Ways to Prevent and
Resolve Conflict in the Church"; emphases in original)

Reflect and Discuss

1. In what ways can it be good for the church that the watching world, as Spurgeon writes, acts as a policeman on the church's conduct? What areas of church life is the world unable to judge?
2. Why is it important that Christians let the government handle criminal cases? In what ways is it better equipped to handle criminal cases than the church?
3. What are Paul's concerns regarding believers taking their civil cases before outside judges? What often motivates one person to sue another person? How does Paul seek to radically reshape what a Christian values most in civil matters?
4. What is the ultimate example of suffering wrong for another's good? Explain.
5. How can your church structures (pastors, membership, small groups, etc.) help your church handle disagreements and civil issues?
6. Why would Paul's language of "brother" and "sister" remind the Corinthians that part of their issue stems from how they view one another?
7. What do the sinful categories on the vice list Paul presents have to do with keeping someone out of the kingdom of God?
8. Why is it important to remember who you were before accepting Christ? Why can your past identity propel you toward holiness without serving as a continual source of shame?
9. Paul speaks of Christ's work in Christians as an ongoing work and a finished one. How are both true?
10. Based on this chapter, how should you finish the initial phrase of 1 Corinthians 6:1: "If any of you has a dispute against another . . ."?

My Body Belongs to God

1 CORINTHIANS 6:12-20

Main Idea: God purchased our bodies by the resurrection of Christ and united us with him so that we would be his temple and glorify him.

I. **God Has Principles for My Body (6:12-13).**
II. **God Has Plans for My Body (6:13-14).**
III. **God Has Protection for My Body (6:15-18).**
IV. **God Has Proprietorship of My Body (6:19).**
V. **God Has Paid for My Body (6:20).**

One of God's most precious gifts to each person is the physical body. In Psalm 139:14 King David says we "have been remarkably and wondrously made." Here, in 1 Corinthians 6:14-15, Paul says the Lord is for the body and that he will resurrect our bodies by his power. In chapter 15 Paul tells us that someday God will give us glorified bodies that are incorruptible, immortal, powerful, spiritual, and heavenly. First John 3:2 provides the capstone to the future destiny of our bodies when it tells us that "we will be like [Jesus] because we will see him as he is." The next verse adds our proper response to such an amazing promise: "Everyone who has this hope in him purifies himself just as he is pure."

God is not indifferent to what we do with our bodies. They matter to him, and they matter a lot. How much do they matter? He paid for them through the death of his Son that he could come to live in them, frail though they are, as his temple (1 Cor 6:19-20). When God saves us, he saves us entirely! He saves a person body, soul, and spirit (1 Thess 5:23).

Many of us have forgotten or neglected this wonderful truth, however, which reveals itself in how we think about our bodies. Many of us are essentially twenty-first-century Corinthians who believe the body counts for little or nothing. Thus, many of us believe we can do whatever we want with them. Even sexual immorality, some believe, is not a big deal to God. To this Paul will respond with conviction and clarity, telling those with such views they could not be more wrong. John Piper helps set the table for our study:

Some of the Corinthians had a view of the body that made what they did with it morally indifferent. In 1 Corinthians 5:2 they actually boasted about an act of incest in the church. In 11:21 some of them even got drunk at the Lord's Supper. They reasoned: the body and food and drink and sex are going to be destroyed in the end. There will only be free spirits. So, the body does not matter. You can eat and drink and have sex any way you like because the body is morally irrelevant. It's what you know and think that really counts (8:1-3).

Paul opposed this view with all his might. He gave them a new and radically different slogan: "The body is for the Lord and the Lord is for the body." The body is not just going to be destroyed; it is going to be raised. The body is not morally indifferent. It is for the glory of God. ("I Will Not Be Enslaved")

Paul lays out five principles in this passage that guide us in glorifying God in our bodies. The body is a great gift from a great God. Each believer must use it wisely and well.

God Has Principles for My Body
1 CORINTHIANS 6:12-13

Two words or phrases control the argument of verses 12-20: "sexual immorality" (Gk. *porneia*), which occurs three times (vv. 13,18 twice, cf. v. 9), and "body" (Gk. *soma*), which occurs eight times (vv. 13 twice, 15,16,18 twice, 19,20). Further, the phrase "Don't you know" occurs three times (vv. 15,16,19) and a total of six times in chapter 6. What you don't know about your body and sexual immorality can hurt you. It can be dangerous to your spiritual health. Paul begins by correcting the Corinthians' faulty theology.

The phrase "Everything is permissible for me" was a Corinthian slogan that Paul quoted (v. 12). It possibly reflects a faulty understanding of grace and liberty in Christ (Fee, *Corinthians*, 2014, 278). Paul counterpunches with a double response:

- "Not everything is beneficial."
- "I will not be mastered by anything."

Before we speak or act, we must ask, "Is it beneficial? Is it helpful? Will it build me and others up in Christ? Is this a good thing to do for the kingdom of my Lord?" We must also ask, "Can this activity take mastery over me? Can it enslave me? Can it bring me into spiritual, emotional, physical, chemical, or psychological bondage?"

Paul continues his argument in verse 13, prefacing it again with a Corinthian slogan. The Corinthians said, "Food is for the stomach and the stomach for food" a stance that assumes God will do away with both of them. I strongly suspect the slogan was an extension of another popular saying: "Sex for the body and the body for sex." This, too, would suggest the body has no use outside this life. Paul fires back against such thinking with a corrective that is grounded in the theology of the body (v. 13) and the resurrection (v. 14): "However, the body is not for sexual immorality but for the Lord, and the Lord for the body." God is pro-body! He made it. He designed it. It is valuable and important!

The body is a good thing when used rightly for God's glory. But, of course, sexual immorality can never bring him honor. Paul Gardner says, "Paul insists that sexual immorality is totally inconsistent with God's design for the body—a body that will eventually be raised and is designed for union with God" (*1 Corinthians*, 278). The precise nature of the sexual immorality in view is not specified. It may involve prostitution, adultery, or even homosexuality (v. 9). Whatever its nature, it violated the marriage bed and covenant God designed for a man and woman. Paul teaches us the body is good and sex is good when used as God intended (cf. ch. 7). I like how Warren Wiersbe puts it:

> Sensuality is to sex what gluttony is to eating; both are sinful and both bring disastrous consequences. . . . Sex outside of [heterosexual] marriage is destructive, while sex in marriage can be creative and beautiful. (*Be Wise*, 71)

God Has Plans for My Body
1 CORINTHIANS 6:13-14

Paul continues his theology of the body by wedding the present to the future, sanctification to glorification. In the present we must remember that our bodies are "for the Lord" (v. 13). Indeed, we are encouraged to "present [our] bodies as a living sacrifice, holy and pleasing to God" (Rom 12:1). The Lord is for the body. He saved you to use you for his glory (1 Cor 6:20) and your good. Never think your body is of little or no consequence. It is important. How important? Look at what God is going to do with it! "God raised up the Lord and will also raise us up by his power" (v. 14). Curtis Vaughn is exactly right: "The fact of the Resurrection shows the importance of the body" (*1 Corinthians*, 65). The resurrection of Jesus is a foretaste and preview of our bodily resurrection. There is a glorified God-Man on the throne in heaven, and there will be glorified bodies filling the kingdom for all of eternity. Our bodies are not finally destined to be eaten by worms. Ultimately, they are headed to a new heaven, new earth, and new Jerusalem (Rev 21–22). Death is not the final word for the Christian. A resurrected and glorified body is. Piper again puts it so well:

> Just as he raised Jesus from the dead and gave him an everlasting resurrection body, so he will raise our bodies from the dead and make them new and whole—with no more pain, no more deformity, no more disability, no more sexual disorientation, no more chemical imbalances, no more insomnia, no more disease of any kind. You will shine like the sun in the kingdom of your Father (Matthew 13:43). ("You Were Bought")

Where we are headed in the future should impact how we live today. What God will do with my body in the future should affect what I do with it today. He has a plan for our bodies now and forever! Let that truth make a difference.

God Has Protection for My Body
1 CORINTHIANS 6:15-18

Paul moves from our resurrection with Christ to our union with Christ. His argument is deeply moving and powerfully convicting. For the first time in verses 12-20 he uses the rhetorical phrase, "Don't you know." Have the Corinthians forgotten that their "bodies are a part of Christ's body" (v. 15)? Have they forgotten that they are united to Christ and that what they do now, in some real and genuine sense, involves him? Specifically, should one "take a part of Christ's body and make it part of a prostitute? Absolutely not!" Driving home how important it is that we treat our bodies well, Paul asks, "Don't you know that anyone joined to a prostitute is one body with her?" If the Corinthians join themselves to prostitutes, they are also joining Christ to prostitutes! Schreiner's comments are spot on:

The relationship between believers and Christ is remarkably intimate such that believers represent Christ in what they do with their bodies. Therefore, joining what belongs to Christ to a *prostitute* is unthinkable and even outrageous. (*1 Corinthians*, 128; emphasis in original)

Paul adds scriptural warrant to his argument in verse 16, quoting Genesis 2:24 of the creation account: "For Scripture says, The two will become one flesh." When God performed the first marriage between Adam and Eve, he united them through sexual intimacy as one flesh, one body. This is one reason we save ourselves sexually for marriage. Sexual intercourse is a union. It is reserved exclusively for the married.

Verse 17 instructs us that there is an even greater union and oneness than that which occurs in sexual union in marriage. It is the spiritual union we enjoy with Christ in salvation. Paul says, "But anyone joined to the Lord is one spirit with him." Verlyn Verbrugge says that through conversion and union with Christ, "a believer belongs body, soul and spirit to the one Lord, and any unholy union with anyone else is a betrayal of our union with Christ" (*1 and 2 Corinthians*, 312). Remembering our sacred union with Christ is a powerful protection against sexual immorality. We should keep that truth continually in our minds.

In verse 18 Paul adds a second protection that is both simple and practical. It comes as a present imperative, an ongoing word of command: "Flee sexual immorality!" (cf. 10:14 on idolatry). Perhaps the apostle had in the back of his mind the story of Joseph and Potiphar's wife as recorded in Genesis 39. Sexual immorality, in all its forms, is something we should run from as fast as we can. Don't let it even get close to you.

Rick Warren, a pastor in California, has crafted what he calls "10 Commandments to Help Church Staff Maintain Moral Integrity." I want to adjust his list slightly so it can apply to all of us. Certain ones may not as readily apply to the unmarried, though there is wisdom here for singles as well.

- Thou shalt not be alone with someone of the opposite sex (even to share a meal).
- Thou shalt not have a person of the opposite sex pick you up or drive you places when it is just the two of you.
- Thou shalt not kiss any attendee of the opposite sex or show affection that could be questioned.
- Thou shalt not visit those of the opposite sex alone.

- Thou shalt not counsel those of the opposite sex alone, including in the office, and thou shalt not counsel anyone of the opposite sex more than once without that person's mate. Refer them.
- Thou shalt not discuss detailed sexual problems with one of the opposite sex in counseling. Refer individuals who need to discuss such matters.
- Thou shalt not discuss your marriage problems with those of the opposite sex.
- Thou shalt be careful in answering emails, instant messages, cards, or letters from those of the opposite sex.
- Thou shalt avoid any and all pornography and also put in place all necessary protective devices on your phone, tablet, and computer.
- Thou shalt pray for the integrity of others, especially fellow staff members. ("10 Commandments")

Paul concludes these verses with an enigmatic statement. Its exact meaning is unclear. The verse reads, "Every other sin [lit. "every sin"] a person commits is outside the body, but the person who is sexually immoral sins against his own body" (v. 18). Because of what we read in the next verse about our bodies being "the temple of the Holy Spirit," Paul appears to say that sexual sin scars the soul and impacts the body beyond all other sins. It scars the psyche and wounds the inner person. As Gordon Fee writes, "No other sin is directed specifically toward one's own body in the way that sexual immorality is" (*Corinthians*, 2014, 290). Calvin adds that sexual immorality "leaves a stain impressed upon the body, such as is not impressed upon it from other sins" (*1 Corinthians*, 220). Sexual sin is serious business. We must listen to the wise counsel of Scripture that provides the essential protection we need.

God Has Proprietorship of My Body

1 CORINTHIANS 6:19

For the third time Paul uses the phrase, "Don't you know." What is it that he fears we may forget? He fears that we may forget that the "body is a temple [Gk. *naos*] of the Holy Spirit who is in [us], whom [we] have from God" (see also 3:16). The body is important and valuable to God. How important and valuable? At conversion he makes it his home, his temple, his holy place. God could live anywhere, and indeed he lives everywhere. But when we repent of sin and trust in Christ, God comes to live inside each one of us by his Holy Spirit.

What a blessing to have God living in us! What an honor! What a privilege! What a responsibility! This God, who is for our bodies, is now in our bodies, and he will never leave (Heb 13:5). That his Holy Spirit comes to live in us is a gift ("[we] have from God"; 1 Cor 6:19). We did not work for this, and we did not earn it. It is all of grace. We are God's possession. Paul says, "You are not your own." We no longer belong to ourselves. We belong to him. Eugene Peterson paraphrases this passage well: "Don't you see that you can't live however you please, squandering what God paid such a high price for? . . . God owns the whole works" (MSG). I am indwelt by the God of my salvation. That should make a difference with what I do with my body.

God Has Paid for My Body
1 CORINTHIANS 6:20

Paul's argument for the value and sacredness of the body reaches its climax in verse 20. He grounds it in the cross work of the Lord Jesus. We are not our own (v. 19). We believers no longer belong to ourselves. We now belong to another who is for us (v. 12) and in us (v. 19). But there is more. He bought us at a price, a great price (v. 20). These words point to the sacrificial death of Jesus on the cross as our ransom. There he paid the full redemption for our sin so that we may be forgiven of our sins, that God's righteousness and justice would be vindicated, and that we may be set free from our enslavement to sin, death, hell, and the grave. Paul does not use the words *ransom* or *redemption* in this verse, but this is what he has in mind. Schreiner notes,

> The word *bought* (*agorazō*) is used elsewhere by Paul to denote
> the ransoming effect of Christ's sacrifice (1 Cor. 7:23; cf.
> 2 Pet. 2:1; Rev. 5:9; 14:3). . . . The *price* here is almost certainly
> the blood of Christ, hence the word "ransom" nicely captures
> what is being communicated. Believers have been freed from
> slavery at the price of Christ's blood, and now they belong to
> God; their bodies are under his lordship (cf. Rom. 6:15-23).
> (*1 Corinthians*, 129–30)

In light of this, there is only one logical and proper response. We must "glorify God with [our bodies]." Our bodies should be a doxology in response to so great a salvation that we have in Jesus. Curtis Vaughn says, "To glorify God seeks His honor as the highest goal" (*1 Corinthians*, 66). Paul will put the capstone on this when he writes in 1 Corinthians 10:31, "So, whether you eat or drink, or whatever you do, do everything for the glory of God." He owns us. He rightly deserves all of us, all the time.

Conclusion

"Jesus Paid It All" by Elvina M. Hall is one of my favorite hymns; I have sung it since I was a small boy. The chorus is so simple and yet so profound. The fourth stanza is a fitting commentary and conclusion to our study:

> And when, before the throne, I stand in Him complete,
> "Jesus died my soul to save," My lips shall still repeat.
> Jesus paid it all, all to Him I owe;
> Sin had left a crimson stain, He washed it white as snow.

Reflect and Discuss

1. In what ways have you heard this text applied before? Does this text match up with Paul's primary concern about sin?
2. How did the Corinthian Christians fail to apply the gospel to beliefs they'd inherited from their surrounding culture?
3. How would Christianity be different if it did not value the body? How would Christianity be different if it only valued the body? How does God's value of body and soul meet the desires of all people?
4. Because the Corinthians did not have a proper view of their bodies, they committed sexual immorality. Are there any sins Christians could be tempted toward today due to an improper view of their bodies? What does "Our bodies should be a doxology" mean?
5. Did what the Corinthians believed have any small piece of truth to it? If so, how was the truth distorted and twisted? What are other sins that are based on twists of truth?
6. How will the resurrection of our bodies help restore God's original design for his creation?
7. Consider the difference between these two statements: "I want to avoid sin because sin is bad" and "Because I'm united with Jesus, I want to avoid sin." Which sentence has the right view of the gospel?

Explain. Can remembering your union with Jesus also teach you to avoid nonsexual sins? If so, how?

8. Believers are "joined to the Lord" (v. 17) and "bought at a price" (v. 20). Why should this help us have confidence in our salvation?

9. Give an example of how sin can rise out of the belief that we are our own (v. 19).

10. Why is reminding one another about the truths of the gospel a fundamental part of the Christian community?

God's Wisdom for a Biblical Marriage

1 CORINTHIANS 7:1-16

Main Idea: Singles and married couples must follow God's design and pursue faithfulness according to their gift.

I. **God Has Helpful Principles for Those Who Are Married (7:1-5).**
   A. Pursue purity (7:1-2).
   B. Pursue partnership (7:3-4).
   C. Pursue prayer (7:5-6).
II. **God Gifts All of Us according to His will (7:7-9).**
   A. Some are gifted for singleness (7:7-8).
   B. Some are gifted for marriage (7:9).
III. **God's Ideal Is for Marriage to Last Until Death Parts (7:10-16).**
   A. A believing marriage should avoid divorce (7:10-11).
   B. Maintaining a mixed marriage depends on the desires of the unbelieving spouse (7:12-16).

Marriage and sex are great gifts from a great God. Unfortunately, sinful humans often make a mess of these great gifts and miss out on all the good things God intended for us to enjoy. In 1 Corinthians Paul addresses incest, fornication, adultery, and homosexuality (5:1; 6:9-10). Ancient records tell us that sexual abuse was common among Greeks and Romans through pederasty and the mistreatment of slaves by their owners (see Johnson and Ryan, *Sexuality*). In chapter 7 Paul addresses those on the other end of the spectrum: ascetics who argued that married people should abstain from sexual relations. What a mess! Sexual libertarians and ascetics were trying to do church together in Corinth, and both were off track from God's design. Paul addresses both groups, and to their credit it seems some Corinthians had sought his counsel through their letter. The repetition of the phrase, "Now in response to the matters you wrote about" (7:1,25; 8:1; 12:1; 16:1,12), would indicate this. Paul will address sex in marriage and other issues related to marriage here. This chapter, then, is one of, if not the most, helpful chapters in the Bible on marriage. Its instructions are as relevant in the twenty-first century as they were in the first.

God Has Helpful Principles for Those Who Are Married

1 CORINTHIANS 7:1-5

God created marriage in the garden of Eden when he joined Adam and Eve together (Gen 2). Prior to the fall (Gen 3) this first couple lived in perfect union and harmony. However, with sin's entrance, things changed for the worse. Ever since, we all have been living on the other side of Eden. And ever since, there has been conflict and confusion in marriage. At Corinth, some were living in unspeakable sexual immorality. Others started believing that abstaining from sex altogether, even in marriage, was the right way. Paul will address both extremes with biblical and practical wisdom. As we walk through these verses we should heed the counsel of Warren Wiersbe:

> Keep in mind that Paul is replying to definite questions. He is not spelling out a complete "theology of marriage" in one chapter. It is necessary to consider as well what the rest of the Bible has to say about this important subject. (*Be Wise*, 75)

Pursue Purity (7:1-2)

Paul received a letter from the Corinthians, who had several questions. One pertained to sex. At Corinth some were saying, "It is good for a man not to have sexual relations with a woman" (v. 1). Celibacy, it was argued, is the higher ideal and the more spiritual way. Paul responded practically: "But because sexual immorality is so common [lit. "because of immoralities"], each man should have sexual relations with his own wife, and each woman should have sexual relations with her own husband" (v. 2). Genesis 1–2 teaches us that God gave us marriage for procreation and partnership. Song of Songs teaches us our Lord gave us sex in marriage for pleasure. Paul teaches the gift of sex in marriage is also for purity. Our sex drives are strong, especially in our youth. Unfortunately, sexual temptation is everywhere. To protect and honor the purity God intends for sexual expression, men and women should find satisfaction exclusively with their mates. This is God's good design for sexual expression and enjoyment. Sex is not bad. Sex is not dirty. By the design of God, it is good and pure within the covenant of marriage between a man and woman. Ray Ortlund highlights four biblical principles for sex in marriage: freedom (Prov 5:18), sensitivity (1 Pet 3:7), agreement (1 Cor 7:5), and exclusivity (Exod 20:14) ("What's Allowed in Married Sex?"). Sex in marriage is normal, and it is good.

Pursue Partnership (7:3-4)

Paul now applies the partnership principle in marriage to a couple's sex life. God's design again is seen as heterosexual and monogamous. Marriage is a relationship in which we seek to honor and serve our mate well. When it comes to sex, "A husband should fulfill his marital duty [ESV, "her conjugal rights"] to his wife, and likewise a wife to her husband" (v. 3). This mutual service to one another is grounded and rooted in the biblical principle of the "one flesh" union between husband and wife (Gen 2:24). They belong to one another because they are one. Therefore, as 1 Corinthians 7:4 affirms, "A wife does not have the right over her own body, but her husband does. In the same way, a husband does not have the right over his own body, but his wife does." The reciprocal and mutual relationship Paul advocates would have been surprising, if not shocking, in his day. Mark Taylor writes, "Commentators . . . frequently note Paul's revolutionary stance regarding the mutuality of the relationship of husband and wife by ancient standards" (*1 Corinthians*, 166). My mate's body is God's gift to me, and my body is God's gift to my mate. Such gifts should be honored and treated with love, care, and respect. They are also to be enjoyed!

Pursue Prayer (7:5-6)

Paul makes one allowance for couples to refrain from sexual activity for a limited time: prayer. And it is a concession, not a command: "Do not deprive one another—except when you agree for a time, to devote yourselves to prayer. Then come together again; otherwise, Satan may tempt you because of your lack of self-control." Sex in marriage is normal and to be expected. It is one means whereby God protects us from the temptations of Satan that could lead to sexual immorality. Now, it is possible, but certainly not necessary, that a couple agree to take a "fast" from sex in order to devote themselves to a season of prayer. That is fine. Nevertheless, such times should be limited. Leon Morris provides a wise comment on this point:

> For married people the breaking off of normal relations, even
> for such a holy purpose, can be only by mutual consent. Then
> the couple must *come together again*. Otherwise the strength of

their natural passions means that they will place themselves at Satan's mercy. (*1 Corinthians*, 103; emphasis in original)

God has good guidelines for the good gifts of marriage and sex. He knows best because they were his ideas to begin with!

God Gifts All of Us according to His Will
1 CORINTHIANS 7:7-9

Paul teaches us that God gifts individuals in terms of singleness and marriage. I believe we will also see that this gifting may be permanent or for a season according to his divine plan for each of our lives. Whatever these plans are, they are best for us.

Some Are Gifted for Singleness (7:7-8)

Paul begins this section with an expression from his heart: "I wish that all people were as I am." Paul was single, and he felt this was a preferable status for serving the Lord. He will expound on this in verses 32-35. Whether Paul was always single, we do not know. Regardless, what he says here reminds us marriage is a blessing, but there are natural and inescapable burdens that come with it. It would have been extremely difficult for Paul to conduct all his missionary work with a wife and family. However, Paul recognizes that not every person has the gift of singleness (cf. Matt 19:12). Most don't. Paul acknowledges this and writes, "But each has his own gift from God, one person has this gift, another has that" (1 Cor 7:7). It is God who gifts us, for a season or permanently, for singleness or for marriage. That is his call. Thus, Paul can say to the unmarried and to widows, "It is good for [you] if [you] remain as I am" (v. 8). Singleness is a blessing for those who have that gift. It is not unnatural, and it is not less than God's best. Indeed, in some practical ways, it is better (cf. v. 32). If this is God's calling for you, be content in it. Rejoice in it. You are free to serve Christ with no strings attached.

Some Are Gifted for Marriage (7:9)

Verse 9 picks up on what Paul said in verses 5-6 as he addresses those God has gifted for marriage. Again, his counsel is practical: "But if they do not have self-control, they should marry, since it is better to marry than burn with desire." In the original text verse 9 ends with the word "burn." This leads some interpreters to believe Paul means to burn in hell (Morris, *1 Corinthians*, 105). However, the understanding of both the CSB and ESV is better. Schreiner writes,

> One indication that one should get married is if one has strong sexual desires. If one has the opportunity for marriage, and sexual desires are strong, marriage is the best option, and one should not try to be what one is not. (*1 Corinthians*, 139)

Some—most—are gifted by God for marriage. A strong desire for sex would be an indication of this. Again, God's design and plan are clear: virginity before marriage and monogamy in marriage; no sex before marriage; no sex outside of marriage; all sex within marriage. God's design does not keep us from sex. His plan is to keep us for sex in marriage. This is a good plan.

God's Ideal Is for Marriage to Last Until Death Parts
1 CORINTHIANS 7:10-16

In a broken world things break. Tragically and too often, sin breaks marriages. In the Western world divorce has become part of the natural ebb and flow of life. It happens. It is becoming odd and exceptional in Western culture, in fact, for a marriage to go the distance until a couple is separated by death. However, divorce is not in God's perfect plan. Jesus himself made this abundantly clear.

A Believing Marriage Should Avoid Divorce (7:10-11)

Paul turns to those who are presently married and draws on the words of Jesus found in Matthew 5:31-32 and 19:3-12 (cf. Mark 10:1-12; Luke 16:18). Paul says these words come as a "command," a divine order: "A wife is not to leave her husband. But if she does leave, she must remain unmarried or be reconciled to her husband—and a husband is not to divorce his wife" (vv. 10-11). Several important points need to be highlighted.

- God desires for marriage to be permanent.
- God allows for separation in a troubled marriage.
- God always desires for reconciliation to take place, if at all possible, in troubled marriages.
- Divorce and remarriage among believers, except for sexual unfaithfulness (see Matt 5:32; 19:9), are wrong and sinful. And,

even when there is sexual unfaithfulness in a believing marriage, God's desire is for reconciliation and restoration.

These are strange-sounding words in a culture that has trivialized the covenantal nature of marriage as designed by God. They sound quaint and old fashioned. Well, they are old, going back to Bible times. As our Lord said in Matthew 19:6, "Therefore, what God has joined together, let no one separate." There is a permanence to marriage that we ignore at great peril to ourselves, our families, and our society.

Maintaining a Mixed Marriage Depends on the Desires of the Unbelieving Spouse (7:12-16)

Paul now moves to address a situation that Jesus did not specifically address. That is why he says in verse 12, "But I (not the Lord) say to the rest . . ." He is not implying his words are less inspired than those of Jesus. In fact, he will conclude this section in verse 40 by saying, "And I think that I also have the Spirit of God." "All Scripture is inspired by God" (2 Tim 3:16). The canonized words of Paul, Peter, and John (and all the writers of Scripture) are just as inspired as the words of our Savior. We can believe and trust all of the Bible.

Paul now addresses a mixed marriage, that is, one in which one spouse is a believer and the other spouse is an unbeliever. Most likely the former became a Christian after they married, though was perhaps unaware a believer should not marry an unbeliever (see 2 Cor 6:14). Paul's instructions here are clear and to the point:

> If any brother [believer] has an unbelieving wife and she is willing to live with him, he must not divorce her. Also, if any woman has an unbelieving husband and he is willing to live with her, she must not divorce her husband. (1 Cor 7:12-13)

The God-ordained permanence of marriage, then, is not dissolved when one partner becomes a Christian. Again, Schreiner's comments are helpful:

> Remaining in a marriage with an unbeliever is pleasing to God even if one has an unbelieving wife or an unbelieving husband. Given the culture of Paul's day, it is remarkable that a wife is given the same status as a husband. (1 Corinthians, 142)

So, remaining in the marriage pleases God. And a further blessing follows, as verse 14 shows us: "For the unbelieving husband is made holy by the wife, and the unbelieving wife is made holy by the husband. Otherwise, [their] children would be unclean, but as it is they are holy."

Now, allow me to address what Paul is *not* saying. He is *not* saying the unbelieving spouse and the children are saved. That would be contrary to all that the Bible teaches about salvation being a personal decision to trust Christ for salvation. I love much of what Leon Morris says, but it is inaccurate to say that "until he is old enough to take the responsibility upon himself, the child of a believing parent is to be regarded as a Christian" (*1 Corinthians*, 107). The Bible never speaks in these terms. So, here Paul teaches that because of the presence of a believing spouse and parent, others in the family are set apart (the meaning of the word "holy" here) in a sanctified relationship and for a gospel witness and the beauty of the Christian life. We see something like this in 1 Peter 3:1-6. I like the insights of Simon Kistemaker at this point:

> Paul is not saying that an unbelieving husband or wife has been made morally holy through his or her Christian spouse. No, man is unable to sanctify or to save a fellow human being. What the apostle means to say is that an unbelieving spouse who lives intimately with a Christian marriage partner experiences the influence of holiness.
>
> To be sanctified means that a person is influenced by the claims of Christ. The converse is equally true: anyone who is not sanctified is influenced by the claims of a world that is opposed to Christ. In the Greek, the verb *to be sanctified* is in the perfect tense, which denotes that from the moment the spouse became a Christian his or her unbelieving partner comes in contact with holiness. (*Exposition*, 224–25)

In verses 15-16, Paul speaks to a situation where an unbelieving spouse wishes to get out of the marriage. Apparently, this too was taking place at Corinth. Paul once more provides counsel: "But if the unbeliever leaves, let him leave." Don't fight it or cause trouble. It is his or her decision, and you should honor it. When that happens, "A brother or sister is not bound in such cases. God has called [us] to live in peace." I take this passage to imply that God has released such a person from the marriage, and he or she is now free to remarry in the Lord (see v. 39). While some commentators do not believe there is permission to remarry here, I think it is the best understanding of the text in light of all the Bible teaches on the issue. A believing divorced person should be at peace in heart and soul if he or she did all that could be done to save the marriage. The spouse who was left does not share the guilt of the one who walked away.

I believe verse 16 concludes this discussion with two rhetorical questions (according to the marginal reading of the CSB): First, "Wife, how do you know that you will save your husband?" Second, "Husband, how do you know that you will save your wife?" We cannot be certain whether Paul's questions are optimistic or pessimistic. However, I like Paul Gardner's hopeful take:

> Paul uses his *covenantal optimism,* based within the workings and promise of God to encourage the believer to persevere in the marriage if possible. With two identical rhetorical questions, "How do you know . . . ?" (τί οἶδας), Paul indicates that for both a Christian wife or a Christian husband, there is a possibility that the unbeliever will be saved. Despite arguments that propose the contrary, it seems likely that Paul would indeed have been hopeful of the possibility of salvation for an unbelieving spouse. (*1 Corinthians*, 315; emphasis in original)

Conclusion

Paul Tripp wrote a wonderful article titled "10 Things You Should Know about Marriage." His main points, summarized below, provide a helpful conclusion to our study of 1 Corinthians 7:1-16.

Your marriage is rooted in worship.

No marriage will be unaffected when the people in marriage are seeking to get from the creation what they were only ever meant to get from the Creator. When we celebrate the Creator, we look at one another with wonder and joy. When you look at your spouse and see the Creator's glory, then you feel blessed by the ways he or she is different.

Marriage will always require work.

Every marriage needs divine wisdom. Every couple will need strength beyond what they have. No husband and wife can do what they were designed to do in marriage without dependency on God.

Marriage requires regular confession of sin.

Confession is the doorway to growth and change in your relationship. It is essential.

A marriage cannot survive without forgiveness.

Forgiveness is the only way to live in an intimate, long-term relationship with another sinner. It is the only way to deal with hurt and disappointment. It is the only way to have hope and confidence restored.

Selfishness is the biggest enemy for your marriage.

Your biggest struggle is with the selfishness that tempts and seduces us all. We must all pull this weed again and again, along with all the weeds of destructive words and actions that attach themselves to it.

Your marriage needs the church.

Right near you in the body of Christ are couples who have been through what you are now going through.

Marriage is the in-between.

God has given us his Word as our guide. Already he has sent his Son to live, die, and rise again for our salvation. Already he has given us his Spirit to live within us. But the world has not yet been restored. Sin has not yet been completely eradicated. We have not yet been formed in the perfect likeness of Jesus.

Your marriage exists in a fallen world.

Somehow, some way, your marriage is touched every day by the brokenness of our world. It is not an accident that you are conducting your marriage in this broken world. It is all a part of God's redemptive plan.

You are a sinner married to a sinner.

Many people get married with unrealistic expectations about whom they are marrying. Here is the point: you both bring something into your marriage that is destructive to what a marriage needs and must do. That thing is called sin.

God is faithful, powerful, and willing to work through your marriage.

You are not alone in your struggle. God is near, so near that in your moment of need you can reach out and touch him because he is not far from each one of us (Act 17:27). The God who determined your address lives there with you and is committed to giving you everything you need. (Tripp, "10 Things You Should Know about Marriage")

Reflect and Discuss

1. Paul corrected issues and answered questions from the church at Corinth. In what ways do people often respond to correction? What must you do to cultivate a heart willing to receive correction? How can someone make sure that the Bible and not the broader culture is their standard for living?

2. Is sexual temptation an external threat that one must avoid or an internal desire that one must change? If someone only perceives sexual temptation as an external threat, how will they fail to walk in holiness?

3. Paul writes that a married couple can abstain from sexual intimacy for a prolonged time for prayer. What does Paul's allowance teach you about the value of prayer? How might abstaining from sex for prayer benefit the Christian?

4. Why are freedom, sensitivity, agreement, and exclusivity important biblical principles for sex in marriage? How would your marriage be affected if you were to remove one of these principles?

5. What is the gift of singleness? What signals the gift of marriage?

6. When it comes to serving the church, what advantages do singles have that married couples do not have? What burdens must singles bear that married couples do not?

7. How does a marriage between a believer and an unbeliever fall short of God's design?

8. What goals for life in the church do married couples and singles share? What beliefs about God must both groups hold to as they pursue these goals?

9. Scripture uses the metaphor of marriage to describe Christ's relationship to the church. What do the principles for marriage found in Corinthians contribute to your understanding of what being part of the bride of Christ means?

10. Which of Paul Tripp's ten points most stands out to you? Why?

Find Your Contentment in Christ

1 CORINTHIANS 7:17-24

Main Idea: Obedience to God matters more than one's social condition.

I.   Be Content in Your Assignment from the Lord (7:17).
II. Be Content in Your Conditions in the Lord (7:18-22).
III. Be Content in Your Relationship with the Lord (7:23-24).

Few things characterize our modern world more than anxiety. Politics, race relations, diseases, social status, and self-esteem dominate so much of people's thinking and stress them out. We live in an anxiety-intoxicated culture. And social media use exacerbates the issue. In an article titled "Tips for Using Facebook When You Have Social Anxiety Disorder," Arlin Cuncic writes,

> Facebook anxiety is a modern-day affliction and a reflection of anxiety that you feel in daily life. Interacting on Facebook carries with it many of the same fears and insecurities that you probably feel in real life. The difference is that when you are alone in front of your computer, there is ample time to start obsessing and spending too much time worrying about what other people think. In this way, Facebook can magnify some of the fears you already experience.

What a difference a relationship with Jesus makes (or should make!). Paul teaches us that because we are in Christ, we should not be anxious "about anything" (Phil 4:6). He teaches us that our Lord enables us to "be content in whatever circumstances" we find ourselves (Phil 4:11). Paul says in 1 Corinthians 7 that we are not to worry whether we are married, single, divorced, or widowed. We should not concern ourselves about ethnic or social distinctions and status. Rather, each should find contentment in his or her identity in Christ and station in life, whatever it is. After all, it is our Lord who put us where we are.

One word dominates this passage: "call." The word occurs eight times in our English text but nine times in the Greek text. It is properly translated as "situation" or "condition" (ESV) in verse 20. Paul will use the word primarily to speak of our call to salvation and identity in Christ, but he will also use it to speak of vocation, one's situation in life. As Stephen Um notes, there is both a vertical and a horizontal dimension to our calling that Paul will unpack (*1 Corinthians*, 135). Both callings have been sovereignly determined by our Lord.

Be Content in Your Assignment from the Lord
1 CORINTHIANS 7:17

Paul has been discussing sex, marriage, and singleness. These are topics that can make us anxious and fill us with discontent. Paul will now move to address basic principles that should undergird our thinking, not only about these matters but all of life. Bottom line: God knows where you are, and he can use you where you are. Paul makes this clear by laying down a certain principle from the Lord and Paul's common practice (his rule or command) for all the churches. The principle: "Let each one live his life in the situation the Lord assigned when God called him." God has an individual plan and purpose for every one of his children. Rest in this. Be at peace in this. When God called you to salvation through his Son, he already had a course for your life in mind. Growing alongside your call to salvation is a definite calling for life predetermined by God. Simon Kistemaker says it well:

> In whatever situation a person becomes a Christian, he or she must remain there. That is the place in life the Lord has designated for everyone. . . . New converts to the Christian faith are often of the opinion that the only way to show gratitude to God for the gift of salvation is to become a minister or missionary of the gospel. This is commendable but not necessary. The Lord calls his people in all walks of life to follow him. He wants them to be Christian fathers and mothers, Christian husbands and wives, Christian employers and employees. Each one should fulfill the role the Lord has assigned to him or her and live (literally, walk) accordingly. (*Exposition*, 230)

Paul tells the Corinthians this is not a word just for them. This is his "command" (CSB) or "rule" (ESV) for everyone, "in all the churches." It is a universal command for all Christians of all times. Service to God can take place in a variety of relationships and vocations within his moral will. Some people may, and probably will, change vocations over time. But that is not something to fret over or worry about. John Piper is right: "Make obedience a big deal; make the *whole* aim of your life to obey the moral law of God . . . you can have fulfillment in Christ whatever your job is" ("Your Job as Ministry"; emphasis in original). By God's grace, my wife Charlotte and I have been content in whatever assignment we have found ourselves given: janitor, associate pastor, courier, teacher, dean, vice president, or president. In each situation, we have found contentment knowing we were exactly where the Lord wanted us to be. There is no better place to be than in the center of God's will (Rom 12:2).

Be Content in Your Conditions in the Lord
1 CORINTHIANS 7:18-22

Paul now illustrates the point he has just made in verse 17. The first illustration has to do with religious distinctions (circumcision), and the second has to do with social distinctions (slavery). These were perhaps the major or "chief" distinctions of the day (Vaughn and Lea, *1 Corinthians*, 77). Paul addresses the issues in a question-and-answer format.

Question: "Was anyone already circumcised when he was called [to Christ and salvation]?"

Answer: "He should not undo his circumcision."

Evidently, according to Gardner, "Such actions to cover a person's Jewishness appear to have taken place from time to time" (*1 Corinthians*, 326). And the reverse situation is true as well.

Question: "Was anyone called while uncircumcised?"

Answer: "He should not get circumcised" (v. 18).

Verse 19 answers why: "Circumcision does not matter and uncircumcision does not matter." So, what matters? "Keeping God's commands is what matters." Galatians 6:15 provides a valuable commentary on Paul's point: "For both circumcision and uncircumcision mean nothing; what matters instead is a new creation" (cf. 2 Cor 5:17). Being in Christ changes everything. Outward ethnic and social distinctions no longer matter as they once did. It is not that they are unimportant, but they no longer have the priority or the weight they previously carried. Piper writes,

> What Paul *was* doing was showing that *obedience* to the commands of God is so much more important than any cultural distinctives, that the mere changing of these distinctives should be of no importance whatever to the Christian. In other words, don't make such a big deal out of whether you are circumcised or not, or whether you are white or black or red or Swedish. But instead make obedience a big deal; make the *whole* aim of your life to obey the moral law of God. Then and only then may circumcision (as Paul implies in Romans 2:25) and other cultural distinctives become beautiful, in a very secondary and derivative way as expressions of the obedience of faith. ("Your Job as Ministry"; emphasis in original)

For a second time in verses 17-24 Paul reiterates the main point of the passage (cf. v. 17): "Let each of you remain in the situation [lit. "in the calling"] in which he is called" (v. 20). God has called you to this "situation" or "condition" (ESV). It is not accidental, nor is it fate.

Reaffirming this cardinal principle, Paul makes a second application. This time he applies it to slavery. When people enslave others, it is a horrible evil in whatever time or form it is practiced. In the Graeco-Roman world it was widespread and common. Unlike the transatlantic slave trade, an atrocity that will always be a stain on America's past, Graeco-Roman slavery was not race based. Further, its manifestations and practice were quite diverse. Schreiner points out,

> One could be born a slave, sell oneself into slavery to pay debts, be sold into slavery or become a slave by being captured in war. Many slaves lived miserably, particularly those that served in the mines. Other slaves served as doctors, teachers, managers, musicians, artisans, barbers, cooks or shopkeepers, and could even own other slaves. In some instances, slaves were better educated than their masters. . . . Slaves in the Graeco-Roman world were under the control of their masters and had no independent existence. They had no legal rights, and they could suffer brutal mistreatment at the hands of their owners: masters could beat them, brand them and abuse them

physically and sexually. Children born in slavery belonged
to masters rather than to the parents who gave them birth.
Seneca's observation exposes the evil of slavery:

You may take (a slave) in chains and at your pleasure
expose him to every test of endurance; but too great violence
in the striker has often dislocated a joint, or left a sinew
fastened in the very teeth it has broken. Anger has left many
a man crippled, many disabled, even when it found its victim
submissive. (*De Ira*, 3.27.3 in Schreiner, *1 Corinthians*, 148–49)

It also should be noted that the slavery of pre-Civil War America most
readily corresponds to what we read in Exodus 21:16 and 1 Timothy
1:10 (of "slave traders"), which the Bible resoundingly condemns.

Paul returns to his Q&A format in verse 21.

Question: "Were you called while a slave?"

Answer: "Don't let it concern you."

In other words, Paul says not to allow your condition to control or consume you. Christ is now your all-consuming passion. He is your everything! How Christ sees you is what ultimately matters. However, Paul
adds a qualification: "But if you can become free, by all means take
the opportunity." This admonition to pursue freedom if the possibility
presents itself finds indirect support in the book of Philemon, when
Paul sends Philemon's slave back to him but says he should consider
Onesimus a brother rather than a slave. It has Old Testament warrant as
well. Schreiner notes,

The admonition, "do not become slaves of human beings"
(7:23), supports the idea that remaining as a slave is not the
ideal . . . [and] this reading fits with the Old Testament, where
enslaving a fellow-Hebrew is frowned upon (Exod. 21:2-11;
Neh. 5:5). (*1 Corinthians*, 150–51)

Paul drives home his argument with a foundational theological
truth in verse 22: "For he who is called by the Lord as a slave is the Lord's
freedman. Likewise, he who is called as a free man is Christ's slave." Paul
will apply this principle in 9:19-23 to the work of evangelism. Here the
point is we are each free from sin but a slave to Christ in our spiritual

status before God. Leon Morris comments on Paul's "paradoxical language" in this verse:

> The slave who is *called* has entered the glorious liberty of the children of God. He has been freed from slavery to sin and this divine liberty matters so much more than his outward circumstances that he should see himself as the *Lord's freedman.* . . . With this goes the complementary truth that he who is a *free man* when called is *Christ's slave.* Once more the point is that outward circumstances matter little. The important thing for the *free man* is his relationship to Christ; his whole life is to be lived in lowly service to his Master. Nothing matters alongside this. (*1 Corinthians*, 110–11; emphasis in original)

Be Content in Your Relationship with the Lord
1 CORINTHIANS 7:23-24

Paul builds on his argument, bringing it to an appropriate climax. He begins by quoting 6:20. However, as Kistemaker notes, "The words are placed in an entirely different context" (*Exposition*, 234). He says, "You were bought at a price," the shed blood of the Son of God. In 6:20 the atonement of Christ sets us free from sexual immorality as we become the temple of the Holy Spirit. Here we are set free from slavery to sin and earthly distinctions as we become slaves of Christ. Therefore, he says, "do not become slaves of people" (v. 23). One's social status according to human standards now means nothing! As a new creation in Christ, then, don't be enslaved to shame or pride. Don't be enslaved to the opinions of others because they don't matter. Christ is Lord, and he says we belong to him. That is what counts! Find your identity, value, and worth in Jesus.

For the third time (vv. 17,20,24) Paul inserts the key that unlocks his argument: "Brothers and sisters, each person is to remain with God in the situation [ESV, "condition"] in which he was called" (v. 24). Warren Wiersbe is right:

> We are prone to think that a change in circumstances is always the answer to a problem. But the problem is usually *within* us and not *around* us. The heart of every problem is the problem in the heart. (*Be Wise*, 80; emphasis in original)

So, whose opinion matters most to you? Yours? Others'? God's? He made you. He saved you. He placed you where you are. So, rest in that. Join with Paul and confess with the apostle the words of Philippians 4:11-13:

> *I don't say this out of need, for I have learned to be content in whatever circumstances I find myself. I know both how to make do with little, and I know how to make do with a lot. In any and all circumstances I have learned the secret of being content—whether well fed or hungry, whether in abundance or in need. I am able to do all things through him who strengthens me.*

Conclusion

"A Prayer for Contentment"

Oh Lord, You are my shepherd and I should not be in want,
but so often I struggle to be content and do want;
forgetting that you have graciously provided me with every
    spiritual blessing in Christ
and everything I need for life and godliness.
Thank you for often not giving me what I want
because my desires would draw my heart from being satisfied
    in You.
Help me to be content in You with what You have given me
and to not be focused on what my flesh wants or what the
    world tells me I should have.
Protect me from coveting possessions or people,
talent or influence, relationships or prestige.
Keep my heart from being anxious for what I don't have
and make me thankful for the numerous gifts that You have
    already given.

According to Your Word and steadfast love,
fill me with the joy and satisfaction of contentment in Christ.
Help me learn to be content in any situation like Paul
and to quickly reject the idolatry that dwells beneath the
    surface of my coveting.
I ask you to continually bring to mind your faithful provision
    for all my needs,
that Christ died for the sin of coveting,

that in Christ I am free to be content and live righteously,
and that godliness with contentment is greater gain than
    pleasing my flesh.
And may I be humbled and changed by the ultimate example
    of contentment;
of Christ becoming poor in order that I could become rich,
and being content to go to the cross to fulfill the Father's will
to rescue a people for Himself who can be free from discontent
    and zealous for good works. (Halloran, "A Prayer")

Reflect and Discuss

1. How often do you feel anxious about life? What areas do you feel most anxious about?
2. In what ways is vulnerability tied to anxiety? How can knowing and relying on God's nearness and sovereignty help with your anxiety?
3. Are anxiety and discontentment ever related? How so? How will focusing on obedience to God help free you from anxiety and discontentment?
4. How are some fears and anxieties a result of trying to be omniscient like God? In what ways can letting God be God free you from anxiety?
5. Should every believer become a pastor or missionary? Why or why not? Why is it important that Christians work in all areas of service, except in those that require actively sinning? In what ways can you work and even minister according to God's design in your job?
6. Why does obedience to God matter more than one's social condition? How does one avoid the two extremes of treating a social condition as ultimate or as unimportant?
7. How does Paul remove the divisions between slaves and free people in the church? How would free people recognizing they are "Christ's slaves" be steered away from pride or superiority?
8. How might Paul's paradoxical inverse (slaves/free) be applied to other social conditions (e.g., wealth, power, status)?
9. How have you seen it to be true that problems in life are usually *within* us and not *around* us?
10. Describe a time when you wanted God to change your situation in life but later realized he instead worked in a way or changed you in a way that was better than what you wanted.

The Savior's Superlative Single

1 CORINTHIANS 7:25-40

Main Idea: Married couples and singles should aim to live in ways pleasing to God and work for his kingdom, yet singles have a special opportunity to serve God and avoid many earthly difficulties.

I. **The Spiritual Single Can Expect Less Distress (7:25-28).**
   A. Singleness can be a good life (7:26).
   B. Singleness can avoid troubles in this life (7:27-28).
II. **The Spiritual Single Can Encounter Fewer Distractions (7:29-31).**
   A. Cultivate the proper priorities (7:29-31).
   B. Cultivate the proper perspective (7:31).
III. **The Spiritual Single Can Enjoy Greater Devotion (7:32-35).**
   A. He or she is freed from many worldly anxieties (7:32).
   B. His or her interest can remain undivided (7:33-35).
IV. **The Spiritual Single Can Exercise a Better Decision (7:36-40).**
   A. Getting married is not sinful (7:36).
   B. Remaining single can be even better (7:37-38).
   C. Getting remarried must be in the Lord (7:39).
   D. Remaining single can result in being happier (7:40).

In an article titled "Single and Satisfied in God," New Testament scholar Tom Schreiner raises the question, "What do the Scriptures teach us about being single?" He then follows up by highlighting an all too familiar attitude toward singleness: "Many in Christian cultures encourage everyone to marry, suggesting that those who are unmarried are strange, or at the very least are not filling their calling." Schreiner, however, then correctly adds, "We see in 1 Corinthians 7:25-40 that the apostle does not agree" ("Single and Satisfied in God," 2). Paul, like our God, is pro-single!

Paul has already informed us in 1 Corinthians 7:7 that God gifts some people for marriage and others for singleness. Jesus said the same thing in Matthew 19:12. In 1 Corinthians 7:25-40 we have the most developed and sustained argument in the whole Bible for the benefits and blessings of a single lifestyle. The God who gave us the gift of marriage also gives us the gift of singleness. Singleness is not a lackluster position in God's kingdom. No one is less spiritual for remaining single. Indeed, God blesses the single state for the Christian in several ways. Paul makes this abundantly clear in these verses.

The Spiritual Single Can Expect Less Distress
1 CORINTHIANS 7:25-28

Paul addresses "virgins" (ESV, "the betrothed") or those who are single. He notes, "I have no command from the Lord, but I do give an opinion as one who by the Lord's mercy is faithful" (v. 25). Jesus did not give a specific command about singleness. So, Paul distinguishes between the inspired words of Jesus and his own inspired judgment, which is assured to be truthful by the Lord's mercy and faithfulness. He reinforces this in verse 40: "And I think that I also have the Spirit of God." Kistemaker puts it well:

> Paul writes his epistle by divine inspiration and not human insight (II Peter 1:20-21). He knows the Lord has given him apostolic authority to speak and to write for the benefit of the church. (*Exposition*, 237)

Singleness Can Be a Good Life (7:26)

Paul informs us that the single life is good, especially when there is a "present distress" (v. 26). Some believe Paul has in view the imminent or soon return of the Lord Jesus here. Fee notes, however, that . . .

> the word distress literally means "necessity." . . . Paul has in view the larger "distress" that is the common lot of those who believe, which was perhaps also being intensified by some present realities. In this case their own "present distress" is but a part of the larger experience of suffering that the church is undergoing until its final redemption at the coming of Christ. (*Corinthians*, 2014, 364)

Life is filled with difficulties and troubles. Sometimes, as it was for the Corinthians, life is extreme and intense. So remaining unmarried is a good thing and lessens one's obligations, pressures, and responsibilities.

Singleness Can Avoid Troubles in This Life (7:27-28)

Paul builds on the point he made in verse 26. His counsel is simple and filled with common-sense wisdom. He begins in verse 27 with two rhetorical questions while also providing the answer to each. Question 1: "Are you bound to a wife?" Answer: "Do not seek to be released." Question 2: "Are you released [ESV, "free"] from a wife?" Answer: "Do not seek a wife." In other words, if you are married, stay married. If you are single, don't feel that you mustn't stay single. Both relationship statuses are pleasing to the Lord. Verse 28 reaffirms this idea and adds a word about the practical value of singleness. Paul writes, "[I]f you do get married, you have not sinned, and if a virgin [ESV, "betrothed woman"] marries, she has not sinned." Marriage is not a sin. It is a good gift from a good God. But on the practical level in this fallen and broken world, those who marry will face many troubles in this life, and Paul wants to spare people from this. Marriage is good, but some troubles will accompany it because the world is under the curse of sin and relationships are thus not easy. Remaining single avoids certain types of concerns, responsibilities, and troubles.

The Spiritual Single Can Encounter Fewer Distractions
1 CORINTHIANS 7:29-31

Verses 29-31 call us to radical Christianity. They call us to be heavenly minded to the point we will wholeheartedly be of earthly good. Paul gives two important principles for careful consideration and reflection.

Cultivate the Proper Priorities (7:29-31)

Christians live in the eschatological tension of the now and not yet. The kingdom has come, but it is not yet here fully and completely. Soon, however, it will be. We must live in the wonderful truth that the end could come anytime, any moment. It is imminent. So, here is Paul's counsel:

> *This is what I mean, brothers and sisters: The time is limited, so from now on those who have wives should be as though they had none, those who weep as though they did not weep, those who rejoice as though they did not rejoice, those who buy as though they didn't own anything, and those who use the world as though they did not make full use of it.*

We must not over-interpret or under-interpret these verses and draw harmful and unbiblical applications. The phrase "the time is limited" in verse 29 provides the controlling principle along with the proper perspective, which we see at the end of verse 31: "This world in its current form is passing away." Paul's point, as Schreiner notes, is that "believers should constantly live in the light of the end (Rom. 13:11-14)" (*1 Corinthians*, 156). Thus, marriage is temporary (v. 29). Mourning and rejoicing over the things of this world are temporary (v. 30). Possessions in this life are temporary (vv. 30-31). None of these things are enduring or eternal. One day they will be gone. This is why we must be sure to have the proper priorities. Understand the value of these things and enjoy them, yes, but do not get glued to them. None of them will last forever. Calvin puts it perfectly:

> All things that are connected with the enjoyment of the present life are sacred gifts of God, but we pollute them when we abuse them. . . . The sum is this, that the mind of a Christian ought not to be taken up with earthly things, or to repose in them; for we ought to live as if we were every moment about to depart from this life. (*1 Corinthians*, 257)

Cultivate the Proper Perspective (7:31)

Proper priorities will grow out of the proper perspective, seeing all of life with kingdom eyes. Paul writes, "[T]his world in its current form is passing away." *The Message* reads, "[T]his world as you see it is fading away." This world is not our home. This world is not our home because we will die. This world is not our home because it will die, too. It will pass away. We should long for an eternal home, a new heaven and new earth, which will arrive in God's timing (Rev 21–22). We are to pine for that "kingdom that cannot be shaken" (Heb 12:28). In Colossians 3:1-2 Paul says, "So if you have been raised with Christ, seek the things above, where Christ is, seated at the right hand of God. Set your mind on things above, not on earthly things." Having been transformed by the gospel, we should have new affections, desires, and passions. This world thus loses its attraction. It no longer controls us. Christ does. It no longer sets our agendas. Christ does. The Lord Jesus Christ and his kingdom will last forever. This world and its stuff will not. Each of us should seek to become heavenly minded, for that will lead to us accomplishing the most earthly good.

The Spiritual Single Can Enjoy Greater Devotion
1 CORINTHIANS 7:32-35

We can see an example of the beauty of a single's devotion to the Lord in the legacy of a woman from the fourth century. The exact dates of her birth and death are unknown. Her name was Anthusa. Widowed at twenty, cultured and attractive, she would choose not to remarry so that she could pour her life into her only son. His name was John Chrysostom (ca. AD 347–407). He is considered by many to be the greatest Christian preacher outside of the prophets, apostles, and the Lord Jesus. Chrysostom praised his mother for nurturing his "enthusiasm for the good, his moral energy . . . his zeal for justice and truth and his steadfast faith" (Deen, *Great Women*, 27). Though he would receive a classical education, he "drank still more deeply of the things of the spirit from his mother at home" (ibid., 27). What a gift, then, this devoted widow, this devoted single mother, gave to the world of her day and ours. What an example she is of the truths we discover in verses 32-35.

He or She Is Freed from Many Worldly Anxieties (7:32)

Paul wants us "to be without concerns." Singleness provides a practical advantage. Why? "The unmarried man is concerned about the things of the Lord—how he may please the Lord." Obeying Matthew 6:33 ("But seek first the kingdom of God and his righteousness") is easier for the single person because he or she can have a singular focus: Christ and his kingdom. Moreover, the single has fewer of the anxieties, concerns, and cares of this world that a married person with a family has.

His or Her Interest Can Remain Undivided (7:33-35)

Verses 33-35 are the flipside of Paul's argument in verse 32. Here he states, "But the married man is concerned [ESV, "anxious"] about the things of the world—how he may please his wife" (v. 33). Paul then drives home his point: "and his interests are divided" (v. 34). It is hard to improve on the paraphrase of *The Message* in terms of offering a brief commentary: "Marriage involves you in all the nuts and bolts of domestic life and in wanting to please your spouse, leading to so many more demands on your attention." Paul continues the same line of argument, but he moves from addressing men to addressing women. His reasoning is the same: "The unmarried woman or virgin is concerned about the things of the Lord" (v. 34). He then adds a specific point of application: "so that she may be holy both in body and in spirit." David Garland helps us grasp what Paul is saying:

> Being holy in body does not mean that she is pure because
> she avoids the sexual relations that marriage imposes. All
> Christians are to be holy in body, whether married or not
> (1 Thess. 5:23; cf. Rom. 6:12,19; 12:1; 1 Cor. 6:13,19–20;
> 2 Cor. 7:1; Phil. 1:20; 1 Thess. 4:4). The combination of body
> and spirit describes the whole person and means that she
> strives to be holy in every way and is totally devoted to the
> Lord. (*1 Corinthians*, 335)

In contrast to the blessing a single woman (or man) enjoys in her (or his) devotion to the Lord, "the married woman is concerned about the things of the world—how she may please her husband" (v. 34). Paul recognizes such concern is unavoidable for the married, as it should be. Godly husbands and godly wives will be concerned about their mates. God intentionally designed marriage this way. Paul's point is that singleness is a blessing from the Lord in terms of lowering responsibilities and concerns, and allowing for undivided devotion.

Paul summarizes these verses by telling us in verse 35 that he is "saying this for [our] own benefit." He uses a picturesque hunting metaphor, informing us he has no desire to put a rope around our necks to restrain us (Fee, *Corinthians*, 2014, 382). His goal is only "to promote what is proper . . . so that [we] may be devoted to the Lord without distraction." I love the way Fee explains what Paul is after here:

> By these words Paul does not want to restrict them, as the
> ascetics would do, but to free them for whatever is appropriate
> in their case (apparently either marriage or celibacy), so that
> they may have constant and unhindered devotion to the Lord.
> For the gifted celibate that would mean celibacy; but for the
> betrothed, whose gift is not celibacy but whose devotion to
> the Lord has been hindered by the ascetics' demanding that a
> person be so, what is appropriate is marriage. . . . Paul has not
> argued that celibacy is the way of life that is most appropriate
> or seemly. Rather, he has given eschatological reasons for
> preferring it. A betrothed person, who is anxious about
> whether or not to marry, is hardly living appropriately or with

unhindered devotion. Thus, at the end, despite his setting out to give new grounds for preferring celibacy, Paul again places that preference in a context that equally affirms the "rightness" of marriage, which is what he will once more spell out in detail in the conclusion that follows. (*Corinthians*, 2014, 383)

The Spiritual Single Can Exercise a Better Decision
1 CORINTHIANS 7:36-40

Paul will now bring everything he has been saying to a conclusion. There are some interpretive landmines in these final verses of chapter 7. Nevertheless, his basic meaning is clear: Find God's will for your life as a single person or a married person and rest in that calling. Both marital statuses are right and good, but there are practical advantages to being single.

Getting Married Is Not Sinful (7:36)

Ascetics, like some Roman Catholic monks and nuns, believe a celibate, single lifestyle is morally and spiritually superior to getting married. Paul says, "Not so!" Rather,

> *If any man thinks he is acting improperly toward the virgin he is engaged to, if she is getting beyond the usual age for marriage, and he feels he should marry—he can do what he wants. He is not sinning; they can get married.*

An engaged man, after all, is possibly acting inappropriately toward his fiancée because of sexual passion. The answer to addressing a problem along these lines is simple: "Get married!" And, I would add, do so sooner than later. Not only is it not sinful, but it is also the good and right thing for most to do. Paul told us in 1 Corinthians 7:2 marriage is one way God protects us from sexual immorality. Those who have the gift of marriage also have the gift of sex. It is God's design and plan for many Christians to enjoy both.

Remaining Single Can Be Even Better (7:37-38)

Again Paul speaks of the practical value of singleness. However, he wants people to be sure such a call is from the Lord. We must not just talk ourselves into it. The person who believes he or she has the call to singleness must be one who "stands firm" in heart, "is under no compulsion," "has control over his [or her] own will," and "has decided" not to pursue marriage. If all these things are present in terms of one who senses a call to remain single, Paul says he [or she] "will do well" to stay single. This is the right thing to do, in fact, because it is a conviction of the heart carefully weighed and considered before the Lord.

Paul brings his discussion of singleness to an end in verse 38, with a small addendum in verses 39-40. He says, "So, then, he who marries his fiancée does well, but he who does not marry will do better." (Of course, she would thus be free to move on.) Marriage is good. Singleness is good. However, there is no denying the practical advantages of the single life. This is especially true in serving Christ in trying and difficult times of life.

Getting Remarried Must Be in The Lord (7:39)

Paul concludes chapter 7 with additional wisdom in the context of marriage and singleness, giving specific attention to the issue of remarriage. Once more he reminds us of the permanence of marriage: "A wife is bound as long as her husband is living." Divorce is never the perfect or desired will of God. However, "if [a woman's] husband dies, she is free to be married to anyone she wants—only in the Lord." When a Christian's mate dies, he or she is free to remarry as long as he or she marries another Christian. This is in keeping with the principle of not being unequally yoked (see 2 Cor 6:14-15).

Remaining Single Can Result in Being Happier (7:40)

Paul concludes by reiterating the practical advantages for those to whom God gives the gift of singleness. Addressing widows, he recognizes God had, for a season, gifted them for marriage. Now, he points out, the Lord may be gifting them for singleness. If so, such a widow is not to weep but rejoice! In his opinion, "she is happier if she remains as she is." Gardner says,

> Paul still gives the Christian woman a clear choice. He does not force his view of these matters on anyone but does remain concerned that people think through the practical issues of how best to serve the Lord and be devoted to him in stressful times. (*1 Corinthians*, 359)

Paul ends this section on a humble but authoritative note: "And I think that I also have the Spirit of God." David Garland argues that others in Paul's day may have been claiming divine inspiration for their extreme views, which Paul has corrected in this chapter. Paul's point is clear and to the point: "The Spirit guides his counsel, and he is not shooting from the hip" (*1 Corinthians*, 345)

Conclusion

Whenever I consider the value of single people, I remind myself of what I find in the Bible:

- The greatest person who ever lived was single: the God-Man, Jesus Christ.
- The greatest mere human who ever lived was single: John the Baptist.
- The greatest missionary and theologian who ever lived was single: the apostle Paul.
- The greatest statesman who ever lived was single: Daniel.
- The greatest prophets of Israel who ever lived were single: Elijah and Elisha.

To this list we can add Joseph, Naomi, Ruth, Boaz, Jeremiah, Nehemiah, Anna, Martha, Mary Magdalene, and Lydia, who were all single for at least a season. The people of God have been blessed by single people in the past. They are blessed by singles in the present and will be in the future. God knows what he is doing when he calls people to marriage, and God knows what he is doing when he calls them to singleness. Whatever God's calling is for you, you can rejoice and be certain that it is his best for you.

Reflect and Discuss

1. What is God's ultimate concern for our lives? How does Paul's opinion in this passage reveal this concern?
2. What lies can married people and singles be tempted to believe about their life situations? What lies could they be tempted to believe about a relational status that is not their own?
3. Why is a married couple *not* excused from serving the church sacrificially despite their increased concerns in the world?

4. Does singleness automatically imply that someone is more dedicated to God's kingdom than married people are? Why or why not? How might a single person cultivate a higher level of sacrificial service?

5. How should the truth that "this world in its current form is passing away" (v. 31) shape all our decisions?

6. Describe some practical ways singles can better serve the church and God's kingdom than married people typically could.

7. If you are single, what are some ways that you can use your singleness for God? If you are married, are there ways that you can better support the singles who are using their time for the Lord?

8. What are examples of the mistaken belief that single Christians are at a disadvantage?

9. How does the Bible's teaching about the church as the family of God ("brothers and sisters") add the necessary foundation for the life Paul calls singles to live? What are the dangers of married couples not weaving singles into their lives?

10. Why is it important to remember that both the married and singles do well before the Lord (v. 38)?

Am I My Brother's Keeper?

1 CORINTHIANS 8

Main Idea: The spiritual good of others should always govern what we Christians do.

I. **All My Actions Are Regulated by the Principle of Christian Love (8:1-3).**
   A. Knowledge alone can make us prideful (8:1-2).
   B. Love for God is evidence God knows us (8:3).

II. **All My Actions Are Regulated by the Truth of Christian Worship (8:4-6).**
   A. Unbelievers worship false gods and false lords (8:4-5).
   B. Christians worship one God and one Lord (8:6).

III. **All My Actions Are Regulated by the Guideline of Christian Deference (8:7-13).**
   A. I will not defile my brother's conscience (8:7-10).
   B. I will not sin against my Christ (8:11-13).

Genesis 4 tells of the first murder recorded in the Bible: the time when Cain killed his brother Abel (4:8). When confronted by the Lord who asked, "Where is your brother Abel?," Cain lied, "I don't know." He then infamously said, "Am I my brother's guardian [ESV, "keeper"]?" (4:9). From Genesis to Revelation Scripture teaches us that we are indeed keepers of our brothers and sisters. Jesus says we are even to love our enemies and pray for them (Matt 5:44).

In 1 Corinthians 8:1-13 Paul informs us that we Christians are the keepers of our brothers and sisters in Christ specifically. We are to always seek their good and avoid any action or word that defiles their consciences (v. 7), destroys their faith (v. 11), or that might prove a stumbling block to their walks with the Lord Jesus (v. 13). The spiritual good of others should always govern what we do. In chapter 8 Paul lays before us the protective check-and-balance system of Christian love (vv. 1-3), Christian worship (vv. 4-6), and Christian deference (vv. 7-13). Three words dominate our text: know(ledge), conscience, and stumble.

All My Actions Are Regulated by the Principle of Christian Love

1 CORINTHIANS 8:1-3

Even Protestant believers do not always agree about the right or wise way to live in a world flooded with idolatry. For instance, should we take the path of withdrawal and become evangelical monastics, essentially living as monks and nuns? Or should we take a different path and immerse ourselves in the culture for the purpose of evangelism? After all, if our hearts are in the right place, isn't that all that matters anyway? When you bring radically different ways of thinking like this alongside each other in a local church, conflict and division are possible. Tim Keller is right in his diagnosis of the twenty-first-century American church: "Today, many Christian believers—who often share virtually identical beliefs—are just as divided over how to relate to our increasingly pagan culture even though the issues are often presented as political." Paul has a strategy for avoiding unnecessary conflicts, fights, and division. Not surprisingly, he begins with the ethic of Christian love. Love must always regulate our liberty.

Knowledge Alone Can Make Us Prideful (8:1-2)

The Corinthians have another question for Paul, introduced by the phrase "Now about" (cf. 7:1,25). The issue is "food sacrificed to idols" (v. 1). Vaughn and Lea help set the table for what the context was in first-century Corinth:

> It was in sacrifice, which was at the center of the worship of all ancient religions, that all the important events of domestic and social life culminated. After the legs of the sacrifice (enclosed in fat) and the entrails had been burned on the altar, and after the priest had been given his share, what was left of the victim's flesh was returned to the family that offered the sacrifice. This consecrated meat was then eaten—either as part of a banquet in the pagan temple (or its precincts) or in the worshiper's home—or it was sold at the marketplace.
>
> If the consecrated meat was used for a banquet—whether at the temple or in the worshiper's house—friends and relatives, among whom there might well be Christians, were invited. Christians would then find themselves confronted

with the question of whether they should eat the idol meat. So also, when meats previously consecrated to a pagan deity were sold in the market, Christians might find themselves having to decide whether to purchase the meat. (*1 Corinthians*, 86)

So, Christians at Corinth were confronted with several dilemmas: How do I respond rightly to the question of meat sacrificed to an idol? Eat? Invite others to eat? Go with my lost, pagan friends and eat (in the temple? in their home?) to maintain a relationship? What about those whose consciences won't allow them to eat? Do I refrain in front of them? Do I help them grow up and see that it is OK because idols aren't real gods anyway? Today we seldom face the problem of meat sacrificed to an idol in western culture, but it has many parallels on the mission field. Further, we have our own questions about the right path when believers disagree about how to act in a world immersed in paganism.

Paul will make clear that his concern above all is for the well-being of brothers and sisters in Christ. To do this, he addresses the know-it-all group at Corinth that was arrogantly spouting, "We know that we all have knowledge" (another Corinthian slogan). This group boasted in their spiritually mature status over those Paul will identify as "weak" in verses 7 and 9. They may have even boasted that they had the spiritual gift of knowledge (cf. 12:8; 13:2). Gardner comments: "Paul has acknowledged that the Corinthians have many grace-gifts including 'knowledge' (1:5). The elitists arrogantly insist they all possess this particular gift" (*1 Corinthians*, 368). Paul hits back hard, telling them the issue is one of love, not knowledge. "Knowledge puffs up," he says (8:1). Knowledge alone makes one arrogant and prideful. However, knowledge wedded to love "builds up" (v. 2). It edifies the body of Christ, making it healthier and stronger. Thinking you know everything reveals you know nothing at all, as verse 2 makes plain: "If anyone thinks [ESV, "imagines"] he knows anything, he does not yet know it as he ought to know it." Something is terribly wrong with alleged spiritual knowledge that tears down rather than builds up. It is broken. Defective. Destructive. It hurts others rather than helping them.

Love For God Is Evidence That God Knows Us (8:3)

Paul does an interesting thing in verse 3. He tells us it is not *what we know* that is of utmost importance—though it is important; cf. 5:6; 6:2,3,9,15, 16,19—but *who knows us*! The ultimate issue in all of life is this: "Does

God know you?" Verse 3 ties together loving God and being known by God. "Those who love God give evidence that they are known by God in electing knowledge and grace (Jer. 1:5; Amos 3:2; Rom. 8:28-30)" (Schreiner, *1 Corinthians*, 169). Further, to love God will supernaturally lead us to love others, especially our spiritual family. Schreiner says it perfectly:

> True knowledge is adorned with humility and accompanied by love, and if these qualities are lacking, one's knowledge has not been applied correctly. Love is the signature and mark of being a Christian (cf. 13:1-13; John 13:34-35), and such love has God supremely as its object, though such love for God is also expressed in love for brothers and sisters. The knowers may have boasted in their knowledge, but what is decisive is whether one *is known by* God. (Ibid.; emphasis in original)

If we know God as we ought through faith in his Son, the Lord Jesus Christ, we cannot help but love our God, who has perfectly loved us. We cannot help but love those "for whom Christ died," our brothers and sisters (8:11). Love regulates our liberty.

All My Actions Are Regulated by the Truth of Christian Worship
1 CORINTHIANS 8:4-6

Sometimes theology is given a bad rap. It is said that theology is boring, deep, irrelevant, and unnecessary. "Just preach the gospel," some say, failing to realize the gospel itself is quite theological. Paul again addresses the pressing issue of "eating food sacrificed to idols." Paul's argument is both theological and pastoral and carefully presented.

Unbelievers Worship False Gods and False Lords (8:4-5)

At Corinth the "knowers" flaunted their theology with two confessional affirmations, both of which were true to a point. First, "We know that 'an idol is nothing in the world'" (ESV, "has no real existence"). Second, alluding to the *Shema* from Deuteronomy 6:4, "There is no God but one" (v. 4). Paul agrees with them. But there needs to be an important qualification theologically and pastorally, especially as it relates to those who have recently been saved out of pagan idolatry.

His argument goes something like this: There are so-called gods in heaven and on earth, many "gods" and many "lords." We know they are not divine, but the lost person doesn't. Further, as Deuteronomy 32:16-17 and 1 Corinthians 10:19-22 teach, while idols are not real, demons are! Lurking and acting behind idols are demons that utilize these false gods and false lords to lead people into false worship and away from the one true God. Demons are real, and they can be worshiped. Some of their favorite tools are idols, false gods to which humans give their ultimate allegiance. Deuteronomy 10:17 is a much-needed corrective: "For the LORD your God is the God of gods and the Lord of lords." There is only one true God, but it is theologically incorrect to deny the existence of the many gods and lords falsely worshiped in this world.

Christians Worship One God and One Lord (8:6)

Paul will now reaffirm the monotheism of biblical teaching within the context of the Christian faith. His words are an early confession of faith. "For us," who know the truth, "there is one God, the Father." This God is the beginning and the end, the A and Z of all things. "All things are from him, and we exist for him" (cf. Eph 4:6). Likewise, and in the same way, "There is one Lord, Jesus Christ. All things are through him, and we exist through him" (cf. Col 1:16-17). With amazing theological ease, Paul affirms a plurality within the divine simplicity of the one God, who exists as Father, Son, and Holy Spirit. No commentary is added. No explanation is given. We are simply left, at this point, to reflect on and worship such an amazing God. Tom Schreiner says,

> Paul reaffirms the Old Testament truth that there is one
> Creator God and thus all glory and praise belong to him. He
> is the Father of believers, and the word "Father" also suggests
> a relationship to Jesus the Son, though the word "Son" is not
> used here. The identity of God, however, is not exhausted by
> the Father. The Son is also the Lord and agent of creation,
> and Paul affirms these astounding truths about the Son
> without compromising or denying the truth that God is one.
> No explanation is given as to how there can be one God when
> the Father and the Son share the same identity. The task
> of working out the implications of what is said here was left
> to later interpreters, but I would argue that such a task was

faithfully carried out in the Nicene-Constantinopolitan and Chalcedonian Creeds. (*1 Corinthians*, 172)

I agree. We can see this task is faithfully carried out in later church history in "The Nicene-Constantinopolitan Creed" (AD 381):

I believe in one God, the Father Almighty,
Maker of heaven and earth, and of all things visible and
   invisible;
And in one Lord Jesus Christ, the only-begotten Son of God,
begotten of the Father before all worlds;
God of God, Light of Light, very God of very God;
begotten, not made, being of one substance with the Father,
by whom all things were made.
Who, for us men and for our salvation,
came down from heaven
and was incarnate by the Holy Spirit of the Virgin Mary,
and was made man;
and was crucified also for us under Pontius Pilate;
he suffered and was buried;
and the third day He rose again, according to the Scriptures;
and ascended into heaven, and sits at the right hand of the
   Father;
and he shall come again, with glory, to judge the living and the
   dead;
whose kingdom shall have no end.
And I believe in the Holy Spirit, the Lord and Giver of Life;
who proceeds from the Father and the Son;
who with the Father and the Son together is worshipped and
   glorified;
who spoke by the prophets.
And I believe in one holy catholic [universal] and apostolic
   church.
I acknowledge one baptism for the remission of sins;
and I look for the resurrection of the dead,
And the life of the age to come. Amen. (Van Dixhoorn, *Creeds*,
   17–18)

The principle of Christian worship is a helpful guide as we consider the question, "Am I my brother's keeper?"

All My Actions Are Regulated by the Guideline of Christian Deference
1 CORINTHIANS 8:7-13

In Philippians 2:3-4 Paul explains to us what it means to have the mind of Christ: "Do nothing out of selfish ambition or conceit, but in humility consider others as more important than yourselves. Everyone should look not to his own interests, but rather to the interests of others." Paul will apply this principle to the controversy that was raging in Corinth.

I Will Not Defile My Brother's Conscience (8:7-10)

The Corinthian know-it-alls claimed all believers have knowledge about idols being nothing. Paul says that's not true: "Not everyone has this knowledge" that idols are nothing and that there is one God (v. 7). Some newer believers are still "weak" and growing in their faith. Worshiping idols has harmed them. Thus, eating food sacrificed to an idol could seriously harm them, defiling their consciences and causing them to question their status before God. Here both the know-it-alls and the "weak" need instruction, which Paul provides in verse 8: "Food will not bring us close [ESV, "commend us"] to God. We are not worse off if we don't eat, and we are not better if we do eat." The Corinthians missed the key point. They should have asked, "What is the loving thing to do for my brothers and sisters in Christ that will build them up in the faith?" So Paul says, "[B]e careful that this right of yours in no way becomes a stumbling block to the weak." Later Paul will bluntly add, "Flee from idolatry" (10:14). All believers, strong and weak, must recognize the seduction of idolatry and our susceptibility to it. In the latter context Paul would forbid eating with friends and associates in an idol's temple, even as he may allow it, in certain situations, in a home. Verse 10 seems to bear this out: "For if someone sees you, the one who has knowledge, dining in an idol's temple, won't his weak conscience be encouraged [lit. "built up"] to eat food offered to idols?" What the know-it-alls call a "right," Paul calls a "stumbling block." The issue was undoubtedly significant and potentially costly to the fledgling Christian community. Do they go to the pagan temples when business is transacted and where people expect to see them as a matter of social convention? Or do they refrain and pay the cost because the spiritual well-being of their brothers and sisters is more important? What would Christ do? The next three verses touch on that question.

I Will Not Sin Against My Christ (8:11-13)

Paul has warned the church about sinning against a brother or sister in the faith. Now he warns them about sinning against their Lord. He drives his plea to the cross and the atoning work of Christ. Their so-called knowledge, flawed and misguided, has defiled the consciences of some among them (v. 7). But the situation is worse than that, as verses 11-12 make clear: "The weak person, the brother or sister for whom Christ died, is ruined [ESV, "destroyed"] by your knowledge. Now when you sin like this against your brothers and sisters and wound their weak conscience, you are sinning against Christ." The word translated "ruined" or "destroyed" is strong, causing some to conclude their eternal destruction is in view. I think, however, Paul employs such a strong word to communicate the severity of arrogantly putting our supposed rights above the well-being of a brother or sister in Christ and seriously damaging his or her faith. We can ruin their faith! And thus we ultimately and more seriously sin against Christ who died for them just like he died for us. Is getting our way and flaunting our rights worth it?

Paul provides the answer to our question. It is not. Verse 13 ends our chapter with an appropriate summation: "Therefore, if food causes my brother or sister to fall, I will never again eat meat, so that I won't cause my brother or sister to fall." We could easily substitute for the word "food" any number of things in terms of application. Paul's words are emphatic and pointed. Love trumps knowledge. Love trumps rights. Love trumps all (see ch. 13).

Conclusion

In reflecting on how to bring this important topic to a close, I felt I could not improve on the words I came across by Paul Gardner. I have been greatly blessed by his insights, as I am once again by these words:

> Those who think they are "something" need to realize they
> can end up leading others into sin. When they no longer see
> love for God and love for neighbor as the true markers of

community standing, then they will behave arrogantly toward others and will replace what is good and of the Lord with what is at best inadequate. This arises from people's desire to place themselves and their actions at the center of their spiritual lives. The ability of Christians to give up what they see as their community rights and privileges—even things they enjoy—for the sake of a Christian brother or sister is ultimately the test of the presence of love. Assurance for those who lack it is found first in looking again to the love of Christ who was crucified for them, but it is then reinforced by a people who build each other up in the faith through their love for one another. (*1 Corinthians*, 382–83)

Reflect and Discuss

1. In what ways does Western culture consistently train you *not* to believe that "the spiritual good of others should always govern what we do" (p. 166)? In what ways does individualism shape how you think and live? What changes can you make to move away from only focusing on your individual needs?

2. When you see culture not reflecting God's design, do you tend to withdraw from it or try to change it? What obstacles do both paths have?

3. Would you describe Christian interaction on social media as filled with love? Why or why not? Do social media create hate or reveal hate in a person's heart? Explain. Do you see any places in your social media interactions where love is not present?

4. In what ways have you used knowing the truth to excuse a lack of love? Why is a lack of love never excusable?

5. What does it look like to use knowledge to tear others down? What attributes of the Spirit must be present for knowledge to build up?

6. How will the "stronger" brother/sister be tempted with pride? How will the "weaker" brother/sister be tempted with judgmentalism? How will each of these heart postures display themselves in actions?

7. Is being a "weak" brother/sister inherently a negative thing? Why or why not? In what ways is the "weaker" brother/sister still glorifying God with how he or she lives?

8. Give examples of how Jesus regulated his actions by humble deference. Where do you see examples of Jesus having knowledge in Scripture and still expressing love?

9. Why is Paul willing to shape his life so drastically for the sake of someone else (v. 13)?

10. How would giving up your rights and privileges for another Christian express your love for God?

The Gospel Above All

1 CORINTHIANS 9:1-18

Main Idea: To advance the gospel, we joyfully and readily give up our rights.

I. **There Is a Right to Compensation for the Minister of the Gospel (9:1-14).**
   - A. It is the right of God's apostles (9:1-6).
   - B. It is the right of a soldier (9:7).
   - C. It is the right of a vinedresser (9:7).
   - D. It is the right of a shepherd (9:7).
   - E. It is the right of an ox (9:8-9).
   - F. It is the right of a plowman (9:10).
   - G. It is the right of a thresher (9:10).
   - H. It is the right of God's servants (9:11-12).
   - I. It is the right of priests (9:13).
   - J. It is the right of those who minister the Word (9:14).

II. **There Is a Compulsion to Preach the Message of the Gospel (9:15-18).**
   - A. We proclaim the gospel out of necessity (9:15-17).
   - B. We proclaim the gospel freely (9:18).

In an interview with *Outreach Magazine*, J. D. Greear, pastor of Summit Church in Raleigh, North Carolina, and a former president of the SBC, addresses the importance and centrality of the gospel for Christianity, what he calls "the gospel above all." He says,

> The apostle Paul said that the gospel was of first importance
> (1 Cor. 15:3-4). This implies that other things were important
> to him, too. But, they weren't of *first* importance. Only the
> gospel was. ("The Gospel"; emphasis in original)

Evangelical Christians have always been gospel people. After all, it's in our name. *Evangelical* is a transliteration of the Greek word "gospel." So, in that sense, the gospel has always been our brand. It's been the heart of Christianity from the beginning. It's what gives our faith life.

The gospel indeed gives our faith life. The gospel affects all areas of life. And some of those areas may surprise us. One such area concerns the question, "Should ministers of the gospel always receive financial support for their work of ministry?" The important word in that question is the word "always." Most of us would recognize that the Bible teaches that ministers are worthy of financial support. One important text on this topic is 1 Timothy 5:17-18, which says,

> *The elders who are good leaders are to be considered worthy of double honor, especially those who work hard at preaching and teaching. For the Scripture says: Do not muzzle an ox while it is treading out the grain* [Deut. 25:4], *and "The worker is worthy of his wages"* [Luke 10:7].

Paul wrote those words, but he also wrote 1 Corinthians 9:1-18, where he will affirm that he gladly laid aside "this right" and preached for free for the sake of the gospel and the souls of men. The salvation of others mattered above all other issues. The gospel above all was the decisive factor in all his decision making. Setting aside personal rights and preferences mattered nothing to him if it meant Christ could use him to save just one more person.

There Is a Right to Compensation for the Minister of the Gospel
1 CORINTHIANS 9:1-14

First Corinthians 8:13 ties chapters 8 and 9 together. Paul will not do anything to cause a brother or sister to stumble in the faith, even if he has the liberty and right to do that thing. That includes eating food sacrificed to a lifeless idol (ch. 8) and receiving compensation for preaching the gospel (ch. 9). Chapter 9 is a personal example that drives home the point Paul is trying to make in chapter 8. He builds a compelling argument for the right of financial compensation for anyone who preaches the gospel and ministers to the church. His argument is filled with rhetorical questions (fifteen altogether) and illustrations. It is a persuasive masterpiece.

It Is the Right of God's Apostles (9:1-6)

Paul begins his rhetorical barrage in verse 1 with four rapid-fire questions, all demanding a yes answer.

- "Am I not free?" Yes! He is free in Christ (Gal 5:1) as much as anyone.
- "Am I not an apostle?" Yes! He was called by Christ on the Damascus Road (Acts 9:1-19; also Gal 1:11-24).
- "Have I not seen Jesus our Lord?" Yes!
- "Are you not my work in the Lord?" Yes! He planted the church in Corinth (Acts 18:1-7; 1 Cor 3:6).

Verse 2 reinforces this last point: "If I am not an apostle to others [of course he was to them too], at least I am to you, because you are the seal of my apostleship in the Lord." As converts under his teaching, they thus authenticate, prove, and validate his work and ministry in the Lord.

Paul continues his "defense" and the rights of his apostleship to those who might want to "examine" his credentials in verses 3 and following. He again uses rhetorical questions, but he is also personal. He asks, "Don't we have the right to eat and drink?" (v. 4). Don't they have the right to financial support to meet the necessities of life like food and water? He asks further in verse 5, "Don't we have the right to be accompanied by a believing wife like the other apostles, the Lord's brothers, and Cephas?" Paul was single. Most, if not all, of the apostles were married like Cephas (Peter). Apparently, the same was true for Jesus's brothers (James, Joseph, Simon, and Judas; Matt 13:55). When they traveled and preached the gospel, the churches cared for them and their wives, and no doubt their entire families. Wasn't Paul entitled to the same rights and support? Paul adds Barnabas to the argument in verse 6. Schreiner notes this "suggests that Barnabas was also unmarried and did not always receive financial support" (*1 Corinthians*, 183). Paul's point is clear. If the other apostles, including Peter and the Lord's brothers, are cared for financially, he and Barnabas would also have that right. It would not be unusual; it would be expected. Yet Paul will gladly forfeit this right for the gospel's sake (v. 12). The gospel above all comes first!

It Is the Right of a Soldier (9:7)

Paul will now add, in rapid-fire succession, nine additional arguments and illustrations to demonstrate his right to financial support. He starts with a military example: "Who serves as a soldier at his own expense?" No one. Warriors are compensated for their service.

It Is the Right of a Vinedresser (9:7)

"Who plants a vineyard and does not eat its fruit?" (Cf. Deut 20:6.) No one. The purpose of planting a garden is to enjoy what it produces.

It Is the Right of a Shepherd (9:7)

"Or who shepherds a flock and does not drink the milk from the flock?" Again, the answer is no one. Labor among the flock is to be rewarded.

It Is the Right of the Ox (9:8-9)

This one may be Paul's most unusual illustration in this section. He again begins with a rhetorical question: "Am I saying this from a human perspective?" The ESV says, "on human authority." Paul asks whether his ideas are just one person's opinion. Then Paul immediately counters with an appeal to Scripture: "Doesn't the law also say the same thing?" What follows is his unexpected appeal to Deuteronomy 25:4 and the rights of an ox: "For it is written in the law of Moses, Do not muzzle an ox while it treads out the grain." He then asks rhetorically, "Is God really concerned about oxen?" While this passage is much debated, here is what I believe Paul is doing. First, Paul is not saying God does not care about animals (see Prov 12:10). He cares for all his good creation. He is, however, more concerned with humans who bear his image (Gen 1:26-31). Second, Paul does not deny the literal meaning of the Deuteronomy text that an ox should be allowed to eat as it works. Third, I believe Paul recognized and considered the greater context of Deuteronomy 25:4 in his appeal to this passage. Gardner writes at this point,

> Paul's use of the Old Testament often provokes questions of this sort, and it is always good to start by looking at the original context in the Old Testament of the verse quoted since frequently this can help explain why he chose the passage. The context for Deuteronomy 25:4 has to do with the way in which men and women are treated. It especially has to do with the care of certain people. To go back no further than 24:14, the passage first speaks to the need to pay workers what they are due. (*1 Corinthians*, 395)

Fourth, Paul is making a lesser-to-greater argument (oxen to humans) and applying the principle contained within the command. Those who work, whoever they are, should reap from their labors. If this is true for an ox, it is certainly true for an apostle!

It Is the Right of the Plowman (9:10)

Paul raises another rhetorical question in verse 10: "Isn't he [God] really saying it for our sake?" This time he provides his answer: "Yes, this is written for our sake," for our benefit and profit. He then adds another illustration: "He who plows ought to plow in hope." The farmer plows a field with the hope and expectation it will provide food in due season for him and his family. It is why he puts in the hard labor.

It Is the Right of a Thresher (9:10)

"He who threshes should thresh in hope of sharing the crop." The reaper in the field works with the anticipation there will be grain to take home at the end of the day. My mind immediately recalls the third chapter of Ruth, in which she visits Boaz at the threshing floor.

It Is the Right of God's Servants (9:11-12)

Paul now makes a precise spiritual application to the Corinthians from his numerous illustrations: "If we have sown spiritual things for you, is it too much if we reap material benefits from you?" Of course, the answer here is no (Rom 15:27). Furthermore, he adds, "If others have this right to receive benefits from you, don't we even more?" That is, if those who have come later receive financial support from them, should not the one who founded the work? Of course, the answer is yes. But Paul then drives home the key point of these verses. He says, "Nevertheless, we have not made use of this right." We have not required or received any financial help. "Instead, we endure everything so that we will not hinder [ESV, "put an obstacle in the way of"] the gospel of Christ." This is the first of seven uses of the word "gospel" in verses 12-18. Its priority is the crux and heart of Paul's argument. The gospel above all was not a mere slogan for Paul. It was the heart and guiding light of his ministry.

It Is the Right of Priests (9:13)

Once more Paul uses a familiar phrase, "Don't you know?" Are they unaware "that those who perform temple services eat the food from the temple, and those who serve at the altar share in the offerings of the altar" (v. 13)? Gordon Fee notes there is ample support for this example

(Lev 6:16-18,26-28; 7:6,8-10,28-36; Num. 18:8-19) (*Corinthians*, 2014, 455). People engaged in spiritual service for God have always been taken care of for their work.

It Is the Right of Those Who Minister the Word (9:14)

Paul's climactic argument appears here. He cites as his support Jesus himself. "In the same way, the Lord has commanded that those who preach the gospel should earn their living by the gospel" (v. 14). Paul probably has in mind the words of our Lord recorded in Luke 10:7: "For the worker is worthy of his wages." Jesus commanded that God's people take good care of God's servants. However, he did not command his servants always to take what was offered. Ultimately God's servants serve him above all. They serve the gospel above all. Whatever best furthers the gospel must guide the minister of the gospel above all other considerations.

There Is a Compulsion to Preach the Message of the Gospel
1 CORINTHIANS 9:15-18

Today it is popular to refer to many things as gospel issues. However, such statements often fail to make a theological distinction between "the gospel" and implications that derive from and are related to the gospel. Issues like the right to life, gender, poverty alleviation, and racial reconciliation are important, and the Bible speaks to them all. Further, and importantly, the gospel will impact our thinking on how we understand and respond to these issues. But—this is crucial—our response to these issues will be implications derived from the gospel. They are not the gospel. As Paul makes clear in 1 Corinthians 15:3-6, the gospel is this: Jesus Christ died for our sins and was raised from the dead according to the Scriptures, and all who repent and believe in him will be saved. That is the gospel. But there are implications and perspectives and actions that the gospel will require and even mandate. Some will relate to how we preach the gospel. In verses 15-18 Paul highlights two.

We Proclaim the Gospel out of Necessity (9:15-16)

Paul again affirms his position that he will receive no financial remuneration for preaching the gospel at Corinth: "For my part I have used none of these rights, nor have I written these things that they may be applied to my case" (ESV, "to secure any such provision"). Paul has the right to financial support, but he will not ask for it. Paul then makes a highly passionate declaration worthy of every minister of the gospel:

> For it would be better for me to die than for anyone to deprive me of my boast! For if I preach the gospel, I have no reason to boast, because I am compelled to preach—and woe to me if I do not preach the gospel.

Paul thus separates himself from any whose motivation for preaching is money. He sees faithful gospel proclamation as a life-or-death issue for himself. So great is this burden, he tells us, that he must preach the gospel. There is no choice. Indeed, he virtually pronounces a curse upon himself: "Woe to me if I do not preach the gospel!" (cf. Jer 20:9). The great Baptist preacher Charles Spurgeon rightly said that any true gospel-called minister knows what Paul is talking about. He writes,

> If a man be truly called of God to ministry, I will defy him to withhold himself from it. A man who has really within him the inspiration of the Holy Ghost calling him to preach cannot help it. He must preach. As fire within the bones, so will that influence be until it blazes forth. Friends may check him, foes criticize him, despisers sneer at him, the man is indomitable. He must preach if he has the call of heaven. ("Preach the Gospel," 267)

Faithful preachers preach the gospel of Jesus Christ whether paid or not. They must. They are under a divine mandate, spiritual obligation, and calling. Paul's only boast is he will not put any hindrance in the way of preaching the gospel. Preaching the gospel itself is no ground for boasting. It is a divinely given compulsion. He must do it. He has no choice, no say in the matter.

Paul's point in verse 17 is open to some confusion and potential misunderstanding. There Paul writes, "For if I do this willingly, I have a reward, but if unwillingly, I am entrusted with a commission" (ESV, "stewardship"). Now, what exactly is Paul saying? Charles Hodge is extremely helpful at this point:

> That Paul preached the gospel willingly, that he esteemed it his highest joy and glory, is abundantly evident from his history and his writings [Rom. 1:5; 11:13; 15:15-16; 1 Cor. 15:9-10; Gal. 1:15-16; Eph. 3:8]. The difference, therefore here

expressed between (ἐκών and ἄκων), *willing* and *unwilling*, is not the difference between cheerfully and reluctantly, but between optional and obligatory. He says he had a dispensation or stewardship (οἰκονομία) committed to him. These stewards (οἰκονόμοι) were commonly slaves. There is a great difference between what a slave does in obedience to a command, and what a man volunteers to do of his own accord. And this is the precise difference to which the apostle here refers. (*An Exposition*, 161–62)

The Message captures the intent of Paul's point: "If this was my own idea of just another way to make a living, I'd expect some pay. But since it's *not* my idea but something solemnly entrusted to me, why would I expect to get paid?" (emphasis in original).

We Proclaim the Gospel Freely (9:18)

Paul concludes this section with one final rhetorical question that informs us he does indeed have a reward, just not a monetary one. He asks, "What then is my reward?" Answer: "To preach the gospel and offer it free of charge and not make full use of my rights in the gospel." To preach the gospel free of charge is his boast (v. 15) and his reward (vv. 17-18). *The Message* paraphrases: "So am I getting anything out of it? Yes, as a matter of fact: the pleasure of proclaiming the Message at no cost to you. You don't even have to pay my expenses!" At Corinth, for the sake of the gospel, Paul felt it was best to serve and preach without financial compensation. It was a decision he made for the spiritual benefit of others. And he was glad to do it. The Corinthians, therefore, would be well served to follow his example regarding eating food sacrificed to idols (chs. 8–10). Not causing a brother or sister to stumble will always trump my rights. Love demands it. The gospel above all demands it too.

Conclusion

Several years ago, I heard a famous athlete say he loved playing his sport so much that he would play for free if he had to. The apostle Paul told a first-century church that he loved the gospel and human souls so much that he would preach for free if necessary. And he did! If there is ever to be a "stumbling block" that keeps a lost person from believing in the gospel of Jesus Christ, let it be the gospel and nothing else (1:23). Let us gladly surrender any and every right necessary so that the lost may hear unhindered the good news of the death, burial, and resurrection of the Son of God for the forgiveness of sins and the gift of eternal life. Jesus surrendered his rights and privileges to go to the cross. It is a small thing for us, like Paul, to follow in his footsteps.

Reflect and Discuss

1. Read Acts 18:1-3. What did Paul have to do because he gave up support from the Corinthians? In what ways did he *not* choose the easier option as he served Christ?
2. In what ways was Paul using his singleness to advance the gospel?
3. How does Paul's example contrast with abusive church leaders'?
4. Paul's life (ch. 9) was an example of how he taught the Corinthians to live (ch. 8). Why is it essential that you live out what you teach others? Are there areas in your life in which you could more faithfully live out an example of what you teach?
5. Paul willingly and joyfully gave up his right to financial compensation. How do you typically feel about giving up your rights?
6. Why does Paul consider it a reward to preach the gospel for free rather than expecting his rights?
7. How does someone decide when giving up a right or privilege is necessary?
8. How will pride keep you from wanting to give up your rights to serve others?
9. What do these verses teach the church about financially supporting those serving God through mission work? Is there anyone you can financially support so that he or she can be freed up to share the gospel?
10. What rights and privileges did Jesus give up to serve us? What did it cost him? What was his reward?

The Heart of a Soul Winner

1 CORINTHIANS 9:19-27

Main Idea: All preferences and rights are worth giving up to bring others to Jesus.

I. **I Deny Myself to Win Souls for Christ (9:19-23).**
   A. I willingly deny myself personally (9:19).
   B. I willingly deny myself religiously (9:20).
   C. I willingly deny myself socially (9:21).
   D. I willingly deny myself completely (9:22-23).
II. **I Discipline Myself to Win the Crown (9:24-27).**
   A. We compete like a runner (9:24-26).
   B. We compete like a boxer (9:26-27).

When I was nineteen, I rededicated my life to Jesus Christ. I had been saved as a young boy, but I did not live faithfully for my Lord as a teenager. In many ways my rededication was more life changing than my conversion. After it, I discovered joy and happiness in Christ I had never known. Immediately I wanted to share about this newfound relationship with others, but I did not know how. I quickly learned that a man named Jack Fordham taught what was called a "soul-winners class" every Wednesday night in the basement of the church I attended. I showed up to the next one. He taught me (and later my wife Charlotte) how to be a soul winner by sharing the "Romans Road," a simple gospel presentation. It goes like this:

- Everyone is a sinner (Rom 3:23).
- Sin's penalty is spiritual death and eternal separation from God (Rom 6:23).
- God loves us and demonstrated his love by sending Christ (his Son) to die for our sins (Rom 5:8).
- We can have our sins forgiven and receive the gift of eternal life by confessing and believing in Jesus (Rom 10:9-10,13).

Soul winning soon became a priority and practice in my life and has been ever since. The term "soul winner" is not as popular as it once was, but it needs to be revived! The Baptist pastor Charles Spurgeon wrote a book titled *The Soul Winner*. He believed soul winning was essential to the life and vibrancy of the church. The apostle Paul would enthusiastically agree. In verses 19-22 he will use the word "win" five times in the context of reaching the lost. Soul winning was a priority for the apostle, and it should be a priority for every follower of Christ. In 1 Corinthians 9:19-27 Paul allows us to examine the heart of a soul winner. Two guiding principles are revealed for our careful consideration.

I Deny Myself to Win Souls for Christ
1 CORINTHIANS 9:19-23

Paul writes for several chapters (chs. 8–10) about surrendering our rights for the blessing and benefit of others. He now applies that spiritual principle to soul winning (see also 10:31-33). Paul gladly flexes and bends to win others to Christ. He, as D. A. Carson writes, "must not do anything that is forbidden to the Christian, and he must do everything mandated of the Christian" to win the lost, both Jew and Gentile (*The Cross*, 120). Paul will highlight four areas where he willingly denies himself to win souls for King Jesus. We do well to follow his example.

I Willingly Deny Myself Personally (9:19)

Paul had one master, and his name is Jesus. Thus, he is free from the opinions and expectations of men. Yet his freedom in Christ entails a certain kind of slavery, as verse 19 makes plain. The apostle says, "Although I am free from all and not anyone's slave, I have made myself a slave to everyone, in order to win more people." Paul belongs only to Christ. He was bought by his blood and redemptive work on the cross (6:20; 7:23). Yet he willingly makes himself a slave to all people so that God can use him to bring (win) them to salvation. Warren Wiersbe says, "What a paradox: free from all men, and yet the servant [slave; Gr. *doulos*] of all men!" (*Be Wise*, 105). We must gladly surrender our rights and make ourselves servants of others so that we "win more" of them to our King.

I Willingly Deny Myself Religiously (9:20)

Paul applies his principle of becoming a slave to all for the souls of all to the Jews. His words are simple, but they contain an important caveat: "To the Jews I became like a Jew, to win Jews; to those under the law [of

Moses], like one under the law—though I myself am not under the law—to win those under the law" (v. 20). Paul flexes his freedom in Christ for his fellow Jewish countrymen. Schreiner is correct when he writes, "[Paul's] ethnic identity as a Jew was . . . no longer the primary reality in his life; Paul identified himself first and foremost as a Christian." Yet "Paul adapted, living as a Jew when with the Jews in order to win them" (*1 Corinthians*, 190–91). Paul did not return to honoring the sacrificial system Christ fulfilled. He did not, as he once incorrectly did, advocate a works-salvation theology. What he would do is have Timothy circumcised so he could more effectively evangelize among Jews (Acts 16:1-3). He himself would take a Nazirite vow and purify himself (Acts 18:18) so that there would be no unnecessary offense in trying to win Jews to faith in Messiah Jesus. Such practical accommodations were small matters in the work of missions and evangelism.

I Will Deny Myself Socially (9:21)

Paul now addresses his soul-winning relationship to Gentiles. His words in verse 21 are like those in verse 20, but they are not identical. He writes, "To those who are without the law, like one without the law—though I am not without God's law but under the law of Christ—to win those without the law." Paul will flex to win Gentiles, too, but his flexing goes in a different direction. Paul, like every Christian, has been set free from the Mosaic covenant and its many ceremonial rules and regulations. Cultural and social separation from so-called Gentile dogs was no longer a practice of his new life in Christ. However, Paul is no antinomian (one with no law). His life is now guided and regulated by a new law, "the law of Christ." Gordon Fee writes, "One should perhaps note the especially high Christology assumed by this phrase, which is unfortunately all too easily overlooked in most discussions of this passage" (*Corinthians*, 2014, 474). Paul lives under a new and different law because he has a new and different understanding of his Lord. It is Christ!

How should we describe the law of Christ? Based on Galatians 5:14-15 and 6:2, the ethic of love must be at the core of any understanding. John 13:34-35 adds weight to this approach. And yet returning to Fee's observation, Paul's Christology should also inform our understanding. The person, work, and teachings of Christ are now preeminent in his life. They color and impact everything! Paul Gardner says it well:

> Paul still concerns himself with the centrality of Christ. In 11:1
> he says, "Be imitators of me as I am of Christ." His concern is
> . . . obedience to Christ in day-to-day service. As a servant to
> all, Paul is first and foremost a servant of Christ. . . . He will
> not do what Christ would not do! (*1 Corinthians*, 408)

Being a faithful soul winner has its limits. The lordship of Jesus Christ trumps all.

I Willingly Deny Myself Completely (9:22-23)

Paul brings his argument full circle. He also adds a third category of persons, those he previously addressed in 8:7-13. He calls them "the weak." As noted in a previous section, this phrase is open to serious misunderstanding. Often, it is incorrectly understood in a derogatory sense. However, Paul uses the phrase to identify new believers who have come out of paganism and idolatry. They contrast with arrogant know-it-alls who valued knowledge above love (cf. 8:1). Gardner makes a particular application to the gift of knowledge (12:8) and those who were flaunting this gift at the expense of others:

> Paul has used the word "weak" to describe a people who have
> been made to feel inferior because they are not exercising
> certain rights related to gifts of the Spirit, such as wisdom
> or knowledge. These people are looked down upon by
> the elitists or "knowers" and so have been made to feel
> weak. Yet, in God's eyes the so-called "weak" belong to him
> even without these (merely) human markers . . . the word
> "weak" should not be seen as a derogatory term or even
> a description of a people who are basically inadequate in
> one way or another. In chapter 8 Paul sided with the weak,
> and ever since 1:27 "weak" has been a term that has been
> used to contrast one group of people against the arrogant.
> (*1 Corinthians*, 409)

Paul will accommodate Jews. He will accommodate Gentiles. He will accommodate those weak in the eyes of people but favored in the sight of God. He even says, "To the weak I became weak, in order to win the weak. I have become all things to all people, so that I may by every possible means save some" (v. 22). Leon Morris provides a good word here:

This whole discussion has underlined Paul's tender concern for *the weak*. But, unlike the Jews and the Gentiles of the previous verses, *the weak* were already Christians. He does not seek *to win* them in the same sense, but to win them for greater strength, or perhaps simply to keep them from slipping. He respected their scruples and conformed his behavior to theirs to help them. (*1 Corinthians*, 136; emphasis in original)

Thus, Paul can summarize his position in verse 23: "Now I do all this because of the gospel, so that I may share in the blessings." The gospel of Christ above all enters the picture again. So does the humility of the apostle. He wishes to share in the blessings of soul winning. We are co-laborers, partners (1 Cor 3). We are in the work of soul winning together. We should work hard to finish our assignment well. Paul will turn to that goal in verses 24-27, drawing from the field of athletics.

I Discipline Myself to Win the Crown
1 CORINTHIANS 9:24-27

The New Testament writers were fond of using athletic imagery to illustrate the Christian life. Second Timothy 2:5 uses the image of an athlete in general; Ephesians 6:12 a wrestler; 1 Corinthians 9:26 boxing; and Galatians 5:7; 1 Corinthians 9:24; 2 Timothy 4:7; and Hebrews 12:1-2 running a race. Here Paul appeals to a race and boxing to urge the Corinthians to finish well, to win. The Isthmian Games of Corinth and/ or the Olympic Games may provide the background for his choices. These were popular events the Corinthians would readily identify with.

We Compete Like a Runner (9:24-26)

Paul begins verse 24 with a familiar rhetorical question: "Don't you know that the runners in a stadium all race, but only one receives the prize?" The purpose of entering a race is to win. Therefore, Paul writes, "Run in such a way to win the prize." Paul is running the race to win souls for Jesus. That is the prize he wants to win, and he is willing to "become all things to all people" (v. 22) to win the prize of their salvation. Achieving this prize requires a certain mindset and lifestyle. In the world of athletics, the strategy of winners is well known: "Everyone who competes exercises self-control in everything" (v. 25). They "do not run like one who runs aimlessly" (v. 26). Runners train hard. They run wind sprints if they are sprinters; they run miles and miles if they run long distance. They watch their diet, they get sufficient rest, and they train their bodies day in and day out to win the next race. Similarly, those who have salvation in Christ should constrain themselves to run the race of the Christian life for his glory.

At the end of verse 25, Paul describes the prize we seek. Athletes in the Isthmian or Olympic Games run "to receive a perishable crown" (ESV, "wreath"), one made of celery, parsley, pine, or some other leafy material. It is nice for a while, but it soon withers away. In striking contrast, we believers run to win "an imperishable crown." Kistemaker notes, "The New Testament teaches that [the imperishable crown] is righteousness, eternal life, and glory" (*Exposition*, 313). I would certainly affirm that to be true. Yet in the context of this passage, the souls of people must be considered as a part of the imperishable crown. Winning Jews and Gentiles to salvation in Christ is an imperishable reward because the gift of God is eternal life. Wiersbe is on target:

> In order to give up his rights and have the joy of winning lost souls, Paul had to discipline himself. That is the emphasis of this entire chapter: Authority (rights) must be balanced by discipline. If we want to serve the Lord and win His reward and approval, we must pay the price. (*Be Wise*, 107)

We Compete Like a Boxer (9:26-27)

Paul introduces the metaphor of a boxer to draw an analogy to the activity of a soul winner. He informs the Corinthians that he does not "box like one beating the air." Vaughn says, "The expression suggests either shadow boxing or missing one's opponent" (*1 Corinthians*, 98). A boxer is not haphazard or aimless in preparation. He works hard in training to prepare himself to deliver effective punches to knock out his opponent and win the match. He recognizes that stamina is essential. Therefore, Paul writes, like a boxer in training, "I discipline [NIV, "I strike a blow to"; CEB, "I'm landing punches on"] my body and bring it under strict control." Morris captures the importance of the Greek text:

> In picturesque language [Paul] speaks of the way he disciplines himself. *Beat* renders *hypōpiazō*, a verb from boxing, with the meaning "give a black eye to." This, coupled with

make it my slave, leaves no doubt as to the vigour with which
Paul subdues his body. (*1 Corinthians,* 138)

Paul works his body over, putting it through whatever is necessary,
making it a slave so that he will win the prize and not come up short
in his holy calling as a soul winner. Paul does not want to preach the
life-changing gospel of Jesus Christ to others only to fail along the way
and become "disqualified." The Greek behind "disqualified" is a strong
word (*adokimos*), leading some excellent scholars to believe Paul is talking about one's salvation. However, the context of being a fit, prepared,
and qualified soul winner for all people groups leads me to conclude
that Paul's fear is that a true Christian could become disqualified from
some service to the Lord, especially the service of being an effective soul
winner to Jew and Gentile alike. Disqualifying actions could be ethical,
moral, or even theological. As 1 Corinthians 3:15 affirms, after all, it is
possible to have one's works consumed by the blazing fire of the judgment seat of Christ (also 2 Cor 5:10), even though he or she is saved.
Paul wants us to begin well, run well, and finish well as soul-winners for
Christ. It will require rigorous discipline, but we will see it was worth it
in the end.

Conclusion

Their names were John Leonard Dober and David Nitschman. They
were Moravian missionaries who were willing to sell themselves into slavery to win the lost with the gospel. Here is their story:

> It was a slave himself who stirred the Moravian church in
> Germany into action [to the West Indies] in 1731, when
> Anthony Ulrich, a former slave from St. Thomas then in the
> country, was invited by Count Zinzendorf to make a plea
> for missionaries to be sent to the West Indies, before the
> congregation of Herrnhut. He told them that no one could
> possibly preach to the slaves unless he first became a slave
> himself. They had to work all day on the plantations, and
> after sunset were not allowed to go out. Thus no one could
> preach who did not work with them. Dober and Nitchsmann,
> two prominent members of the congregation, volunteered
> to go, and Dober was actually prepared to see himself into
> slavery, had not the law of the Danish West Indies prohibited

it. Instead, Dober started his work as an overseer on a cotton plantation, and Nitchsmann did jobs as a carpenter. (Furley, "Moravian Missionaries," 3)

There is a tradition that says as the two men said goodbye to their weeping families, they shouted from their ship, "May the Lamb that was slain receive the reward of this suffering." Here are the hearts of soulwinners. May our Lord grant to us hearts like theirs, a heart like Paul's, a heart like our King's.

Reflect and Discuss

1. Do you know how to share the gospel with someone? If so, who in your life can you share the gospel with this week? If not, who in your local church can equip you to share the gospel?
2. What does it mean to be "free from all" (v. 19)?
3. In what practical ways would Paul have made himself a slave to Jews or Gentiles to win them to Jesus? How can you make yourself a slave to others to win them?
4. What reasons might Christians give for why they will not change or bend themselves for others? Why are these reasons *not* valid excuses?
5. In order to bend yourself for others, what must you believe about Jesus? What must you believe about yourself?
6. Could giving up your preferences so that you might win others to Jesus open the door to temptations for bitterness? If yes, how so? What must be done to prevent bitterness as you give up rights and preferences to win others to Jesus?
7. What blessings does a Christian receive when an unbeliever starts following Jesus?
8. Would you describe yourself as "disciplined" and "self-controlled" in the way Paul describes? Why or why not? If not, what do you need to change to become more self-controlled for the sake of others?
9. Is receiving a reward from the Lord a regular motivation for how you live your life? Why or why not?
10. In what ways is Jesus the supreme example of this passage's teaching?

A History Lesson from God

1 CORINTHIANS 10:1-13

Main Idea: Avoid sin by remembering God's work in the past among the Hebrews and by depending on God's faithfulness.

I. **Spiritual Blessings Do Not Guarantee Us God's Pleasure (10:1-5).**
   A. We see God's guidance (10:1).
   B. We see God's deliverance (10:2).
   C. We see God's provisions (10:3-4).
   D. We see God's wrath (10:5).

II. **Spiritual Blessings Do Not Insulate Us from Divine Judgment (10:6-10).**
   A. God punishes the sin of lust (10:6; cf. Num. 11:18-34).
   B. God punishes the sin of idolatry (10:7; cf. Exod 32).
   C. God punishes the sin of sexual immorality (10:8; cf. Num 25:1-9).
   D. God punishes the sin of testing him (10:9; cf. Num 21:4-9).
   E. God punishes the sin of grumbling (10:10; cf. Num 16:41-50).

III. **Spiritual Blessings Do Not Protect Us from Personal Temptations (10:11-13).**
   A. Remember our susceptibility to evil (10:11-12).
   B. Remember God's way of escape (10:13).

In 1948, in a speech to the House of Commons, British Prime Minister Winston Churchill famously said, "Those who fail to learn from history are condemned to repeat it." The apostle Paul, no doubt, is in full agreement with Churchill's warning, as 1 Corinthians 10:1-13 makes clear. Twice he tells us that events in Israel's past serve as "examples" (10:6,11) warning us not to repeat their sinful behavior, which had devastating consequences for the Hebrew people. Paul has challenged us to discipline ourselves so that we may win imperishable crowns and not suffer disqualification (9:24-27). Unfortunately, such determination and discipline "found no place in the lives of many of the Israelites who followed Moses out of Egypt" (Vaughn and Lea, *1 Corinthians*, 99). Though they made a good start, they failed to finish well. Paul wants us to learn from their tragic example so that we do not repeat their history.

193

Spiritual Blessings Do Not Guarantee Us God's Pleasure
1 CORINTHIANS 10:1-5

Paul gives us a history lesson in these verses, drawing parallels between Israel ("our ancestors") and the church. He uses the event of the exodus under Moses as his teaching tool. Israel experienced, as have we Christians, extraordinary blessings and privileges from our God. These past blessings, however, did not guarantee they would successfully finish the race (9:24).

We See God's Guidance (10:1)

We should never lose sight ("be unaware") of the past blessings and kindnesses of God to his people. Take the great exodus of God's people out of Egyptian slavery. Note the repetition of the word "all." Paul writes, "Our ancestors [or "fathers," AMP] were all under the cloud, all passed through the sea." The pillar of cloud (Exod 13:21) guided them through the wilderness day and night. God was with them every day and every step of the way (cf. Ps 105:39). And all passed through the sea (Exod 14). God delivered the Hebrews and crushed the Egyptians! God was his people's divine guide through the sea and in the wilderness.

We See God's Deliverance (10:2)

Paul draws an analogy between Moses (a type of Christ) leading the people to pass through the waters of the Red Sea and Christian baptism (Rom 6:1-14). Moses delivered the Hebrews out of Egyptian slavery. He seemed like their savior. After all, trusting him and pledging their allegiance, they followed him in the cloud and out of the waters of the sea. In a sense they were baptized (identified) into Moses just as Christians are baptized (identified) into Christ. Wiersbe summarizes it nicely:

> Israel had been delivered from Egypt by the power of God,
> just as the Christian believer has been redeemed from sin (in
> 5:7-8, Paul has already related Passover to salvation). Israel was
> identified with Moses in their Red Sea "baptism," just as the
> Corinthians had been identified with Christ in their Christian
> baptism. (*Be Wise*, 91)

We See God's Provisions (10:3-4)

Paul now draws another analogy from Israel's experience in the wilderness, this one involving the Christian ordinance of the Lord's Supper or

Communion. The Hebrews "all ate the same spiritual food." They all ate the manna, "bread from heaven," that God provided (Exod 16). "And all drank the same spiritual drink" (Exod 17:1-7; Num 20:2-13). Here, Paul adds a very instructive word of commentary: "For they drank from the spiritual rock that followed them, and that rock was Christ" (v. 4). Paul uses the word "spiritual" three times in verses 3-4. Kistemaker is right: "The material substance of food, drink, and rock points to a spiritual source. Through his Spirit, God actively engages in providing for the basic needs of his people" (*Exposition*, 324). Who was the "who" not the "what" that gave them the water of life that sustained them? It was Christ! John MacArthur comments:

> The source of their spiritual drink was a spiritual rock which
> followed them; and the rock was Christ. Even at the time of
> the Exodus, the Messiah was with Israel providing for them!
> The Jews had a popular legend, still known and believed by
> many in Paul's day, that the actual rock that Moses struck
> followed Israel throughout her wilderness travels, providing
> water wherever they went. I believe the apostle may have been
> alluding to this legend, saying, "Yes, a rock did follow Israel
> in the wilderness. But it was not a physical rock that provided
> merely physical water. It was a spiritual rock, the Messiah (the
> Hebrew term for Christ) whom you have long awaited, who
> was with our fathers even then." (*1 Corinthians*, 220)

We See God's Wrath (10:5)

Jim Hamilton summarizes verses 1-5: "Paul's point is that no Corinthian claiming to be a Christian should think [partaking in] baptism and the Lord's Supper prevent God's wrath on idolatry and sexual immorality" (*Typology*, 279). How right he is. Israel had experienced the equivalence of Christian graces. They followed Moses, went through baptism, and enjoyed the sacramental blessings of food and drink. "Nevertheless God was not pleased with most of them, since they were struck down [NASB, "*their dead bodies* were spread out"] in the wilderness." God had blessed the Hebrews beyond measure. He delivered them, guided them daily, and met every need. How did they respond? With idolatry, sexual immorality, and grumbling (10:7-10). The result? Most died in the wilderness and never made it to the promised land (e.g., Num 14). Leon Morris says,

> *Most of them* is a masterly understatement. Of all the [adult]
> host of Israel only two men [Joshua and Caleb] entered
> Canaan; the rest perished in the wilderness . . . the wilderness
> [was] strewn with bodies. (*1 Corinthians*, 140)

Such a great beginning, but such a tragic ending! This gets to the heart
of Paul's concern for the Corinthians and Paul's concern for us. To
begin well is no guarantee one will finish well. We must not presume on
God's blessings. There are too many spiritual corpses all around us for
us to make that error.

Spiritual Blessings Do Not Insulate Us from Divine Judgment
1 CORINTHIANS 10:6-11

Paul's history lesson continues with specific examples drawn mostly
from the book of Numbers, which catalogues much of what happened
during the forty years Israel was in the wilderness. It is not a pretty picture. Further, Paul will cite events and sins that were relevant for the
Corinthians and the vexing issue of food sacrificed to idols, which he
began addressing in chapter 8. Flirtation with the world is the way of the
fool. These verses should leave no doubt of that truth.

God Punishes the Sin of Lust (10:6; cf. Num 11:18-34)

Verse 6 begins the record of five specific sins Israel committed in the wilderness, sins that the church too often gets cozy with. These historical
events are "examples for us, so that we will not desire [NIV, "[set] our
hearts on"] evil things as they did." Paul alludes to Numbers 11:18-34.
The Hebrews whined and complained about only having manna to eat.
They wanted (lusted for) meat and complained that they had it better
back in Egypt (11:5-6). Obviously, God's plan was not to their liking. God
responded to their discontent by giving them an abundance of quail
(11:31-34). The people greedily gathered them and gorged themselves
on the meat, only to have God punish them with a great plague for their
lust and lack of trust in him (cf. Ps 106:14). Indulging evil desires will
always lead to divine judgment. Don't fail to learn from history.

God Punishes the Sin of Idolatry (10:7; Exod 32)

Israel continually danced with idolatry in violation of the first and second commandments (Exod 20:3-4; Deut 5:7-8). They always paid a

heavy price when they did. Paul warns, "Don't become idolaters as some of them were; as it is written, The people sat down to eat and drink, and got up to party" (NIV, "indulge in revelry"). The verse is a quotation from Exodus 32:6 about worshiping a golden calf. Schreiner is right on target when he writes,

> It is no accident that Paul selects the verse which describes Israel committing idolatry while eating and drinking. The warning to the Corinthians is clear: they too will be guilty of idolatry if they eat and drink in an idol's temple. The words *indulge in revelry* in the citation, according to Paul, denote idolatry, and the Corinthians will be guilty of the same if they eat food offered to idols in temples. (*1 Corinthians*, 203)

The word translated "party" may also indicate sexual immorality. God would command the death of three thousand Hebrews who "instigated [their] idolatrous and immoral orgy at Sinai" (MacArthur, *1 Corinthians*, 222). The sin of idolatry always has a very high price tag.

God Punishes the Sin of Sexual Immorality (10:8; Num 25:1-9)

Paul urges the Corinthians not to "commit sexual immorality." He has already told them to "flee sexual immorality" in 6:18. How often it is that idolatry and sexual immorality are bedfellows. How seriously does God take this duo? Citing the story of Numbers 25:1-9, where Israel committed idolatry and sexual immorality with the women of Moab, Paul notes that God punished them "and in a single day twenty-three thousand people died." Numbers 25:9 reveals another thousand eventually died in connection with that incident. Indulging evil cravings and lust of the flesh (1 John 2:16) will not be ignored by God. Such sins always bring a bitter harvest.

God Punishes the Sin of Testing Him (10:9; cf. Num 21:4-9)

The fourth sin Paul raises is testing (or questioning) Christ. He admonishes the Corinthians to "not test Christ as some [Israelites] did and were destroyed by snakes." Yes, Israel tested Christ, who was there with them on multiple occasions (Exod 17:2-7; Deut 6:16). Paul's high Christology is present once again. Here Paul has in mind Numbers 21:4-9 where the people became impatient in their journey in the wilderness and spoke against both God and Moses. God punished them by sending "poisonous snakes" (ESV, "fiery serpents") that bit them. The result was "many

Israelites died" (Num 21:6). Once again, we see a food issue present.
Israel wanted to dine again in Egypt. The Corinthians wanted to dine
again in pagan temples. Both scenarios would dishonor God, ignore
what was best for others, and accommodate idols, pagan gods. In both
situations the people tested Christ (God!) and invited his swift and
severe discipline. Compromise is not the way of Christ. Faithfulness to
Christ means we will not consort with the world.

God Punishes the Sin of Grumbling (10:10; cf. Num 16:41-50)

Paul's fifth and final warning is against grumbling. He is direct and to
the point: "And don't grumble." The focal word means to murmur or
complain. Learn a lesson from history. It will be most instructive. The
Hebrews grumbled, at least "some of them did, and were killed by the
destroyer" (NIV, "the destroying angel"). It is not easy to know what Old
Testament passage Paul has in mind. The Hebrews, after all, grumbled
all the time! Schreiner notes,

> Israel grumbled about lack of food (Exod. 16:1-3, 7, 8) and
> water (Exod. 15:24; 17:7), about the difficulty of travelling in
> the wilderness (Num. 11:1), about the leadership of Aaron
> (Num. 16:11), about the death of Korah, Dathan, Abiram and
> their families (Num. 16:41) and especially about the Lord's
> promise that he would bring them into the land of promise
> (Num. 14:2, 27, 29, 36; Deut. 1:27; Ps. 106:24). (*1 Corinthians*, 205)

Numbers 16:41-50 is most likely in view. When Israel grumbled
about the leadership of Moses and Aaron, God killed 14,700 with a
plague. The destroying angel (not mentioned directly in Numbers) may
be the same angel of judgment who also struck the Egyptians by means
of a plague. If so, David Garland's insight is worth our careful reflection:

> If the destroying angel who killed the firstborn in Egypt
> (Exod. 12:23) is in view, it reveals a terrifying mystery
> that God's instrument to liberate the people can return,
> in boomerang fashion, to strike them dead for their
> disobedience. (*1 Corinthians*, 464)

Why does Paul mention grumbling? Perhaps it is because the
Corinthians continually complained about the prohibition against eating in pagan temples. Just as the Israelites complained about the leadership of Moses, the church at Corinth complained about the leadership

of Paul. But remember and learn from history. God gives us godly leaders for our good. Perhaps we should listen more and grumble less!

Spiritual Blessings Do Not Protect Us from Personal Temptations
1 CORINTHIANS 10:11-13

Paul does not want us to repeat the mistakes of the past. He wants us to learn from the examples of our ancestors and make better and wiser decisions. Lessons from the past are good, but having a strategy for the present provides a helpful companion. This is exactly what Paul provides in verses 11-13.

Remember Our Susceptibility to Evil (10:11-12)

Paul again reminds us that "[t]hese things [events in the Old Testament] happened to them as examples." Indeed, "they were written for our instruction." The Corinthians, then, should learn valuable lessons from the Hebrews, and so should we. However, there is something unique about our situation. Since the coming of Jesus Christ, a new age has dawned. We are among those "on whom the ends of the ages have come." The last days have been inaugurated with the first coming of Christ. But the consummation or climax awaits his return (Rev 19:11-21). Gardner writes, "This is the age toward which all history and all God's activities with his people have been leading" (*1 Corinthians*, 437). In that light we need to heed the warning of verse 12—"So, whoever thinks he stands must be careful not to fall." *The Message* has a colorful paraphrase: "Don't be so naïve and self-confident. You're not exempt. You could fall flat on your face as easily as anyone else." Pride is always a problem for the people of God. But a know-it-all posture is foolish and dangerous. Be careful. Watch out! God is the one who keeps you standing. You are incapable of doing that yourself. Taylor notes,

> In context, the meaning of "fall" is to die (10:8), which has already occurred in Corinth over abuses of the Lord's supper (11:27-30). "Falling" may also be synonymous with standing before God "unapproved" (9:27). Both certainly entail God's judgment. (*1 Corinthians*, 236–37)

So, remember Proverbs 16:18 (NIV): "Pride goes before destruction, a haughty spirit before a fall."

Remember God's Way of Escape (10:13)

Verse 12 contains a grave warning. Verse 13 contains a great promise. It is one of the most encouraging promises in the whole Bible. "No temptation has come upon you except what is common to humanity." Your temptations not to trust God are not new or unique. People everywhere and in every age have experienced the same things. But now the promise! "God is faithful." He is faithful in a precise way: "[H]e will not allow you to be tempted beyond what you are able." He places limits on how far the temptation can go. He will help you stand and not fall! How? "With the temptation he will also provide the way out [ESV, "way of escape"] so that you may be able to bear [ESV, "endure"] it." Leon Morris provides a beautiful illustration of this verse:

> The imagery is that of an army trapped in rugged country, which manages to escape from an impossible situation through a mountain pass. The assurance of this verse is a permanent comfort and strength to believers. Our trust is in the faithfulness of God. (*1 Corinthians*, 142)

He will not fail us. He never has. He never will.

Conclusion

God has given us more than history lessons to learn from. He has given us Jesus Christ to lean on. We resist temptation for Christ's glory and through his power. We avoid idolatry, sexual immorality, and grumbling by running to Jesus. The hymn "What a Friend We Have in Jesus" concludes these verses well by reminding us how Jesus is our faithful friend who provides us a way out of sin, a way through troubles, and the way into eternal life with him. In 1855 Joseph Scriven wrote,

> What a friend we have in Jesus,
> All our sins and griefs to bear!
> What a privilege to carry
> Everything to God in prayer!
>
> Oh, what peace we often forfeit,
> Oh, what needless pain we bear,
> All because we do not carry
> Everything to God in prayer!

Have we trials and temptations?
Is there trouble anywhere?
We should never be discouraged;
Take it to the Lord in prayer.

Can we find a friend so faithful
Who will all our sorrows share?
Jesus knows our every weakness,
Take it to the Lord in prayer.

Reflect and Discuss

1. How do we effectively use the Old Testament stories as examples to learn from without being legalistic? How does drawing a connection to Christ help avoid legalism?
2. What is another Old Testament example of God's guidance, deliverance, provision, and/or wrath? How can that story function as an example for Christians today? Does that story have a type of Christ like the exodus narrative?
3. Why is participation in Christian graces (e.g., baptism, the Lord's Supper) not a substitute for trusting in saving grace? What are some ways that Christians can subtly lean more on these acts rather than God's grace?
4. How does the New Testament's teaching about punishment compare to the Old Testament's? What are some similarities and differences?
5. Why must God punish sin severely?
6. Sin has such severe consequences, so why do Christians choose to sin? How can Christians better remember the consequences of sin to guard themselves from believing its lies?
7. Why is grumbling such a severe sin that it appears in Paul's list?
8. How can confessing temptations help Christians to support one another and avoid falling into sin?
9. Does not being tempted "beyond what [one is] able" (v. 13) have to do with someone's personal strength or God's ability to help? Explain. How might Christians escape temptation when it comes?
10. Are you ever surprised that you must regularly fight temptations to sin? How can verse 13 encourage you as you bear temptations until Jesus returns?

Don't Dine with Demons

1 CORINTHIANS 10:14-22

Main Idea: Avoid idolatry and practices that bring you near idols, knowing that demonic activity promotes them.

I. **Communion with the Lord Is Essential (10:14-17).**
    A. We are to flee idolatry (10:14-15).
    B. We are to fellowship with our Savior (10:16-17).
    C. The cup emphasizes our communion (10:16).
    D. The bread emphasizes our union (10:17).
II. **Association with Demons Is Evil (10:18-22).**
    A. It distorts our worship (10:18-20).
    B. It compromises our loyalty (10:21).
    C. It provokes our God (10:22).

C. S. Lewis (1898–1963) was a British scholar who taught at both Cambridge and Oxford. He was one of the finest Christian thinkers of the twentieth century, writing classics such as *The Chronicles of Narnia*, *Mere Christianity*, *The Problem of Pain*, and *The Screwtape Letters*. That last one is a fictional conversation between an older, wiser demon named Screwtape and his young apprentice named Wormwood. In the preface to this imaginary correspondence Lewis sounds a warning for all who have ears to hear:

> There are two equal and opposite errors into which our
> race can fall about the devils. One is to disbelieve in their
> existence. The other is to believe, and to feel an excessive
> and unhealthy interest in them. They themselves are equally
> pleased by both errors, and hail a materialist or magician with
> the same delight. (*Screwtape Letters*, xi)

Lewis is right, and his counsel is extremely valuable. But at Corinth in AD 55, the Corinthians had an issue with demons that did not fall into either of these categories. They believed in demons, but they failed to understand how dangerous and seductive they are. When it came to eating food sacrificed to an idol in a pagan temple, for instance, they did not realize they were dining with demons there! Paul knew if one dances with the devil, he or she should not be surprised to get burned. Just as we must "flee sexual immorality" (6:18), we must also "flee from idolatry" (10:14). These two sins are like twins. They often go around together. Therefore, we must always be on guard against both.

Communion with the Lord Is Essential
1 CORINTHIANS 10:14-17

Paul will address at some length Communion, the Lord's Supper, in 11:17-34. However, he will address it briefly in these verses, too, drawing a contrast between dining at the Lord's table and dining at the tables of demons. There are similarities and differences we must recognize and understand. The consequences of how we respond are massive.

We Are to Flee Idolatry (10:14-15)

Paul speaks tenderly but directly. "So then" draws attention to the importance of the verse and connects it to the previous paragraph, especially verse 13. The address "Dear friends" (ESV, "beloved") communicates his affection and love for the church. God will provide for them a way of escape from the danger of idolatry. His "way out" (v. 13) is this: "Flee from idolatry!" The warning is a present imperative, a word of command calling for continuous vigilance and attention. Keep fleeing. Keep running away from idolatry. Paul adds to his command, saying, "I am speaking as to sensible people" (v. 15). In other words Paul's words make sense if the Corinthians will reflect on them. He adds, "Judge for yourselves what I am saying." If you run from idolatry, it will be hard for it to catch you. Stay away from it, and the temptation to give in to it will not present itself. If you are not at the wrong place at the wrong time with the wrong people, the wrong thing will not happen. That is good common sense and a word of wisdom we should all listen to.

We Are to Fellowship with the Savior (10:16-17)

Paul informs us that there is a table of communion to which we should draw near. There is a right place, a right time, and a right people with whom we should regularly fellowship. At the Lord's Supper we draw close to Christ in participation with our spiritual family. This too is a way to flee idolatry and the worship of false gods.

The Cup Emphasizes Our Communion (10:16)

Paul writes, "The cup of blessing that we bless, is it not a sharing (ESV, "participation") in the blood of Christ? The bread that we break, is it not a sharing in the body of Christ?" Tom Schreiner comments: "At the Supper a believer's relationship and communion with Christ are deepened, and the solidarity between believers and Christ is attested" (*1 Corinthians*, 210). Religious meals are more than taking in physical nourishment. They have great spiritual value and significance. At Communion we draw near to our God as a community, a family of faith. We seek his presence and pledge our allegiance and devotion to our Lord. This is no mere ritual we thoughtlessly perform. We reflect on the love of the Lord Jesus demonstrated by his broken body and shed blood on Calvary's cross. We recall his perfect atoning sacrifice that bore the full penalty and paid the full debt of all our sins. The Lord's Supper reminds us of the truth stated in Robert Lowry's hymn: "What can wash away my sins? Nothing but the blood of Jesus."

The Bread Emphasizes Our Union (10:17)

Verse 17 anticipates Paul's discussion of spiritual gifts in chapter 12 and the one/many analogy with the human body and the body of Christ. The repetition of the word "one," which occurs three times, is the key to unlocking this verse. Consider, Paul writes, what is being communicated when we observe Communion: "Because there is one bread," not many, "we who are many are one body, since all of us share the one bread." There is a breathtaking beauty to this verse. The body of Christ is one! We are fed by one source, the Lord Jesus Christ. We share a common bond and unity as one body even though we have different cultural, economic, social, and ethnic backgrounds. In Christ we are one family, which is beautifully testified to by the meal of Communion shared at the Lord's Table. John MacArthur summarizes the truth of this verse so well:

> Christ's body also symbolizes our unity in Jesus Christ. . . .
> Because we are one with Christ, we are one with each other.
> As we come into fellowship with Christ through Communion,
> we come into fellowship with each other in a unique and deep
> way (cf. 1 Cor. 6:17). All believers stand on the same ground
> at the foot of the cross as forgiven sinners who possess the
> eternal life principle within them. (*1 Corinthians*, 239)

Association with Demons Is Evil
1 CORINTHIANS 10:18-22

Paul will now deliver his knockout punch concerning the foolishness of going to an idol's temple and eating food offered to an idol. Participants essentially end up eating dinner with demons! They also wind up "provoking [our God] to jealousy" (v. 22), which only compounds the foolishness of flirting with the world and its gods. Paul provides three reasons why knowingly eating food sacrificed to idols is foolish and why we should heed his counsel to flee idolatry.

It Distorts Our Worship (10:18-20)

Once again Paul appeals to the history of the Hebrews. He calls us to "[c]onsider [NASB, "Look at"] the people of Israel." He then raises a rhetorical question: "Do not those who eat the sacrifices participate in the altar?" Given the context, Paul is likely referencing Israel's sinful behavior in the wilderness where they were guilty of gross idolatry and sexual immorality. Mark Taylor writes,

> When the Israelites partook of idolatrous sacrifices, they participated in the altar and what the altar represented. Those who ate the food of the sacrifice entered into a partnership with all that the altar stood for. (*1 Corinthians*, 242)

That is, they fellowshipped and dined with false gods and the demons lurking behind them. Paul raises a second and a third question for us to consider. The second is, "What am I saying?" The ESV says, "What do I imply then?" The idea is "What do I mean by writing these words?" The third question asks, "That food sacrificed to idols is anything, or that an idol is anything?" He then follows with a devastating and eye-opening truth: "No, but I do say [ESV, "imply"] that what they sacrifice, they sacrifice to demons and not to God." Then follows his prophetic and pastoral concern: "I do not want you to be participants with demons!" Wow, what a thing to say! Let's unpack this.

Verses 20-21 are the only time Paul mentions demons in 1 Corinthians. Apparently, he assumes the Corinthian Christians know what he is talking about. Since I am not convinced we should make that assumption of most in the twenty-first-century secular and biblically illiterate West, let me provide a quick outline summary of demonology.

Who Are Demons? (Four Possibilities)

1. The spirits of a pre-Adamic (though merely theoretical) evil race.
2. The spirits of evil men.
3. The product of angels cohabitating with women in Genesis 6:1-4. (Note, however, that the identity of "the sons of God" is open to multiple interpretations.)
4. Fallen angels.

The fourth answer is most likely correct and is the one the church has affirmed throughout its history.

What Are Some Basic Biblical Facts about Demons?

- Possibly one-third of the angels fell with Satan (Rev 12:4).
- Some demons are free to roam now (Mark 1:21-34).
- Some demons will be free to roam during the great tribulation (Rev 9:13-19).
- Some demons are confined now, never to roam the earth again (2 Pet 2:4; Jude 6).
- Demons are powerful but not omnipotent (Mark 1:24). Only God is omnipotent.
- Their activity may have increased during the time of Christ, and it may also increase again at the end of the age before Christ returns (see Rev 6–19).
- They are set up under Satan's control (Eph 6:11-12), probably in rank, possibly in geography (Dan 10:12-14).
- They have authority and can promote disunity, false doctrine, and false worship, cause mental difficulties, and hinder Christian growth.
- Demons can oppress but not possess believers.
- Demons use idolatry to further false worship of false gods.

So, demons are real (Jesus certainly agreed!), and they like to use idols for their nefarious work of promoting false worship. They have unbelievers in their clutches, but they present an ever-present danger to believers in Jesus as well. When we choose to dine with demons, "we get entangled in their power. We submit to them. We become vulnerable to them. We enter into some kind of fellowship. We affirm them in some way and give them leeway in our lives" (Piper, "Idolatry").

It Compromises Our Loyalty (10:21)

Paul draws an irrefutable conclusion in verse 21 from his argument in verses 18-20: "You cannot drink the cup of the Lord and the cup of demons. You cannot share in the Lord's table and the table of demons." *The Message* says, "You can't have it both ways, banqueting with the Master one day and slumming with demons the next." So, who will feed and nourish our souls? Christ or demons? Who will provide our spiritual sustenance? Christ or demons? Whom will we dance and dine with? Christ or demons? We cannot do both! We cannot have it both ways! Gordon Fee provides food for thought on this verse:

> Those who eat at the Lord's Table, proclaiming his death until
> he comes (11:26), are thereby also bound to one another
> through the death of the Lord that is thus celebrated. So also
> with pagans. Theirs is a sacred "fellowship" in honor of demons.
> Those who are bound to one another through Christ cannot
> also become "fellows" (= be in partnership) with those whose
> meals are consecrated to demons. (*Corinthians*, 2014, 522)

In 1 Kings 18:21 Elijah asked the people, "How long will you waver between two opinions? If the LORD is God, follow him. But if Baal, follow him." Paul essentially calls the Corinthians to make the same decision. He calls on us to decide as well.

It Provokes God (10:22)

Paul concludes this section with a powerful word of warning through two rhetorical questions. First he asks, "Or are we provoking the Lord to jealousy?" Second, "Are we stronger than he?" The second of the Ten Commandments may be in view here. There Moses writes,

> *Do not make an idol for yourself, whether in the shape of anything*
> *in the heavens above or on the earth below or in the waters under the*
> *earth. Do not bow in worship to them, and do not serve them; for I, the*
> *LORD your God, am a jealous God.* (Exod 20:4-5)

C. K. Barrett asks,

> Do we suppose that we (even though we regard ourselves as
> "the strong"—cf. viii. 7, 10) can play fast and loose with our

> loyalty to [God] (as some in Corinth were disposed to do),
> and get away with it? . . . God is not mocked. (*First Epistle*, 238)

God's position on idolatry has a long history, and he has not changed his mind. Provoking Christ to jealousy is clearly the way of the fool, not the wise, no matter what one says. "Are we stronger than he?" Does not the history of the Old Testament and our Lord's empty tomb teach us anything? We are ants before an elephant in comparison to our God. Warren Wiersbe captures what Paul wants us to understand in this final question:

> "Are we stronger than he?" (1 Cor. 10:22) is directed at the
> strong Christian who was sure he could enjoy his liberty in
> the pagan temple and not be harmed. "You may be stronger
> than your weaker brother," Paul intimated, "but you are not
> stronger than God!" It is dangerous to play with sin and tempt
> God. (*Be Wise*, 94)

Conclusion

The wonderful theologian, pastor, and author A. W. Tozer (1897–1963) wisely said,

> Christianity at any given time is strong or weak depending
> upon her concept of God. And I insist upon this, and I have
> said it many times, that the basic trouble with the church today
> is her unworthy conception of God. . . . Our religion is little
> because our god is little. (*Attributes of God*, 41)

Tozer is right. Think little of God and you will think that dining with demons and dancing with idols is no big deal. What fools that makes us! What dishonor we bring to the one whose body was broken and whose blood was shed for sinners like you and me. No demon or idol died for you. Why would you even go near one's place of worship?

Reflect and Discuss

1. Instead of fleeing idolatry, how do Christians sometimes treat idolatry and sin?
2. What divisions or issues could be solved if Christians would remember that they share one bread and one cup in the Lord's Supper?
3. In what areas can Western Christians apply Paul's teaching to avoid food sacrificed to idols?

4. Would you describe yourself as someone who generally does not think about spiritual warfare and demons or someone who regularly thinks about them? Explain your answer.

5. Why do Western Christians often dismiss or ignore the presence of demonic work?

6. Why is it dangerous to ignore spiritual warfare and the reality of demons?

7. How is demonic activity portrayed in movies and pop culture? How do these images contrast with the biblical portrait of demonic work?

8. This chapter teaches that demons want to further false worship. How does this goal demonstrate the true danger they pose?

9. Although Christians should be fighting against demonic work and false worship, Christians do not need to be afraid of demons. Why?

10. Have you seen evidence that Tozer's comment that "our religion is little because our god is little" is true in American church culture? If yes, how so? How have you seen it to be true at times in your life?

My One Ambition: Glorifying God

1 CORINTHIANS 10:23–11:1

Main Idea: Glorify God by doing whatever you can to serve others and bring them to salvation.

I.   I Will Always Pursue What Is Helpful and Builds Up (10:23).
II. I Will Always Pursue What Is Good for Others (10:24).
III. I Will Always Pursue What Is in the Best Interest of Another's Conscience (10:25-29).
IV. I Will Always Pursue a Thankful Heart (10:29-30).
V. I Will Always Pursue the Glory of God in All Things (10:31).
VI. I Will Always Pursue What Is Best for the Salvation of Others (10:32-33).
VII. I Will Always Pursue the Principles of WWPD and WWJD (11:1).

Who am I? Why am I here? These fall under the heading of "life's ultimate questions." And they are good questions. We all ask them. More productive, however, would be to put them in a biblical context. For a believer, the questions then become, "Why did God create me?" "Why did God save me through the Lord Jesus?" Interestingly, the answer to both of those is the same. God created us and saved us so that we may glorify him every day and in every way throughout our lives (1 Cor 10:31; cf. Rom 11:36).

This text concludes the conversation about food sacrificed to idols begun in chapter 8. In the process of dealing with this situation, Paul will put forward seven principles to help us navigate difficult issues the Bible does not directly address. There is some repetition with what we have seen in 1 Corinthians 6:12–10:22. But repetition is a very good teacher. We often need to hear truths repeated before they sink in. Glorifying God may be a lofty theological concept, but it is also extremely practical, affecting every area of our lives. In motive and action the glory of God must be preeminent for the believer. Bringing him glory is essential to the mission of the church. His glory should be our one ambition.

I Will Always Pursue What Is Helpful and Builds Up
1 CORINTHIANS 10:23

The Corinthians said, "Everything is permissible" (cf. 6:12), but this slogan reveals a misunderstanding of grace and the Christian life. We now live "under the law of Christ" (9:21), a law that focuses on loving others. Thus, we are not free to do anything we want. We must live in a way that advances the gospel among the nations. The proper perspective is to remember that "not everything is beneficial" as 6:12 says, or "not everything builds up" (NIV, "is constructive") as 10:23 does. In 6:12 the context is sexual immorality; here it is spiritual idolatry. Sexual immorality and spiritual idolatry are often together in the Bible. Should a believer be tempted to compromise with either, two questions should be asked: "Will my actions be helpful to others? Will my actions build others up?" Vaughn is right: "Liberty should be limited by consideration for the well-being of others" (*1 Corinthians*, 106). The edification of fellow believers must always be a major guideline for our words and actions. Oswald Chambers says, "The stamp of the saint is that he can waive his own rights and obey the Lord Jesus" ("Unblameable Attitude").

I Will Always Pursue What Is Good for Others
1 CORINTHIANS 10:24

Schreiner notes, "Verse 24 sharpens the point of verse 23" (*1 Corinthians*, 214). Paul writes, "No one is to seek his own good, but the good of the other person" (ESV, "his neighbor"). This principle appears several times in the New Testament. In Romans 15:2-3 Paul writes, "Each one of us is to please his neighbor for his good, to build him up. For even Christ did not please himself." In 1 Corinthians 13:5 we read that love "is not self-seeking" (cf. Phil 2:3-4). Christians are never to act in ways that harm and hurt others. Rather, we are to help them grow in Christlikeness and build them up in their faith. Glorifying God in relation to others means we seek to do the right thing, the right way, at the right time, and for the right reason. An evangelistic, Great Commission focus should inform everything that we do.

I Will Always Pursue What Is in the Best Interest of Another's Conscience
1 CORINTHIANS 10:25-29

One final time, Paul will address the vexing issue of food sacrificed to idols. He lays down a basic principle, grounding it in the Word of God: "Eat everything that is sold in the meat market, without raising questions for the sake of conscience" (v. 25). In modern language we could say, when you go to the grocery store to buy steaks, buy what you want without making an issue about where the meat came from. Do this as a matter of conscience for yourself and others. After all, "the earth is the Lord's, and all that is in it" (v. 26; cf. Ps 24:1). Beale and Carson note, "Paul is thoroughly Jewish and biblical in his understanding that creation is good and that the food we receive has been provided for us by God and should be received with thanksgiving" (*Commentary*, 730). The meat you eat is a part of God's good creation and God's provision for your nourishment. Eat it. Enjoy it! No need to ask any questions about it.

Different circumstances, however, may require a different response. "If any of the unbelievers invites you over and you want to go, eat everything that is set before you, without raising questions for the sake of conscience" (v. 27). That means if an unbeliever invites you to his or her home for a meal, pray about it, give the invitation consideration, and decide if you will accept the invite. If you choose to go, recognize it as an opportunity to share the gospel and be a witness for Jesus. When the meal is served, have at it. No need to ask questions. However—and this is a big however—"if someone says to you, 'This is food from a sacrifice,' do not eat it, out of consideration of the one who told you, and for the sake of conscience. [Paul does] not mean your conscience, but the other person's" (vv. 28-29a). These verses address a specific situation that can potentially arise when a Christ-follower goes to the home of an unbeliever for missions and evangelism. Godly wisdom is essential. We do not want to offend anyone unnecessarily. But we cannot send mixed signals and foster confusion for unbelievers and believers alike. Blomberg is concise and to the point: "In this situation, one might decide to refrain so as to not risk leading the other person into sin or confusing his or her conscience" (*1 Corinthians*, 203). Morris adds,

> The strong Christian knows that offering meat to an idol
> cannot really alter its character, for the idol is nothing; his

conscience is clear. But a pagan observer thinks the idol is a god, and thus sees the Christian who [knowingly] eats the meat as sanctioning his idolatry. A weak Christian observer will be in danger of being harmed in the way noted earlier (8:10-13). Whatever the status of the informer, then, the wise and kindly course for the strong Christian is to abstain from eating. (*1 Corinthians*, 147)

For the sake of evangelizing the lost and edifying a fellow believer, no uncertain sound should be trumpeted. The gospel is at stake, and your witness is on the line. The spiritual well-being of others takes precedence. On this occasion, a vegetarian meal will be just fine.

I Will Always Pursue a Thankful Heart
1 CORINTHIANS 10:29-30

Paul picks back up with his main argument in verse 26. "The earth is the Lord's, and all that is in it." Therefore, "why is my freedom judged by another person's conscience?" Paul's point is this: we should not be paranoid and overly concerned about what others think. We can "partake with thanksgiving," not asking unnecessary questions or making a big deal about something we don't need to raise. We should be thankful for God's gracious provisions of drink and nourishment. It all belongs to him and comes from him. We know that. Why make an issue of something when there is no issue and draw criticism over "something for which [we] give thanks?" Doing so would be foolish, silly, and unprofitable for everyone. We must each choose to pursue a thankful heart and place no unnecessary stumbling blocks before anyone. Sometimes the wise and godly thing to do is remain silent rather than raise questions.

I Will Always Pursue the Glory of God in All Things
1 CORINTHIANS 10:31

First Corinthians 10:31 is a verse every Christian should memorize. It has been one of my life verses. I believe Paul intended it to be a foundational pillar in our lives that offers direction 24/7. It is comprehensive and all-encompassing in nature. It says, "So, whether you eat or drink, or whatever you do, do everything for the glory of God." Isaiah 43:7 teaches that God created us for his glory. Paul would add that he saved us for his glory, too. God, not man, then, is to be at the center of all things. Moreover, nothing is outside of the command to glorify God in all things. The question we must answer is, "What does it mean to bring God glory?" In its simplest expression, it means to make much of God in all things, to magnify and show his unsurpassing worthiness in all we do. John Piper has famously said, "God is most glorified in us when we are most satisfied in him" (*Don't Waste Your Life*, 46). He also says glorifying God means we love him, trust him, are thankful to him, obey him, enjoy him, and take pleasure in him. In other words, "when he created us for his glory, he also created us for our joy . . . the way he seeks to be glorified in us is by making us satisfied in him" ("Joyful Duty"). Paul shows in this section several ways we glorify God:

- We do what is beneficial or helpful to others (10:23).
- We do what builds others up (10:23).
- We seek what is good for others (10:24).
- We acknowledge all of creation is God's good gift to us (10:26).
- We care well for the consciences of others (10:29).
- We put no unnecessary stumbling blocks in the path of Jews, Greeks, or the Lord's church when it comes to the gospel and the salvation of others (10:32-33).
- We always put the well-being of others ahead of our own (10:33).
- We find and follow worthy and godly role models (11:1).
- We seek to be like Jesus (11:1).

There are lots of ways to glorify God mentioned in these verses alone! Maybe that is why C. S. Lewis wrote, "A man can no more diminish God's glory by refusing to worship Him than a lunatic can put out the sun by scribbling the word 'darkness' on the walls of his cell" (*Problem of Pain*, 46). Bringing glory to God should be our one ambition in all we do. "Will this glorify God?" should always be the question in our minds, its answer ultimately influencing even the words that pass through our lips.

I Will Always Pursue What Is Best for the Salvation of Others

1 Corinthians 10:32-33

These are what I call soul-winner verses (cf. 9:19-22). My friend James Merritt, co-author of this book, says believers' number one desire for everyone on this planet is stated in the last five words of verse 33: "that they may be saved." Because the winning of souls to the Savior is a priority in our lives, we will "give no offense [NIV, "not cause anyone to stumble"] to Jews or Greeks or the church of God" (v. 32). Paul says that he does not want to be a stumbling block to an unbeliever coming to Jesus or a stumbling block to a believer living for Jesus. Rather, as verse 33 affirms, "[He tries] to please everyone in everything, not seeking [his] own benefit [ESV, "advantage," NIV, "own good"], but the benefit of many, so that they may be saved." Others may be offended when we share the gospel, but they should never be offended by how we live out the gospel. Their souls and eternal destinies matter more than any right, privilege, or desire you or I may have. Paul's phrase "I . . . try to please everyone" could be wrongly understood and misapplied if we rip it out of its context. Warren Wiersbe clarifies that Paul . . .

> was not suggesting that he was a compromiser or man-pleaser (Gal. 1:10). He was affirming the fact that his life and ministry was centered on helping others rather than on promoting himself and his own desires. (*Be Wise*, 96)

We must consistently prize the spiritual welfare of others above any personal preferences we have. The eternal destinies of men, women, and children hang in the balance.

I Will Always Pursue the Principles of WWPD and WWJD
1 CORINTHIANS 11:1

The acronyms WWPD and WWJD stand for "What would Paul do?" and "What would Jesus do?" If 1 Corinthians 10:31 is one of those verses every Christian should memorize, then 1 Corinthians 11:1 is its close companion. In fact, the verse fits better with the end of chapter 10 than the beginning of chapter 11. It is, I think, an unfortunate chapter division (remember, verse and chapter divisions were not a part of the original texts). Regardless, a cursory read of it makes Paul sound puffed up and arrogant, but only if we fail to read all the verses around it! Once more, then, we are reminded of the importance of reading a text within context.

Paul begins with a clear and simple command that literally reads, "Imitators of me become." The word "imitate" reflects the Greek word *mimetai*, from which we get our word "mimic." Paul calls us to become like him, to follow his example in the same way he has imitated and followed Christ (cf. 4:16). Gordon Fee is right: "The emphasis here is certainly on the example of Christ, which for Paul finds its primary focus in his sacrifice on the cross" (*Corinthians*, 2014, 540). In other words, sacrificial service for the benefit and blessings of others is at the heart of what it means to imitate our Lord. We all need role models, examples we can follow and imitate. For the Christian the ultimate example is Christ. To glorify God by being like Jesus should be our consuming passion that helps fuel our ambition. But we need flesh-and-blood role models, too. Paul knew he could provide that for the Corinthians. But who is providing that for you? Are you providing that for anyone else? How often do you consider the questions, "What would Paul do?" and "What would Jesus do?"

Several years ago I was listening to an address by the brilliant and famous British scholar N. T. Wright. As he addressed the issue of Christian ethics, he noted that several of his British friends had poked fun at and dismissed the silly, shallow American phenomena of the WWJD (What Would Jesus Do?) bracelet. However, he then pointed out that several of his children were in their teenage years. In light of that, he said, he did not find the WWJD idea to be a silly and shallow consideration at all. In fact, he said, he rather hoped his children would adopt such an ethic in this postmodern, anything and everything goes culture of the West (Wright, *A Lenten Devotional*, 22, 29). I agree with N. T. Wright 100 percent here. I would only add that it is essential to know what Jesus said and did if asking WWJD is going to have any benefit. In other words, the gospel-centered, Christ-centered mind requires immersion in Scripture and calls for the heart of a servant, even a slave. To live like Jesus, you must know Jesus. To live like Jesus, you must love Jesus. So, let me ask a question we all must answer. If others were to follow your example and imitate you, would they in some real and genuine sense be imitating Jesus? Or, to put it another way, can your children follow in your footsteps and in the process be walking in the footsteps of Jesus?

Conclusion

One of the most famous statements in church history, which is often taught to young children to help them understand our relationship to God, is located in the Westminster Shorter Catechism. It raises this question: "What is the chief end of man?" And it answers, "Man's chief end is to glorify God and enjoy him forever." This is the theme of 1 Corinthians 10:23–11:1. This is the theme for the Christian life. This is the theme of the Bible. May it be the theme that captures your life and mine, reflecting our shared and holy ambition. Nothing could be greater.

Reflect and Discuss

1. What biblical principles can Christians apply to issues the Bible does not directly address? What principles in these passages about food sacrificed to idols have you learned to apply better?
2. How does Paul's understanding of God's rule (v. 26) shape how he lives?
3. Why is a lack of love for Jesus a core reason someone will not seek the good of others?
4. Why is it wrong to fail to seek the good of others by ignoring or avoiding them?
5. When should Christians be concerned about the opinions of others? When should they not be?
6. Have you learned anything new about verse 31 as a result of studying it in the context of the passage?
7. What does it mean that "God is most glorified in us when we are most satisfied in him"?
8. In what way do we glorify God by seeking the good of others and caring for the consciences of others?
9. Are there things you should change in order to better seek the benefit of others so that they might be saved? Explain.
10. If others follow your example and imitate you, will they also be imitating Jesus? Why or why not?

Seven Principles for Worship That Pleases God

1 CORINTHIANS 11:2-16

Main Idea: God's instructions, not past experiences, must govern Christian worship if it is to be pleasing to him.

I. **We Must Honor the Principle of Divinely Ordained Authority (11:2-3).**

II. **We Must Honor the Principle of Proper Social Expectations (11:4-6).**

III. **We Must Honor the Principles of Glory, Creation, and Purpose (11:7-9).**

IV. **We Must Honor the Principles of Angelic Observation and Submission (11:10).**

V. **We Must Honor the Principle of Interdependency (11:11-12).**

VI. **We Must Honor the Principle of Nature (11:13-15).**

VII. **We Must Honor the Principle of Common Practice (11:16).**

I am an unapologetic complementarian when it comes to gender and gender roles in the church and the home. I believe "The Danvers Statement on Biblical Manhood and Womanhood" (1987) and "The Nashville Statement on Human Sexuality and Gender Roles" (2017) faithfully reflect biblical and theological truth. Among their affirmations and denials, we find the following statements, which are relevant to 1 Corinthians 11:2-16.

- Both Adam and Eve were created in God's image, equal before God as persons and distinct in their manhood and womanhood ("Danvers").
- Distinctions in masculine and feminine roles are ordained by God as part of the created order ("Danvers").
- WE AFFIRM that divinely ordained differences between male and female reflect God's original creation design and are meant for human good and human flourishing. WE DENY that such differences are a result of the Fall or are a tragedy to be overcome ("Nashville," article 4).

- The Old Testament, as well as the New Testament, manifests the equally high value and dignity which God attached to the roles of both men and women (Gen. 1:26-27; 2:18; Gal. 3:28). Both Old and New Testaments also affirm the principle of male headship in the family and in the covenant community (Gen. 2:18; Eph. 5:21-33; Col. 3:18-19; 1 Tim. 2:11-15) ("Danvers").
- Redemption in Christ aims at removing the distortions introduced by the curse.
- In the family, husbands should forsake harsh or selfish leadership and grow in love and care for their wives; wives should forsake resistance to their husbands' authority and grow in willing, joyful submission to their husbands' leadership (Eph. 5:21-33; Col. 3:18-19; Tit. 2:3-5; 1 Pet. 3:1-7) ("Danvers").
- In the church, redemption in Christ gives men and women an equal share in the blessings of salvation; nevertheless, some governing and teaching roles within the church are restricted to men (Gal. 3:28; 1 Cor. 11:2-16; 1 Tim. 2:11-15). ("Danvers").
- WE AFFIRM our duty to speak the truth in love at all times [Eph. 4:15], including when we speak to or about one another as male or female. WE DENY any obligation to speak in such ways that dishonor God's design of his image-bearers as male and female ("Nashville," article 11).

Such statements sound countercultural (and they are!) in a society awash in so much confusion about gender and sexuality. When we have a Supreme Court justice who cannot define the word "woman," we have a serious issue in our culture. And we should not think the church is immune to such confusion. This problem existed in the first-century church, and it is also making inroads in the twenty-first-century church. Paul tells us that "God is not a God of disorder but of peace" (1 Cor 14:33) and that in his church "everything is to be done decently and in order" (1 Cor 14:40). Such principles are not intended to stifle excitement, exuberance, or spontaneity in worship. They are, however, intended to provide divinely ordained parameters and patterns that will build up the body (1 Cor 14:26) and provide a positive witness to unbelievers who attend our services (1 Cor 14:23-25). First Corinthians 11:2-16 beautifully complements these principles as it provides a Trinitarian lesson for the proper roles of men and women in corporate worship. Seven principles are set forth for our instruction.

We Must Honor the Principle of Divinely Ordained Authority
1 CORINTHIANS 11:2-3

Paul will need to say some tough things in these verses, so he begins with a word of affirmation: "Now I praise [ESV, "commend"] you because you remember me in everything and hold fast to the traditions just as I delivered them to you" (v. 2). Thus Paul begins tactfully, wanting to establish goodwill as he addresses headship and proper decorum in worship, areas in which the Corinthians were deficient. The traditions that the church held fast are not specified, but they probably included "the basic facts of the gospel, plus some training in conduct" (Vaughn and Lea, *1 Corinthians*, 111). Further, as Taylor notes, "The traditions were not Paul's own but rather those handed down to him (11:23; 15:1-3)" (*1 Corinthians*, 257). The basics of the gospel were not Paul's creation. He passed on, as we must, the good news he had received. Paul then, in verse 3, lays down the basic theological truth that will serve as the foundation for the remainder of this section: "But I want you to know that Christ is the head of every man, and the man is the head of the woman [ESV, "the head of a wife is her husband"; CSB marginal reading is similar], and God is the head of Christ."

Immediately we are struck by the repetition of the word "head" here. It appears nine times in the Greek New Testament in this text. Sometimes it refers to a person's literal head (vv. 4a,5a,7,10). However, at other times, the word is used symbolically of having authority over another. Schreiner writes, "[T]he notion of authority is the most likely contextually. . . . The most important evidence here is the parallel in Ephesians 5:23" (*1 Corinthians*, 222). Because of what we read in the context of this text, "wife" and "husband" are the more likely meanings and better translation. The issue of male headship is taught to apply to the home and church, yet Scripture nowhere teaches male headship in general with application to the whole of society. And the issue is one of function, not essence. It is an issue of assignment, not nature. We know this because men and women, husbands and wives, equally bear the image of God. They are equal in essence and essential being. Further, and more importantly, Christ the Son is equal in essence and essential being to God the Father. This is classic and biblical Trinitarianism.

Now, there is one caveat. Christ, as Son of God, is essentially superior to man (husbands) as well as superior in spiritual authority over him. That truth is also taught throughout the whole of inerrant and infallible Scripture. So, to summarize our foundation verse by way of paraphrase, this is what Paul is saying: We must understand that the spiritual authority over every man is Christ, the spiritual authority for a wife is her husband (or a father for an unmarried daughter), and the spiritual authority of Christ (God the Son) is God (the Father). There is no inferiority in submitting to one's divinely ordained head. It is for humanity's good and the glory of the triune God.

We Must Honor the Principle of Proper Social Expectation
1 CORINTHIANS 11:4-6

These verses address the specific topic that demands Paul's attention: proper adornment in public worship. In an honor-shame culture, this matter would be extremely important. Though most commentators argue the issue is whether one should wear a hat (men) or a veil (women), and the text could certainly be applied to cultures where such is an issue, I am persuaded by the argument of my friend Chuck Quarles that the issue is different and more acute. I will quote him at some length to get the proper context:

> Paul's construction does not refer explicitly to an article of clothing. The only time he mentions a "head covering" is in vs. 15 in the statement that God has given a woman long hair "instead of" or "in place of" a head covering. When this statement is combined with the numerous references to hair length and shortness in vv. 5, 6, 14, and 15, it appears that the issue is the length of the hair of men versus women, not the wearing of an article of clothing though Paul's rationale could apply by extension to that (i.e., if an article of clothing is worn on the head in worship, this should be reserved for women exclusively). "Having down the head" refers to hair hanging down the back of the head. Paul says that men should not have long hair covering their head, but women should have long hair covering their head in worship. Paul addresses the hair length of both men and women. It appears that not only were women adopting the very short hair length that was characteristic of men, but men were also adopting the significantly longer hair length that was characteristic of women. . . .

The Corinthians consistently blended together elements of the Christian faith with practices from their pagan past. Some members of the church continued to participate in the idol feasts of the pagan temple (1 Cor. 10:7, 14-22; 2 Cor. 6:14-18). Some were turning the Lord's Supper into the kind of drunken and gluttonous feast they had celebrated in pagan temples. Some misunderstood prophecy and tongues as ecstatic utterances like those practiced in the pagan temples. Confused interpretation influenced by their pagan background likely influenced the practice addressed in 1 Corinthians 11 as well.

One of the most prominent religions in Corinth was the worship of Dionysius. In Greek mythology, Dionysius was conceived through Zeus's union with the human woman Semele. In one account, Dionysius was a male god who had been raised as a girl in order to protect him from Hera, Zeus's wife, who was determined to kill him. Dionysius dressed as a girl, kept long flowing locks, doused himself with perfume, walked with a feminine gait, and imitated the female voice when he spoke. His worshippers described him as androgynous, both male and female, and would celebrate Dionysius's gender confusion by their own gender reversal. In the worship of Dionysius (which was mixed with the worship of Demeter in Corinth according to McRay's *Archaeology and the New Testament*) men would wear feminine clothing and long hair, and women would wear men's garments and wear men's short hair style, sometimes even having their heads shaved. Archaeologists have discovered vase paintings from Corinth depicting Dionysius worship that show some female worshippers would go to shocking extremes to make themselves fully male. Thus, men would masquerade as women and women as men and similar practices appear in the worship of Cybele, Demeter, Artemis, and Diana. Paul may well have taught in Corinth what he taught in Galatians 3:28, in Christ "there is no male and female." But in context, that means that both male and female Christians are the seed of Abraham and are equal heirs of the promise. It most certainly did not mean that we are to seek to undo the distinction between male and female that was part of God's creation ordinance.

> Yet the Corinthians apparently latched onto the mantra, "no
> male or female," and interpreted that against their pagan
> background and consequently incorporated elements of pagan
> worship into the Christian church. By interpreting Christian
> claims against their own pagan background, they perverted
> and distorted the Christian faith. That is the almost inevitable
> result of using our own past experience as the primary guide to
> biblical interpretation. (Quarles, "Confusion at Corinth")

Now we have the proper context to understand Paul's meaning in
these verses. Allow me to paraphrase the focal passage while also sup-
plying the fresh perspective Quarles suggests: "Every man who prays or
prophesies [the latter is to be equated with Holy Spirit-inspired speech,
not the authoritative teachings of the elders; see 1 Tim 2:12], with
something on his head [giving him a female appearance], dishonors
his head" [who is Christ!] (v. 4). In short, a man should look like a man.

Verses 5-6 mean this: "Every woman who prays or prophesies [Paul
affirms that women may do this when the church gathers for worship;
see Acts 2:17-18; 21:9] with her head uncovered [giving her a male-like
appearance], dishonors her head [her husband], since this is one and
the same as having her head shaved." In fact, if a woman wants to shame
her husband, act like a pagan, and flaunt her so-called freedom, then
she should just go ahead and cut it all off. Shave it off and look like a
bald man (a *reductio ad absurdum* argument). "For if a woman doesn't
cover her head [with long hair], she should have her hair cut off." (v. 6).
However, this is absurd and shameful. Indeed, "it is disgraceful for a
woman to have her hair cut off or her head shaved." A woman should
look like the glorious female God created her and designed her to be.
Therefore, "let her head be covered." In short, men should look like
men, and women should look like women. There should be no gender
or cultural confusion. What a critically important word for our day!

We Must Honor the Principles of Glory, Creation, and Purpose
1 CORINTHIANS 11:7-9

Paul appeals to creation's order and design in these verses about proper
conduct in worship. Like his Trinitarian argument in verse 3, there is a
timelessness to his argument here. What he says is true anywhere, any

place, and in any era. He begins by again affirming that "[a] man should not cover his head" when he prays or prophesies in worship (v. 7). Yes, it is shameful (v. 4), but every believing man should also remember that "he is the image and glory of God." And "so too, woman is the glory of man" (v. 7). Further, "man did not come from woman, but woman came from man. Neither was man created for the sake of woman, but woman for the sake of man" (vv. 8-9).

Now, let's be clear about what Paul is saying and what he is not. First, what is he *not* saying? Paul is not suggesting a woman is not in the full image and likeness of God. He is *not* saying a woman is inferior to a man. He knows Genesis 1:27 very well. The key to these verses is the word "glory." As Gardner points out, "It is notable that Paul does not say in verse 7c that woman is the 'image' of man" (*1 Corinthians*, 491). So, what *is* he aiming for here? The greatest thing in all of creation that brings glory to God is man (humanity). Similarly, the greatest and most magnificent thing that ever came out of a man is his female counterpart. My friend Andy Davis puts it like this: "What is the greatest thing that ever physically came out of a man, not any of his works, but woman. . . . The crowning achievement of man . . . is a woman" ("Headship"). Further, as Genesis 2:18 teaches, God made the woman as "a helper corresponding to [the man]," someone that perfectly fits and complements him. Again, all of this points to the essential Christocentric nature of authentic worship. Gardner again proves helpful:

> Whatever the reason for the head covering in terms of social mores at the time, Paul's point is that this created difference between husbands and wives has not changed simply because people have become Christians. The created order should still be respected. In this way, as worship takes place, it is ultimately only Christ to whom glory is given. (*1 Corinthians*, 492)

We Must Honor the Principles of Angelic Observation and Submission
1 CORINTHIANS 11:10

Verses 2-16 are not about our rights but our responsibilities in worship. Why, even the angels know and understand this. Paul says, "This is why a woman should have a symbol of authority on her head, because of the angels" (v. 10). Now, just because the angels know what is going on here does not mean we do! As David Garland wisely and humbly notes, "No interpretation [of v. 10] can be held with great confidence" (*1 Corinthians*, 524). Still, some basic biblical facts can help us grasp the main idea Paul is seeking to make. First, angels, like us, were created to glorify God (Ps 148:2). Second, angels delight in worshiping and serving God (Rev 7:11-12). Third, angels gladly submit to the authority of God in all things (Ps 103:20). Fourth, angels attend our worship services and observe what is going on (Rev 1:20). Fifth, they celebrate when we worship properly and are disappointed when we don't (Acts 12:23). Therefore, we should be sure to worship in a God-glorifying way because our fellow servants, the angels who minister to us (Heb 1:14), want to join us in humble, proper worship that focuses on Christ and honors and glorifies our heavenly Father (cf. Isa 6:2-3).

We Must Honor the Principle of Interdependence
1 CORINTHIANS 11:11-12

I believe Paul was aware that his argument to this point could be open to misunderstanding. So he moves to make sure his meaning is clear. There is no superiority of men over women or women over men. There is a divine design of both complementarity and interdependence. "In the Lord . . . woman is not independent of man, and man is not independent of woman. For just as woman came from man, so man comes through woman" (vv. 11-12). The first woman (Eve) came from the first man (Adam), as Genesis 2 makes clear. However, ever since the original creation acts, every man (and woman) has come from a woman, a mother. A woman coming from a man's rib was a unique event. Since then, there has been a beautiful and necessary interdependence in marriage, procreation, parenting, and church life. Males and females stand equal before God and in need of one another. Neither exists without the other. We cannot flourish without each other. Schreiner summarizes well Paul's intention in these two verses:

> Paul wants to avoid any thought that women are ontologically inferior; thus, he emphasizes the interdependence of men and women in the Lord. Women came into existence through men, but men come into the world through women. The first woman was from the first man, but now all men come into the world through women, that is, through their birth via a

mother. A difference in function between men and women
does not negate the equality and value of the two sexes.
(*1 Corinthians*, 235–36)

It is important to note how Paul begins and ends his argument in
verses 11-12. Our design is "in the Lord" (v. 11) and "all things come
from God" (v. 12). Thiselton is on target in explaining Paul's meaning
when he writes,

Paul almost certainly means to say that gender differentiation
is decreed in creation, expressed in societal convention, and
not abrogated in the order of the gospel. . . . [I]n the gospel
differentiation is determined more explicitly by a principle of
mutuality and reciprocity. (*First Epistle*, 842)

God is the origin and source of all of this, and it is for our good and
his glory. This should especially be on glorious display when we gather
for worship.

We Must Honor the Principle of Nature
1 CORINTHIANS 11:13-15

Paul has appealed to theology proper (God), social convention, and creation. Now he appeals to nature and common sense. The latter, unfortunately, is often in short supply. Paul begins with a rhetorical question,
the first of three. First, he asks, "Judge for yourselves: Is it proper for a
woman [ESV, "wife"] to pray to God with her head uncovered?" (v. 13).
The expected and proper answer is no, it isn't. Second, Paul asks, "Does
not even nature itself teach you that if a man has long hair it is a disgrace to him?" (v. 14). Debates about what is too long and too short are
of little value, especially in missiological contexts where cultural norms
vary. The point, however, is clear. Men should look like and be easily recognized as men, and women should look like and be easily recognized
as women. There should be no gender blurring or gender confusion.
Third, Paul asks whether nature also teaches: "[I]f a woman has long
hair, [isn't it] her glory?" (v. 15). Yes! Long hair on a woman's head
honors her; "it functions as something that distinguishes the splendor
of the woman" (Fee, *Corinthians*, 2014, 583). A female who wears her
hair in a feminine manner, then, testifies and witnesses to the goodness
and rightness of God's good creation in distinguishing the differences

between a male and a female. Therefore, Paul can conclude, "for her hair is given to her as a covering." God himself is the implied agent of this act. God himself gives hair to a woman to be maintained as an appropriate sign of respect for and submission to the divine ordering. Such a covering honors her head, her husband, and it also glorifies her Creator, her God. Attention thus is directed where it should be directed in worship: on God and not on us.

We Must Honor the Principle of Common Practice
1 CORINTHIANS 11:16

Paul ends this section acknowledging that his instruction is not just for Corinth. This is the way things are done everywhere in all the churches. Paul is direct and leaves no room for debate: "If anyone wants to argue about this, we have no other custom, nor do the churches of God" (v. 16). When it comes to corporate worship, there are nonnegotiable guidelines and parameters. Men acting like redeemed men and women acting like redeemed women is one of those areas. Wiersbe wisely notes that it is essential to rightly worship and rightly honor God.

> In my ministry in different parts of the world, I have noticed that basic principle of headship applies in every culture; but the means of demonstrating it differs from place to place. The important thing is the submission of the heart to the Lord and the public manifestation of obedience to God's order. (*Be Wise*, 114)

Conclusion

Gender confusion and perversion pervade our culture, especially in the worlds of education, media, and sports. It should not find a home in the church. Rather, God's good design should be on public display among those who have been redeemed by Christ and transformed by the power of the gospel. Bisexuals, homosexuals, lesbians, and transgenders should know we love and care for them. But one way we do this is by modeling and telling the truth. It may not be the popular thing to do, but it is the right thing to do. After all, Jesus teaches in John 8:32, "You will know the truth, and the truth will set you free." There is real freedom in Christ. There is real freedom in being who God created you to be.

Reflect and Discuss

1. What is the specific situation that Paul addresses? How does Paul's concern for the Corinthians' worship shape how you interpret and apply the passage?

2. When it comes to the discussion of the length of hair for men and women, what is Paul's biggest concern? What is not Paul's concern?

3. Why does it matter that Christianity teaches that male headship applies in the church and home, but not society?

4. What is the difference between function and essence concerning husbands and wives?

5. How does having Christ as a spiritual authority shape all spiritual authority a husband may have?

6. Why does having spiritual authority *not* mean the husband makes all decisions in a marital relationship? Why is having spiritual authority *not* an excuse to be a domineering or abusive husband?

7. How do Christians avoid the Corinthian error of using one's past experiences as the primary guide to biblical interpretation?

8. How do verses 11-12 provide a corrective for possible misunderstandings of this passage?

9. What is the relationship hierarchy between the various principles outlined in this passage (e.g., ordained authority, social expectations, nature, common practice, etc.)?

10. When should social expectations and common practice play a role in Christian worship? When should these not have as much influence?

The Lord's Supper Manuscript

1 CORINTHIANS 11:17-34

Main Idea: Examine yourself when taking the Lord's Supper, repenting of all sin and selfishness and uniting with believers around the work of Christ.

I. **We Must Deal with Problems When We Come (11:17-22).**
    A. We must deal with divisiveness (11:17-19).
    B. We must deal with selfishness (11:20-22).
II. **We Must Honor the Meal's Purposes When We Come (11:23-26).**
    A. It is a commemoration of the Lord's death (11:23-25).
    B. It is a proclamation that anticipates the Lord's return (11:26).
III. **We Must Make Preparation When We Come (11:27-34).**
    A. There must be personal examination of ourselves (11:27-32).
    B. There must be humble consideration of others (11:33-34).

The Lord's Supper (Communion) is so important to the Christian faith that the Bible addresses it five times. It appears in Matthew 26:26-29; Mark 14:22-25; Luke 22:14-20; 1 Corinthians 10:16-22; and 1 Corinthians 11:17-34. Along with baptism, it constitutes the two ordinances of the church. Some, however, view foot washing as a third ordinance (John 13:1-20), and the Roman Catholic Church recognizes seven sacraments (Baptism, Eucharist [the Lord's Supper], Confirmation, Penance, Holy Orders, Matrimony, and Extreme Unction). Evangelicals and Baptists limit the number of ordinances to two because only baptism and the Lord's Supper meet five important criteria:

1. They were prescribed by the Lord.
2. They were proclaimed among the saints.
3. They were practiced by the churches.
4. They were participated in only by the saved.
5. They picture the atoning sacrifice and bodily resurrection of Jesus.

Now, one other issue must be addressed before examining this text. How are we to understand the nature of the Lord's Supper? What is the relationship of Christ to this ordinance? Four basic views have been held in the history of the church. I closely follow Mark Dever's excellent presentation from *Theology for the Church*:

1. **Transubstantiation**—Communion is an "unbloody sacrifice" of Christ that is continual and ongoing. The elements change in substance but not appearance. Effectual grace is communicated to the participant. This is the Roman Catholic position.

2. **Consubstantiation**—The elements are not changed (transubstantiated), but Christ is "in, with, and under" the substance of the bread and wine. The sacrament, therefore, is the true body and blood of Christ. This is the Lutheran position.

3. **Spiritual presence**—Christ is present in the Lord's Supper spiritually but not physically. By faith we enjoy a unique and special presence of our Lord when we come together as the body of Christ. This is the view of John Calvin (1509–64) and one I believe is compatible with the fourth position held by most Baptists.

4. **Memorial**—In a sense all hold this view, though as Dever notes, "the other three positions go beyond the supper as memorial, but no one denies this is an aspect of the Lord's Supper" ("The Church," 648). The memorial view sees Communion as symbolic of the atoning work of the Lord Jesus on our behalf.

As I noted, I believe views three and four are so close in understanding they can be held together. Dever writes, "Baptists have historically used language so rich about Christ's presence in the Lord's Supper for those who come by faith that little difference is perceptible between their position and the Reformed idea of Christ's spiritual presence" ("The Church," 648).

The Lord's Supper is a holy and sacred practice in which believers come together as a body to remember, meditate on, and celebrate the atoning death of the Lord Jesus for the forgiveness of sins. It is not something to be trifled with or handled flippantly. To do so invites the severe reprimand of the apostle and the judgment of our God. First Corinthians 11:17-34 makes this clear.

We Must Deal with Problems When We Come
1 CORINTHIANS 11:17-22

When a local church deserves to be praised, we should praise it. But when a church needs to be rebuked and corrected, we should do that too. Speaking the truth in love (Eph 4:15) requires that we do both.

We Must Deal with Divisiveness (11:17-19)

Paul began with a word of commendation in 11:2. Now he discusses the church's behavior at the Lord's Supper with a word of criticism (v. 17): "Now in giving this instruction I do not praise you." Why? "[S]ince you come together not for the better but for the worse." The church's gathering for worship and observing Communion was neither glorifying to God nor edifying for the body. In particular ("For to begin with"), Paul says, "I hear that when you come together as a church there are divisions among you, and in part I believe it" (v. 18). Schreiner notes as we move through the passage, we discover the divisions were "sociological instead of theological" (*1 Corinthians*, 241). They were between the "haves" and the "have nots." Further, although the divisions were wrong, they were still used by God for redemptive purposes. While Paul regrets the divisions that have arisen at the gathering of the Lord's Supper, he recognizes that these "factions" are "necessary . . . that those who are approved may be recognized among [the rest]" (v. 19). Schreiner says, "The factions that break out have, it seems, a refining and purifying effect on the church in that they clarify who truly belongs to God and also uncover those who do not truly belong to God" (*1 Corinthians*, 241). How we love and defer to one another speaks volumes about our walks with God.

We Must Deal with Selfishness (11:20-22)

The Corinthians were operating in self-deception when they came together to observe this sacred communal meal. In reality, when they gathered it was "not to eat the Lord's Supper" at all (v. 20). What is the apostle's evidence? "For at the meal, each one eats his own supper" (v. 21). Their self-focus meant "one person is hungry while another gets drunk!" (v. 21). The Corinthians were guilty of letting their rich take precedence over their poor and of gluttony. Perhaps being influenced by the pagan festivals they once indulged in, the wealthy gorged themselves. All the while the poor (many of whom were probably slaves) went hungry, receiving little or nothing to eat and drink because it was soon gone. Wiersbe is almost certainly correct:

> It is likely that the weekly agape feast was the only decent meal some of the poorer members regularly had; and to be treated so scornfully by the richer members not only hurt their stomachs, but also their pride. (*Be Wise*, 115)

Paul is outraged by such selfish and sinful behavior and delivers a stern rebuke in verse 22: "Don't you have homes in which to eat and drink? Or do you despise the church of God and humiliate those who have nothing? What should I say to you? Should I praise you? I do not praise you in this matter!" *The Message* concludes verse 22 with, "I never would have believed you would stoop to this. And I'm not going to stand by and say nothing!" A sacred meal that should have been building up the church had become a means of tearing it down. Selfish and narcissistic behavior insults God and embarrasses brothers and sisters in Christ. There is no place for it in the faith family.

We Must Honor the Meal's Purpose When We Come
1 CORINTHIANS 11:23-26

Paul provides clear and careful instructions on the purpose and significance of Communion. It shares nothing in common with a pagan feast or wild party. It is a solemn act of worship that has historical roots in the Last Supper our Lord had with his disciples on the night he was betrayed. Theologically it calls us to look backward, forward, inward, and outward.

It Is a Commemoration of the Lord's Death (11:23-25)

In words that follow closest the account in Luke 22:14-20, Paul informs the Corinthians he is passing on what he "received from the Lord" (v. 23). Paul was passing on the tradition that originated with Jesus and was then relayed to others by the apostles, including himself. The words are simple and yet powerful: "On the night [before he was crucified] when he was betrayed [by Judas], the Lord Jesus took bread, and when he had given thanks, broke it, and said, 'This is my body, which is for you. Do this in remembrance of me'" (vv. 23-24). The taking of the bread and its breaking commemorate and illustrate the sacrifice of Jesus as his body was beaten and broken for us. Paul continues in verse 25: "In the same way also he took the cup, after supper, and said, 'This cup is the new covenant in my blood. Do this, as often as you drink it, in remembrance of me.'" The "new covenant" recalls the language of Exodus 24:8 and Jeremiah 31:31-34. Mention of Jesus's blood points to his brutal death and the atoning blood sacrifice poured out on the cross. Leviticus 17:11 reminds us that life "is in the blood," and Hebrews 9:22 affirms, "without the shedding of blood there is no forgiveness." The hymn writer Lewis Edgar Jones wonderfully reminds us, "Would you be free from the burden of sin? There's power in the blood." Indeed, there is power in the blood of the Lord Jesus for the forgiveness of sin. We remember this truth every time we celebrate the Lord's Supper.

It Is a Proclamation That Anticipates the Lord's Return (11:26)

The Lord's Supper calls us to look to the past as we remember our Savior's sacrifice for our sins on the cross. But now Paul tells us we should also look to the future. Why? Verse 26 provides the answer: "For as often as you eat this bread and drink the cup, you proclaim the Lord's death until he comes." The Lord's Supper should certainly be a time of careful meditation and reflection. But it should also be a time of joyful anticipation and celebration! Yes, Jesus died. But he rose from the dead, and he is coming again! Sorrow and joy are partners in this meal. I think John Piper says it well: "Should the Lord's Supper be solemn or cheerful? I'm saying it should not be either-or and should not be sequentially. There is a solemnity with explosive joy, and there is sweet cheerfulness whose eyes are brimming with tears" ("The Lord's Supper"). In the Lord's Supper we testify to a Savior who died but is alive, one who came and is coming again!

We Must Make Preparation When We Come
1 CORINTHIANS 11:27-34

The Bible does not tell us how often believers should gather to celebrate and observe Communion. I would say, however, it should be regular and often enough to prompt the careful introspection of soul that each one of us needs for spiritual health and nourishment. This is especially the case for those going through trials, difficulty, and suffering. There are

many precious testimonies from the persecuted church of their observance of Communion. Paul has told us to look backward and forward.
Now he teaches us to look inward and outward.

There Must Be Personal Examination of Ourselves (11:27-32)

Verse 27 begins the conclusion of Paul's discussion joined to a stern
warning: "So, then, whoever eats the bread or drinks the cup of the Lord
in an unworthy manner will be guilty of sin against the body and blood of
the Lord." The divisiveness and selfish behavior of the Corinthians make
them unworthy to come to the Lord's table. John Calvin writes, "To eat
unworthily, then, is to pervert the pure and right use of it by our abuse of
it" (1 Corinthians, 385). Such actions do not honor Christ. They are grievous sins against Christ and his atoning sacrifice. Paul, therefore, issues a
strong word of command: "Let a person examine himself [note the present imperative here]; in this way let him eat the bread and drink from
the cup" (v. 28). Examine yourself. Look at your life and take inventory
of your heart. If you are not right with God and others, then it would be
better for you not to draw near the table of Communion (cf. Matt 5:23-
24). The consequences of coming in an unworthy manner are strikingly
detailed in verses 29-30: "For whoever eats and drinks without recognizing [ESV, "discerning"] the body, eats and drinks judgment on himself"
(v. 29). Exactly what Paul means by "the body" here is unclear. Is it Christ?
Is it the church? I like Schreiner's both/and response to this question:

> Perhaps the best solution does not opt for an either-or. In
> partaking of the bread, believers participate "in the body of
> Christ" (1 Cor. 10:16); and "Because there is one loaf, we, who
> are many, are one body" (1 Cor. 10:17). Paul has already forged
> a close connection between the broken body of Christ and the
> one body which is the church. The same connection and link is
> probably present here as well. Those who discriminate against
> other members of the congregation while eating and drinking
> of the elements do not discern the significance of Christ's
> death, nor do they perceive the unity of the body. Indeed,
> Christ by his death has made all believers one. Those who fail
> to perceive the significance of Christ's broken body and the
> unity of the church incur judgment. (1 Corinthians, 247)

The precise nature of the judgment is now explained in verse 30. The words are shocking, to say the least: "This is why many are sick [ESV, "weak"] and ill among you, and many have fallen asleep." God's judgment was quite severe for those who desecrated his table. Some became sick, and some had died. The metaphor of sleep is often used in the Bible for the death of a believer and never an unbeliever. Such persons do not lose their salvation, but their earthly lives are cut short. As Leon Morris says, "Spiritual ills may have physical results" (*1 Corinthians*, 161). Indeed, some may even be fatal.

Paul explains in verses 31-32 that it does not have to be this way if the church is acting like the church: "If we were properly judging ourselves, we would not be judged" (v. 31). That is, if we properly take care of things, then God does not have to step in. But if we don't, he will. And there will be redemptive value for the church: "when we are judged by the Lord, we are disciplined, so that we may not be condemned with the world" (v. 32). These words are sobering and comforting. God will discipline us believers as his children (cf. Prov 3:11-12; Heb 12:5-13), but he will not condemn us with the world in final judgment. He loves us too much to let us continue acting like fools. We cannot lose our spiritual life because we are secure in Christ (John 10:27-28). The same, however, cannot be said for our physical lives.

There Must Be Humble Consideration of Others (11:33-34)

Curtis Vaughn reminds us why self-reflection is necessary when taking Communion:

> Paul's stern warnings in this section are a reminder that
> participation in the Lord's Supper is no trivial matter. It is
> a solemn privilege to be undertaken by those who come in
> earnestness and commitment. The Supper is a memorial
> to Christ, an anticipation of His return, and it becomes a
> source of much help and encouragement to the participant.
> It should be undertaken only by a believer serious about his
> fellowship with God and other brothers in Christ. It must be
> preceded by rigorous self-examination and not be performed
> superficially at each quarterly, monthly, or weekly observance.
> (*1 Corinthians*, 123)

Paul drives these truths home in the final verses of chapter 11. Again, he is tender as he concludes: "Therefore, my brothers and sisters, when you come together to eat, welcome [ESV, "wait for"] one another" (v. 33). Be kind and gracious to one another. Defer to one another. Adopt the mind of Christ as is so beautifully expounded in Philippians 2:3-4. First Corinthians 11:34 parallels verse 22. If one is concerned about getting enough to eat, which is not the focus or point of Communion, "he should eat at home, so that when [the church gathers] together [he] will not come under judgment" and receive God's discipline.

There were other matters Paul needed to discuss with the church at Corinth, but those could wait until another time, "whenever [he came]." These may or may not be related to the Lord's Supper. We cannot be sure. What we do know is he feels that he has said enough for now. If they listen to his counsel laid out in verses 17-34, he will be satisfied.

Conclusion

In the Lord's Supper believers unite as a body to remember, meditate on, and celebrate the atoning death of the Lord Jesus for the forgiveness of sins. Twila Paris's song "Lamb of God" provides a proper reflection on that atoning death to close this chapter.

Your only Son no sin to hide
But You have sent Him from Your side
To walk upon this guilty sod
And to become the Lamb of God

Your gift of love they crucified
They laughed and scorned Him as he died
The humble King they named a fraud
And sacrificed the Lamb of God

Oh Lamb of God, Sweet lamb of God
I love the Holy Lamb of God
Oh wash me in His precious Blood
My Jesus Christ the Lamb of God

I was so lost I should have died
But You have brought me to Your side
To be led by Your staff and rod
And to be called a lamb of God

Oh Lamb of God, Sweet lamb of God
I love the Holy Lamb of God
Oh wash me in His precious Blood
My Jesus Christ the Lamb of God

("Lamb of God," Words and Music by Twila Paris. © Copyright
1985 Mountain Spring Music (ASCAP) Straightway Music
[ASCAP] [adm. at CapitolCMGPublishing.com] All rights
reserved. Used by permission.)

May we continually remember and worship the God who washed us with
his precious blood.

Reflect and Discuss

1. What do the elements of the Lord's Supper teach about Christ's past and future work? How does the regular taking of the Lord's Supper remind you of your continual need for Christ?
2. What does the Lord's Supper teach about the unity of believers?
3. Why was a division among believers at the Lord's Supper so severe in Paul's eyes?
4. How might Christians identify whether there are factions in their churches (or whether they are unknowingly part of a faction)?
5. How do the Corinthians' actions warn Christians not to assume that their coming together will automatically glorify God?
6. Why must the church never be divided into those who have wealth and those who do not?
7. What does deferring to others suggest about one's walk with God?
8. Why should the Lord's Supper never seem boring or dull to Christians, no matter how often it's practiced?
9. How can you rightly practice sorrow and joy in the Lord's Supper?
10. In what ways does the Lord's Supper sound a warning and offer hope?

You Are a Gifted Child

1 CORINTHIANS 12:1-11

Main Idea: Every believer has spiritual gifts that are to be exercised, not for personal gratification, but for corporate edification in the church.

I. **How the Gifts Are Described (12:1,4,7)**
   A. They are spiritual gifts (12:1).
   B. They are supernatural gifts (12:4).
   C. They are service gifts (12:7).
II. **How the Gifts Are Distributed (12:5-7,11)**
   A. They are distributed individually (12:5-6, 11).
   B. They are distributed intentionally (12:7).
III. **How the Gifts Are Distinguished (12:4-6)**
   A. There is a motivation for the gifts (12:4).
   B. There is a ministry with the gifts (12:5).
   C. There is a might behind the gifts (12:6).

There was nothing boring about the church at Corinth. Hollywood executives would salivate over making a movie about this church. What went on there would make for great reality TV, too. One could almost call the Corinthian church the "drama queen of the New Testament." At the same time, some of the most interesting and richest teaching of Christian doctrine and practical Christian living is found in 1 Corinthians, and perhaps no part of the book is more interesting from that perspective than chapters 12–14, which deal with spiritual gifts.

Anyone preparing commentary on this passage must do so with care and humility. After all, Anthony Thiselton, in his magisterial commentary, said, "Hardly any statement about chapters twelve and fourteen remains uncontroversial" (*First Epistle*, 902). Needless to say, there is neither a guarantee nor an expectation that there will be unanimity of agreement on the interpretation given on some of the gifts that are listed and their relevance and application today. But the truth remains: we are to give ourselves not only to studying these gifts and trying to understand them but just as importantly to using them for the glory of God and the good of the church.

Spiritual gifts were obviously a hot topic at the church in Corinth if we are to judge by the extent of Paul's discussion of them in the book. One of the reasons Paul wrote to the Corinthians in such detail, in fact, was because of their ignorance of spiritual gifts. He specifically states, "Now concerning spiritual gifts: brothers and sisters, I do not want you to be unaware" (12:1).

It is very easy to be ignorant of spiritual gifts, and having served as a pastor for four and a half decades, I've come to believe most Christians are. After all, I went to a Southern Baptist college, grew up in Southern Baptist churches, went to Southern Baptist Sunday schools, and never heard one sermon on spiritual gifts and was never taught about spiritual gifts.

The Greek word behind "unaware" is the word that gives us the English word "agnostic." Unfortunately, when it comes to the church there are many spiritual agnostics. They know very little about spiritual gifts, and those who do are not even sure what their spiritual gifts might be. I have learned by personal experience there is a great cost involved in being educated, but there is a greater cost if you are not. This is especially true in regards to spiritual gifts. What you don't know can hurt you.

One other thing must be kept in mind. Exercising a spiritual gift is no guarantee of spiritual maturity, nor is it a guarantee that one belongs to a great church. Spiritual gifts, unfortunately, were not uniting the church in Corinth; they were dividing the church. It was obvious that some of the Corinthians were placing such an inordinate emphasis on showy displays of spirituality, particularly speaking in tongues, that it was disrupting the church's worship, dividing the church's fellowship, and demeaning the witness of the gospel (Hays, *Interpretation*, 206). This church was exercising the gifts of the Spirit, but they were not exhibiting the fruit of the Spirit!

We are going to do a deep dive into these next few chapters. I do so humbly, realizing there will be difference of opinion as we go. I hope to shine more light on rather than give more heat to the topics we will encounter. May we as ministers and teachers better understand God's Word so that others might be edified.

How the Gifts Are Described
1 CORINTHIANS 12:1,4,7

They Are Spiritual Gifts (12:1)

"Now concerning spiritual gifts." The word translated "gifts" does not appear in the original Greek. The word *pneumatikon* means "the spirituals" or "the things of the spirit." There is a debate among scholars as to whether the term refers to "spiritual things," "spiritual people," or "spiritual gifts." I agree with Schreiner: "A reference to spiritual gifts is most likely, given the ensuing discussion, for Paul does not discuss spiritual things or people, but spiritual gifts" (*1 Corinthians*, 253).

Gifts are actually Trinitarian in nature. God the Father has given us the gift of God the Son for our salvation. God the Son has given us God the Holy Spirit for our sanctification, but God the Holy Spirit has given us spiritual gifts for our service. The point is, these are not material gifts. These are spiritual gifts. They are gifts of and from the Holy Spirit.

They Are Supernatural Gifts (12:4)

The word for "gifts" in verse 4 is different from the word translated "spiritual gifts" in verse 1. Here the word is *charismata*. The root word is *charis*, which literally means "grace." These gifts are grace gifts—not only gifts of the Spirit, but gifts of grace.

Spiritual gifts are supernatural gifts granted by the grace of God. They are not just glorified natural abilities. They are not something you gain by going to school or practicing or inheriting. They are literally charismatic gifts, which means if you are a Christian in the truest sense of the term, you are a charismatic Christian by default. Spiritual gifts, simply put, are supernatural endowments that enable us to carry out God's work in God's way. They are provided by the grace of God, and they are powered by the Spirit of God. They truly are supernatural gifts.

They Are Service Gifts (12:7)

These gifts are not to be stored; they are to be shared for the "good" of others. That expression can be literally rendered "with a view to profiting" (Carson, *Showing*, 35). Spiritual gifts are given to every believer to bless the church, build up the body of Christ, and edify believers. But if a spiritual gift does not in some way edify the church, it is no longer a *used* gift; it is an *abused* gift. My mentor, Dr. Adrian Rogers, used to say, "Spiritual gifts are not given for your enjoyment, but for his employment." They are not toys for playing; they are tools for building.

To be sure, this does not mean there would not be any private benefit to the one exercising the gift. But this verse would certainly rule out using any gift strictly or merely for personal gain or self-satisfaction. It certainly does not rule out any and all benefits for an individual (Carson, *Showing*, 35).

How the Gifts Are Distributed
1 CORINTHIANS 12:5-7,11

Spiritual gifts are not given out arbitrarily, by flipping a coin, drawing lots, or playing favorites. They are given out under the sovereign control of the Holy Spirit, who controls specifically how they are distributed.

They Are Distributed Individually (12:5-6,11)

Verse 11 says, "One and the same Spirit is active in all these, distributing to each person as he wills." Spiritual gifts are distributed "to each." Keep in mind Paul is talking to believers. Every Christian has received at least one spiritual gift. Unfortunately, I have pastored some people who assumed they had the spiritual gift of criticism, which is not a thing! No one Christian has every gift, but every Christian has at least one.

Paul said to the Christians in Corinth, "There are different ministries, but the same Lord. And there are different activities, but the same God works all of them in each person" (vv. 5-6). Every Christian has received the grace of God, which is the essence of being a Christian. Every Christian has received a spiritual gift, too. (See also 1 Pet 4:10.)

You may not have graduated first in your class. You may not be very athletic. You may not be one of the world's most talented people, but if you are a follower of Jesus, you are a gifted child! You have a gift that God wants you to use in his church in service and ministry that might not get done unless you do it. No Christian should ever say, "God couldn't use me," or "This church doesn't need me," or "I pray God could use someone like me." Every Christian is a minister, and every Christian has a ministry. The ministries of the church are to be carried out as followers of Jesus exercise their spiritual gifts in ministering to one another. Again, they are distributed independently. Verse 11 reminds us that these gifts are given "to each person as [the Spirit] wills." That means the Holy Spirit decides the gift or gifts you are going to have. You can't determine your spiritual gift any more than your birthplace or the color of your eyes. The Holy Spirit sovereignly distributes all gifts as he wills, not as we will, because he knows what is best for the body.

This should remind us that no believer should ever be jealous of another believer who may have a different gift. All of us have been gifted differently, but all of us have been gifted perfectly. The Holy Spirit, in his divine wisdom and sovereignty, has given to each of us precisely the gift, or gifts, that will enable us to function most effectively in the body of Christ.

They Are Distributed Intentionally (12:7)

Why does the Holy Spirit distribute these gifts in such a fashion? Why doesn't the Holy Spirit give every Christian every gift, or why doesn't he give every Christian the same gift? The intention of the Holy Spirit is found in verse 7. The word for "common good" or "profit *of all*" (NKJV; emphasis in original) implies "to bring together" or "to join together." In other words, God has made us different that he might make us one. The gifts serve to help show us we are a puzzle made up of different pieces. When we exercise our gifts within a local context, we find that we fit together perfectly and create a beautiful representation of God's greater family.

Although what we perceive God to be doing sometimes doesn't make sense to us, there is always a method to his seeming madness, and he knows what he is about and what he is doing. As we think about spiritual gifts, we should rejoice knowing that we are each gifted, that we can be used, that God has a purpose and a plan for us and a work for us to do, and that with his gifts and by his power we can do things in a way that brings glory and honor to him and serves to bless others.

How the Gifts Are Distinguished
1 CORINTHIANS 12:4-6

I refer to this passage as "Trinitarian" in both a theological and a homiletical way. In it, two words are used three times; they are also antonyms: the word *different* and the word *same*. But we also see all three Persons of the Trinity mentioned. There is a parallelism that is hard to miss. There are three differentiations:

of different *gifts* (*charismatōn*), but the same *Spirit*;
of different *ministries* (*diakoniōn*), but the same *Lord*;
of different *activities* (*energēmatōn*), but the same *God.*

Compared to some scholarship, I agree with Carson, who says, "There are some, of course, who cannot detect here or elsewhere in the New Testament any Trinitarian thought; but this appears to me to owe more to a doctrinaire reconstruction of early historical theology than to exegesis" (*Showing*, 32). Thiselton notes, "While the trinitarian stance is implicit in 2 Cor. 13:13 and Eph. 4:4-6, here we encounter the earliest 'clear' trinitarian language" (*First Epistle*, 934; so Fee, *Corinthians*, 1987, 588; see 1 Cor 2:10). The point is that the work God was doing among the Corinthians through spiritual gifts was a triune work and was not limited only to the Holy Spirit (Schreiner, *1 Corinthians*, 255).

Paul is looking at the gifts from three different angles, though Bruce is correct in saying they are not distinct categories (*1 & 2 Corinthians*, 118). Yet Thiselton is surely right when he says, "More than a difference of aspect is entailed, on the part of the subject or the reader's observation" (*First Epistle*, 933). Hence, I would delineate them this way.

There Is the Motivation for the Gifts (12:4)

In effect, these are grace gifts. The original key word in this passage is *charismatōn* (v. 4), which means "gifts of grace." The motivation for all our ministry and acts of service should be a gratitude for the grace of God that both saves us and strengthens us to serve him, the gift giver. Not only are we saved by grace, but we serve by grace and because of grace.

There Is a Ministry with the Gifts (12:5)

Verse 5 tells us, "There are different ministries." The key word behind that translation is *diakoniōn*. This is not "ministry" in a technical or formal sense; this is putting any gift to work in serving the church (Thiselton, *First Epistle*, 931). Gifts show up in different ways in different ministries. Even though two Christians may have the same basic gift, that gift may be manifested and applied in different ways. So, for example, one person with the gift of teaching may be especially gifted in teaching young children, while someone else may be especially gifted in teaching PhDs (MacArthur, *1 Corinthians*, 291). The truth is, all ministry is done and should be done through the exercise of spiritual gifts, and all spiritual gifts are to be displayed in ministry.

There Is a Might behind the Gifts (12:6)

Verse 6 speaks of "different activities." The Greek word for that is *energēmatōn*, which gives us the word "energy." We exercise these gifts not only by the grace of God but through the power of God. It is his power that fires engines and leads us to exercise these gifts effectively.

So you might say that the first category represents the essence of the gifts (they are grace gifts). The second category represents the expression of the gifts (they are to be used for service). The third category represents the effects of the gifts. They result is a display of the power of God through his people.

Conclusion

This chapter reminds us that spiritual gifts exist to glorify God. They exist to edify the church. They exist because God, in his sovereign wisdom, has graciously given them to every member of the church so that we can proclaim Jesus as Lord to all nations. We Christians exercise our gifts best when we depend on the Spirit and faithfully use them in our local ministries.

Reflect and Discuss

1. What costs might arise if Christians remain uninformed about spiritual gifts?
2. Why is exercising a spiritual gift no guarantee of spiritual maturity nor an indicator that one belongs to a great church?
3. What is the difference between a used gift and an abused gift? Can someone abuse his or her gifts while appearing to use them faithfully? If so, how?
4. How must people depend on God as they use their spiritual gifts? Why is dependence on God crucial?
5. Have you ever been jealous of another person's spiritual gift? Why is it significant that no one Christian has every spiritual gift? How can you cultivate joy in seeing others using their gifts?

6. Why don't spiritual gifts necessarily match up with the personalities of those who have them? Why are spiritual gifts able to be used effectively and faithfully by people of all dispositions?
7. In what ways is God the beginning, middle, and end of spiritual gifts?
8. What role does the Christian community play in helping people discern their spiritual gifts?
9. Why will relying on talent and man-centered power for ministry result in fatigue and frustration?
10. Do all spiritual gifts have the same value in God's eyes? Why or why not? Do all spiritual gifts have the same value in your eyes? Why or why not? Explain any differences in how you answered these two questions.

Unwrapping Spiritual Gifts

1 CORINTHIANS 12:8-31

Main Idea: Different gifts are given to different believers, and all gifts are for the glory of God and the good of the church.

I. **The Gifts of Wisdom (12:8,10)**
   A. The message of wisdom (12:8)
   B. The message of knowledge (12:8)
   C. The work of distinguishing between spirits (12:10)
II. **The Gifts of Worship (12:9-10)**
   A. The work of faith (12:9)
   B. The word of prophecy (12:10)
III. **The Gifts of Wonders (12:9-10)**
   A. The work of healings (12:9)
   B. The performing of miracles (12:10)
   C. The word of tongues (12:10)
   D. The work of interpretation of tongues (12:10)
IV. **Unity in Diversity (12:11-31)**
   A. The unity that binds the body (12:11-13)
   B. The diversity that blesses the body (12:14-31)

As we dive into the individual gifts that are listed in this chapter, keep in mind that every Christian has at least one basic gift as a primary gift. As that gift is exercised in the body of Christ, the believer will be fulfilling his or her role of ministry and service to which all of us are called. This does not mean that everyone has only one gift, however. Someone with the gift of teaching may in his or her teaching exercise the gift of exhortation. Someone with the gift of service may in her service exercise the gift of mercy. Someone with the gift of prophecy may in his preaching exercise the gift of leadership. Also keep in mind that this list is not necessarily exhaustive. However, I believe it is fairly comprehensive; most areas of service and ministry could be positioned under the rubric of one of these gifts.

Now, I do have one final plea: Regarding some of the gifts, there are differences of opinion on what exactly the gift is, how the gift is manifested, and how the gift is to be used. Still, every gift is to be used for the glory of God and the good of the church.

The Gifts of Wisdom
1 CORINTHIANS 12:8,10

I call the following gifts of wisdom because I see these gifts as those through which God supernaturally imparts insight about the Scriptures or reveals how the Word of God may be applied to certain situations, how the will of God may be preserved, and how the work of God may be continued.

The Message of Wisdom (12:8)

Carson points out that the emphasis here is not exactly on the wisdom, but on the "message," the *logos*, which literally means "word" (*Showing*, 38). Nevertheless, to properly understand this gift, we must first define what we mean by wisdom. Wisdom is not just knowing the ways of the world. It is not just being a clever person, nor it is just common sense.

Wisdom is not just education. You can have a PhD, but if you don't believe in God, the Bible calls you a "fool" (Ps 14:1). On the other hand, some of the wisest people I've met had little traditional education. Wisdom is supernatural in origin (Jas 1:5). You can get knowledge from a book and education in a school, but true wisdom comes only from God.

I consider a message of wisdom a special spiritual insight into the ways and Word of God that gives one the ability to see a situation from his point of view. It is the ability to see things as God sees them.

The Message of Knowledge (12:8)

Now there is some debate among scholars as to whether or not there is to be a distinction made between wisdom and knowledge. I believe Bruce sums it up best: "Paul presumably intends some distinction between *sophia* (wisdom) and *gnōsis* (knowledge), but the distinction is not clear to us" (*1 & 2 Corinthians*, 119). I agree there must be some distinction or it would not be distinguished as a separate gift in Paul's delineation.

At issue here is the gift of the *message* of knowledge, not knowledge itself. No one knows everything. Neither is this necessarily the kind of knowledge that comes from a book. You don't study to achieve and receive this kind of knowledge.

A word of knowledge, then, is perhaps when God reveals something to someone that he or she would not know or could not know about a particular situation unless it was revealed supernaturally. It is a special message of insight into a particular situation that may reveal a hidden motive or even a future action.

Two examples might be found in Acts. The first is in chapter 5, where Peter uncovered the fact that Ananias had kept back some of the money he claimed to have given to the church. The second is in Acts 27, where the apostle Paul warned the entire crew of the ship they had to stay together or else they would all perish. How would either one of these men have known to say what he did apart from the word of knowledge?

Both wisdom and knowledge reflect the God-given ability to bring spiritual insight beyond human understanding to bear in a situation. Blomberg notes, "If Paul intends any difference between the word of wisdom and the word of knowledge it may be that wisdom is knowledge applied, particularly in moral contexts" (*1 Corinthians*, 244).

The Work of Distinguishing between Spirits (12:10)

I put "distinguishing between spirits" in the category with wisdom and knowledge because I believe this is also a wisdom gift. It takes insight to be able to distinguish between what is true and what is false (Schreiner, *1 Corinthians*, 258). The Greek word translated "distinguishing" comes from a word that literally means "to see through." In other words, this gift refers to the ability to see through false teaching, false prophets, and false doctrine. I like to think of it as spiritual x-ray vision.

In the spirit of what's said in 1 John 4:1-3, I believe the gift is also the ability to discern not just by what is being said but sometimes by the person who is saying it. I have found by personal experience that some of the finest, most eloquent speakers can also be the best at deception. More than ever before, the exercise of this gift is desperately needed both in the church and in the academy.

The Gifts of Worship
1 CORINTHIANS 12:9-10

I place two gifts, faith and prophecy, under this category because I believe these two are linked very closely. Most worship will involve some prophecy because God always speaks in and through worship, but no worship can take place apart from faith because "without faith it is impossible to please God" (Heb 11:6). The work of God is expanded through faith. The Word of God is expounded through prophecy.

The Work of Faith (12:9)

The next gift up is faith. This most certainly is not referring to saving faith because that is not just a gift. It is a necessity that all Christians possess in order to have a relationship with God. Hays is certainly correct when he says, "[P]resumedly 'faith' here refers not to ordinary Christian faith in God, but to the sort of special faith that can 'move mountains'" (*Interpretation*, 212). Bailey notes that "faith in the New Testament is composed of intellectual assent, a response in obedience, and a daily walk of trust. . . . Many are gifted in one or more of these three aspects of faith" (*Paul*, 337). I have had the privilege of being around some of the greatest people of faith you can imagine. There are just certain people who have the ability not only to see what no one else can see, go where no one else will go, risk what no one else will risk, but do it with a quiet confidence and unshakable assurance that God is going to come through. Theirs is in effect an unshakable faith in God's unequalled faithfulness that is far more abundant than all that we ask or think.

The Word of Prophecy (12:10)

This one word, this one gift, has generated volumes of debate and discussion as to exactly what should be included in its definition. Carson puts it succinctly when he says, "The answers to that question are legion" (*Showing*, 91). There is neither enough time nor space here to categorize and investigate all the various definitions that have been posited for this gift, but at a minimum I define at least the major part of this gift this way: *The spiritual ability to proclaim God's truth in such an authoritative and powerful fashion that lives are changed, the lost are saved, and believers are motivated for greater service and maturity.* Carson notes there is in fact a sustained tradition that identifies the New Testament prophecy with what we today call "preaching" or "expounding Scripture" (*Showing*, 92). Bailey is helpful when he says, "*Prophecy* is at least preaching at its best. Many have experienced it to be more; it cannot be less" (*Paul*, 337; emphasis in original).

In one sense, all the gifts should have a prophetic function. Every gift should be used in such a way that people better hear the voice of

God and see the work of God. I believe all true preaching should have a prophetic element, and indeed I would venture to say that all true preachers should have at least a measure of this gift. In fact, this is one of the gifts that requires speech. Paul goes on to say two chapters over, "[T]he person who prophesies speaks to people for their strengthening, encouragement, and consolation" (14:3).

To be clear, I agree with Blomberg when he points out,

> Both inside and outside of the canon, prophecy consistently included both "foretelling" (predicting future events) and, *more predominantly*, "forthtelling" (exhorting God's people . . . about his will for their present circumstances). (*1 Corinthians*, 244, emphasis added)

On the other hand, I do not agree with his assessment that in the New Testament prophecy would refer to both what we would call "preaching" directly from the Word of God and then at times "more spontaneous, unpremeditated utterances" (ibid.).

The Gifts of Wonders
1 CORINTHIANS 12:9-10

To put it mildly, some of the gifts described in this section are among the most intriguing and mysterious gifts of all. There are some who believe that these gifts are no longer in existence today. I have difficulties with that view, though I respect those who hold it. My position is that rather than throwing the baby out with the bathwater here, we simply need to clean up the bathwater. That said, we need to understand that these gifts, though normative to Paul, are neverthless exceptional. In the Bible, they are neither more prominent nor more prominently displayed than other gifts. In fact, church history would suggest they are rarely used except in special situations. With that caveat, I accept all these gifts as legitimate for today.

The Gift of Healings (12:9)

In Greek, the words for "gifts" and "healing" are plural. I believe this may be so for two reasons. First, there are different kinds of healings. Surely a doctor can be used by God to bring physical healing, a counselor may be used to bring about emotional healing, and a pastor may be used to bring about spiritual healing. Bailey puts it this way: "Gifts of *healing* are given at times to doctors and also to simple people of faith" (*Paul*, 337; emphasis in original).

Second, I believe it is plural to illustrate that there is no one gift of healing. There are "gifts" of healings. That is, at certain times, in certain situations, and through certain people God brings healing to those who are sick.

Many times in my role as a pastor I have been asked, "Do you believe God still heals people?" My answer to that is, "Not only do I believe it, but only God *can* heal people." Indeed, at the end of the day, all healing is divine healing. Surgeon Ambroise Paré, known as "the first of the moderns," wisely said, "I apply the dressing, but God heals the wound" ("The Journey to Turin, 1537").

Considering the time when Paul wrote this also strongly suggests that not all healings would fall under one simple category. Different people were healed through different people, and as Carson rightly points out, there may have been certain persons with one of these gifts of healing for a certain disease at certain times. However, no Christian should think of the gift of healing as something he or she has on a permanent basis and begin "a healing ministry" (*Showing*, 39–40).

In sum, I do believe in faith healing, though I do not believe in faith healers. God still heals. He sometimes uses medicine to heal, he may use the prayer of faith to heal, or he may use other means to heal. Not since the days of the apostles has there been anyone with the singular gift to heal, nor is it always God's will to heal, but God does still heal.

The Performing of Miracles (12:10)

At the outset, the presupposition that miracles cannot happen must be jettisoned if God is still God. Bailey offers cautionary insight to any who would argue: "In areas of our world traditionally closed to the gospel, astounding *miracles* are taking place that cannot be forced into a post-Enlightenment worldview" (*Paul*, 337; emphasis in original). One clear example of this is that God is using dreams to draw Muslims to faith in Christ, driving them to the Word of God, to the gospel, and to salvation by grace through faith even as they sleep! I have personally met some of these, in fact. And I am not ever going to deny the gift of miracles, not just because I've seen evidence God still does them, but because I might need one at some point!

The word "miracles" in the plural literally means "the workings of powers." The fact that it is in the plural is noteworthy, referring back to the discussion of healings. Carson notes that healings may be a demonstration of miraculous powers, but not all miraculous powers can be limited to healings (*Showing*, 40). Indeed, one could argue both theologically and even practically that the greatest miracle of all is that of regeneration: a sinner who trusts in Jesus is made a new creation! If you have no problems with God, then, you should have no problem with miracles. However, Thiselton cautions, "Deeds of power . . . *does* [sic] *not exclude the miraculous, but neither does it narrowly specify it* as the entire content and range of these deeds of power" (*First Epistle*, 952; emphasis in original). My bottom line is this: When it comes to spiritual gifts— whether it be miracles, healings, messages of wisdom and knowledge, prophecy, or any other gift—I refuse to put God in a box. I am not prepared to tell God what he can do, when he can do it, and where he can do it.

The Word of Tongues (12:10)

Of all the gifts, this one most consistently proves itself a topical land mine. Unfortunately, the gift of tongues has become one of the most controversial and divisive issues among God's people. I would say, based on my pastoral observation, that regardless of what one believes about this gift as it relates to this time, the rules for the exercise of this gift as presented in chapter 14 are seldom followed. Regardless, I believe the gift of tongues is the supernatural ability to speak in a foreign language previously unknown by the speaker so that the gospel and biblical truth might be communicated to people that need to hear it. I realize there are some who believe that this is a gift of what might be called "ecstatic utterance," too. There is, however, no evidence in Hellenistic literature that the word translated "tongues" ever has the connotation of ecstatic utterances (Schreiner, *1 Corinthians*, 261–62). As Mare and Harris point out,

> The only concrete evidence we have as to the nature of the
> tongues-speaking in the early church is to be found in the only
> clear scriptural example we have—that given in Acts 2 where
> the speaking is a speaking in foreign languages that were to be
> understood and were understood. (*1 & 2 Corinthians*, 91)

Bruce concurs that the word "different" or "various" would include languages intelligible to some hearers and those that could not be understood by some hearers and would need interpretation (*1 & 2 Corinthians*, 119).

I believe, therefore, the gift of tongues is a missionary gift. Indeed, there are reports it has been heard on mission fields before. And while in this day and age, given all of the translation technology at our fingertips, it may be growing unnecessary. Nevertheless, the gift of tongues is still a reality.

The Work of Interpretation of Tongues (12:10)

In light of what I said above, this gift would be the spiritual ability to translate a supernaturally given message from an unknown language into the native language of those overhearing it. This missionary gift is specifically for one who is involved with gospel witness but who does not speak the foreign language in question.

Unity in Diversity
1 CORINTHIANS 12:11-31

The Unity That Binds the Body (12:11-13)

So why has the Holy Spirit distributed these gifts in such a fashion? Why doesn't the Holy Spirit give every Christian every gift, or why doesn't he give every Christian the same gift? These gifts are not given arbitrarily but with a definite purpose in mind. Again, the phrase "common good" (v. 7) implies "to bring together" or "to join together." God has made us different so that he might make us one. Why are the pieces of the puzzle all different? So they will all fit together. We have different gifts so that we might all fit together in the body of Christ. Beginning in verse 12 Paul uses the analogy of a body to illustrate that, just as the different parts of a body are joined together to work together, so is Christ's body, the church. The emphasis is not on the word "many" but on the word "one." That is why verse 13 naturally follows: "For we were all baptized by one Spirit into one body—whether Jews or Greeks, whether slaves or free—and we were all given one Spirit to drink."

Paul first describes the unity of the body. We are many members, but we are one body. Now, unity is not to be confused with *union*. It's possible to be in union but not in unity. You can take a dog and a cat and put them in the same house. You may have a union, but you won't have unity.

Unity is not *uniformity*. It does not mean that we have to agree on everything. It does not mean that everyone has to be a copy or a clone of anyone else. To illustrate, an orchestra must have three sections—wind, strings, and percussion—or else it is not an orchestra. It does not mean that everyone plays the same instrument. It means they play the same song in the same tempo and key in harmony with one another. The point is, the same Holy Spirit who gives us different gifts (v. 11) binds those gifts together in the body of Christ, and unity is the result.

The Diversity That Blesses the Body (12:14-31)

God is not only a God of unity, but he is a God of diversity. No two snowflakes are alike; there is a wide spectrum of colors in a rainbow; the world is made up of different ethnicities; and so we read, "Indeed, the body [of Christ] is not one part but many" (v. 14). We are to be different from one another. There is nothing wrong with being different. There is, however, something wrong with being divided. No person should be jealous of another person's spiritual gifts or God-given abilities. Rather, as we come to understand the whole dynamic of spiritual gifts, we celebrate the differences and the point that we are all unique.

But we are also to be *dependent on one another* (vv. 14-17). It takes every part of the body working together to have a healthy, properly functioning church body. Each part of the body is dependent on other parts of the body to do its work. When you drive a car, after all, you need your eyes to guide the car, your hands to steer the car, and your feet to propel the car. Your eyes, hands, and feet are not competing with one another; they are completing one another. Many parts are needed because each part is dependent on others.

One thing to keep in mind is that even though we believers are different members of the body, we are still members of the same body (vv. 18-23). The eye can do things the foot cannot do, and the foot can do things the eye cannot do, but both need each other. There is no such thing as Lone Ranger Christianity. *There is no such thing as a Christian who does not need to be involved in a local church.*

Perhaps you feel disappointed to be only a foot in the body of Christ; if so, remember that when a foot is injured, it cripples the body. You may be only an eye in the body of Christ, but if a body is missing an eye, that whole body will feel its lack. As the human body needs every part working together, so does the body of Christ. Everybody is needed.

This passage tells us not only that every member of the body is equally needed, but every member of the body is equally important. We all have different gifts, different passions, and different interests. Yet every gift should be unwrapped and put into the service of the body. *Everybody is somebody in Christ's body.*

Then, we are to be devoted to one another (vv. 23-26). No matter what functions, gifts, or ministries other people have, we each honor and respect all others, and we empathize with one another. That is exactly the way a body functions. If I have a splinter in my right hand my mouth says, "Ouch!" My brain tells my left hand to try to remove the splinter. My tongue might even lick my hand to offer comfort. Not until that right hand stops hurting will my body feel happy again.

Oftentimes, the church forgets that when one member hurts the body should hurt because the many members are one. We are to be one in sorrow. We are to be one in success. We are to be one in remorse, and we are to be one in rejoicing, for we are all one body (v. 26).

Paul concludes this chapter in verses 27-31. Here we realize the list of spiritual gifts in verses 4-11 is not all-inclusive because Paul mentions two other gifts in these verses, namely "helping" and "leading" (or "administrating"; Bailey, *Paul*, 337). Furthermore, he reminds us that not only is the church given spiritual gifts but also spiritually gifted people—apostles, prophets, and teachers (Schreiner, *1 Corinthians*, 268). Paul specifically numbers in order of importance apostles, prophets, and teachers, which is the same order given in Ephesians 4:11. They are placed first because their jobs are considered of the greatest importance (Mare and Harris, *1 & 2 Corinthians*, 94; Bruce, *1 & 2 Corinthians*, 122). In a sense, though, every Christian has the apostolic ministry of bearing witness to the truth of the resurrection of Jesus. God still calls preachers and prophets who are indeed a prophetic witness of the truth of God's Word to a world full of believers and unbelievers. And in every area of life, people who clearly articulate fundamental truths of the Christian faith are teaching.

Thiselton suggests "helping" (v. 28) means "administrative support" (*First Epistle*, 1019). In every orchestra there is a need for a stage manager. I can tell you no pastor is better than the staff around him and is often reliant on the administrative support that a personal assistant gives. I can certainly testify to that, having had two of the best any pastor could have ever asked for!

"Leading" (v. 28) originally referred to the helmsman of a ship, and it speaks of people who are especially adept at handling details, overseeing finances, and formulating strategies for effective church ministry and leadership.

Paul brilliantly uses the last few words of verse 31 to set up one of the greatest chapters in all of the Bible. It is, in fact, one of the greatest discourses of any kind concerning what makes the world go around as well as on what is truly the glue that holds any church together and makes its witness effective. That topic in not another spiritual gift but love.

Conclusion

The thing to keep in mind about spiritual gifts is not only that they have a theological basis, but they also have a very practical application. We need to remember they are still in existence today, and we should each use our own in the service of the church under the authority of the pastor in a way that brings unity to the body.

Reflect and Discuss

1. What specifically is the gift of wisdom in your understanding? Who do you know who possesses that gift?
2. Explain your understanding of a message of knowledge and share about a time you have given or received such a message.
3. Why is the gift of distinguishing between spirits so very important in the day and age in which we live?
4. What do you understand to be the difference between saving faith and the spiritual gift of faith?
5. What do you believe should always be the connection between the gift of prophecy and the plain teaching of Scripture?
6. Why is it important to believe there is a gift of healings at work in the church even today? What about miracles?
7. Why does Paul link the gift of tongues with the gift of interpretation of tongues?
8. Describe how spiritual gifts used properly will both express the diversity of the church and also bring unity to the church.

Love from Above

1 CORINTHIANS 13

Main Idea: No spiritual gift, no natural ability, no human achievement is greater or more important than love.

I. **The Matchless Value of Love (13:1-3)**
   A. Love is greater than beautiful speech (13:1).
   B. Love is greater than brilliant scholarship (13:2a).
   C. Love is greater than bold spirituality (13:2b).
   D. Love is greater than benevolent sacrifice (13:3).
II. **The Marvelous Virtues of Love (13:4-7)**
   A. Love is patient (13:4a).
   B. Love is kind (13:4b).
   C. Love does not envy (13:4c).
   D. Love is not boastful or arrogant (13:4d).
   E. Love is not rude (13:5a).
   F. Love is not self-seeking (13:5b).
   G. Love is not irritable (13:5c).
   H. Love does not keep a record of wrongs (13:5d).
   I. Love finds no joy in unrighteousness but rejoices in the truth (13:6).
   J. Love bears all things, believes all things, hopes all things, endures all things (13:7).
III. **The Majestic Victory of Love (13:8-13)**
   A. Love is permanent (13:8-12).
   B. Love is preeminent (13:13).

First Corinthians 13 may be one of the most written about, talked about, and preached on passages of Scripture that the apostle Paul wrote. In it, a particular Greek word for love, *agapē*, is used ten times. While some have suggested this is an early version of a Christian hymn or perhaps a stand-alone, independently composed chapter on love, it is clear within the context this chapter is an integral part of a discussion Paul is giving on spiritual gifts and worship in the church. Hays is certainly right when he says, "The purpose of chapter 13 is to portray love as the *sine qua non* of the Christian life and to insist that love must govern the exercise of all the gifts of the Spirit" (*Interpretation*, 221). In the context of all of Paul's writings concerning the Holy Spirit, certainly one principle we can derive from this chapter is that the fruit of the Spirit, namely love, is more important than the gifts of the Spirit (so says Bruce, *1 & 2 Corinthians*, 124). This chapter neatly divides into three basic sections.

The Matchless Value of Love
1 CORINTHIANS 13:1-3

Love Is Greater Than Beautiful Speech (13:1)

One may have the ability to move the minds of men through soaring oratory, but without love no speech can move the heart of God. The language of "angelic tongues" here should not be pressed, for it is most certainly hyperbolic (Schreiner, *1 Corinthians*, 273). Paul likely is trying to draw as sharp a contrast as possible with love (Carson, *Showing*, 58). Have you ever been to a cymbal concert? I am sure you have not. You couldn't stand it very long if you did! The point is, you may have the gift of beautiful speech, but without love your words are just noise.

Love Is Greater Than Brilliant Scholarship (13:2a)

You may have a PhD—perhaps even more degrees than a thermometer— and display great insight into deep truths that no one else can even fathom, yet without love it is not just that your scholarship is nothing. Tragically, you yourself are nothing. In other words, you may have knowledge bursting from your head, but if you do not have love bursting from your heart, you are just a big bust. Pharisees, after all, were brilliant theologians. They knew the law and the Scriptures inside out. They could split a theological hair into sixteen equal divisions, yet even a high-powered microscope would be unable to find love for God and others in most of their hearts.

Love Is Greater Than Bold Spirituality (13:2b)

This passage is not about saving faith or the gift of faith Paul previously referred to. This is the kind visionaries, entrepreneurs, and risk-takers may have. You may have mountain-moving faith that you can go out and accomplish great things for God, but if you do not have love, you are just one big molehill.

Love Is Greater Than Benevolent Sacrifice (13:3)

Even should you offer the ultimate sacrifice of your life for a cause or a belief with the goal of being able to boast about yourself (apparently in eternity) or to give others reason to boast about you, you gain nothing if you are not also motivated by love. Here some translations, including the CSB, use manuscripts with the verb *kauchēsōmai*, "to boast."[3] Others follow different manuscripts with the verb *kauthēsōmai*, "to burn." All in all, I agree with Thiselton that "to boast" is "the more probable reading on both external and internal grounds" (*First Epistle*, 1042–43).

The Marvelous Virtues of Love
1 CORINTHIANS 13:4-7

As we enter this second section in the chapter, I need to be clear that Paul is not deprecating or depreciating the importance of spiritual gifts. His point is that any and all spiritual gifts are dispensable, but love is indispensable (Carson, *Showing*, 61). Paul engages in describing love not in theoretical, philosophical, or even theological terms, but mainly in practical terms (ibid.).

Love Is Patient (13:4a)

If you can imagine love being a fleet of ships, then the flagship of love is patience. In contrast to that virtue, we use the term *short-tempered* to describe someone who loses his or her temper quickly or has a short fuse. Here the word that Paul uses is made up of two words. The first word is *macro*, which is the opposite of *micro*. It means "long." The second word is *thymia*, which refers to heat or passion. So, literally, "love is long-tempered." Love has a long fuse. Love also has a short memory.

Love Is Kind (13:4b)

The word translated "kind" was used to describe food that was tasty as well as healthy. It is the only time this phrase is used in the whole New Testament. It is not just an action toward one to whom it is easy to be kind but a reaction to one who is not. Love is "quick to pay back with kindness what it received in hurt" (Carson, *Showing*, 62). Mark Twain

---

[3] Thiselton: "This verse constitutes one of the most widely known examples of the crux of textual criticism in the New Testament" (*First Epistle*, 1042).

reportedly said, "Kindness is a language the deaf can hear and the blind can see."

Love Does Not Envy (13:4c)

True love isn't envious. Both AMP and NLT use the word "jealous" here. The only being in the universe who has a right to be jealous in this sense is God because he is the only God there is. Not only is it the case that a person who loves is not envious because of what someone else has or does, but he or she actually rejoices that the Lord has given someone a gift or ability. This is especially relevant today for pastors because nothing is more dangerous to one's self-esteem or to one's spiritual attitude than pastoral jealousy. Loving allows you to say "Amen!" to another church's revival!

Love Is Not Boastful or Arrogant (13:4d)

Love does not boast or feel arrogant because it always deflects praise to others and glory to God. Perhaps this is why it can prove particularly difficult to love when you are a successful person. What I am saying is well worth emphasizing. As Alfred North Whitehead reportedly said, "No one who achieves [true] success does so without acknowledging the help of others. The wise and confident acknowledge this help with gratitude." In fact, you might say that one of the great measurements of love is humility. You will see this amplified with everything else Paul says about love.

Love Is Not Rude (13:5a)

I prefer the NIV's translation here: love "does not dishonor others." Indeed, it isn't rude. It doesn't put another person down and doesn't cut other people off. It doesn't interrupt when another person is talking and doesn't ignore the one who is trying to talk. Simply put, love is always courteous. It doesn't cut in line. In fact, it lets others go first.

Love Is Not Self-Seeking (13:5b)

Jesus Christ exemplified that true love is selfless love. It is a loving-you-before-you-love-me and even-if-you-don't-deserve-it kind of love. If Jesus had been looking out only for himself, he would not have gone to the cross. If Jesus had been self-seeking, we would all be on the ocean of sin in a boat without sails or oars. But his love, which is true love, says, "I am making a commitment to place your needs above my comfort." The love from above doesn't ask, "What can you do for me?" It asks, "What can I do for you?"

Love Is Not Irritable (13:5c)

Be honest: sometimes it is very easy to get irritable with people who are irritating, isn't it? True love realizes we can all be irritating at times. True love recognizes that we all have bad days. Therefore, extending grace, love does not look for reasons to nitpick. James offers helpful counsel: "Everyone should be quick to listen, slow to speak, and slow to anger" (Jas 1:19).

Love Does Not Keep a Record of Wrongs (13:5d)

Having been an accounting major in college, I appreciate this word translated "record" here because it is actually an accounting or book-keeping term. Literally, the passage means, "Love does not keep a ledger on evil." Love does not hold a grudge. It leaves a lot of room for people to make mistakes, and when they do, to forgive them and over-look the offenses. Love doesn't keep a list in a back pocket to pull out whenever a certain person needs to be reminded of how he or she did us wrong. Love doesn't need a file cabinet or a backup on the computer for grievance storage. It releases things people have done to hurt us.

Love Finds No Joy in Unrighteousness but Rejoices in the Truth (13:6)

Here is the most difficult part of real love (the hardest of all of these virtues): "it rejoices in the truth." That means that when you really love someone you will be willing both to tell them the truth when they need to hear it but also to receive the truth from them when you need to hear it, regardless of pain and unpleasantness. If you have friends who cannot hear truth or will not tell you the truth, they really are not your friends.

Love Bears All Things, Believes All Things, Hopes All Things, Endures All Things (13:7)

Something is repeated four times in this verse: the word translated *all.* It is derived from the Greek word *panta.* You see reference to it all the time in your dictionary. *Pan*theism is the belief that God is in *all things.* A *pan*acea is a cure for *all things.* A *pan*oply is an array of *all things. Panta* means *all things*. What Paul is saying is that love always sees the glass not just half-full but totally full. It always looks for the good, the positive. It does not look over people's faults, but it overlooks people's faults.

There is a staying power to true love, like a flame that cannot be quenched. Love takes the long view not the short view. It keeps the big picture in mind. It hangs in there with other people even under their worst circumstances and refuses to quit. For married couples, it takes seriously those words "until death do us part." You simply cannot kill a love that bears, keeps believing and hoping through, and endures all things. That is a love that will last through all adversity and stand the test of time.

The Majestic Victory of Love
1 CORINTHIANS 13:8-13

As if Paul has not already said enough about one of the most powerful words in the English language, he drives the point home with a sledge-hammer blow in his closing passage.

Love Is Permanent (13:8-12)

Three words say it all: "Love never ends" (v. 8). As necessary, as profitable, as needed are spiritual gifts, they are temporary. The gifts most highly valued by the Corinthian church, such as tongues, knowledge, and prophecy, will all cease to exist. They will do so "when the perfect comes" (v. 10). There is some debate over what "the perfect" references. The context and the overarching revelatory context of Scripture convinces me this is referring to "the arrival of the eschaton, when all God's purposes for human beings will be realized and fulfilled" (Schreiner, *1 Corinthians*, 280). In other words, it refers to the "life in the world to come after Jesus reappears on earth" (Blomberg, *1 Corinthians*, 260). The gifts mentioned simply won't be needed then. One cautionary note, though: "'Perfection' is not the Parousia itself, but the state of affairs brought about by the arrival of the Parousia" (Carson, *Showing*, 69).

Love can never end, for if God is love and God cannot end, then certainly love cannot end either. The moments each of us arrives in heaven will be the first time that we will experience perfect love—not just a perfect love from God but a perfect love for God and a perfect love for each other.

Love Is Preeminent (13:13)

Though my interpretation goes against the grain of much scholarship, I believe what Paul means here is very simple. The reason that love is the greatest is because love is the one virtue of the three mentioned that we will take into eternity. Faith becomes sight in heaven, hope is completely fulfilled in heaven, but love, again, never ends. Love never ceases. Moreover, it is because of the magnificent love of God that our faith will be rewarded by sight and our hope will be rewarded by total fulfillment.

I agree with John MacArthur: "Because faith and hope will have no purpose in heaven, where everything true will be known and everything good will be possessed, they are not equal to love" (*1 Corinthians*, 167). In my opinion, this even goes with the entire sense of all that Paul has stated in 1 Corinthians 13, putting love on the top of the Mount Everest of spiritual qualities. Of faith, hope, and love, the most Godlike is love because "God does not have faith or hope, but 'God *is* love' (1 John 4:8)" (ibid.; emphasis in original). God did not send his Son into the world because he believed in the world and had hope in this world, but because he loved this world.

Conclusion

There is a divine element to true love that can never be dismissed. It is impossible for this world to comprehend what real love is without knowing the God who is love and the God who gives love.

Reflect and Discuss

1. In what ways have you tried to substitute other things, such as speech and scholarship, for loving? What was the result?
2. Which of the virtues of love do you find easiest to practice?
3. Which of the virtues of love do you find most difficult to practice?
4. How does the concept of true love relate to the issue of bitterness and the lack of forgiveness that we find so prevalent both in the church and outside it?
5. How is love even greater than faith and hope?
6. What are some practical ways you can express love that you have heretofore not done effectively?

Control Your Tongues

1 CORINTHIANS 14

Main Idea: The gift of tongues comes with a reminder that the most important thing about all spiritual gifts is not the experience of a gift but the effectiveness of the gift.

I. **Determine the Meaning of the Gift (14:1-25).**
   A. The definition of the word *tongue* (14:1-4)
   B. The difference between prophecy and tongues (14:5-25)
II. **Describe the Ministry of the Gift (14:7-9,12,14-15,19,22).**
   A. The ministry of communication (14:7-9,12,14-15,19)
   B. The ministry of confirmation (14:22)
   C. The ministry of conversion (14:19)
III. **Direct the Management of the Gift (14:26-40).**
   A. There was confusion from the gift (14:26-31).
   B. There was conflict with the gift (14:20,32-33).
   C. There was to be control over the gift (14:28,33-40).

Dealing with the subject of 1 Corinthians 14 relative to speaking in tongues is akin to handling spiritual nitroglycerin: one false move and everything can blow up! No biblical subject, in fact, has caused more consternation, fueled more debates, ignited more arguments, or divided more churches, perhaps, than the subject that is likely properly termed *glossolalia*. The difficulty is immediately signaled when one realizes that, unlike in the case of any other spiritual gift, one entire chapter of the New Testament is devoted to discussing it.

Carson notes there are three distinct issues in play in the matter of tongues (*Showing*, 78): Is ecstasy involved? Is the utterance contemptuous or not? Is it a known human language?

The underlying cause of contention may be in the very meaning of the word "tongues." Again, Carson puts the matter succinctly. What does one mean by the term *tongues*? Are they . . .

"real languages" or something else? . . . Is the phenomenon in
1 Corinthians 14 an instance of xenoglossia (that is, speaking
in unlearned human languages) or glossolalia (that is,

speaking in verbal patterns that cannot be identified with any human language)? (*Showing*, 79)

One thing to keep in mind when attempting to interpret this chapter is Paul's conclusion words in verses 39-40: "So then, my brothers and sisters, be eager to prophesy, and do not forbid speaking in tongues. But everything is to be done decently and in order." So, putting my cards on the table, I do not believe that the gift of tongues has ceased, nor do I believe we should forbid someone to speak in tongues. I do not believe we should forbid the exercise of any spiritual gift as long as it is done legitimately and scripturally. I do not intend to be dogmatic in the interpretation that I will put forth. I realize there are many wonderful, godly Christians who both see this gift differently than I do and would exercise it accordingly. So, my only caveat would be that the gift should be exercised biblically, following all the regulations laid down in this chapter.

It should also be said that believers should not be opposed to enthusiasm and excitement in worship. Certainly it would be great for all of our churches if people were more participative in worship and not less. Sadly, some of what may be seen as excesses in worship are perhaps a reaction to the dead formalism we have in many churches today. So as we tackle this difficult chapter, I ask for grace and that you agree with me on three criteria: *the exercise of any spiritual gift should always be for the glorification of God, the edification of the church, and (ultimately) the evangelization of the lost.*

Determine the Meaning of the Gift
1 CORINTHIANS 14:1-25

The Definition of the Word "Tongue"

The word translated "pursue" (v. 1) refers to a hunter chasing after prey (Thiselton, *First Epistle*, 1082). While there is nothing wrong with spiritual gifts, the exercise of them, and desiring them, what we must note here is that the ultimate prey we are after is love. If spiritual gifts are not clothed in love, those exercising them are in effect naked and should be ashamed.

Now, the moment Paul refers to "the person who speaks in a tongue" (v. 4), this question comes up: "What is this gift?" Is it some form of esoteric, ecstatic, angelic babbling that is known only to God? Or is it something else? Before we can deal with the gift, we have to define the gift.

The Greek word translated here as "tongue" is *glossa*. The word is used fifty times in the New Testament. Sometimes it refers to a literal human tongue (a physical organ in the mouth). In Acts 2:3, however, it is used figuratively to refer to tongues of fire. The other thirty-three times the word means "language." My studied opinion is it always refers to a foreign language, an earthly language that is spoken by some group or nation on this earth. For example, see Revelation 5:9:

> And they sang a new song: You are worthy to take the scroll and to open its seals, because you were slaughtered, and you purchased people for God by your blood from every tribe and language and people and nation.

The CSB properly translates this use of *glossa* as "language." Every tribe and nation, yes, some from every language spoken on earth, will be in heaven.

Admittedly, there are those who hold that the gift spoken of in 1 Corinthians 14 is an altogether different gift. It is some sort of an angelic heavenly language or an unknown language. However, there are several things to consider in opposition to this view.

We are fortunate to find that in the King James Version the word "unknown" is supplied (see 14:2 KJV). In my copy, it is italicized, though, which means that adjective is not in the original. This means people were not speaking in an unknown tongue, as has been held by some, but simply "another language." As we know, there are all kinds of foreign "tongues" or languages. Hebrew, Greek, Aramaic, Italian, Spanish, Russian, or English: they are all simply different kinds of languages. Furthermore, I do not believe it is coincidental that Paul uses this very type of illustration in verses 10-11. It is obvious there that Paul is referring to a human language that is foreign to him.

Further down, Paul quotes a prophecy in verse 21. In it, taken from Isaiah 28:11-12, Isaiah was prophesying the Assyrian takeover of the Jewish people. His point was that God had tried to speak in the Hebrew language to call the nation to repent, but when they refused, God brought a people speaking another language; it would be a real language, but one the Hebrews would not understand as a sign of his judgment.

Furthermore, it is extremely relevant to me that the first evidence of any type of speaking in tongues is found in the book of Acts, where what Luke describes are real known human languages (Carson, *Showing*, 80). In fact, word studies have shown that never does the term *glossa* denote noncognitive utterance (ibid., 83; Gundry, "Ecstatic Utterance," 299–307).

So to summarize, I define the gift of speaking in tongues as a gift of speaking in a foreign language that is totally unknown to the one who is speaking and to some who may be hearing. This is what we find in the very first occurrence of the gift in the book of Acts.

The Difference Between Prophecy and Tongues

In the beginning verses Paul is putting prophecy and tongues on a scale, as it were, to see which of the two is more weighty. He immediately notes that *prophecy is to be desired above tongues* (vv. 1-5).

Paul makes it plain that, between the two gifts, the greater gift and the better gift is prophecy. That is not necessarily the best spiritual gift, but it is one that the Corinthians should desire. The reason can be boiled down to one simple truth. When the gift of tongues stands alone without interpretation, it is unintelligible and only benefits the speaker, but prophecy builds up the church (Hays, *Interpretation*, 235). It should be noted immediately that there is something unique about tongues: *it is the only gift that needs a corollary spiritual gift to complete its function as a gift.* Tongues can neither edify the church, glorify God in the greatest sense, nor evangelize the lost unless there is understanding. That is simply undeniable in this chapter (Bruce, *1 & 2 Corinthians*, 130).

Next we see that *prophecy is distinguished from tongues* (vv. 6-12). As we discuss these verses and in fact the entire chapter, keep in mind that for Paul two things are paramount: (1) communication in the church must be intelligible and delivered in such a way that people as well as God understand what is being said, and (2) the building up of the church and the stabilizing of the community are purposes behind the gifts. In verses 6-12 Paul uses various analogies to make the point.

The first analogy Paul uses involves musical instruments (v. 7). Musical instruments don't exist to make random sounds; they are intended to actually play music that has melody and meaning. Music that is unintelligible to the mind will never move the heart.

An even more pertinent illustration involves the military bugler (v. 8). A soldier must always know whether the bugler is sounding retreat or attack. Getting that wrong can lead to a disastrous defeat instead of thrilling victory. The fact that Paul has to emphasize this point with examples from music and the military shows just how deeply committed at least some of the Corinthians were to trying to argue for the superiority of tongues (Carson, *Showing*, 103).

Of course, the third analogy one might expect from Paul is here, too. He speaks of the variety of *known* languages in the world, noting that every language has meaning that can be understood when properly heard or interpreted (vv. 9-11). In fact, languages are given to do just that—communicate intelligibly (Schreiner, *1 Corinthians*, 288).

The word "therefore" signals that Paul is drawing a conclusion from the analogies he just listed (vv. 13-19). A word and a phrase stand out in this passage: "understanding" and "built up." Edification, being built up (v. 17), always comes only through understanding (v. 14). Paul points out the redundant *sine qua non* of interpretation accompanying tongues. There is no question that in this passage Paul is putting a premium on understanding because edification comes through the mind and through understanding (Schreiner, *1 Corinthians*, 289).

Simply but strongly put, when believers come together for both personal and corporate worship, understanding and intelligibility should rule the day. The ultimate goal, after all, is the edification of the church. Carson rightly says, "Edification in the church depends utterly on intelligibility, understanding, coherence. Both charismatic and non-charismatic churches need to be reminded of that truth again and again" (*Showing*, 106).

In verses 20-25 Paul draws the only conclusion anyone could from all that he has said: *prophecy is over tongues*.

Whether for the benefit of believers or unbelievers, prophecy should always be first in line over tongues. Any spiritual gift that puts a barrier between unbelievers and God rather than a bridge is simply out of place. F. F. Bruce points out, "Over concentration on glossolalia is a mark of immaturity" (*1 & 2 Corinthians*, 132). Spiritual maturity would never under any circumstance stress something that is noncognitive over what is cognitive. It would never emphasize what is unintelligible over that which is intelligible (Blomberg, *1 Corinthians*, 270). Paul focuses his attention on "people on the periphery of the church community"; they need to understand what they hear for it to benefit them (Hays, *Interpretation*, 238). It cannot be stated strongly enough, in fact, that the most important aspect of any spiritual gift is not the personal experience of the gift but the spiritual effect of the gift. Any gift falls short of its God-intended function if it does not edify the believer and help evangelize the unbeliever. One cannot deny the plain teaching in this passage that prophecy—speaking plain truth from God—is a powerful tool for evangelism, but tongues, if uninterpretable, is a hindrance to making the gospel clear (Hays, *Interpretation*, 239).

Though Schreiner is certainly correct that verses 20-25 are some of the most difficult in the letter (*1 Corinthians*, 290), the thrust of the passage is clear. Prophecy not only edifies believers every time, since it is understandable and fosters maturity, but prophecy evangelizes unbelievers, producing belief when unbelievers are convicted of their sins and brought to faith through hearing the gospel plainly presented (Schreiner, *1 Corinthians*, 292).

Describe the Ministry of the Gift
1 CORINTHIANS 14:7-9,12,14-15,19,22

When tongues are properly interpreted, what is the purpose and function of the gift? The gift of speaking in tongues, which is speaking in a foreign language by the supernatural power of God, is a threefold ministry.

The Ministry of Communication (14:7-9,12,14-15,19)

Every verbal spiritual gift—whether it is prophecy, teaching, exhortation, or speaking in tongues—should communicate truth that correlates with the Word of God. Whether it is a human language or a heavenly language, anything that is not interpretable doesn't communicate anything. Just as a flute communicates music or a bugle communicates military orders (vv. 7-8), words must communicate to serve any purpose (v. 9). It is better never to say a word, in fact, than to say a thousand words that cannot be understood because that only results in confusion rather than communication. The gift of speaking in tongues is not so much to communicate to God but to communicate for God.

But Carson believes that verse 9, along with verses 18-19, provides an extremely strong defense of the private use of tongues. He dogmatically states, "The only possible conclusion is that Paul exercises his remarkable tongues gift *in private*" (*Showing*, 105; emphasis in original). Though it is difficult to find solid evidence of tongues of any sort being used this way in Scripture, for sure a gift used privately in a closet cannot possibly edify the church—only the discipline of prayer works that way. One thing that chapter 14 should tell us all is that we need to get a lot of spiritual gifts out of the closet and into the pews so the church can be truly edified.

Nevertheless, Scripture sheds light in verses 14 and 15 on what Paul means here, and note that it does fit within the context of prayer. In effect, Paul is saying, "We are not only to pray with our hearts; we are to pray with our heads, and we are to understand what we say when we pray." Any speaking gift is, by the very nature of its function, to exercise the ministry of communication.

The Ministry of Confirmation (14:22)

What did Paul mean when he said that tongues were a sign for unbelievers (v. 22)? We have already stated it could refer, as it did in the reference to Isaiah, to the judgment of God, but I would go further.

Tongues when interpreted can also show unbelievers the power of God when they hear the gospel in their own languages, knowing full well there would be no way the speaker could have possibly known the language beforehand. Certainly in the book of Acts tongues was a sign of confirmation. It made unbelievers sit up and take notice. Jews from all over the world asked, "How is it that each of us can hear them in our own language? . . . [We all] hear them declaring the magnificent acts of God in our own tongues" (Acts 2:8,11).

The Ministry of Conversion (14:19)

Paul was primarily a missionary and a church planter. What Paul was saying in verse 19 was that in the church he would prophesy. Five words of prophecy spoken in the common language of a congregation of believers would be better "than ten thousand words in" a tongue foreign to them. On the foreign mission field, things might sometimes be far different.

As stated previously, I believe speaking in tongues is primarily a missionary gift. It was a gift that God gave and that God can still give so that people around the world can hear the gospel in their own languages. With current technology a gift like this is less necessary than it once was, but it can still be useful in certain parts of the world.

Could this reality be what Paul had in mind when he said, "I wish all of you spoke in tongues" (v. 5)? I think so. After all, one would meet all kinds of foreigners in those days. It would make sense that Paul was saying in effect, "I wish every time you met people whose language you didn't speak, and they didn't speak yours, that you could exercise this gift of tongues so that they might hear the gospel, understand it, and come to know Jesus."

It cannot be overemphasized that spiritual gifts are not gifts primarily for our enjoyment but for God's employment. They are a means to an end: teaching biblical truth to believers and reaching unbelievers with the gospel.

Direct the Management of the Gift
1 CORINTHIANS 14:26-40

To reiterate, I am not denouncing the legitimate biblical gift of speaking in tongues, and neither did Paul. He made that very plain when he said, "[D]o not forbid speaking in tongues" (v. 39). So whatever you believe about this gift, it is a legitimate biblical spiritual gift. Though we should not denounce the use of the gift, we must direct the management of it. This gift was being grossly misused in the Corinthian church, and we know that for two reasons.

There Was Confusion from the Gift (14:26-33)

Unlike any other gift listed in any other New Testament book, these two gifts, tongues and prophecy, are to be highly regulated. Why? Verse 33 says it all: "since God is not a God of disorder but of peace." There was confusion in the Corinthian church. The worship services were chaotic. Praise had been replaced by pandemonium. Their worship services at times resembled Grand Central Station in New York on Monday morning: mass confusion.

Where there is confusion, you will find the absence of God. God is not the author of confusion or disorder. He is the author of peace and order and purpose. I believe we are confused about tongues in particular today for the same reason they were confused two thousand years ago: the gift is misunderstood and misused. It had been given a place of prominence in the church when in fact it should not have been. Paul does not hesitate to say that the gift of prophecy is much more productive and fruitful than the gift of tongues, particularly in a service where there is no one to interpret. What is certainly also clear is that not every Christian has this gift or should seek the gift, but those who have the gift should make sure it is used properly.

There Was Conflict Over the Gift (14:20,32-33)

The Corinthians were acting like children (v. 20). They were at each other's throats over the gift of tongues. Sadly, there is still much conflict over this gift. There are many born-again Christians who love Jesus, who believe the Bible, who want God to be glorified, who are filled with the Holy Spirit, but who have been led to believe they are deficient since they do not exercise the gift of tongues. Then there are those who won't even fellowship with anyone who believes he or she has the gift, particularly if such a person thinks of it as some type of angelic or heavenly, unintelligible language. There is also ridicule of those with the gift and rejection of the gift itself.

This is not from God. Spiritual gifts were intended by God to bring harmony not disharmony, to bring unity not disunity, to be a rallying point not a dividing line. So what was Paul's solution?

There Must Be Control of the Gift (14:28,33-40)

There were very strict safeguards on this gift, not to eliminate it but to regulate it. Let me reiterate. In a service, the gift must be accompanied by interpretation (v. 28). Speaking in tongues and interpretation are joined at the hip, and in a public assembly they are never to be used apart from one another. A speaker should not exercise the gift unless there is someone to interpret the tongues; sometimes the one speaking in tongues can interpret.

Then comes this kicker. Paul says,

> [T]he women should be silent in the churches, for they are not permitted to speak, but are to submit themselves, as the law also says. If they want to learn something, let them ask their own husbands at home, since it is disgraceful for a woman to speak in the church. (14:34-35)

Frankly, I grew up in a church tradition that took these verses out of context and taught that a woman could not pray or say anything at all in church. That is an impossibility, since Paul gives clear instructions in chapter 11 that a woman can not only pray but also prophesy. Though these verses are hotly debated, a viable position has been proposed. Verse 29 calls for prophecy to be evaluated. I agree with Blomberg when he says, "Perhaps the best perspective, therefore, is to take Paul's commands as prohibiting women from participating in the final church decisions about the legitimacy of any given prophecy" (1 Corinthians, 281). He is surely right when he says that the evaluation of any prophecy would most likely have been the responsibility of the church leadership, which at least in the first century was exclusively male (ibid.). Carson concurs that, in light of the call to submission and obedience to the law, this seems to be the most plausible interpretation (Showing, 129–31).

Anticipating objections, Paul closes with firm words (vv. 37-40). Spiritual gifts are to be subject to two authorities: the Word of God and the man of God. The Corinthians should recognize that what he wrote to them is the Lord's command, and they should also understand that "the prophets' spirits are subject to the prophets" (v. 32).

Conclusion

The bottom line is that every gift must be exercised in a way that is fitting and orderly, ultimately meeting all three criteria of glorying God, edifying the church, and evangelizing the lost. The goal for all the gifts is to strengthen and build up the church.

Reflect and Discuss

1. What is your past experience with the use of spiritual gifts in the church? In what ways does your experience shape how you think about spiritual gifts today?

2. Why should those wielding spiritual gifts feel naked and ashamed if they have failed to exercise their gifts in love? How do we endanger the church if we promote someone who boldly uses spiritual gifts but lacks love?

3. How will one's perception of spiritual gifts change if speaking in tongues employs a coherent, foreign language as opposed to an incoherent, angelic language? How does the purpose of the gift change?

4. How do you determine if you are using your spiritual gifts for the glory of God or the glory of self? What might cause people to shift from using their gifts to edify the church to using their gifts to promote themselves?

5. Why should you not equate having spiritual gifts with being holy? Are there examples in Scripture of people having gifts and not holiness? If so, identify one.

6. What is the difference between the "experience" of a spiritual gift and the "effectiveness" of that spiritual gift? Why is the latter more important?

7. What is the relationship between God's Word and spiritual gifts? What will happen when you use spiritual gifts without any relationship to God's Word? Are there also dangers if you neglect spiritual gifts as you promote God's Word?

8. How did speaking in tongues fuel the early church's missionary work?

The Gospel

1 CORINTHIANS 15:1-11

Main Idea: The gospel is the most important message in the history of the world, for it alone is an eternally saving message and is therefore to be a universally shared message.

I.   We Must Prioritize the Message of the Gospel (15:1-3).
II. We Must Recognize the Meaning of the Gospel (15:3-8).
III. We Must Emphasize the Might of the Gospel (15:2,9-11).

One of the reasons George Washington was so revered and respected by his countrymen and was chosen to be the first commander in chief and the president of the United States is he was "first in war, first in peace, and first in the hearts of his countrymen." To put that simply, he knew how to keep first things first.

Never has doing that been more important in the life of the church than today. The church has been given one mission, and that always will be the first activity we are to be about: fulfilling the Great Commission—making disciples of all nations. The church is unique in many ways compared to any other institution or entity in the world, not the least of which is because *the mission of the church is actually determined by the message of the church.* The church must put above everything else the proclamation of the message of the church, which is called "the gospel." Certainly, the gospel is not the only message of the Bible or the church, but it is the first and most important message of both. Essentially, this is what the most prolific writer of the New Testament and perhaps the most famous Christian who ever lived said in the chapter we are going to study.

It is accurate to say that the primary reason Jesus came was so we would have a gospel to embrace and so we would proclaim the gospel. Yet I believe we are living in a day when more and more churches and more and more pastors and teachers are putting less and less emphasis on the gospel—to our detriment. I will admit that I write this particular part of this commentary with the rock-ribbed conviction that at every opportunity, both in church buildings and outside them, the gospel should be heard and clearly explained, and people should have a chance to respond to that gospel.

This is keeping first things first.

We Must Prioritize the Message of the Gospel
1 CORINTHIANS 15:1-3

Paul begins this chapter with a somewhat surprising but also helpful statement (v. 1). The word translated "make clear" is the Greek word *gnōrizō*, the translation of which, Thiselton points out, "is more difficult than might appear" (*First Epistle*, 1183). Paul uses this verb in 12:3 to mean "I give you to understand" (ibid.). I believe the CSB translation "make clear," both by context and force, is most fitting. Obviously, these Corinthians knew and understood the gospel enough to be saved by it. But for reasons to be seen, Paul obviously felt the need to make crystal clear the true essence of the gospel again. In the early church there was a need to continuously clarify the heart of the gospel.

Verse 2 contains an amazing statement we will return to at the end of this section. Simply put, Paul said the gospel is so important because it is how anyone is saved. How can people come to know God through faith in Jesus Christ unless they hear and respond to the gospel? With that being true, Paul's next statement logically follows. Paul says the "most important" message of the church is the gospel of Jesus Christ (v. 3). It is the one message, the foremost message that should always make the cut in our preaching and teaching. In the context of this letter, this statement carries even more force.

Paul had to deal with so many subjects in this church—from incest, to sex, to spiritual gifts, to marriage, to the single life, to temptation, to the Lord's Supper, to speaking in tongues—but he declares that the most important subject is and always will be the gospel. To reiterate, it is not the only message of the church, but it is the main message of the church. Schreiner says, "The gospel is the priority as it represents 'the fundamentals of the Christian faith'—the baseline and touchstone for all that is taught" (*1 Corinthians*, 303).

We Must Recognize the Meaning of the Gospel
1 CORINTHIANS 15:3-8

Paul feels a need to define exactly almost to the last letter of the last word what the gospel is. He lets us know there are three key components to the gospel. Paul refers to the fact that he is passing on what he had "received" (v. 3). Hays points out that this is the same terminology he uses in describing how he received the tradition of the Lord's Supper

(11:23). This indicates that this confession likely dates back to the time when Paul was called to be an apostle, within about three years after Jesus was crucified (Hays, *Interpretation*, 255).

The first truth of the gospel is that "Christ died for our sins according to the Scriptures" (15:3). The Greek word translated "for" could be translated "concerning." Jesus died concerning the sins of the world, and because of the sins of the world he died as our substitute.

There is nothing unusual about people dying. People die every day. It wasn't even unusual back in the days of Jesus for people to be crucified. Thirty thousand Jews were crucified during the time of the Roman occupation of Israel (MacArthur, "The Wickedness of the Crucifiction"). What made his death stand out above every other death in history is first that he died *concerning our sins*. The emphasis is surely on the fact that Christ died. The verb is in the aorist tense denoting a single past event setting up for these Corinthians the main theme of the chapter, which is both the resurrection of Jesus and our own resurrection. He died but also rose "never to die again" (cf. Rom 6:9; Thistelton, *First Epistle*, 192).

There is another part of the gospel we don't pay much attention to, but it is also important. We don't often note in conversation "that he was buried" (v. 4). To some that mention may seem redundant or even unnecessary, but obviously Paul did not think it was a small detail at all because the point is that only dead men get buried. In fact, I have informed my wife that before she buries me my only request is that she truly makes sure I am dead! The detail of burial is not only a necessary part of the story of the gospel, it was actually a fulfilment of biblical prophecy. Isaiah prophesied seven hundred fifty years before this event, saying, "He was assigned a grave with the wicked, but he was with a rich man at his death, because he had done no violence and had not spoken deceitfully" (Isa 53:9). It is entirely possible that Paul was anticipating objections to the resurrection of Jesus, too, because if you deny the resurrection, you either have to deny that he was raised (as many skeptics do) or you have to deny that he really died (as some other religions do).

Of course, contemporary readers would have realized this clear statement that he was buried also addressed the rumor that someone had stolen a corpse. The very rumor itself substantiates the fact that Jesus was indeed buried. Furthermore, the process involved in preparing the body, putting it in a sealed tomb, and guarding it by a crack garrison of Roman soldiers—all of which goes against any so-called Swoon

Theory, which claims that Jesus really didn't die but somehow revived from his Calvary experiences and broke out of the tomb on his own.

The gospel emphasizes three parts: part 1—Jesus literally died; part 2—Jesus was actually buried; part 3—Jesus was physically raised to be a resurrected Lord. Paul says, "[H]e was raised on the third day according to the Scriptures" (v. 4). It should go without saying that the other two parts of the gospel do not matter if this third part is not true. There is only one way to know that his death for our sins was efficacious, and that is the resurrection. In modern-day financial terms, the resurrection is God's receipt to us that our sins have been paid in full. Christ's death is the payment.

The reference to Christ's burial in verse 2 confirms the reality of his death, but then Paul trots out a line of eyewitnesses to underscore he really was raised from the dead (vv. 5-8). Hays is correct in stating,

> This shows that Paul did not think of the resurrection of Jesus
> as some sort of ineffable truth beyond history; rather, it was
> an event that had occurred in the immediate past, an event
> for which historical eyewitness testimony was readily available.
> (*Interpretation*, 257)

We Must Emphasize the Might of the Gospel
1 CORINTHIANS 15:2,9-11

Next, Paul feels the need to point out why he is qualified to talk about the gospel. This he does in a powerful, personal way that relates to the impact the gospel has had in his own life.

Why is the gospel the most important message in the Bible? Why is the gospel the most important message of the church? Why is the gospel the most important message of the Christian? Because, as Paul stated elsewhere, "[I]t is the power of God for salvation to everyone who believes" (Rom 1:16). It is by the gospel "you are being saved," Paul notes, "if you hold to the message I preached to you—unless you believed in vain" (1 Cor 15:2). There is no deliberation, equivocation, or hesitation. The gospel is the only message that has the power to take anyone from sin to salvation, from hell to heaven, from death to life, and from darkness to light. Having experienced this, Paul naturally points to himself as the supreme example of the power of the gospel (vv. 9-11).

The transparency and honesty of perhaps the greatest Christian who ever lived is both heartwarming and breathtaking. He fully admits he is the least of all apostles. He should not even be called an apostle. In fact, he had been the ultimate anti-apostle by persecuting God's church. Nevertheless, it was the resurrected Lord who saved Paul by grace, changed him by grace, and empowered him with grace to do the work that he did and become the person he became.

Suffice to say that every true child of God could put his or her name in a similar paragraph. I freely admit I am the least of all preachers, the chief of all sinners. I, too, have broken God's heart, fallen short of God's glory, and failed in doing God's will. Yet because of the resurrected Lord, I as a believer can say, "By the grace of God I am what I am, and his grace toward me was not in vain" (v. 10).

Conclusion

Of all the messages we can glean from the Scriptures to share with the world, far and away the most important, the one that should take first priority and never last, is the gospel. Other biblical messages can encourage, correct, and exhort, but only one message can bring eternal salvation, and that is the gospel.

Reflect and Discuss

1. Why is the message of the gospel so vital and in fact of first importance?
2. With the gospel as a priority, what should that say practically to what is heard in the church when the Word of God is preached every Sunday?
3. What is the gospel, and why are each of the three parts Paul mentioned so important to the whole?
4. What does the gospel have to say about the literal, physical resurrection of Jesus?
5. What is it about the gospel that makes it so different from every other message that every other religion in the world has to offer?
6. When is the last time you shared the gospel with an unbeliever?
7. What did Paul mean in verse 2 when he spoke about holding to the message of the gospel?
8. How do you see the gospel being compromised in the church today?

What If?

1 CORINTHIANS 15:12-19

Main Idea: If Christ has not been raised from the dead, Christianity collapses like a house of cards.

I.   **Our Message Is Meaningless (15:12-14).**
II. **Our Witness Is Worthless (15:15-16).**
III. **Our Faith Is Foolish (15:17a).**
IV. **Our Sin Is Sovereign (15:17b).**
V.   **Our Loved Ones Are Lost (15:18).**
VI. **Our Existence Is Empty (15:19).**

Why is it that Christians who truly understand their faith dogmatically assert that Christianity cannot be lumped in with any other religion in the world? Why is it that one who truly understands Christianity dogmatically asserts that Christianity is not even a religion?

What makes our faith so different and so distinct is not just the teaching of Jesus, or the life of Jesus, or even the death of Jesus. What makes Christianity so different can be traced to a simple moment in time—maybe even less than a moment. It may be a period that cannot be measured because what happened in that infinitesimally small segment of time was something that had never happened before in history and has never happened since: a man was permanently and eternally *raised from the dead, having received a body that could never die.* In that moment, Jesus Christ was ressurected from the dead in an incorruptible, immortal, eternal, heavenly body. On that rock lies the foundation of Christianity.

But what if? What if the corpse of Jesus were hidden away somewhere? What if it turned out Jesus Christ has not been raised from the dead and there is no resurrection of the dead? People in the Corinthian church were raising the last question at least. Paul will point out in his reply that if you question the latter, you question the former. If there is no resurrection and therefore Christ has not been raised, the results are truly catastrophic for both the church and the world.

Our Message Is Meaningless
1 CORINTHIANS 15:12-14

We are about to see why Paul begins this chapter with his recitation of the gospel; it is because the gospel of Christianity and the Christianity of the gospel have one thing in common: both are meaningless apart from the resurrection of Jesus. The general resurrection of believers and the particular resurrection of Jesus are inextricably linked (vv. 12-13).

Garland points out that evidently, there were those in the church who had adopted the thinking of many in the Graeco-Roman world that the soul is immortal, but once the body dies it stays dead forever (*1 Corinthians*, 700). So, in effect, these wanted to have their heaven cake and eat the world's way of thinking about the body, too. They wanted to hold to the resurrection of Jesus in particular but not the resurrection of believers in general. Paul categorically denies that possibility. You cannot say that believers will not be raised from the dead but Christ has been risen, since being in Christ, we are linked with Christ, and our destiny is the same.

Then, beginning in verse 14, Paul lays out the consequences of a still-dead Jesus—of a savior who is still in the tomb. In the original Greek, conditional sentences throughout this section begin with *ei de*, "and if," the condition being an assumed fact. That is, if one thing is assumed to be true, then the conclusion must be true (Mare and Harris, *1 & 2 Corinthians*, 111). So the first conclusion is this: "and if Christ has not been raised, then our proclamation is in vain, and so is your faith" (15:14). A dead Jesus affects not just the messenger but also the message. If Jesus Christ has not been raised from the dead, then ministers are wasting their time preaching the gospel and people are wasting their time listening to it.

When Peter was convinced that Jesus really had died and was not coming back from having gone to his Father, do you remember what he did? He simply went back to fishing (John 21:3; see Matt 4:18). If Jesus's death were the end of the story, Peter would no longer be fishing for men because he had no more bait. He could only fish for fish.

Without a risen Savior, no sermon—regardless of how beautiful, how oratorial, how logical, or how stimulating it might be—is really worth hearing. Paul calls messages that leave out the resurrection "vain," which literally means "empty." If Jesus Christ is dead, not even the great apostle Paul had anything worth saying to anyone about this life or the next. There was nothing worth hearing.

Our Witness Is Worthless
1 CORINTHIANS 15:15-16

Paul in effect goes from "the pulpit to the pew," or if you will, from "the pastor to the people." The facts concerning the resurrection are not just an issue for ministers; they are crucial for every Christian.

The Greek wording for "false witnesses" (v. 15) is actually a combination of two words. The first word is *pseudo*, which means "false." A *pseudo*-intellectual is someone who thinks he is smart when he really is not. A *pseudo*nym is a false name. The other half of that Greek phrase gives us the English word *martyr*. Originally the word meant "witness." Simply put, if Jesus Christ has not been raised from the dead, then those of us who are witnesses of the gospel, who are sharing and proclaiming the gospel, are liars. We are guilty of spiritual perjury.

In fact, and I say this with the deepest respect: Paul essentially said that if Jesus Christ has not been raised from the dead, then he would be a liar, since he claimed repeatedly he would be raised from the dead. If Jesus Christ has not been raised from the dead, once again, Christianity collapses.

In verse 16, Paul then reiterates the only possible conclusion: if there is no resurrection for anyone, then Christ has not been raised. You cannot have your feet in both worlds: if you believe in the particular resurrection of Jesus, you must believe in the general resurrection of believers.

Our Faith Is Foolish
1 CORINTHIANS 15:17A

If Jesus is still dead and buried in the tomb, it strikes a deathblow to even the very concept of Christian faith (v. 17a). We live in a world today where most people say it doesn't really matter what you believe so long as you are sincere in your belief. This statement's nonsensical reasoning is revealed in that if Jesus Christ has not been raised from the dead, our faith is foolish, since faith's value can be no greater than its object. All the faith in the world will not allow you to sit safely in a two-legged chair, fly an airplane with no fuel, or drive a car with no wheels.

The truth of the matter is, the Jesus who is worthy of our faith is a resurrected Jesus. The Jesus who makes it worthwhile to live a life of faith is a resurrected Jesus. The one who serves as the foundation of our faith, gives feet to our faith, and replaces fear with faith is only a resurrected Jesus. It is simply foolish to place your faith in anyone—regardless of the quality of his life, the brilliance of her teaching, or the quality of his or her example—if that person died only to stay dead.

Our Sin Is Sovereign
1 CORINTHIANS 15:17B

Since Paul said in Ephesians we are "saved by grace through faith" (Eph 2:8), then there is no salvation if there is no risen Jesus to believe in; without his completed work, there would be no grace to receive. Because that is true, then Paul's conclusion here is logical: those assuming there is no resurrection "are still in" their sins (v. 17b). Sin is sovereign. Sin wins. Salvation is an illusion. If Jesus is still physically dead, we are still spiritually dead. Sin is still a chain that binds us, a load that burdens us, and a hammer that breaks us.

Our Loved Ones Are Lost
1 CORINTHIANS 15:18

A dead Jesus offers no hope for those of us who are living, but would a dead Jesus give us any hope for those believers who have died before us? No, because that would imply they "have also perished" (v. 18).

The Greek verb Paul uses here, *apōllumi*, denotes not just physical death but spiritual death, a final death, a sleep from which no one ever wakes up, eternal eschatological destruction (Schreiner, *1 Corinthians*, 310). Death still has its sting; the grave still has its victory. If Jesus has not been raised from the dead, there is no hope now, and there is no positive afterlife. Our loved ones may as well have been lost.

Our Existence Is Empty
1 CORINTHIANS 15:19

Not only does a dead Jesus kill any hope for life beyond this life, but it also kills any hope for any meaning in this life (v. 19). It might be argued that the Christian life is worth living on its own merits, and obviously this world would indeed be a better place if everyone were to live the Christian life the way the Word of God teaches. But any advantage is short-lived, temporal, and—at the end of the day—in some sense futile. Schreiner draws this devastating conclusion: "Paul does not salute the nobility and sacrifice of Christians even if their faith is not true. Instead, if Christ was not crucified and is not risen for their sins, believers have wasted their lives in believing fables" (*1 Corinthians*, 310).

Thankfully, this is all hypothetical. The sad conclusions are not true, since Christ has indeed been raised from the dead, which is the theme not only of this chapter but of the entire New Testament.

Conclusion

I attended both a supposedly Christian college and a theological seminary where professors did not believe in the literal, physical resurrection of Jesus. The Bible passage we have studied in this chapter, however, leaves no doubt that without the literal, physical resurrection of Christ, the house of Christianity collapses like a deck of cards. It is great foolishness to believe in a still-dead Jesus.

Reflect and Discuss

1. Why is the literal, physical resurrection of a Jewish peasant so important in the twenty-first century?
2. Does it really matter for the Christian and the whole church to believe in a literal, physical resurrection as opposed to a simply "spiritual" resurrection? Explain your answer.
3. What happens to the most important message of the church, "the gospel," if Jesus has not been raised from the dead?
4. Why would it be wrong to try to witness to anyone about a Jesus who is dead, even if people might learn from his great moral teachings?
5. Without the resurrection, what benefit is it to have faith in Jesus? Why?
6. How does the resurrection impact our ability to be forgiven of our sins?
7. If Jesus has not been raised from the dead, what does that say about our family and friends who believed in Jesus and then died?
8. Without the resurrection of Jesus, what possible meaning to life can you glean?

Resurrection Guaranteed

1 CORINTHIANS 15:20-34

Main Idea: The resurrection of Jesus was not a one-off event; it guarantees our resurrection as well, and much more!

I. Jesus's Resurrection Guarantees the Certainty of Future Resurrection (15:20-22).

II. Jesus's Resurrection Guarantees the Priority of Future Resurrection (15:23).

III. Jesus's Resurrection Guarantees the Finality of Future Resurrection (15:24-26).

IV. Jesus's Resurrection Guarantees the Totality of Future Resurrection (15:27-28).

V. Jesus's Resurrection Guarantees the Reality of Future Resurrection (15:29-34).

The pundit Mark Twain is reported to have said, "It ain't what you don't know that gets you into trouble; it is what you know for sure that just ain't so." There was obviously some misunderstanding and misconception in Corinth both about the necessity of a general resurrection and about the quality of any resurrected body. Up to this point in the chapter, Paul has corrected the faulty supposition that one can believe in the resurrection of the Savior but not the resurrection of the saints. He argued that if there is no general resurrection, then one cannot possibly believe in a particular resurrection. He showed the devastating consequences of a non-resurrected Jesus.

Thankfully, here Paul quickly pivots from the gloom and doom of a purely hypothetical situation to the joyful actuality that Christ has indeed been raised from the dead. His resurrection is actually a guarantee of our resurrection. As we will see, the past resurrection of Jesus also guarantees several facets of the future resurrection to come.

Jesus's Resurrection Guarantees the Certainty of Future Resurrection

1 CORINTHIANS 15:20-22

All of the "if" clauses of the previous section are "counterfactual conditions" (Hays, *Interpretation*, 262). The first four words of verse 20 set the stage for what Paul is going to say: "But as it is." The two Greek words behind this, *nuni de*, mean literally "but now." It is Paul's way of emphasizing he is about to introduce some extremely important affirmations that are absolutely true. He goes on to say that since there is an implication that none of these Corinthian believers deny the resurrection of Jesus, they must accept the corollary truth, which is that his resurrection guarantees their resurrection (Mare and Harris, *1 & 2 Corinthians*, 113).

This is a great word of comfort to these Corinthian believers, who had seen many loved ones precede them in death. Jesus is the firstfruits of those who have died. Hays points out this is a new element in the resurrection story. It is an aspect of the resurrection of Jesus that was left out of Paul's explanation of the gospel in verses 3-5. His resurrection did not just confirm his identity; it also confirms our identification with him (Hays, *Interpretation*, 263)! This leads into mention of the Old Testament-era practice where the firstfruits or the first harvest that came in would be given to the Lord to demonstrate the believers' confidence in a future harvest to come. So, it is safe to say, *if he was raised from the dead, we will be raised from the dead.* Jesus is not only the firstfruits, but he is surely the last Adam. The first Adam brought death; the last Adam brought life. The first Adam brought sin; the last Adam brought salvation. The first Adam caused separation between humanity and God; the last Adam brought reconciliation between humanity and God. This is only a good thing for those who are "in Christ," for these are the only ones who will be resurrected to life eternal. (See the fate of the risen unrighteous in Rev 20:11-15.) Note that Paul surely believed in a literal Adam just as much as he believed in a literal Christ.

Jesus's Resurrection Guarantees the Priority of Future Resurrection

1 CORINTHIANS 15:23

Paul moves from an agricultural metaphor to a military metaphor. There is a certain priority in the future resurrection. The word behind "order" is the Greek word *tagma*, which is usually used of a unit of soldiers. This military metaphor dominates verses 23-28 (Hays, *Interpretation*, 261). Earlier Paul spoke about everything being done in the services of the church "decently and in order" (14:40). That way of doing things is exactly what you should find in the military. Such will prevail at the resurrection. There is an interval between the resurrection of Jesus and the resurrection of believers in part because the resurrection of believers takes place at the second coming of Jesus. (The Greek word for "coming," *parousia*, is commonly used for the second coming of Christ; e.g., Matt 24:3,27,37; 1 Thess 2:19; 3:13; 2 Thess 2:1,8; Jas 5:7.) The resurrected Lord will descend, and at that time those who belong to Christ will also be raised and given their new resurrection bodies.

Jesus's Resurrection Guarantees the Finality of Future Resurrection

1 CORINTHIANS 15:24-26

The return of the resurrected Lord actually sets off a chain reaction of eschatological events that brings life as we know it to a close. Paul gets right to the point with four more words: "Then comes the end" (v. 24). Though scholars debate what the phrase "the end" refers to, one should not overthink it. Simply understand that this refers to the "end of this age or world-order to be followed by the age to come" (Bruce, *1 & 2 Corinthians*, 146). This is "when [Jesus] hands over the kingdom to God the Father, when he abolishes all [other] rule and all authority and power" (v. 24). To that, Schreiner would add, "This almost certainly refers to demonic powers" (*1 Corinthians*, 314). Demonic powers will not merely be subjugated; they will be annihilated. Make no mistake. We need to understand this comprehensively and rejoice that "any kind of structural opposition to God, whether social, political, economic, ethical, or spiritual" will all be placed under the feet and the authority of Jesus (Thiselton, *First Epistle*, 1250).

Paul declares that Jesus must reign from heaven until this occurs, and then "the last enemy," death, will be destroyed (vv. 25-26).

Jesus's Resurrection Guarantees the Totality of Future Resurrection
1 CORINTHIANS 15:27-28

Everything and everyone in every place is brought to this grand conclusion. Just as God has promised over and over and as Jesus predicted, everything is put under him, except of course the one who put everything under him, God the Father (v. 27). This is not readily apparent to us today, but at Christ's return, no one will be able to question it.

The final climax comes in the next verse (v. 28). Without question, this verse carries with it inherent difficulties. It is safe to say nothing in the verse should be construed as even implying the Son's ontological inferiority to the Father. Any thought of an eternal submission of the Son ontologically should be rejected. It is, rather, a "functional subordination" (Schreiner, *1 Corinthians*, 316). Perhaps Bruce puts it best and most succinctly: "The kingdom of Christ comes to an end in its present phase, but only to merge in the eternal Kingdom of God, so there is no failure of the prophetic promise that the Messiah's kingdom will know no end (Isa. 9:7; Lk. 1:33)" (*1 & 2 Corinthians*, 148).

Jesus's Resurrection Guarantees the Reality of Future Resurrection
1 CORINTHIANS 15:29-34

Paul now brings the Corinthians back to the matter of daily life and shows how the reality of their coming resurrection should impact how they live. Paul leaves the realm of the theological and enters the realm of the experiential. He begins with an allusion to a very strange practice: baptism for the dead (v. 29)

Whatever this was, this point should not be missed: the practice makes no sense if there is no resurrection. Paul does not make either a positive or a negative comment about the practice, but, unfortunately, he does not explain it either (Schreiner, *1 Corinthians*, 317). Thiselton gives no less than thirteen possibilities. The first ten he believes to be unconvincing. Three are widely considered or in one case (in his opinion) highly probable (*First Epistle*, 1242). I personally believe, as does Thiselton, that baptism for the dead is referring to a practice meant to honor believers who'd shared the gospel with a friend or relative even as their own deaths neared. Then subsequent to their deaths, in cases where the friend or relative came to faith in Christ, he or she could request to receive baptism on behalf of the dead person (Thiselton, *First Epistle*, 1248).

Regardless, if there is no resurrection, then to face persecution, enemies of the faith, or even martyrdom is senseless (vv. 30-32). Suffering, in fact, is senseless if this life is all there is. The logical alternative would be to embrace a party-it-up lifestyle in which one grabs all the pleasure he or she can. There were obviously people espousing this in Corinth, which gives credence to Paul's statement: "Do not be deceived: 'Bad company corrupts good morals'" (v. 33). I would go further and say that anyone who denies not only the resurrection in general but the resurrection of Christ specifically—or argues against the trustworthiness of the Word of God—is bad company.

Paul's conclusion of the whole matter is pointedly made in verse 34. Thiselton states that verses 33-34 (especially v. 34) expressed the theological heart of the chapter and are the linchpin of Paul's entire argument (*First Epistle*, 1253). To deny the resurrection shows a breathtaking ignorance of God in both his power and his purpose. To deny the truth of the resurrection is not just ignorance but wickedness. There is no excuse for being seduced into following heresy when the truth of the Word of God is before us. Jesus was right: "You will know the truth, and the truth will set you free" (John 8:32). There is no greater truth than the truth that, because Jesus was raised from the dead, so shall we be.

Conclusion

Whether or not Jesus was raised from the dead has tremendous implications for our own eternal future. Just as Paul has shown the foolishness of believing in a still-dead Jesus, he shows the tremendous benefits of believing in a risen one. Jesus's resurrection is the firstfruits that guarantees our resurrection as well.

Reflect and Discuss

1. What commonality will our own burial sites one day share with Jesus's?
2. What does Paul mean by Jesus being the firstfruits, and how and why is that so important to us?
3. What is the order of the resurrection, and when will our part in resurrection take place?
4. Since the return of Jesus sets off a chain reaction of eschatological events, what does Paul mean by "the end"?
5. How is the subjection of the Son to the Father at the end to be properly understood in terms of their relationship to each other?
6. What do you believe being baptized for the dead actually refers to?
7. How should we deal with church members who are either confused about the resurrection of Jesus or deny it?

No Body Like This Body

1 CORINTHIANS 15:35-58

Main Idea: Like the Savior, every saint will be physically raised in a supernatural body impervious to sin and death forever.

I. **Paul Receives a Puzzled Interrogation concerning the Resurrection (15:35).**
II. **Paul Gives Practical Illustrations of the Resurrection (15:36-41).**
   A. The agricultural world (15:36-38)
   B. The animal world (15:39)
   C. The astronomical world (15:40-41)
III. **Paul Provides Pertinent Information about the Resurrection (15:42-49).**
   A. The promise of the transformation (15:42-46)
   B. The perfection of the transformation (15:47-49)
IV. **Paul Applies the Powerful Inspiration of the Resurrection (15:50-58).**
   A. The inspiration of eternal life (15:50-57)
   B. The inspiration for effective labor (15:58)

One thing we all know is that we are going to die, unless Jesus returns first. There is no escaping it: "It is appointed for people to die once" (Heb 9:27). Almost everyone has an appointment with death. We will each be on time for those, and we will not be able to avoid them. We don't know where, when, or how our deaths will come, but we will keep our appointments.

Yet from time immemorial, humanity has thought not only about the certainty of death but also the possibility of life after death. Four thousand years ago, an ancient thinker named Job asked the question, "When a person dies, will he come back to life?" (Job 14:14). I believe God has planted within every person a desire for a resurrection—an eternal existence. In the remaining part of this chapter, Paul deals with that hope, but he doesn't just speak about the hope of the resurrection but also about the fact of the resurrection. Continuing his argument, he moves from the resurrection of the Savior to the resurrection of the saint, holding to the thesis that the former guarantees the latter.

In fact, you might say the remainder of chapter 15 is Paul's doctoral thesis on the subject of the resurrection because we read more here about the resurrection of believers than what we are told in all of the rest of the Bible put together. As we will see, this entire passage is a fitting ending to one of the greatest chapters in the Bible.

Paul Receives a Puzzled Interrogation Concerning the Resurrection
1 CORINTHIANS 15:35

Paul shifts from dealing with the *necessity* of the resurrection body (that is, since Jesus was raised from the dead one should not doubt that we will be raised from the dead) to the *nature* of the resurrection body. He is dealing with two specific questions: "How are the dead raised? What kind of body will they have?" Some people in the church were questioning not just the possibility but the pattern of the resurrection.

Keep in mind, Paul is speaking here to the resurrection of the body, not of the soul. There is a difference. My body is going to die, but thanks to God's grace through my faith in Jesus the essence of who I am—my soul, my spirit—will not. Jesus himself said, "Everyone who lives and believes in me will never die" (John 11:26). Obviously, he was not speaking of the body; therefore, when the Bible speaks of death and resurrection it always refers to that of the physical body. It is important to keep that distinction.

Still, the question remains, "How can a natural sinful body become a supernatural spiritual body?" Now on the surface the question seems like an innocent one, but then two words tell us otherwise: "You fool!" (v. 36). There were still skeptics, you might even say troublemakers, who disputed the credibility of any idea of a resurrection (Schreiner, *1 Corinthians*, 320). So Paul launches into his brilliant apologetic for the bodily resurrection of believers.

Paul Gives Practical Illustrations of the Resurrection
1 CORINTHIANS 15:36-41

To answer the question about the resurrection, Paul turns to the outside world just as Jesus did so often. He shows how the visible can help us understand the invisible. The natural world informs us about the spiritual world.

The Agricultural World (15:36-38)

Paul goes back to the farmer and his field to illustrate the possibility and the nature of the resurrection (vv. 36-38). Since Paul is writing to an agrarian society, this metaphor would easily be understood. You sow a seed in the earth, and in a real sense it dies, decays, dissolves, and disintegrates; but over a period of time, out of the death of that seed comes life. The new life is different from the seed, but it comes from the seed.

So our current bodies are like a seed. Just as a seed is buried, so is the body. Just as a seed comes back made better, so does the body. Later, Paul even refers to burial as a seed "sown in dishonor, raised in glory" (v. 43).

The great nineteenth-century evangelist Dwight L. Moody said, "As I go into a cemetery I like to think of the time when the dead shall rise from their graves. . . . Thank God our friends are not buried; they are only sown!" ("Shall We Meet Our Loved Ones Again?").

The Animal World (15:39)

Next Paul goes from the world of agriculture to the world of the animals (v. 39). Simply put, animals are different from humans. The flesh of a human being is different from the flesh of a bird, and it is smooth unlike the scales of a fish.

Similarly implied, there are no two birds exactly alike, no two fish alike, and no two humans alike. In a technical sense, there is no such thing as identical twins because their fingerprints, for one thing, are different. We are not going to be carbon copies of one another post resurrection. We are going to be different then just as we are now, but our resurrected bodies will be of the same quality.

The Astronomical World (15:40-41)

Paul now moves to the astronomical world. We know from the study of astronomy that some of what tend to be called stars are accurately planets, similar to the earth. True stars are in themselves suns. The stars generate their own light, but the moons and planets only reflect light produced by the stars. Each celestial body has its own glory. The point is, you can tell the difference between the sun, the moon, and the faraway stars. You know when you are looking at the sun. You know when you are looking at the moon.

I think there is an implication here that we will recognize each other in heaven. In a sense, we will be the same in kind as we are here, but we will be different. Charles Spurgeon comments: "I have not the slightest doubt that you will know me. At any rate, you will be bigger fools in heaven than you are here if you do not" ("Believer's Deathday," 153). Paul's point is essentially this: there is simply no reason you have to check your mind at the door to believe that a corruptible, sinful, physical body can be raised into a supernatural, spiritual, perfect body. After all, there is nothing too difficult for God!

Paul Provides Pertinent Information about the Resurrection
1 CORINTHIANS 15:42-49

Beginning in verse 42, Paul gets down to the nitty-gritty of the resurrection. He gives as much detail as divine revelation allows in describing the resurrection of the body. This event can be summed up in one word: *transformation*. Our aging, dying bodies will one day be transformed into ageless, everlasting bodies.

The Promise of the Transformation (15:42-46)

There is going to be both a continuity and a discontinuity between our earthly bodies and our eternal bodies. We will maintain our identities and be the same people, but out bodies will be wonderfully different (Schreiner, *1 Corinthians*, 321). The difference, which is hard to grasp, is probably best explained with the verbs *sown* and *raised*.

Paul writes, "So is it with the resurrection of the dead. What is sown is perishable; what is raised is imperishable" (v. 42 ESV). Here I prefer the English Standard Version's *perishable* and *imperishable*. We are all born dying. We are all living in dying bodies. We all suffer from a terminal disease called life-on-a-fallen-planet. There is an expiration date on every human body that will go into effect unless Christ returns first.

When a person dies, a mortician can preserve the body with embalming fluid, put it in the finest casket money can buy, and even have it sealed in a vault. Still, every body is going to totally and completely decay, whereas our resurrected bodies—our risen and reformed dust—will be invincible to time and impenetrable by death. They will indeed be truly filled with eternal life.

Again, listen to the language of verse 43: "sown in dishonor, raised in glory." It is not that the body is intrinsically evil or bad; rather, it does not yet have the glory that God intended for it to have thanks to the presence of sin in the world. So, think of a coal and a diamond.

A diamond is the most precious jewel on earth, made up of carbon, the same stuff of which coal is made. A diamond and a piece of coal are made up of the same element, but they are so different. Someone said, "Coal is carbon in humiliation, but a diamond is carbon in glory." Someday, the coal-like body you have will be transformed into the bodily equivalent of a beautiful diamond formed by the grace of God.

The idea of "sown in weakness, raised in power" (v. 43) means our current bodies are limited by time, space, sickness, and breakdown, but our new bodies will be freed from the shackles of fallen humanity. They will no longer be limited by time, space, or material substance. Such bodies will be filled with the power that can only come from the God who raised them.

When a person becomes a believer, he or she remains in his or her natural body. We thus experience Christ first in these sinful bodies, but the resurrection means that won't be the case in eternity (vv. 44-46).

It should be noted that these resurrection bodies to come are not *spirit bodies* but *spiritual bodies*. It was not, after all, the spirit of Jesus alone that was raised from the dead but his physical body too. Post-resurrection those who encountered him could touch his physical body, feel his body, see that he was not a ghost. When Paul refers to a spiritual body, then, he is not thinking at all of an immaterial, invisible body. Again and again, Paul emphasizes that the resurrection of the saints will be just like the resurrection of the Savior: physical.

The Perfection of the Transformation (15:47-49)

Now Paul compares the first Adam to the last Adam. In our natural bodies we are in the image of Adam, humanity's shared father (see Gen 3:20; Acts 17:26). It is a marred image. Adam was created in the image of God, but when Adam fell that image was scarred by sin, and every person from then until now has been born bearing that same flawed image.

One day, though, believers will truly bear the image of God. In fact, the simplest way to explain the resurrection body of the saint is to remember it is going to be much like the resurrected body of the Savior. John concurred with this when he said, "Dear friends, we are God's children now, and what we will be has not yet been revealed. We know that when he appears, we will be like him because we will see him as he is" (1 John 3:2). We are not only going to *see* what Jesus is like, but we are going to *be* what Jesus is like. Not divine, but perfected.

Paul Applies the Powerful Inspiration of the Resurrection
1 CORINTHIANS 15:50-58

Everything that Paul has said in this section, he restates in one sentence: "What I am saying, brothers and sisters, is this: Flesh and blood cannot inherit the kingdom of God, nor can corruption inherit incorruption" (v. 50). Let me be clear. What Paul means by "flesh and blood" here is not simply the physical body, because the point he has been making all along is that a resurrected physical body will indeed inherit the kingdom of God. What he is referring to is the corrupted, dishonored, weak, natural bodies that are yet under the curse. Then Paul fleshes out what all of this means, not just for our future but also for our present.

The Inspiration of Eternal Life (15:50-57)

Realizing that one day these decayed, deficient bodies are going to be raised glorious and victorious is a tremendous source of inspiration.

Paul is revealing "a mystery"; there were some things about the resurrected body that Christians didn't understand, but Paul gives a startling revelation. Not every Christian is going to die, but every Christian is going to "be changed" (vv. 50-53). "In the twinkling of an eye," at the blast of a trumpet, nearly at the same time, both those who have died before the second coming of Jesus and those who are still alive at the time are going to receive their divinely custom-built, tailor-made, new, glorified, immortal, everlasting, resurrected bodies! First Thessalonians 4:13-18 explains this in more detail.

So, two groups are going to be present when this transformation takes place: those who are alive will be raptured and changed and the spirits of those who have already died will be resurrected. Then, those who've been raptured can ask, "Where, death, is your sting?" Those resurrected from the grave will be able to say, "Where, death, is your victory?" Indeed, death will be swallowed up in victory, and a song will ring out all over heaven: "Victory in Jesus!"

Jesus, then, has taken the doom out of death and the gloom out of the grave. Where the grave was once a period to close the sentence of life, Jesus has made it a comma. Where the grave was once a wall that separated us from God, it is now a bridge that takes us to God.

You most likely remember the little poem you learned as a kid that went like this:

> Humpty Dumpty sat on a wall;
> Humpty Dumpty had a great fall;
> All the king's horses and all the king's men
> Couldn't put Humpty together again.

Chuck Swindoll rewrote that little poem and put it this way:

> Jesus Christ came to our wall;
> Jesus Christ died for our fall.
> He slew Queen Death.
> He crushed King Sin.
> Through grace He put us together again. (*Growing Deep*, 209)

Jesus never sinned, never broke God's law. Yet he gave his life for ours at the cross, taking the sting out of death and, in coming out of his tomb, ensured his people will one day come out of their own. Every heart should be filled with gratitude to God, who has given us tremendous victory through the Lord Jesus Christ!

The Inspiration for Effective Labor (15:58)

To be clear, the resurrection is not just about pie in the sky. It is about the future, and it is about the present. Our bodies are truly going to be raised from the dead never to die again, and there is one practical conclusion that we can draw. If we know that God is able to put together a body, even one that has decayed into nothing but ashes or particles of dust, then we should know that God never forgets even the smallest deed done in his service. "Therefore," Paul says, we ought to be *constant* in God's work: "be steadfast." We ought to be *committed* to God's work: "immoveable." We ought to be *consistent* in God's work: "always excelling." We ought to be *confident* in God's work: "because you know that your labor in the Lord is not in vain."

I say to all of my fellow believers, and especially to those in what we would call full-time Christian ministry, you may get tired in the work, but don't ever get tired of the work.

> The work is solemn—therefore don't trifle:
> the task is difficult—therefore don't relax:
> the opportunity is brief—therefore don't delay:
> the path is narrow—therefore don't wander.

the Prize *is glorious*—therefore don't faint. (Panton,
"Counsels," 2; emphasis in original)

We have the promise of the resurrection before us. We have the person
of the resurrection above us. We have the power of the resurrection
already at work within us. Until that day comes, when we are raised up
or taken up, we each should use the body that we have now to do all the
good we can for as long as we can, knowing we are getting ready for the
body that is unlike any other body that has ever been born.

Conclusion

Though what Paul speaks of is tremendous mystery in many ways, it
is nevertheless exciting. However our bodies will differ from their current state, they will be just like the body of Jesus. His is perfect, eternal,
impervious to sin, and cannot face disease or death again.

Reflect and Discuss

1. Do you believe that God has planted within every person a desire
   for an eternal existence after this life? Why or why not?
2. What are the two major questions that Paul addresses in this chapter about the resurrection of the body?
3. What would you say to a skeptic who does not believe that a
   natural sinful body can become a supernatural spiritual body?
4. What is the agricultural example Paul uses as an analogy to the resurrection, and what lessons can we draw from it?
5. What is the zoological example Paul uses as an analogy to the resurrection, and what lessons can we draw from it?
6. What is the astronomical example Paul uses as an analogy to the
   resurrection, and what lessons can we draw from it?
7. How does Adam's natural body relate to Jesus's resurrected body?
8. How would you explain the major differences between the bodies
   we live in today and the bodies we will live in for all eternity?
9. What does the certainty of our future resurrection say to us about
   both the life that is to come and the kind of lives that we are to
   live now?

Now about the Collection

1 CORINTHIANS 16:1-4

Main Idea: Giving will always be a part of the church's worship, and it should follow some specific guidelines.

I.   We Should Give with Sincere Dedication (16:1).
II. We Should Give to a Specific Destination (16:2a).
III. We Should Give with Steadfast Determination (16:2a).
IV. We Should Give with Studied Deliberation (16:2b).
V.   We Should Give with Sober Discrimination (16:3-4).

Oftentimes I have heard people whom I have pastored say, "Wouldn't it be great if we could go back to the time of the early church?" Of course, perhaps in some ways it would be, but more than a few might be disappointed to find that even in the earliest days the church took up offerings! Regardless, I imagine Paul was glad to get to this last chapter where the subject is discussed. Not only is there really nothing of any controversy mentioned here, but it allows him to end on a positive note in what was, by any account, a very difficult letter to write.

Though no local church has ever been perfect, including the best congregations in history, it is refreshing to note that with all the flaws and foibles of the Corinthian church, it was a generous church. Paul is giving directions here on "the collection for the saints" (v. 1). We know from another letter that Paul wrote that this collection was for the poor and suffering among the Jewish Christian brothers and sisters in Jerusalem (Rom 15:26). The Greek words *peri de*, translated "and about," introduce a subject that had not been discussed before, also indicating it got included in response to a question the Corinthians had asked about participating in this offering (Blomberg, *1 Corinthians*, 323). The Corinthians evidently wanted to be included in it, thus working alongside other churches that Paul was appealing to for help. So Paul proceeds in an extremely practical section of this book to talk about the "where," "when," and "what" of giving. While Paul was dealing with a specific situation, Blomberg is surely right when he says, "We may take Paul's principles for giving . . . as widely applicable to comparable situations of need and not as a unique respond to an idiosyncratic problem that could have been avoided" (*1 Corinthians*, 126).

So as we examine a patten of giving in the early church, we can readily see some giving guidelines that should help every believer who wants to exercise the stewardship of both supporting the work of ministry and meeting the needs of those believers who are requiring assistance. In several solid and practical ways, Paul gives us a model that shows how Christians should be financially faithful to the church and how the church should be forensically faithful in managing what is given.

We Should Give with Sincere Dedication
1 CORINTHIANS 16:1

The instructions for this giving are found in verse 1: "Now about the collection for the saints: Do the same as I instructed the Galatian churches." Since almost the beginning of the church, the first or mother church in Jerusalem had experienced great difficulty. It was mainly made up of Jewish believers, which means that almost the entire body would have been persecuted for their faith from the very beginning, both by the Jewish community and even by some pagans. There was a high cost tied to faith in those days; in fact, in many parts of the world there still is. Back then, you could expect to be socially ostracized, economically compromised, and religiously disenfranchised. As a Jew claiming Jesus as your Messiah, you likely would be excommunicated from the synagogue and considered *persona non grata* in the community. Besides that, the church in Jerusalem was in the middle of a great economic depression. They were having to minister to thousands of new converts who had come to Christ, and many of them were in desperate need of financial help. Well aware of this, Paul had sent out a communiqué to several Gentile churches he had founded, asking them to help their brothers and sisters in Jerusalem. Everyone knew what this offering was to be dedicated to; it had a specific purpose.

These Corinthian Christians, then, were motivated by a love for and a brokenness over their Jerusalem brothers and sisters. They eagerly agreed to give to this offering because they realized Christianity is a team sport and everyone is on the same team. From this, we can draw a key principle about giving.

When you give you should give with sincere dedication to Jesus, his kingdom, and your fellow people of God, not worrying about tax breaks or public recognition. The truth is, one will only give away money from either a blessed heart or a burdened heart. Christians are to give out of gratitude or compassion, never out of guilt or compulsion (see 2 Cor 9:7). So, every believer should take from this that we should all give not out of obligation but with sincere dedication.

We Should Give to a Specific Destination
1 CORINTHIANS 16:2A

Now, when was this offering to be set aside and given? "On the first day of the week." Why specifically the first day of the week? This refers, of course, to Sunday. Blomberg is correct when he says this verse is the first known reference to a weekly offering as a part of Christian worship when the church gathered together (*1 Corinthians*, 324). The fact that this was to be done on Sunday strongly suggests that the first day of the week (Sunday), not the seventh day of the week (the Sabbath), had come to be the special day for Christians to gather in worship (ibid.).

Because it was on Sunday that Jesus left his tomb, the day came to be called "the Lord's day," and Christians apparently would gather together on that day to celebrate the resurrection of Christ (Schreiner, *1 Corinthians*, 328).[4] Now it must be conceded that the text did not specifically say the gift was to be collected at church, but Mare and Harris raise a great question:

> But then why mention doing it on Sunday, when they could just as well do it regularly at home at other times? The meaning must rather be that the Christians were to bring their offerings to church on Sunday since that was the day they were to assemble for worship (Acts 20:7; Rev. 1:10). (*1 & 2 Corinthians*, 121)

I would add a theological reason why this makes sense. When the church gathered on the first day of the week, it was always to worship the risen

---

[4] Thiselton points out that how quickly the full principle of Sabbath observance was actually replaced by worship on Sunday is disputed. At the very least, Thiselton notes, "The replacement of the Jewish Sabbath by the Christian *Lord's Day*, *First Day*, or **Sunday** has, it seems, begun to be in process within the New Testament period" (*First Epistle*, 1322–23; emphases in original).

Lord, and giving should be a part of worship. The early church could not conceive of having a worship service without people giving.

In its purest form, worship is not about getting; it is about giving. *You can give without worshiping, but you cannot worship without giving.* It needs to be said that worship is not primarily about getting something from God but giving something to God. When you worship, you give your voice in exaltation as you praise the character of God. You give your ear in concentration as you listen to the Word of God. You give your mind in meditation as you think about the things of God. You give your heart in adoration as you bask in the love of God. Surely we should also bring our offerings in commemoration as we remember the goodness of God. This is not to be understood as saying that all giving should only be given to any specific church, but I do believe this passage suggests the first financial gifts we give to God should be to the work of the church. If you love God, you will love God's church, and if you love God's church, you will give to its work.

We Should Give with Steadfast Determination
1 CORINTHIANS 16:2A

There are three important words not to be missed in verse 2: "each of you." To state the obvious, "each of you" means "every one of them." Paul makes it plain that everybody should give something to this offering. There is no room for exemptions, exceptions, or excuses. Nobody gets a pass. Nobody gets a get-out-of-giving card. When it comes to giving, we are to participate whether we are rich or poor, whether the offering looks like a gold coin from a rich man or a little mite from a widow (Mare and Harris, *1 & 2 Corinthians*, 121).

So, everyone was to come together on the first day of the week as the church gathered, and giving was to be systematic—not haphazard. Every first day of the week, everyone was to be determined to give something.

I have discovered that Christian givers typically fall into three categories. Most people give only *spontaneously.* When presented with a cause or an emergency or something that burdens them, they will give. That is one way to give, and some giving should be spontaneous, but I think there is room for improvement here.

Some people give *sporadically.* They just give when the mood hits them. So depending on their frame of mind, the performance of the stock market, how high or low interest rates are, or how much confidence they have in the economy, they give. Here, too, I see room for improvement, and I think Paul would agree.

There is one more thing to say here. I have also witnessed that people who give only spontaneously and sporadically, for the most part, give *sparingly*. For many of them, giving is not generous or sacrificial; they just want that good feeling that comes of knowing they have at least given something.

The best way to give, though it may certainly be supplemented with spontaneous offerings, is *systematically*. We should give with a steadfast determination to give as often as our income is refreshed or we have an unexpected inflow of money. We should have a steadfast determination to give some portion of that back to God's work and to people who are more needy than we are. Though there may be times to give beyond this pattern, we should have a system of calculating what we are going to give ahead of time, where we are going to give it, and when we are going to give it. Once we do, that just leads to the next characteristic of giving.

We Should Give with Studied Deliberation
1 CORINTHIANS 16:2B

Giving is not merely a cookie-cutter exercise where everybody offers exactly the same amount. Paul says, "in keeping with how he is prospering" (v. 2b). This means giving is to be in proportion to one's means and what one has at his or her disposal. Now Blomberg's observation is, "Neither here nor in any other New Testament text is the tithe taught as incumbent on Christians" (*1 Corinthians*, 236). With respect to this great scholar, I do not believe that ends the matter; after all, giving is a topic appearing throughout the whole of Scripture. Moreover, I find nothing in the New Testament that either would abrogate the desire of a New Testament Christian under grace to give any less than a Jew was required under the law to give or that would abrogate the benefit that God specifically promises to those who do (Mal 3:10).

We must remember the context of the prior chapters of 1 Corinthians and in fact of this entire book. The emphasis has been on the gospel: the message that Christ gave his life to pay for the sins of the world. Therefore, our lives as those he has redeemed should be lived in gratitude for all that God has given to us and done for us. So Thiselton says,

In this light, it is theologically entirely appropriate to speak of the collection not as a mundane chore of "maintaining" the church in any routinized mechanistic sense, but of "maintaining" . . . others by passing on *freely received grace*. (*First Epistle*, 1319; emphasis in original)

The operative word is indeed "grace." No one put it better than my mentor Dr. Adrian Rogers when he said, "Any Christian who would give less under grace than a Jew would give under the law is a disgrace to grace."

My mom and dad taught me from the time I received my first dollar to give God ten percent of each one before I did anything with the rest. I will just simply say, God is not a heavenly slot machine, and we should not give expecting to get. On the other hand, I will also say, I am one extremely satisfied giver. I have witnessed how God blesses generosity.

We should keep in mind there are two things we will never ever be able to do again once we die. One is to share the gospel with a lost person, but the other is to give financially to God's work. In light of this, it is appropriate to see how much we can give, not how little.

We Should Give with Sober Discrimination
1 CORINTHIANS 16:3-4

Paul shifts the focus from the people who are giving their gifts to the church representatives of Corinth who are both going to collect the offering and give the offering to the church in Jerusalem (vv. 3-4). We indeed have a responsibility to give to God's work, but the corollary to that is, when we give to God's work, we have the right to know where our money is going to be used and what we are giving it for. Paul told the Corinthians to recommend men of integrity and honesty to transport the money collected for a stated purpose. Some things never change since, as Schreiner points out, "[w]e know from II Cor 8:16-24, that Paul was concerned about the men who would bring this gift since religious hucksters often would make off with the money" (*1 Corinthians*, 329).

With responsibility comes accountability, and in this instance, of course, the entire gift had to be transported in cash. There was no other way. There were no credit cards, wire transfers, ATMs, or even checks back then. You had to know exactly how much money was originally given and take care that all that money finally arrived. There was accounting for what was given and where the money ended up, and a final accounting would be given back to the church that gave the money in the first place. In other words, the money was not only to be given in the church, to the church, and for the church, it was to be managed by the church. It is incumbent on those of us who give money to God's work to do everything possible to make sure that dollars given toward his work are always used correctly, properly, and wisely.

One final thing should not be missed here. It is not coincidental or incidental that the offering of these Gentiles to these Jewish believers would be delivered by the Gentile believers themselves. Paul wanted to make sure that the Jewish believers not only received what was given but knew who gave it (Hays, *Interpretation*, 285).

Conclusion

This chapter is a refreshing reminder that even the early church understood the importance of giving and its role in worship. It gives us some wonderful insights into how money should be given, distributed, and managed in such a way that the needy are ministered to, the gospel is spread, and the church is blessed.

Reflect and Discuss

1. Why is giving so important for the individual Christian?
2. Why is giving so important in corporate worship?
3. What should be the motivation behind all our giving?
4. Why should we give to causes and people who may never directly benefit our church?
5. Why is the offering plate the best place to give at least the firstfruits of your gift to God?
6. Why was it important to the early church that the offering discussed be given and collected on the first day of the week?
7. What does the principle of proportionality have to do with the discipline of giving?
8. Do you believe the concept of tithing is still relevant today? Why or why not?
9. What policies and procedures does your particular church have in place to guarantee that offerings are handled with integrity?

Parting Words

1 CORINTHIANS 16:5-24

Main Idea: If possible, parting words should always be encouraging and uplifting, particularly after having to speak tough truths in love.

I.   **A Word of Anticipation (16:5-12)**
II. **A Word of Exhortation (16:13-14)**
III. **A Word of Commendation (16:15-18)**
IV. **A Word of Salutation (16:19-24)**

In what was probably the toughest, hardest letter Paul ever had to write to a church, you can almost hear the relief in his voice once the need for tough love is over. This last section is written on a very upbeat note. Paul is anticipating a visit to these Corinthian Christians, exhorting them to be open and supportive to others who may want to come work alongside them as well as to stand firm in their faith.

A Word of Anticipation

1 CORINTHIANS 16:5-12

Paul wants to encourage the Corinthians by letting them know that his plans are ("if the Lord allows") to spend some time with them personally (vv. 5-7). Paul left unstated that it is obvious that one of the main reasons he wants to spend a good deal of time with this church was that he hoped to rebuild bridges and help them to improve their witness for Christ and their unity in the body (Blomberg, *1 Corinthians*, 332).

But Paul may have had an even more practical motive. He could find more gainful employment in Corinth than in almost any other city he visited. Tentmakers were in demand there because of the Isthmian Games, which had high attendance, and because of the two harbors there. Bailey points out that tentmakers would also manufacture sails, and small ships would naturally use "the winter" to get their vessels ready for their shipping season (*Paul*, 486).

Regardless, in the spirit of a traveling evangelist and missionary, Paul was going there to give them the chance to contribute financially to his traveling expenses and the ministry of the gospel. In verse 6 the phrase "send me on my way" is a verb used for supporting and helping people engaged in mission (cf. 15:24; Rom 1:16; Titus 3:13; 3 John 6; Schreiner, *1 Corinthians*, 331). "*Propempō* is used technically to denote helping someone on their journey with food, money, or arranging for companions" (BAGD, 709).

But for the time being, Paul needs to stay in Ephesus (vv. 8-9). It is interesting to note that Paul faced the two variables every person in ministry faces—every pastor, every evangelist, every missionary, every layperson living the Christian life: opportunity and opposition. The encouraging part is Paul makes it very plain that all the opposition in the world cannot slam the door on the gospel when the opportunity to share the gospel presents itself.

Then Paul prepares them for multiple visits: one from Timothy and one from Apollos (vv. 10-12).

Timothy was one of Paul's most valued co-workers. Paul, in his fatherly spiritual relationship to the younger man, wants to pave the way for both his visit and his departure. He does not want Timothy to be looked down on in a condescending way; he wants him to be received with respect. Moreover, he is to receive "the practical support and necessary provisions" he needs (Thiselton, *First Epistle*, 1331).

On the other hand, though Timothy was certainly willing to go, Apollos was hesitant. We are not told specifically why he was so adamant about not going at the present time. The related sentence itself is somewhat ambiguous; the literal translation would read, "It was not the will for him to come now" (Hays, *Interpretation*, 287). It may well be that he did not want to visit Corinth because he was unhappy with some using his name to promote the claims of "Paul's fan club" (Thiselton, *First Epistle*, 1332).

A Word of Exhortation
1 CORINTHIANS 16:13-14

Paul, within one verse in rapid fire, gives some exhortatory words all in the imperative that are in a sense a call to arms. Blomberg calls these "military metaphors to encourage resoluteness in the faith" (*1 Corinthians*, 117). The Corinthians were to always be on their guard and never go to sleep at their theological post, making sure that false teaching did not corrupt the church. They were to "stand firm in the faith," where in the context "faith" most likely means the gospel (Schreiner, *1 Corinthians*, 333). Of course, this would entail staying strong, but everything should be wrapped up in a package of love. Paul here is directing the Corinthians back to chapter 13, his encomium on what true love is all about.

We should never ever apologize for standing firm in the faith and standing for truth and being strong, but we must remember that our tone is extremely important. If truth is not offered in love, even the greatest defense of the faith in the world will fall on deaf ears.

A Word of Commendation
1 CORINTHIANS 16:15-18

Paul wants to commend some who had come to visit him from Corinth. Paul had baptized the entire household of Stephanas (1:16). As so-called firstfruits (16:15), these most likely were the very first believers of Corinth (Schreiner, *1 Corinthians*, 333). Because of their devotion to serving the saints (particularly within their own local church), they deserved both respect and submission because they had certainly proven their servant leadership.

Fortunatus and Achaicus evidently filled a void in Paul's life, rescuing him at times from loneliness, discouragement, and perhaps even depression, which is something all Christ-followers should do for one another. We can refresh one another's spirits. Even though people like this serve mostly behind the scenes, Paul reminds the Corinthians, we should always give honor to whom honor is due.

A Word of Salutation
1 CORINTHIANS 16:19-24

Paul closes a tough letter with words of tenderness, affection, and greetings from the churches in Asia. The term translated "Asia" is used by Paul for what would be an area now located in western Turkey (Mare and Harris, *1 & 2 Corinthians*, 124). The reference to a house church in this passage is not unusual; in fact, now we are seeing a resurgence of this type of church in the twenty-first century.

From the time I was a child I have always been interested in verse 20 in particular: "Greet one another with a holy kiss." While growing up, I had to be reminded more than once that the emphasis was on the word "holy" and not the word "kiss"! That word "kiss" is also mentioned in Romans 16:16; 2 Corinthians 13:12; and 1 Thessalonians 5:26. Apparently, such kissing was a public practice among early believers to show their love for one another and their unity (Mare and Harris, *1 & 2 Corinthians*, 124). It was not a church ritual, nor was it confined only to community gatherings on the first day of the week (Schreiner, *1 Corinthians*, 335).

Up to this point, an amanuensis had been writing this letter as Paul dictated it to him, but now Paul takes the pen in his own hand (v. 21). As in today's business practice of dictating a letter to an assistant and then signing it, Paul similarly dictated his correspondence before adding his "John Hancock" on the finished product (cf. Gal 6:11; Col 4:18; 2 Thess 3:17; Phlm 19).

Paul perhaps drew attention to that here because of the way he closes this letter (again in extremely strong language). He wanted to make sure the Corinthians knew this was coming not just from his own heart, but his own hand. He says, "If anyone does not love the Lord, a curse be on him. Our Lord, come!" (v. 22). The Greek behind "curse" is the word *anathema*, which has a ring of final eschatological destruction and condemnation (Schreiner, *1 Corinthians*, 335). But right after this warning, Paul reverts back to love as the *sine qua non* of the Christian life—specifically a supreme love for the Lord. Of course, one indicator that someone truly does love the Lord is that he or she has a desire for him to return. It is not folly to say that one of the marks that you truly love the Lord Jesus is a longing for and an anticipation of his return.

Interestingly, in the original text, Paul uses the Aramaic words *marana tha* here without translating them into Greek. He might have done so because the early church used the Aramaic phrase, meaning "Our, Lord come," even in primarily Greek speaking churches (Bruce, *1 & 2 Corinthians*, 162).

Perhaps to end this letter on the highest note possible, he closes with two of the greatest words in the Christian language: grace and love (vv. 23-24). The gospel of which we should never be ashamed is all about grace. And once you experience the grace of the gospel, you should be filled with the love of the God of the gospel. This is not a bad way to end a very difficult letter! Not at all.

Conclusion

If possible, even when conversations are tough by their nature, it is always good to end them on a positive note that includes encouragement and exhortation. Paul actually teaches us in this chapter how to end a low conversation on a high note. He thus reminds us of the importance of maintaining personal relationships and friendships.

Reflect and Discuss

1. Have you ever had to have a tough communication with or write a difficult letter to someone? If so, how did you try to bring it to a positive conclusion?

2. When and how is it appropriate to let others know that you have a need that they can help meet in your own life?

3. How do you discern when God opens a door for ministry and closes another one? Can you give an example of a time this happened to you?

4. Why is it important for a local church to treat others, especially those who minister over them, with hospitality and respect?

5. What role does love play in keeping true to the faith, holding firm in convictions, and communicating hard truth?

6. How often do you take the time to give honor privately or publicly to those who often work behind the scenes and sacrifice greatly for you or the church? Can you think of someone in your life who deserves to receive such commendation this week?

7. How might we express love to each other apart from holy kissing, a practice that might be misinterpreted in today's Western world?

8. Why should the phrase *marana tha*, "Our Lord, come," still be used today in our conversations with fellow believers? What encouragement does it bring to you?

WORKS CITED

Bailey, Kenneth E. *Paul Through Mediterranean Eyes: Cultural Studies in 1 Corinthians.* Downers Grove, IL: IVP Academic, 2011.

Baptist Hymnal. Nashville, TN: Lifeway Worship, 2008.

Barrett, C. K. *First Epistle to the Corinthians.* Harper's New Testament Commentaries. New York: Harper & Row, 1968.

(BAGD) Bauer, Walter, William F. Arndt, F. Wilbur Gingrich, and Frederick W. Danker. *A Greek-English Lexicon of the New Testament and Other Early Christian Literature.* 3rd ed. Chicago: The University of Chicago Press, 2000.

Begg, Alistair. "Discipline in the Fellowship—Part Two." *Truth for Life,* June 23, 1985. Accessed Sept 7, 2022. https://www.truthforlife.org /resources/sermon/discipline-in-the-fellowship-part-2.

Blomberg, Craig L. *1 Corinthians.* The NIV Application Commentary. Grand Rapids, MI: Zondervan Academic, 1994.

Boice, James Montgomery. *Philippians.* Expositional Commentary. Grand Rapids, MI: Zondervan, 2006.

Bonhoeffer, Dietrich. *Life Together.* San Francisco: HarperOne, 1954.

Bridges, Jerry. *Respectable Sins: Confronting the Sins We Tolerate.* Colorado Springs, CO: NavPress, 2007.

Broadus, John A. *A Gentleman and a Scholar: Memoir of James P. Boyce.* Vestavia Hills, AL: Solid Ground Christian Books, 2004.

Bruce, F. F. *1 and 2 Corinthians.* New Century Bible Commentary. Grand Rapids, MI: Eerdmans, 1971.

Calvin, John. *1 Corinthians.* Grand Rapids, MI: Baker Book House, 1993.

Carmichael, Amy. *Candles in the Dark: Letters of Hope and Encouragement.* Fort Washington, PA: CLC Publications, 2012.

———. *Gold Cord: The Story of a Fellowship.* London: Society for Promoting Christian Knowledge, 1952.

Carson, D. A. *The Cross and Christian Ministry: Leadership Lessons from 1 Corinthians.* Grand Rapids, MI: Baker Books, 2003.

————. *Showing the Spirit: A Theological Exposition of 1 Corinthians 12–14.* Grand Rapids, MI: Baker Book House, 1987.

Carson, D. A., and G. K. Beale, editors. *Commentary on the New Testament Use of the Old Testament.* Grand Rapids, MI: Baker Academic, 2007.

Chambers, Oswald. "The Unblameable Attitude." *My Utmost for His Highest.* September 26. https://utmost.org/classic/the-unblameable -attitude-classic.

"Cult of Personality." *Merriam-Webster.* https://www.merriam-webster.com /dictionary/cult+of+personality.

Cunic, Arlin. "Tips for Using Facebook When You Have Social Anxiety Disorder." *Verywell Mind,* December 27, 2020. Accessed Sept 7, 2022. https://www.verywellmind.com/ten-things-not-to-do-on-facebook -when-you-have-sad-3024849.

Dagg, J. L. *Manual of Theology: A Treatise on Church Order.* Charleston, SC: Southern Baptist Publication Society, 1858.

Davis, Andy. "Headship, the Trinity, and Headcoverings, Part 2." *Two Journeys,* October 13, 2019. Accessed Sept 7, 2022. https://two- journeys.org/sermon/headship-the-trinity-and-headcoverings-part -2-1-corinthians-sermon-37.

————. "Wisdom Through the Spirit (1 Corinthians Sermon 8)." *Two Journeys,* November 4, 2018. Accessed Sept 7, 2022. https:// twojourneys.org/sermon/wisdom-through-the-spirit-1-corinthians -sermon-8.

Deen, Edith. *Great Women of the Christian Faith.* New York: Harper, 1959.

Dever, Mark. "The Church." Pages 603–68 in *A Theology for the Church.* Edited by Daniel L. Akin. Rev. ed. Nashville, TN: B&H Academic, 2014.

Dillon, Kyle. "What Does It Mean for the Saints to Judge Angels?" *The Gospel Coalition,* September 1, 2021. Accessed Sept 7, 2022. https:// www.thegospelcoalition.org/article/saints-judge-angels.

Drummond, Henry. *The Greatest Thing in the World.* New York: James Pott & Company, 1890.

Edwards, Jonathan. *Memoirs of the Rev. David Brainerd: Missionary to the Indians on the Borders of New-York, New-Jersey, and Pennsylvania: Chiefly Taken from His Own Diary.* New Haven, CT: S. Converse, 1822.

Elliot, Elisabeth. *Shadow of the Almighty: The Life and Testament of Jim Elliot.* San Francisco: HarperOne, 1956.

Fee, Gordon D. *The First Epistle to the Corinthians.* The New International Commentary on the New Testament. Grand Rapids, MI: Eerdmans, 1987.

————. *The First Epistle to the Corinthians*. Rev. ed. The New International Commentary on the New Testament. Grand Rapids, MI: Eerdmans, 2014.

Finney, Charles Grandison. *Lectures to Professing Christians*. New York: Milner, 1837.

Furley, Oliver W. "Moravian Missionaries and Slaves in the West Indies." *Caribbean Studies* 5, no. 2 (1965): 3–16.

Gardner, Paul D. *1 Corinthians*. Zondervan Exegetical Commentary on the New Testament. Grand Rapids, MI: Zondervan Academic, 2018.

Garland, David E. *1 Corinthians*. Baker Exegetical Commentary on the New Testament. Grand Rapids, MI: Baker Academic, 2003.

Greear, J. D. "The Gospel Above All—Part 1." *Outreach Magazine*, October 2, 2019. Accessed Sept 7, 2022. https://outreachmagazine .com/interviews/46343-j-d-greear-the-gospel-above-all-part-1.

Gundry, R. H. "'Ecstatic Utterance' (N.E.B)?" *The Journal of Theological Studies* 17 (1966): 299–307.

Halloran, Kevin. "A Prayer for Contentment." *Anchored in Christ*, March 14, 2016. https://www.kevinhalloran.net/a-prayer-for-contentment.

Hamilton, James M., Jr. *Typology: Understanding the Bible's Promise-Shaped Patterns*. Grand Rapids, MI: Zondervan Academic, 2022.

Hays, Richard B. *First Corinthians*. Interpretation: A Biblical Commentary for Teaching and Preaching. Louisville, KY: Westminster John Knox, 2011.

Henry, Matthew. *The Communicant's Companion*. Boston: Crocker & Brewster, 1828.

Hodge, Charles. *An Exposition of the First Epistle to the Corinthians*. New York: Robert Carter and Brothers, 1860.

House, H. Wayne. *Chronological and Background Charts of the New Testament*. Grand Rapids, MI: Zondervan, 1981.

Jeschke, Marlin. *Discipling the Brother: Congregational Discipline According to the Gospel*. Scottdale, PA: Herald Press, 1972.

Johnson, Marguerite, and Terry Ryan. *Sexuality in Greek and Roman Society and Literature: A Sourcebook*. Abingdon, VA: Routledge, 2005.

Jowett, John Henry. *Apostolic Optimism and Other Sermons*. London: Hodder and Stoughton, 1901.

Kempis, Thomas à. *The Inner Life*. New York: Penguin, 2005.

Kistemaker, Simon J. *Exposition of the First Epistle to the Corinthians*. New Testament Commentary. Grand Rapids, MI: Baker Books, 1993.

Köstenberger, Andreas J., et al. *The Cradle, the Cross, and the Crown: An Introduction to the New Testament.* 2nd ed. Nashville, TN: B&H Academic, 2016.

Laney, J. Carl. "The Biblical Practice of Church Discipline." *Bibliotheca Sacra* 143, no. 572 (1986): 353–64.

Lassen, Eva Maria. "The Use of the Father Image in Imperial Propaganda and 1 Corinthians 4:14-21." *Tyndale Bulletin* 42, no. 1 (1991): 127–36.

Lawless, Chuck. "11 Reasons Churches Don't Practice Discipline." *Chuck Lawless,* January 26, 2021. Accessed Sept 7, 2022. https://chucklawless.com/2021/01/11-reasons-churches-dont-practice-discipline.

Lewis, C. S. *Mere Christianity.* San Francisco: HarperOne, 2015.

———. *The Problem of Pain.* San Francisco: HarperOne, 2015.

———. *The Screwtape Letters.* San Francisco: HarperOne, 2015.

Lightfoot, Joseph Barber. *Notes on Epistles of St. Paul from Unpublished Commentaries.* London: Macmillan, 1895.

MacArthur, John. *1 Corinthians.* The MacArthur New Testament Commentary. Chicago: Moody, 1984.

———. "Church Discipline." *Grace to You.* Accessed Sept 7, 2022. https://www.gty.org/library/articles/DD02/church-discipline.

———. "The Wickedness of the Crucifixion, Part 1." Grace to You. Accessed November 28, 2022. https://www.gty.org/library/sermons-library/2395/the-wickedness-of-the-crucifixion-part-1.

Mare, W. Harold, and Murray J. Harris. *1 & 2 Corinthians.* NIV Expositors Bible Commentary. Grand Rapids, MI: Zondervan, 1995.

Moody, Dwight L. "Shall We Meet Our Loved Ones Again?" Jesus Site. Accessed November 28, 2022. https://www.jesussite.com/resources/articles-papers/shall-we-meet-our-loved-ones-again.

Morris, Leon L. *1 Corinthians.* Tyndale New Testament Commentaries. Downers Grove, IL: IVP Academic, 2008.

Origen. *Against Celsus.* https://www.ccel.org/ccel/schaff/anf04.vi.ix.iii.xliv.html.

Ortlund, Ray. "What's Allowed in Married Sex?" *The Gospel Coalition,* September 23, 2021. Accessed Sept 7, 2022. https://www.thegospelcoalition.org/article/allowed-married-sex.

Panton, David Morrieson. "Counsels for Young Workers." *Present Day Leaflets.* Eastbourne: "Living Waters" Unions, 1949. Accessed August 4, 2022. http://www.ccofstarke.com/Site/Panton/ECYW.pdf.

Paré, Ambroise. "The Journey to Turin, 1537," in *Journeys in Diverse Places.* Trans. Stephen Paget. New York: Collier & Son, 1909–1914.

"Patricians." Pages 539–40 in *The Oxford Dictionary of the Classical World*. Edited by John Roberts. Oxford: Oxford University Press, 2007.

Piper, John. "Battling the Unbelief of a Haughty Spirit." December 18, 1988. Accessed September 2, 2022. https://www.desiringgod.org /messages/battling-the-unbelief-of-a-haughty-spirit.

———. *Don't Waste Your Life*. Redesign. Wheaton, IL: Crossway, 2018.

———. "How Satan Saves the Soul." *Desiring God*, September 5, 1993. Accessed September 3, 2022. https://www.desiringgod.org/messages /how-satan-saves-the-soul.

———. "How the Spirit Helps Us Understand." *Desiring God*, May 20, 1984. Accessed September 3, 2022. https://www.desiringgod.org /messages/how-the-spirit-helps-us-understand.

———. "I Will Not Be Enslaved by Anything." *Desiring God*, September 1, 1985. Accessed September 3, 2022. https://www.desiringgod .org/messages/i-will-not-be-enslaved-by-anything.

———. "Idolatry, the Lord's Supper, and the Body of Christ." *Desiring God*, October 4, 1992. Accessed September 3, 2022. https://www .desiringgod.org/messages/idolatry-the-lords-supper-and-the-body -of-christ.

———. "Is It Ever Okay for a Christian to Sue a Non-Christian?" *Desiring God*, September 30, 2009. Accessed September 3, 2022. https:// www.desiringgod.org/interviews/is-it-ever-okay-for-a-christian -to-sue-a-non-christian.

———. "The Joyful Duty of Man." *Desiring God*, January 22, 1989. Accessed September 3, 2022. https://www.desiringgod.org /messages/the-joyful-duty-of-man.

———. "Let Him Who Boasts Boast in the Lord!" *Desiring God*, January 31, 1988. Accessed September 3, 2022. https://www.desiringgod .org/messages/let-him-who-boasts-boast-in-the-lord.

———. "The Lord's Supper—Somber or Cheerful?" *Desiring God*, September 25, 2017. Accessed September 3, 2022. https:// www.desiringgod.org/interviews/the-lords-supper-somber-or -cheerful.

———. "Sustained by the Faithfulness of God." *Desiring God*, January 17, 1988. Accessed September 3, 2022. https://www.desiringgod.org /messages/sustained-by-the-faithfulness-of-god.

———. "The Wisdom We Speak." *Desiring God*, July 20, 1980. Accessed September 3, 2022. https://www.desiringgod.org/messages/the -wisdom-we-speak.

————. "You Were Bought with a Price: Glorify God with Your Bodies." *Desiring God*, November 22, 1992. Accessed September 3, 2022. https://www.desiringgod.org/messages/you-were-bought-with-a-price.

————. "Your Job as Ministry." *Desiring God*, June 14, 1981. Accessed September 3, 2022. https://www.desiringgod.org/messages/your -job-as-ministry.

Polhill, John B. *Paul and His Letters*. Nashville, TN: B&H Academic, 1999.

"Preaching." *Christianity Today*, July 2002.

Quarles, Charles L. "Confusion at Corinth: Biblical Interpretation, Sex, and the Glory of God." Unpublished paper.

Sande, Ken. "20 Ways to Prevent and Resolve Conflict in the Church." *NC Baptist*, November 10, 2020. Accessed Sept 7, 2022. https://ncbaptist .org/article/20-ways-to-prevent-and-resolve-conflict-in-the-church.

————. "Judging Others: The Danger of Playing God (Part 2)." *Christian Counseling & Educational Foundation*, March 21, 2009. Accessed Sept 7, 2022. https://www.ccef.org/judging-others-danger-playing-god -part-2.

————. "Judging Others: The Danger of Playing God (Part 3)." *Christian Counseling & Educational Foundation*, August 23, 2009. Accessed Sept 7, 2022. https://www.ccef.org/judging-others-danger -playing-god-part-3.

Saucy, Robert L. *The Church in God's Program*. Chicago: Moody, 1972.

Schreiner, Thomas R. *1 Corinthians: An Introduction and Commentary*. Tyndale New Testament Commentaries. Downers Grove, IL: IVP Academic, 2018.

————. "'Single and Satisfied in God,' An Exposition of 1 Corinthians 7:25–40." *Towers*, February 18, 2002, pp. 2, 7.

Sproul, R. C. *In Search of Dignity*. Ventura, CA: Regal Books, 1983.

Spurgeon, Charles Haddon. "The Believer's Deathday Better Than His Birthday." Pages 145–56 in *The Metropolitan Tabernacle Pulpit, Volume 28: Sermons Preached and Revised by C. H. Spurgeon, During the Year 1881*. London: Passmore & Alabaster, 1882.

————. "Confirming the Witness of Christ." *The Metropolitan Tabernacle Pulpit*. Volume 50. Pasadena, TX: Pilgrim Publications, 1978.

————. *Lectures to My Students*. Grand Rapids, MI: Zondervan, 1977.

————. "The Parent's and Pastor's Joy." *The Metropolitan Tabernacle Pulpit*. Volume 19. Pasadena, TX: Pilgrim Publications, 1981.

————. "Preach the Gospel." *The Metropolitan Tabernacle Pulpit*. Volume 1. Pasadena, TX: Pilgrim Publications, 1990.

Swindoll, Charles R. *Growing Deep in the Christian Life: Essential Truths for Becoming Strong in the Faith*. New York: Harper Collins, 1995.

Taylor, Mark. *1 Corinthians: An Exegetical and Theological Exposition of Holy Scripture*. New American Commentary. Nashville, TN: Holman Reference, 2014.

Thiselton, Anthony C. *The First Epistle to the Corinthians: A Commentary on the Greek Text*. New International Greek Testament Commentary. Grand Rapids, MI: Eerdmans, 2000.

Tozer, A. W. *The Attributes of God*. Chicago: Christian Publications, 1997.

———. *God's Pursuit of Man*. Abridged ed. Chicago: Moody, 2015.

Tripp, Paul. "10 Things You Should Know about Marriage." *Ten Things You Should Know*, October 1, 2021. Accessed Sept 7, 2022. https://www.crossway.org/articles/10-things-you-should-know-about-marriage.

———. *Journey to the Cross: A 40-Day Lenten Devotional*. Wheaton, IL: Crossway, 2021.

Um, Stephen T. *1 Corinthians: The Word of the Cross*. Preaching the Word. Wheaton, IL: Crossway, 2015.

Van Dixhoorn, Chad. *Creeds, Confessions, and Catechisms: A Reader's Edition*. Wheaton, IL: Crossway, 2022.

Vaughn, Curtis, and Thomas D. Lea. *1 Corinthians*. Bible Study Commentary. Grand Rapids, MI: Zondervan, 1984.

Verbrugge, Verlyn. *1 and 2 Corinthians*. Expositor's Bible Commentary. Grand Rapids, MI: Zondervan Academic, 2008.

Warren, Rick. "10 Commandments to Help Church Staff Maintain Moral Integrity." *Pastors.com*, April 25, 2017. Accessed Sept. 3, 2022. https://pastors.com/maintaining-moral-purity-in-ministry.

Waters, Guy P. "1–2 Corinthians." Pages 195–248 in *A Biblical-Theological Introduction to the New Testament: The Gospel Realized*. Edited by Michael J. Kruger. Wheaton, IL: Crossway, 2016.

Watson, Thomas. *A Body of Practical Divinity*. Aberdeen: D. Chalmers and Co., 1838.

Whitehead, Alfred North. https://www.brainyquote.com/quotes/alfred_north_whitehead_119000. Accessed July 26, 2022.

Wiersbe, Warren W. *Be Wise*. The BE Series. Wheaton, IL: Victor Books, 1983.

Wray, Daniel E. *Biblical Church Discipline*. Carlisle, PA: Banner of Truth, 1978.

Wright, N. T. *A Lenten Devotional*. 2017. Accessed Sept 7, 2022. http://ntwrightonline.org/wp-content/uploads/2017/03/Lenten-Devotional-v3.pdf.

SCRIPTURE INDEX

Genesis
1 *xiii*
1–2 *138*
1:26-27 *51, 219*
1:26-31 *179*
1:27 *224*
2 *138, 225*
2:18 *219, 224*
2:24 *132, 139*
3 *138*
3:20 *294*
4 *166*
4:8 *166*
4:9 *166*
6:1-4 *206*
39 *132*

Exodus
12 *109*
12:23 *198*
13:21 *194*
14 *194*
15:24 *198*
16 *195*
16:1-3,7-8 *198*
17:1-7 *195*
17:2-7 *197*
17:7 *198*
20:3-4 *196*
20:3-6 *119*
20:4-5 *207*
20:14 *139*
21:2-11 *152*

21:16 *152*
24:8 *233*
25:8 *66*
29:45 *66*
32 *196*
32:6 *197*

Leviticus
6:16-18,26-28 *181*
7:6,8-10,28-36 *181*
17:11 *233*
18:8 *103*
18:22 *119*
20:13 *119*
26:11-12 *66*

Numbers
11:1 *198*
11:5-6 *196*
11:18-34 *196*
11:31-34 *196*
14 *195*
14:2,27,29,36 *198*
16:11 *198*
16:41 *198*
16:41-50 *198*
18:8-19 *181*
20:2-13 *195*
21:4-9 *197*
21:6 *198*

25:1-9 *197*
25:9 *197*

Deuteronomy
1:27 *198*
5:7-8 *196*
6:4 *169*
6:5 *27*
6:16 *197*
7:7 *36*
10:17 *170*
17:7 *112*
17:7,12 *112*
19:19 *112*
20:6 *179*
21:21 *112*
21:23 *30*
22:21-22,24 *112*
22:30 *103*
24:7 *112*
25:4 *177, 179*
27:20 *103*
32:16-17 *170*

Joshua
7:11-12 *103*

1 Samuel
2:1-10 *37*
16:7 *79*

2 Samuel
24:24 *68*

1 Kings
18:21 *207*

Ezra
9 *105*

Nehemiah
5:5 *152*

Job
2:6 *107*
5:13 *71*
14:14 *290*
42:6-7 *107*

Psalms
14:1 *247*
22 *30*
24:1 *212*
24:10 *49*
44:21 *79*
83:16,18 *37*
84:11 *10*
94 *71*
94:5-7,16 *71*
94:11 *71*
103:20 *225*
105:39 *194*
106:14 *196*
106:24 *198*
110 *48*
114:2 *66*
139:14 *128*
148:2 *225*

Proverbs
1:8 *93*
2:1-5 *93*
3:1-2 *93*
3:11-12 *100, 235*
4:1-2 *93*

5:18 *138*
6:20-22 *94*
8:22-31 *39*
10:13-14 *81*
11:14 *81*
12:10 *179*
13:24 *98*
15:1 *91*
15:22 *81*
16:2 *79, 81*
16:18 *199*
18:13 *81*
19:11 *126*
20:18 *126*
22:6 *98*
23:22 *94*
29:15 *98*

Isaiah
6:2-3 *225*
9:7 *287*
28:11-12 *266*
29:14 *28*
40:13 *56*
40:31 *11*
43:7 *213*
52:15 *49*
53 *30*
53:9 *276*
55:8-9 *28*
64:4 *49*
65:17 *49*

Jeremiah
1:5 *169*
3:16 *49*
9:23-24 *39*
20:9 *182*
31 *48*
31:31-34 *233*

Lamentations
3:45 *91*

Daniel
2 *47*
2:18-19,27-30,47
    47
4:9 *47*
10:12-14 *206*

Amos
3:2 *169*

Malachi
1:11 *9*
3:10 *302*

Matthew
1:21 *33*
3:17 *73*
4:18 *280*
5:11-12 *68*
5:23-24 *234*
5:31-32 *141*
5:32 *141*
5:39-42 *118*
5:44 *166*
6:4,6,18 *67*
6:6,18 *68*
6:20 *67*
6:25-34 *92*
6:33 *160*
7:1-5 *81*
7:12 *81, 121*
8:20 *90*
9:38 *62*
10:42 *68*
11:20-24 *65*
12:38-42 *30*
13:43 *131*
13:55 *178*

15:8-9 *28*
16:1-4 *30*
18:12-14 *80, 126*
18:15 *126*
18:15-17 *112*
18:15-20 *16, 102, 106, 126*
18:16 *126*
19:3-12 *141*
19:4-6 *119*
19:6 *142*
19:9 *141*
19:12 *140, 156*
19:24 *35*
19:28 *116*
20:26-28 *68*
22:37 *27*
22:37-40 *18, 122*
23:14 *65*
24:3,27,37 *286*
26:26-29 *229*
26:67 *89*
28:18-20 *20*

Mark
1:21-34 *206*
1:24 *206*
8:34 *70*
10:1-12 *141*
10:42-45 *77*
14:22-25 *229*

Luke
1:33 *287*
1:46-53 *37*
2:26-38 *37*
6:28 *90*
10:7 *177, 181*
14:12-14 *68*
16:18 *141*

21:3 *68*
22:14-20 *229, 232*
22:29-30 *116*
23:34 *90*
24:25-26 *48*
24:25-27,44-47 *xiv*

John
1:1 *73*
1:14 *114*
2:18-22 *30*
3:2 *128*
3:27,30 *86*
4:34-38 *62*
5:39,46 *xiv*
6:30-66 *30*
7:53–8:11 *81*
8:32 *227, 288*
10:27-28 *235*
10:27-29 *13*
11:26 *291*
13:1-20 *229*
13:34-35 *169, 187*
13:35 *115*
14:16 *53*
17:11,21-23,26 *16*
17:17-19 *111*
17:18 *111*
21:3 *280*

Acts
2 *252*
2:3 *266*
2:8,11 *270*
2:17-18 *223*
2:41-47 *20*

4:27-28 *49*
4:28 *48*
5:1-11 *107*
7:58–8:3 *7*
9:1-2 *7*
9:1-19 *178*
9:15-17 *7*
12:23 *225*
13:9 *7*
15:36–18:22 *5*
16:1 *97*
16:1-3 *187*
17:14-15 *97*
17–18 *42*
17:26 *294*
17:27 *146*
18:1-3 *184*
18:1-7 *178*
18:1-17 *4–5, 95*
18:3 *90*
18:5 *97*
18:8 *21*
18:11 *5*
18:17 *7*
18:18 *187*
18:18-21 *4*
19:8-10 *5*
19:21 *5*
19:22 *4, 97*
20:2-3 *5*
20:4 *97*
20:7 *300*
20:28 *66*
21:9 *223*
27 *248*
28 *7*

Romans
1:5 *182*

1:16 *26, 277, 306*
1:18-25 *119*
1:22 *29, 47*
1:26-27 *119*
1:29 *19*
1:29-31 *118*
2:12 *26*
2:16 *13*
2:25 *151*
3:23 *185*
5:8 *185*
5:9 *26*
6:1-11 *21*
6:1-14 *194*
6:9 *276*
6:12,19 *161*
6:19 *109*
6:23 *185*
8:9,15 *54*
8:28-30 *48, 169*
8:28-39 *13*
8:29 *73*
8:29-30 *48*
8:35-39 *73*
10:9-10,13 *185*
11:13 *182*
11:36 *210*
12:1 *130, 161*
12:1-2 *111*
12:2 *54, 150*
12:3-8 *10*
12:17 *90*
13:1-5 *115*
13:11-14 *159*
13:13 *19*
14:1-6,13-23 *81*
14:7-12 *82*
14:10 *64*
15:2-3 *211*

15:15-16 *182*
15:26 *298*
15:27 *180*
16:16 *308*
16:17-18 *16, 102*
16:21 *97*
16:23 *21*

1 Corinthians
1 *7*
1:1 *7*
1:1-3 *7*
1:1-4,6-9 *8*
1:1-9 *3*
1–2 *57*
1:2 *8, 13–14, 120*
1:2-3 *8*
1:2,9 *31*
1–3 *75*
1:3 *9–10, 44*
1:3-4 *44*
1:4 *10*
1:4-7 *10*
1:5 *11, 168*
1:5-7 *10*
1:6 *11*
1:7 *11–12*
1:7-8 *12*
1:7-9 *11–12*
1:8 *13*
1:8-9 *12*
1:9 *13–14*
1:10 *17–19, 85, 94*
1:10–2:9 *69*
1:10–4:21 *17, 94, 99*
1:10-12 *58*
1:10-17 *3, 17, 25*

1:11 *4–5, 18–19, 103*
1:12 *17, 19*
1:12-13 *19*
1:13 *20*
1:14-16 *21*
1:14-17 *20*
1:16 *307*
1:17 *21, 25*
1:18 *25–26, 28, 30, 42, 44, 51–52*
1:18–2:5 *25, 99*
1:18–3:23 *25*
1:18–4:21 *111*
1:18-25 *24–25, 30, 34*
1:18-31 *46*
1:19 *28*
1:19-21 *27*
1:20 *28*
1:21 *29*
1:22-23 *30, 51*
1:22-25 *30*
1:23 *42, 184*
1:24 *25*
1:24-25 *31*
1:26 *34, 36*
1:26-29 *70*
1:27 *36, 88, 188*
1:27-28 *36*
1:27-29 *34, 36*
1:28 *37*
1:28-29 *37*
1:30 *34, 39*
1:30-31 *38*
1:31 *31, 34, 39, 49, 53, 71, 105*
2:1 *43, 50*

2:1,4 *50*
2:1-5 *43, 46, 99*
2:1-9 *43, 53*
2:2 *43, 45, 52,*
    61, 63, 69, 77
2:2,7 *48*
2:3-4 *44*
2:4 *44–45*
2:5 *45–46*
2:6 *46–47, 49*
2:6-7 *50*
2:6-8 *70*
2:6-9 *46*
2:7 *47–48, 50*
2:7-9 *47*
2:8 *47–50*
2:9 *49*
2:10 *53–54, 243*
2:10–3:4 *51*
2:10-11 *53*
2:10-13,15-16 *47,*
    53
2:12 *54*
2:12-13 *54*
2:13 *54*
2:14 *52, 54, 56*
2:15 *53, 55*
2:15-16 *55*
2:16 *56, 70*
3 *69, 71, 189*
3:1 *47, 57, 70*
3:1-2 *57*
3:1-3 *59*
3:1-4 *52, 56, 59*
3:2 *57*
3:3 *58*
3:3-4 *58*
3:5 *61*
3:5–4:5 *85*

3:5-6,8-9 *61*
3:5-9 *60–61*
3:5-17 *60, 69*
3:6 *61–62, 178*
3:6-7 *62*
3:7 *61–62, 68*
3:8 *61–62*
3:8-9 *61*
3:9 *61–62*
3:9-15 *60, 62, 65*
3:10 *62*
3:10-15 *80*
3:11 *61, 63*
3:12-13 *63*
3:13 *63–64*
3:13-15 *64*
3:15 *191*
3:16 *53, 65–66,*
    133
3:16-17 *60, 65*
3:17 *66–68, 70*
3:18 *69–70, 73*
3:19 *70–72*
3:19-20 *70*
3:20 *71*
3:21 *69, 71, 105*
3:21-23 *71–72*
3:22 *61*
3:22-23 *72*
3:23 *69, 73–74*
4 *99*
4:1 *61, 76*
4:1-2 *76*
4:2 *77*
4:3-5 *77, 81*
4:4 *77, 83*
4:4-5 *77, 82*
4:5 *61, 64, 80*
4:6 *85–86, 98*

4:6-7 *85*
4:6,18-19 *105*
4:7 *86*
4:8 *12, 87, 89*
4:8-9 *87*
4:8-13 *87, 91, 94*
4:9 *87–88*
4:9-13 *97*
4:10 *88*
4:11 *89*
4:12 *90*
4:13 *90–91*
4:14 *94*
4:14-15 *17, 94*
4:15 *94*
4:16 *95–96, 216*
4:16-17 *96*
4:17 *4, 97*
4:18 *98*
4:18-19 *98*
4:19 *98*
4:20 *99*
4:20-21 *99*
4:21 *85, 94, 100,*
    105
5 *16, 81, 103,*
    111–12
5:1 *81, 103, 111,*
    137
5:1-13 *3, 102*
5:2 *104–5,*
    107–8, 112,
    129
5:3 *106*
5:3-5 *106*
5:4 *107*
5:4-5 *106*
5:5 *26, 107, 112*
5–6 *94, 126*

5:6 *108, 116, 168*
5:6-8 *105*
5:7 *109*
5:7-8 *109, 194*
5:8 *109*
5:9 *110, 113*
5:9-11 *103, 110*
5:9-13 *4*
5:10 *110*
5:10-11 *110, 119*
5:11 *106, 111*
5:12 *103*
5:12-13 *111*
6 *114, 116–17,
    120–21, 129*
6:1 *115, 127*
6:1-2 *115*
6:1-3 *115*
6:1-6 *126*
6:1-11 *3, 111*
6:2 *116*
6:2,3,9,15-16,19
    168
6:3 *116*
6:4 *117*
6:4-5 *126*
6:4-8 *117*
6:5 *114, 117, 120*
6:5-8 *117*
6:6 *117*
6:7 *114, 117–18*
6:8 *118*
6:9 *118–20,
    129–30*
6:9-10 *118, 120,
    137*
6:9-11 *57, 118*
6:9,13-18 *111*
6:9,13,18 *103*

6:11 *121*
6:12 *129, 134,
    211*
6:12–10:22 *210*
6:12-13 *129*
6:12-20 *3, 129,
    131*
6:13 *129–30*
6:13-14 *130*
6:13,18 *129*
6:13,19–20 *161*
6:14 *130–31*
6:14-15 *128*
6:15 *131*
6:15-16,18 *129*
6:15-16,19 *129*
6:15-18 *131*
6:16 *132*
6:17 *132, 136,
    204*
6:18 *132–33,
    197, 203*
6:19 *65, 133–34,
    136*
6:19-20 *53, 128*
6:19,20 *129*
6:20 *130, 134,
    136, 153, 186*
7 *130, 137, 148,
    162–63*
7:1 *4–5, 138*
7:1-2 *138*
7:1-5 *138*
7:1-6 *111*
7:1-16 *144*
7:1,25 *137, 167*
7:1-40 *3*
7:2 *103, 138, 162*
7:3 *139*

7:3-4 *139*
7:4 *139*
7:5 *138*
7:5-6 *139–40*
7:7 *140, 156*
7:7-8 *140*
7:7-9 *140*
7:8 *140*
7:9 *140*
7:10-11 *141*
7:10-16 *141*
7:12 *142*
7:12-13 *142*
7:12-16 *142*
7:14 *142*
7:15-16 *143*
7:16 *144*
7:17 *149–51*
7:17,20,24 *153*
7:17-24 *151*
7:18 *150*
7:18-22 *150*
7:19 *150*
7:20 *148, 151*
7:22 *152*
7:23 *134,
    152–53, 186*
7:23-24 *153*
7:24 *153*
7:25 *157*
7:25-28 *157*
7:25-40 *156*
7:26 *157–58*
7:27 *158*
7:27-28 *158*
7:28 *158*
7:29 *159*
7:29-31 *158*
7:30 *159*

7:30-31 *159*
7:31 *159, 165*
7:32 *140, 160*
7:32-35 *140, 160*
7:33 *160*
7:33-35 *160*
7:34 *160–61*
7:35 *161*
7:36 *162*
7:36-40 *162*
7:37-38 *162*
7:38 *163, 165*
7:39 *143, 163*
7:39-40 *163*
7:40 *142, 157,
    163*
8 *111, 166, 177,
    184, 188, 196*
8:1 *137, 167–68,
    188*
8:1-2 *167*
8:1-3 *129,
    166–67*
8:1–11:1 *3*
8:1-13 *166*
8:2 *168*
8:3 *168–69*
8:4 *169*
8:4-5 *169*
8:4-6 *166, 169*
8:6 *170*
8:7 *166, 172–73*
8:7,9 *168*
8:7-10 *172*
8:7,10 *207*
8:7-13 *166, 172,
    188*
8:8 *172*
8–9 *177*

8–10 *183, 186*
8:10 *172*
8:10-13 *213*
8:11 *166, 169*
8:11-12 *173*
8:11-13 *173*
8:13 *166, 173,
    175, 177*
9 *177, 184*
9:1-6 *177*
9:1-14 *177*
9:1-18 *177*
9:2 *178*
9:3 *178*
9:4 *178*
9:5 *178*
9:6 *178*
9:7 *178–179*
9:8-9 *179*
9:10 *180*
9:11-12 *180*
9:12 *178*
9:12-18 *180*
9:13 *180*
9:14 *181*
9:15 *183*
9:15-16 *181*
9:15-18 *181*
9:17 *182*
9:17-18 *183*
9:18 *183*
9:19 *186, 192*
9:19-22 *186, 214*
9:19-23 *152, 186*
9:19-27 *186*
9:20 *186–87*
9;21 *187*
9:21 *187, 211*
9:22 *188–89*

9:22-23 *188*
9:23 *189*
9:24 *189, 194*
9:24-26 *189*
9:24-27 *189, 193*
9:25 *189–90*
9:26 *189*
9:26-27 *190*
9:27 *199*
10 *111, 215*
10:1 *194*
10:1-5 *194–95*
10:1-13 *193*
10:2 *194*
10:3-4 *194–95*
10:4 *195*
10:5 *195*
10:6 *196*
10:6-11 *196*
10:6,11 *193*
10:7 *196*
10:7-10 *195*
10:7,14 *119*
10:7,14-22 *222*
10:8 *197–99*
10:9 *197*
10:10 *198*
10:11-12 *199*
10:11-13 *199*
10:12 *199–200,
    204*
10:13 *200–201,
    203*
10:14 *132, 172,
    203*
10:14-15 *203*
10:14-17 *203*
10:15 *203*
10:16 *204, 234*

10:16-17 *203*
10:16-22 *229*
10:17 *204, 234*
10:18-20 *205,*
207
10:18-22 *205*
10:19-22 *170*
10:20-21 *205*
10:21 *207*
10:22 *205, 207–8*
10:23 *211, 214*
10:23–11:1 *217*
10:24 *211, 214*
10:25 *212*
10:25-29 *212*
10:26 *212–14,*
217
10:27 *212*
10:28-29 *212*
10:29 *214*
10:29-30 *213*
10:31 *53, 67–68,*
135, 210, 213,
215
10:31-33 *186*
10:32 *215*
10:32-33 *214*
10:33 *214–15*
11 *215, 222, 236,*
272
11:1 *96–97, 100,*
188, 214–15
11:2 *220, 231*
11:2-3 *220*
11:2-16 *3,*
218–19, 224
11:3 *220, 223*
11:4 *223–24*
11:4-5,7,10 *220*

11:4-6 *221*
11:5-6 *223*
11:5-6,14-15 *221*
11:6 *223*
11:7 *224*
11:7-9 *223*
11:8-9 *224*
11:10 *224–25*
11:11 *226*
11:11-12 *225–26,*
228
11:12 *226*
11:13 *226*
11:13-15 *226*
11:14 *226*
11:15 *221, 226*
11:16 *227*
11:17 *231*
11:17-19 *231*
11:17-22 *231*
11:17-34 *3, 203,*
229–30
11:18 *231*
11:19 *231*
11:19-20 *16*
11:20 *231*
11:20-22 *231*
11:21 *111, 129,*
231
11:22 *232, 236*
11:23 *220, 232,*
276
11:23-24 *232*
11:23-25 *232*
11:23-26 *232*
11:25 *233*
11:26 *12, 207,*
233
11:27 *105, 234*

11:27-30 *199*
11:27-32 *234*
11:27-34 *233*
11:28 *234*
11:29 *234*
11:29-30 *234*
11:30 *107, 235*
11:31 *235*
11:31-32 *235*
11:32 *235*
11:33 *236*
11:33-34 *235*
11:34 *236*
12:1 *137, 239–40*
12:1,4,7 *240*
12:3 *275*
12:4 *240, 243*
12:4-6 *242*
12:4-11 *255*
12:4-11,28-30 *10*
12:5 *243*
12:5-6 *241*
12:5-6,11 *241*
12:5-7,11 *241*
12:6 *244*
12:7 *240, 242,*
253
12:8 *11, 168,*
188, 247
12:8,10 *247*
12:9 *249–50*
12:9-10 *248, 250*
12:10 *248–49,*
251–53
12:11 *241, 254*
12:11-13 *253*
12:11-31 *253*
12:12 *253*
12:13 *253*

12–14 *3, 10, 238*
12:14 *254*
12:14-17 *254*
12:14-31 *254*
12:18-23 *254*
12:23-26 *255*
12:26 *255*
12:27 *65*
12:27-31 *255*
12:28 *255–56*
12:31 *256*
13 *173, 257, 307*
13:1 *258*
13:1-3 *258*
13:1-13 *169*
13:2 *168, 258*
13:3 *259*
13:4 *259–60*
13:4-7 *259*
13:5 *211, 260–61*
13:6 *261*
13:7 *261*
13:8 *262*
13:8-12 *262*
13:8-13 *262*
13:10 *262*
13:13 *263*
14 *10, 252, 264, 266, 269*
14:1 *265*
14:1-5 *267*
14:1-25 *265*
14:2 *266*
14:3 *250*
14:4 *265*
14:5 *270*
14:6-12 *267*
14:7 *267*
14:7-8 *269*

14:7-9,12,14-15,19 *269*
14:7-9,12,14-15,19,22 *269*
14:8 *267*
14:9 *269*
14:9-11 *268*
14:10-11 *266*
14:13-19 *268*
14:14 *268*
14:14-15 *269*
14:17 *268*
14:18 *282*
14:18-19 *269*
14:19 *270*
14:20 *271*
14:20-25 *268–69*
14:20,32-33 *271*
14:21 *266*
14:22 *270*
14:23-25 *219*
14:26 *219*
14:26-33 *271*
14:26-40 *271*
14:28 *272*
14:28,33-40 *272*
14:29 *56, 272*
14:32 *273*
14:33 *219, 271*
14:34-35 *272*
14:37-40 *272*
14:39 *271*
14:39-40 *265*
14:40 *219, 286*
15 *3, 128, 291*
15:1 *275*
15:1-3 *220, 275*
15:1-20 *26*
15:2 *275, 277*

15:2,9-11 *277*
15:3 *275–76*
15:3-4 *176*
15:3-5 *285*
15:3-6 *20, 44, 181*
15:3-8 *275*
15:4 *276–77*
15:5-8 *277*
15:9-10 *182*
15:9-11 *277*
15:10 *278*
15:12-13 *280*
15:12-14 *280*
15:14 *280*
15:15 *281*
15:15-16 *281*
15:16 *281*
15:17 *281–82*
15:18 *26, 282*
15:19 *282*
15:20 *285*
15:20-22 *285*
15:23 *286*
15:23-28 *286*
15:24 *286, 306*
15:24-26 *286*
15:25-26 *287*
15:27 *287*
15:27-28 *287*
15:28 *287*
15:29 *287*
15:29-34 *287*
15:30-32 *288*
15:33 *288*
15:33-34 *288*
15:34 *288*
15:35 *291*
15:36 *291*

15:36-38 *292*
15:36-41 *291*
15:39 *292*
15:40-41 *292*
15:41 *65*
15:42 *293*
15:42-46 *293*
15:42-49 *293*
15:43 *292–94*
15:44-46 *294*
15:47-49 *294*
15:50 *295*
15:50-53 *295*
15:50-57 *295*
15:50-58 *295*
15:58 *296*
16:1 *298–99*
16:1,12 *137*
16:2 *300–302*
16:3-4 *303*
16:5-7 *305*
16:5-12 *305*
16:6 *306*
16:8 *4*
16:8-9 *306*
16:10 *4*
16:10-11 *97*
16:10-12 *306*
16:13-14 *306*
16:15 *307*
16:15,17 *21*
16:15-18 *307*
16:17 *103*
16:19-24 *307*
16:20 *307*
16:21 *308*
16:22 *308*
16:23-24 *308*
24:14 *179*

2 Corinthians
1:19 *97*
2 *112*
2:1 *4*
2:3-9 *5*
2:5-11 *102*
2:12-13 *5*
2:15 *26*
4:3 *26*
5:8 *73*
5:10 *60, 63–64, 67, 82, 191*
5:17 *109, 118, 150*
5:21 *39*
6:14 *142*
6:14-15 *163*
6:14-18 *222*
6:16 *66*
7:1 *161*
7:6-16 *5*
7:8-12 *5*
8:16-24 *303*
9:6-7 *68*
9:7 *300*
10:10 *4*
11:21-23 *4*
11:23-29 *89*
12:6-7 *4*
12:7 *107*
12:7-10 *88*
12:10 *44*
12:14 *4*
13:1 *4–5*
13:1-3 *102*
13:12 *308*
13:13 *243*

Galatians
1:4 *47, 71*

1:8-9 *66*
1:10 *215*
1:11-24 *178*
1:15-16 *182*
1:16 *7*
3:2,14 *54*
3:10-14 *30*
3:28 *219, 222*
4:6 *54*
5:1 *178*
5:7 *189*
5:14-15 *187*
5:19-21 *118*
5:20 *19, 119*
6:1 *80*
6:1-2 *81, 102, 112*
6:2 *187*
6:11 *308*
6:14 *20, 40, 42, 53*
6:15 *150*

Ephesians
1:5,11 *48*
1:13-14 *13*
2:1 *52*
2:10 *67*
2:19-22 *66*
3:8 *182*
4:1-16 *20*
4:4-6 *243*
4:6 *170*
4:11 *10, 255*
4:12 *65*
4:15 *81, 219, 231*
5:1 *96*
5:3-6 *118*
5:5 *119*

5:18 *119*
5:21-33 *219*
5:23 *65, 220*
5:25-27 *103*
5:26 *120*
6:4 *98*
6:11-12 *206*
6:12 *189*

Philippians
1:6,10 *13*
1:9-10 *80*
1:20 *161*
1:21 *72–73*
2:2 *18*
2:3-4 *172, 211, 236*
2:3-5 *33*
2:5 *17, 96*
2:6 *73*
2:12-13 *98*
2:16 *13*
2:19-24 *97*
3:4-6 *7*
3:20 *12*
4:2 *17*
4:6 *148*
4:8-9 *125*
4:11 *148*
4:11-12 *89*
4:11-13 *154*

Colossians
1:15 *73*
1:16-17 *170*
1:18 *20*
3:1-2 *159*
3:5 *119*
3:5-9 *118*
3:18-19 *219*

3:20-21 *98*
4:18 *308*

1 Thessalonians
1:10 *12*
2:16 *26*
2:19 *68, 286*
3:2 *97*
3:13 *286*
4:3 *8*
4:4 *161*
4:11-12 *68*
4:13-18 *12, 295*
5:15 *90*
5:23 *128, 161*
5:23-24 *12*
5:26 *308*

2 Thessalonians
2:1,8 *286*
2:10 *26*
3:6-12 *102*
3:17 *308*

1 Timothy
1:2,18 *97*
1:10 *119, 152*
1:19-20 *107*
2:11-15 *219*
2:12 *223*
5:17-18 *177*
6:4 *19*
6:17 *47*
6:20 *97*

2 Timothy
1:2-5 *97*
1:12 *13*
2:5 *189*
3:16 *142*
4:7 *189*

Titus
2:3-5 *219*
3:5 *53, 120*
3:9 *19*
3:9-11 *16*
3:9-15 *102*
3:13 *306*

Philemon
19 *308*

Hebrews
1:3 *73*
1:14 *225*
5:12 *57*
6:10 *68*
9:22 *233*
9:27 *290*
11:6 *249*
12:1-2 *189*
12:5-6 *100*
12:5-13 *13, 235*
12:28 *159*
13:5 *134*

James
1:5 *247*
1:19 *261*
2:1 *49*
3:1 *xiii, 60*
3:14-15 *27*
3:14-17 *80*
3:17 *27*
3:18 *127*
4:1 *122*
4:5 *78*
4:12 *77*
4:15-16 *98*
5:7 *286*
5:15-16 *81*

1 Peter
1:10-12,20 *48*
1:18-19 *39*
2:2 *57*
2:9-10 *39*
2:21 *96*
3:1-6 *143*
3:1-7 *219*
3:7 *138*
4:10 *241*
4:10-11 *10*
5:2-3 *96*

2 Peter
1:20-21 *157*
2:1 *134*
2:4 *206*

1 John
2:16 *197*
3:2 *294*
4:1-3 *248*
4:8 *263*

3 John
6 *306*
11 *96*

Jude
6 *206*
7-8 *119*
24-25 *13*

Revelation
1:10 *300*
1:20 *225*
2:20-24 *103*

5:9 *134, 266*
6–19 *206*
7:11-12 *225*
9:13-19 *206*
12:4 *206*
14:3 *134*
19:11-21 *12, 73, 199*
19:12 *64*
20:4 *116*
20:11-15 *64, 285*
20:14-15 *119*
21:8 *119*
21–22 *118, 131, 159*
22 *xiii*